Dollars over Dominion

THOMAS DAVID SCHOONOVER, a
native of Minnesota, received his
doctorate from the University of
Minnesota. He has taught American
history and foreign relations in both
Europe and the United States.

DOLLARS OVER DOMINION

The Triumph of Liberalism in Mexican–United States Relations, 1861–1867

Thomas David Schoonover

LOUISIANA STATE UNIVERSITY PRESS
Baton Rouge and London

Designer: Dwight Agner
Type face: VIP Janson
Typesetter: The Composing Room of Michigan, Inc.
Printer and binder: Kingsport Press, Inc.

LIBRARY OF CONGRESS CATALOGING IN PUBLICATION DATA

Schoonover, Thomas David, 1936–
  Dollars over dominion.

  Bibliography: p.
  Includes index.
1. United States—Foreign relations—Mexico. 2. Mexico—
Foreign relations—United States. 3. United States—Foreign
relations—1861–1865. 4. United States—Foreign
relations—1865–1898. I. Title.
E183.8.M6S36   327.72'073   77-21287
  ISBN 0-8071-0368-3

To Ebba, Paco, Harriet, Bush, Erna,
Elisabeth, and Werner

Contents

Acknowledgments

IN THE course of writing this book, I have benefited from the aid and encouragement of many people. My advisor, Kinley Brauer, while reading through three drafts in the dissertation stage and several chapters in later revised form, has constantly reminded me to write more precisely. More important, he never tired of posing the questions that stimulated me to rethink and reanalyze my views. Beyond his earlier guidance during my graduate training, T. Harry Williams twice took time to read and to offer extended criticism on my dissertation manuscript during its revision. In addition, I found encouragement from talking to him about writing, history, and politics. Others who have helpfully criticized all or portions of the manuscript are David Pletcher, Norris Hundley, Milton Lyman Henry, Jr., Richard Sinkin, Judith Fenner Gentry, James Dormon, James E. Sefton, Martin Martell, Matthew Schott, Hans Trefousse, and Rodney Loehr. I wish to publicly express my gratitude to each of them for their comments and suggestions.

In 1968–1969, I spent six months in Mexico doing research under the sponsorship of the very generous Chicago Civil War Round Table Fellowship. I wish to thank Lloyd D. Miller, Clement Silvestro, Jerry Warshaw, Marshall Krolick, and the rest of the Chicago Civil War Round Table not just for myself, but for all my colleagues. We are all helped by the interest and action these men have taken to promote historical scholarship.

During my numerous visits to Mexico, three people facilitated my research by guiding me to useful materials: Guadalupe Monroy, historian and curator of the Archivo Histórico de Matías Romero, Martín Quirarte, professor of history at the University of Mexico and former director of the Archivo de la Secretaría de Relaciones Exteriores, and Enrique Florescano of El Colegio de México. Their friendly assistance is appreciatively remembered.

I wish to thank the staffs of the following archives and libraries for their generous assistance: the libraries at the University of Minnesota, the University of Southwestern Louisiana, and Louisiana State University, as well as the Latin American Collection of the University of Texas, Tulane University Middle America Library, the Manuscript Division and Reader Room of the Library of Congress, and the Houghton Library of Harvard University; the archives at Duke University, the University of Rochester, the University of Virginia, and Stanford University, as well as the National Archives, the Indiana State Historical Archives, and the Dallas Historical Society. I am especially grateful for use of these libraries and archives outside the United States: the Archivo Histórico de Matías Romero in the Banco de México, the Biblioteca Nacional, the Hemeroteca Nacional, the library of the Universidad Nacional Autónoma de México, the Archivo de la Secretaría de Relaciones Exteriores, the Biblioteca de la Secretaría de Hacienda, the Archivo de la Cámara de Diputados, the Archivo General de la Nación, the Archivo Histórico del Museo de Antropología y Historia, the Centro de Estudios de Historia de México, the library of El Colegio de México, and the Austrian Staatsarchiv.

My wife Ebba typed all the drafts. She has also been my research assistant, proofreader, and indexer. Although she is a born and bred German, her suspicions of my use of English have often proved well founded. A good part of the labor that went into producing this book has been hers. Ebba knows how much I appreciate her. Finally, I wish to acknowledge the patience of Ebba and my son Paco with my need to be alone to work on this book.

I wish to thank the *Pacific Historical Review* for permission to reprint, in a slightly revised form, my article "Dollars over Dominion: United States Economic Interests in Mexico, 1861–1867," which appeared in Volume XLV (February, 1976), 23–45, and the *East Tennessee Historical Society's Publication* for permitting me to reprint, in revised form, my article "Mexican Affairs and the Impeachment of President Andrew Johnson," which appeared in Volume XLVI (1974), 76–93. The first item appears here as Chapter IX, the second item as part of Chapter VIII.

Introduction

LIBERAL ideology in the nineteenth century presented a theoretical, spiritual, and humanitarian form when the faction was in opposition; however, upon obtaining political power, the liberals confronted the need to construct a legal, practical, concrete system. Politics, involving the concretization of abstract political concepts and the practical organization of the political economy, is the institutional method of transforming ideology into the actual. While the (Whig-)Republicans, profoundly influenced by nineteenth-century liberalism, were out of power in the 1840s and 1850s, they espoused the more abstract aspects of their Weltanschauung. Faced with the task of reducing ephemeral, multifaceted ideas into one specific form upon assuming power in 1861, the Republicans confronted the practical phase of implementing liberalism, only imperfectly visualized in their ideal world.

During the early 1860s, the Republican party not only fought a Civil War but also found time to transform its version of liberalism from a stage emphasizing the abstract humanitarian concerns—not only antislavery, but also many other reforms—into a set of laws and codes governing the political economy. For the encouragement and preservation of the necessary free flow of goods, labor, and capital, there were, according to Adam Smith, four legitimate areas of operation for a central government: (1) the police power, including court functions; (2) the currency system, a medium of exchange which holds confidence throughout the nation; (3) the transportation and communication system; and (4) the means to raise the revenue necessary to fulfill these necessary functions. Thus basic liberal economic order was encased in the Homestead Act, the transcontinental railroad and telegraph legislation, the national banking acts, the Morrill Tariff, and the encouragement for agricultural and mining development encompassed in the Morrill Act's authorization of land-grant colleges and the creation of an immigration bureau and a bureau of agriculture. The Homestead Act, the Immigration Bureau, the Bureau of Agriculture, the agricultural and mining emphasis of the land-grant colleges, and the railroad legislation were necessary if the land in the West was to be included in a liberal, free-flowing economic system. Otherwise citizens in the West would be excluded from the national market place. The national banking legislation was also necessary since Secretary of the Treasury Salmon Chase's report in 1861 pointed out that there were over three thousand different currencies circulated in the United States, ranging from valueless to full face value. It would be impossible to move goods through the national market place until there was only one currency of uniform value throughout the country. Then even the Morrill Tariff, a mild protective bill, takes on new light. Admittedly it ran counter to free trade. However, it did generate the revenue to fight the war, to finance the moderately costly development of the West, and to revamp the nation's currency system. Moreover, these problems had to be faced when a traditional major source of revenue, land sales, was removed in the name of liberal "progress."

The post-Civil War years revealed the concerted effort of the Republican party to preserve their conception of the future, not so much from a sense of reform and alteration, but from a feared wholesale attack which might destroy the very structure of the liberal socioeconomic system they had legislated during the Civil War. The return of the South, whose leaders had uniformly opposed the implementation of the liberal Weltanschauung before 1861, threatened the liberal economic program. During the Reconstruction era the "New Order," the political economy liberals found absolutely essential for a developing progressive, modern society in the nineteenth century, had to be defended.

Of course, in the real world, many abstract liberal ideas were altered, transformed, or even forgotten. One "core" liberal idea, never more than an abstraction for many United States liberals, was the concept of free trade. In interesting comparison, free trade was also an idea which British liberals could not apply very well in practice—hence the imperial preference system and the preservation of other regulations that always qualified British "free trade." Later, during the world economic crisis of 1873, the British discussed the possibility of restricting free trade even further. Given the heavy burden of Civil War expenses confronting the Republican party immediately upon arriving in power, and given the realization that open competition with Britain, France, and the advanced European export economies would place them at great disadvantage, many United States liberals justified a course which temporarily postponed the implementation of free trade. Later, the long, disruptive, worldwide economic crisis lasting from 1873 until 1897, compelling worldwide recognition that industrial countries needed expanded markets, preserved United States protectionism. Since the United States market could not consume American production, the free traders' call for the United States to open its interior market to foreign competition received little heed. Many liberals refused, reluctantly, to institute an abstract principle which would sharpen already grave economic burdens. After all, liberals no more than any other breed of men could be expected to follow their ideas to personal and national ruin. Liberals learned that abstract principles bend much easier than laws, institutions, and economic realities. This does not mean that liberals intended to withdraw from the "free" competition for foreign raw materials and trade or the search for external investment opportunities for their surplus capital. In fact, recognizing the inability of domestic consumption to purchase the national production, they sought expanding foreign markets and the preservation of "free trade" access to other areas, *i.e.* the "open door."

Within the Republican party the radical faction was not necessarily a more dedicated group, although it may have contained more than its fair share of dedicated liberals. The radicals, however, tended to be impetuous in both domestic and foreign policy, in their urgency to institute free labor, resolve the transportation, communication, currency, and banking roadblocks to the creation of a domestic free market place, and in their strong opposition to the conservative monarchical intervention in Santo Domingo and Mexico. Broadly and generally conceived, the Republican party's support for Mexican President Benito Juárez was derived from the liberal Weltanschauung. However, although the radicals urged action, the conservative faction, of which William H. Seward was a chief spokesman in foreign policy (and domestic policy for that matter), was every bit as committed to the ultimate goal—removal of the foreign influence. The Seward faction was more willing to take time to consider alternative solutions. Thus, while the Republican party as a whole advocated a liberal world order, the differences which arose derived largely from the speed as well as the precise implementation of programs which both sides agreed upon.

Since the days of Monroe, United States politicians, businessmen, military leaders, and geopoliticians had considered Latin America their special preserve. This old idea was reinforced first by the "no-transfer" principle and the Monroe Doctrine, then by the acquisitions of the Mexican War, later by the need for Pacific transit routes, and finally by the ever-increasing export surpluses of agricultural raw materials, along with the growing list of processed foodstuffs and semi- and fully manufactured products which the American domestic market could no longer absorb. The announced goal of Napoleon III's intervention in Mexico between 1861 and 1867 to permanently block United States growth and influence south of the Rio Grande intensified the desire of many North Americans, not only to eliminate his puppet Maximilian from the

Cactus Throne, but also to firmly reassert United States domination throughout the New World.

Thus, in the 1860s United States–Mexican affairs took on a very special significance. Since European markets were restricted for practical competitive reasons to American businessmen, with the outstanding exception of the surpluses of agricultural businessmen, European action in Latin America, if successful, threatened United States economic progress and growth. For the United States, with only limited immediate prospects in the highly industrialized and technologically advanced European market and without the courage or ideological strength to develop the domestic market, the most attractive areas for future growth and progress were in Latin America and Asia. Since trade with Asia required the cheap, quick communications possible in Panama, Nicaragua, or Tehuantepec, access to both promising markets depended upon United States power and security in Latin America. After 1861, the Republican party, responding to the internal economic growth and aspirations, and sharing the pre–Civil War Democratic party's concern for protecting Latin America from foreign political and territorial encroachment, developed an interest in preventing new and reducing old foreign commercial and investment inroads into an area which had long been considered bound geographically and ideologically to the United States economic sphere.

The terms economic expansionism and imperialism require explanation and clarification. The pre–Civil War period in United States–Mexican relations can be labeled one of territorial expansionism. In the Civil War and post–Civil War periods, the annexationist drive gave way to economic infiltration. United States economic interests wanted to develop trade, build transportation systems, acquire mines and land, obtain commercial and manufacturing privileges, export technology and engineering skills, invest capital, and, very important, acquire political influence in Mexico. What term best described this type of economic activity? I considered several alternative terms: commercial expansionism, business expansionism, and capital expansionism. Each term describes only a part of the total economic activity. Given the total economic relationship and the desire to obtain internal, political influence, the terms economic expansionism or imperialism strike me as the most realistic and accurate descriptive terms. Both will be used.

In interpreting and analyzing United States–Mexican relations in the 1860s, most standard and recent works, operating from a narrow concept of diplomatic history, have relied heavily upon United States State Department records, Confederate State Department records, and newspapers and other printed sources. Beyond these sources, this study utilizes extensive holdings of private manuscript collections in the United States, official and private manuscript holdings in Mexico, and some archival materials, newspapers, and secondary literature from Latin America and Europe in order to broaden the perspective for viewing the two wars in a world setting.

Significantly, many Civil War and Reconstruction historians have either ignored or slighted the interrelationship between foreign and domestic affairs. For example, differing views of the French intervention and its relationship to the southern rebellion played a significant role in the conflict between Lincoln's administration and the moderate and Radical Republicans. During the Johnson administration, significant elements of the controversy between radicals and moderates on one hand and conservatives on the other were based upon different foreign as well as domestic policies. This should not be so astounding if one considers that foreign policy can be meaningfully viewed as the goals, hopes, objectives of the domestic elite as shaped by the needs, pressures, and demands of the domestic socioeconomic order.

The historiography of United States–Mexican relations during the 1860s has not adequately recognized the decisive start which American capitalists obtained in Mexico's economy during this era. The often-cited bromide that United States penetration of Mexico was a product of Porfirio Díaz' policy overlooks the pivotal attitudes and policies of Juárez' Liberal government.

In addition to these interpretative matters, historians have not placed United States–Mexican relations within a broad conceptual framework. The late David Potter's suggestive essay, "Civil War," in *The Comparative Approach to History*, argues that the United States Civil War was part of the worldwide struggle of liberalism with conservatism—a thesis apparently supported by several others, notably Raimundo Luraghi, A. R. Tyrner-Tyrnauer, and Hans-Ulrich Wehler. No historian, however, has done more than touch lightly and suggestively upon this theme. This book attempts to explore a new interpretative structure for the Civil War period, using United States–Mexican relations as a testing ground.

By mid–nineteenth century, the European conflict between liberalism and conservatism was in full flourish in the New World. Liberal revolutions were ousting conservative forces in Mexico and elsewhere in Latin America. The United States Civil War and Reconstruction era can be most meaningfully understood as a liberal revolution. On the international level, the French and Spanish intervention in the New World was interpreted as part of this worldwide contest between liberalism and conservatism.

The central thesis of this work is that the Liberal party in Mexico and the Republican party in the United States shared an ideology—laissez-faire liberalism—which led them to define their respective problems and the solutions to their problems as interrelated, and which alleviated some of the stress on United States–Mexican relations during the crisis years of the 1860s, while permitting the mutually desired American economic penetration of Mexico during the 1860s and 1870s. Many American and Mexican liberals considered the French-Confederate alliance as one of aristocratic, agrarian conservatives who intended to destroy republicanism, liberty, and freedom in the New World, while the Confederates and Franco-Maximilianists regarded "radical republican" efforts as aimed at destroying the superior talent and institutions of their elite societies. The friendly relationship between the governments of Juárez and Lincoln for the eleven months before the French intervention hence was not merely a leaning for help on the United States. It was even consummated before there was much of a secession crisis, since the instructions which sent Romero on the mission to Springfield, Illinois, in January, 1861, were written by Juárez' secretary of foreign relations before Mexico learned of South Carolina's secession. Behind their coming together was an ideological substance: the Mexicans wanted to model their social, political, and economic institutions on patterns similar to those of the Republican party's version of the United States. Romero made clear in his address to Lincoln that the old, southern-influenced version of the United States offered nothing for Mexico, except the threat of the loss of their territory. The Mexican liberals around Juárez truly believed that this threat had all but disappeared by the simple act of the right party (*i.e.*, ideological outlook) coming to power.

Besides a theoretical agreement and a similar definition of the enemy, Mexico and the United States discovered their fundamental economic interests and needs were mutually supporting. Mexico sought manufactured goods, investment capital, and technology to develop its economy, while the United States sought new markets for its manufactured goods and areas for speculation and investment. Economic cooperation in this pattern lead to United States economic predominance, which eventually demanded political influence to protect the "humanitarian" and "property" rights of the numerous United States citizens who constituted the thrust of economic expansionism. Thus, American imperialism in Mexico, and probably elsewhere in Latin America, was not the product of undesired United States penetration or of United States international power politics, but rather, initially at least, a phenomenon heartily welcomed by the governing liberal elite in Mexico.

I An End to Forty Years of Enmity in Mexican–United States Relations

SPRINGFIELD, Illinois, was a bustling town from November of 1860 until mid-February, 1861. Scores of important Republican politicians descended upon it to request favors of Abraham Lincoln, president-elect of the United States, as rewards for their support during the recent election campaign. Among these visitors, one, a foreigner, came not to request a favor, but to acknowledge the significance of the Republican victory, both to his country and to the United States. On December 22, 1860, Benito Juárez, president of Mexico, had instructed Mexico's twenty-three-year-old chargé d'affaires in Washington, the talented, diligent Matías Romero, to visit Lincoln at his home in Springfield. Romero's instructions were to stress the ideological bond between the two governments.[1]

During a meeting on January 19 Romero presented Lincoln with a note from Juárez. Romero next explained at considerable length that the church and army had been jointly responsible for the disorders in Mexico since independence. Now both groups were defeated and incapable of further rebellion. The republic

---

1. Melchor Ocampo to Matías Romero, December 22, 1860, in Matías Romero (comp.), *Correspondencia de la legación mexicana en Washington durante la intervención extranjera* (10 vols.; Mexico, 1870–1892), I, 274; hereinafter cited as Romero (comp.), *Correspondencia.*

wished friendly, intimate relations with the United States, under which all rights of United States citizens would be protected, while commercial and other mutual interests would be facilitated. Mexico wished to adopt the same "principles of liberty and progress" as the United States, hoping thereby "to take the same path to prosperity." Romero also informed Lincoln that the Mexican government viewed with satisfaction the victory in the United States of "republican ideas," since such principles were closer to those held by Mexicans. It was expected that the policy followed by the new administration would be more fraternal than that of the Democratic administration which had attempted to despoil Mexico to extend slavery.[2]

Lincoln, responding to Romero's speech, expressed a strong wish for peace and prosperity for Mexico and promised that his administration would treat Mexico with consideration, sympathy, and justice in all pending and future questions between the two republics. Romero reported to his government Lincoln's particular interest in the condition of the *peones*; Lincoln inquired if peonage was not worse than Negro slavery. Romero admitted the abuses, but indicated they were contrary to law in Mexico, requiring only the firm establishment of a liberal government to initiate the needed corrections.[3]

After taking leave of Lincoln on January 21, Romero summarized his impression of this first meeting as particularly opportune since Lincoln appeared ill-informed about, if well disposed towards, Mexico. Romero evaluated Lincoln as a simple, honest, sincere person whose policies would conform to his expressed sentiments. Furthermore, Mexico's haste in congratulating Lincoln

2. Romero to the Ministro de Relaciones Exteriores, January 23, 1861, in Correspondencia General con los Estados Unidos, Archivo Histórico de la Secretaría de Relaciones Exteriores. Romero's views were affirmed in the official Mexican newspaper, *El Siglo Diez y Nueve*, in an editorial by Juárez' future minister of foreign relations, Manuel María Zamocona, "Los Estados Unidos y México," *El Siglo Diez y Nueve*, March 29, 1861, p. 1.

3. Romero to Ministro de Relaciones Exteriores, January 23, 1861, in Correspondencia General con los Estados Unidos; and Lincoln to Romero, January 21, 1861, in Roy P. Basler (ed.), *The Collected Works of Abraham Lincoln* (8 vols. and index; New Brunswick, N.J., 1953), IV, 177–78.

upon his election victory ought to have convinced the incoming administration of Mexico's friendly sentiment.[4]

The amiability of the interview between Romero and Lincoln was unusual in the uneasy and troubled course of Mexican–United States relations. Since its interests were served by having a weaker, republican, independent state on its frontier in place of a colony of Spain, the United States had responded sympathetically to Mexico's struggle for independence. Mexico was properly grateful for the aid received, as well as the early recognition extended by the United States in 1822. This air of friendship and good feelings died quickly for a number of reasons, among which were expressions of ethnocentricism, racism, and expansionism current in the United States, a border disagreement, a legacy from Spanish–United States relations, and the United States' delay in reciprocally appointing a minister to Mexico. While Mexican skepticism toward the United States appeared within the first few months after recognition, additional suspicions developed within the first years of recognition.[5]

Between the early 1820s and the Mexican War, the several major problems disturbing Mexican–United States relations included: the growth of British influence in Mexico; the condition of Cuba, which both Mexico and the United States desired to annex; Mexico's limitation on American use of the Santa Fe Trail; various

4. Romero to Ministro de Relaciones Exteriores, January 23, 1861, in Correspondencia General con los Estados Unidos; and Romero to Lincoln, January 21, 1861, in Abraham Lincoln Papers, Library of Congress.

5. This summary of Mexican–United States relations 1820 to 1861 has been drawn from the following works: Luis G. Zorrilla, *Historia de las Relaciones entre México y los Estados Unidos* (2 vols.; Mexico, 1965–1966); J. Lloyd Mecham, *A Survey of United States–Latin American Relations* (Boston, 1965); and J. Fred Rippy, *The United States and Mexico* (New York, 1926). See also Karl M. Schmitt, *Mexico and the United States, 1821–1973: Conflict and Coexistence* (New York, 1974); Carlos Bosch García, *Historia de las Relaciones entre México y los Estados Unidos, 1819–1848* (Mexico, 1961); José Fuentes Mares, *Poinsett, Historia de una Gran Intriga* (Mexico, 1958); Alberto Mariá Carreño, *La Diplomacia Extraordinaria entre México y los Estados Unidos, 1789–1947* (2 vols.; Mexico, 1951); Samuel Flagg Bemis, *The Latin American Policy of the United States* (New York, 1943); James M. Callahan, *American Foreign Policy in Mexican Relations* (New York, 1932); and William R. Manning, *Early Diplomatic Relations Between the United States and Mexico* (Baltimore, 1916).

commercial problems which hindered the writing of a satisfactory commercial treaty; and disagreement on the Texas-Mexican boundary. In addition, during the pre–Mexican War years the United States' insistence upon territorial expansion at Mexico's cost in California and New Mexico destroyed any basis for compromise or negotiation between the two countries. After the Mexican War, "the Golden Age of Anglo-American filibustering" maintained United States expansionism continuously in the view of Mexicans.[6] In addition to the legacy of ill feeling growing out of the Mexican War, other problems played significant roles in preventing the relaxation of tension between the neighboring countries. The major problems were the depredations by Indians along the frontier, for the most part raiding out of the United States into Mexico; United States requests for transit rights in Tehuantepec and elsewhere in Mexico; and the disagreement over the boundary described in the Treaty of Guadalupe Hidalgo.

The economic and political problems disturbing Mexican–United States relations have always been in part traceable to the diverse cultures of the two countries.[7] The United States was an Anglo-Saxon, Protestant, democratic society which asserted the separation of the New World from the Old with the Monroe Doctrine. Mexican society was Latin, Roman Catholic, and aristocratic, with strong economic and cultural ties to Europe. It is easy to understand why Joel R. Poinsett, first United States minister to Mexico and representative par excellence of Yankee culture, left behind memories of interference in internal affairs which a Mexican historian refers to as "*la gran intriga.*"[8] It is not surprising that Poin-

6. Rippy, *The United States and Mexico*, 85.

7. Don E. Fehrenbacher, *The Era of Expansion: 1800–1848* (New York, 1969), esp. 120–38; and William R. Brock, *Conflict and Transformation: The United States, 1844–1877* (Baltimore, 1973), 11–120. David M. Pletcher has convincingly developed the thesis that "the Mexican War, Texas, and Oregon were not simple family quarrels in the Western Hemisphere. Instead, they formed a truly international question of first importance in which Britain, France, and occasionally even Spain played lively roles, both political and economic." See *The Diplomacy of Annexation: Texas, Oregon, and the Mexican War* (Columbia, 1973), 5.

8. Fuentes Mares, *Poinsett.*

sett's tour of service encompassed the period when Mexican gratitude for aid and sympathy, rendered during her war for independence, turned to fear and distrust of Yankee expansionism.

The debate over whether southern slave society was or was not expansionist will undoubtedly rage long into the future. Equally clear is the fact that the Mexican liberals were convinced that the South was expansionist and that it desired to annex all or part of Mexico.[9] In support of the slave-based political economy, by the late 1840s some sections of the South became increasingly interested in commercial expansion. New Orleans' economic interests sought to develop a railroad across the Tehuantepec Isthmus. This route would lend New Orleans geographic advantages in commercial relations with California, Oregon, and the Pacific area in general. Operating under President James Buchanan's instructions, United States Minister to Mexico John Forsyth intended to turn the financial need of the conservative government in Mexico City to the advantage of the South by offering to purchase Baja California, parts of Chihuahua and Sonora, as well as certain transit rights.[10] When the conservative government rejected this proposal, Forsyth broke relations with it and returned to the United States.

Later, when the Juárez-led Liberal government in Veracruz indicated it could be persuaded to cede Baja California, perpetual

9. For contemporary and recent arguments asserting the expansionist nature of the slave-based society, see José Mata to Benito Juárez, July 2, 1858, in Archivo Benito Juárez, Biblioteca Nacional, Mexico, #1–32; Matías Romero, *Estudio sobre la anexión de México a los Estados Unidos* (Mexico, 1890), 5–17; Eugene D. Genovese, *The Political Economy of Slavery* (New York, 1967), 243–74; James Edward Southerland, "Mexican–United States Relations, 1857–1860: The Failure of Manifest Destiny" (Ph.D. dissertation, University of Georgia, 1970), 181; Major L. Wilson, "Ideological Fruits of Manifest Destiny: The Geopolitics of Slavery Expansion in the Crisis of 1850," *Journal of the Illinois Historical Society*, LXIII (Summer, 1970), 132–57; Brock, *Conflict and Transformation*, 15–16; and William L. Barney, *The Road to Secession: A New Perspective on the Old South* (New York, 1972), xiv–xv, 5–11, 65–72, 102–108. See also Ernest Charles Sheaver, "Border Diplomatic Relations Between the United States and Mexico, 1848–1860" (Ph.D. dissertation, University of Texas, 1940), 309, for an unconvincing effort to argue: "Slavery played a very little part in causing diplomatic tension between the United States and Mexico."

10. Marvin Lyle Durham, "American Expansionism into Mexico, 1848–1862" (Ph.D. dissertation, Fletcher School of Law and Diplomacy, 1962), 138–39.

transit rights over Tehuantepec and rights-of-way from the Rio Grande to Guaymas and Mazatlán, Buchanan sent Robert McLane to recognize the Liberal government, thereby deviating from the traditional United States policy of granting recognition de facto to whichever government controlled the main parts of the country. At that time the capital, many harbors, and a large majority of the land area and population were controlled by the Conservative government in Mexico City.

Nationalistic pressures of the domestic Mexican struggle prevented any territorial cession by Juárez' government; however, McLane and Melchor Ocampo, Juárez' foreign minister, signed a treaty granting the United States transit rights, special privileges, and broad powers to protect those transit rights without prior consultation with the Mexican government. In the Senate in 1860, however, a sectional vote defeated the McLane-Ocampo treaty. Whereas the South supported the acquisition of territory or privileges which would augment its political power and raise New Orleans to a dominant position in trade with the Pacific coast areas, northern congressmen from both parties sought to prevent trade and commercial advantages from falling to New Orleans and the South, as well as to deny expansion to the southern slave system.[11]

In the 1850s, the issue of government-subsidized private transportation became intertwined with the dominant domestic problem of slavery expansionism. The sectional conflict over location of the transcontinental line arose from the incompatibility of the Northeast's democratic laissez-faire capitalism, which sought to expand its marketplace, with southern staple-crop, oligarchical agricultural system, which was content with the English-French market.[12] The

11. In addition to the items in footnote 5, see Marvin L. Durham, "American Expansionism"; Jay M. Maisel, "The Origin and Development of Mexican Antipathy toward the South, 1821–1867" (Ph.D. dissertation, University of Texas, 1955); Norman A. Graebner, *Empire in the Pacific: A Study in American Continental Expansion* (New York, 1955); and Agustín Cue Canovas, *El Tratado McLane-Ocampo, Juárez, los Estados Unidos y Europa* (3rd ed.; Mexico, 1968), 4–5.

12. Douglass C. North, *Growth and Welfare in the American Past: A New Economic History* (Englewood Cliffs, N.J., 1966), 77–78; Bernard A. Weisberger, *The New Industrial Society* (New York, 1969), 29, 68–69; William A. Williams, *The Roots of the Modern American Empire*

fact that both the Northeast and the South produced capitalist groups interested in transit rights in Mexico does not contradict the difference in basic economic structure of the two sections. It shows rather that sections geographically as large as the Northeast and the South can share internally certain basic social, economic, and cultural patterns and a sectional pride while nevertheless tolerating minor divergences from the normal sectional patterns. The southern capitalist group stemmed from New Orleans, the one city in the South which considered itself a great world-commercial city. New Orleans, with its banking structure and its location at the mouth of the Mississippi, had become the exporter of a sizable share of the newer South's and the Midwest's exportable agricultural surpluses. New Orleans' slump in trade and commercial growth in the mid-1840s was followed by the increasing interest of its bankers and businessmen in Tehuantepec. Although New Orleans' position was deteriorating, perhaps its nearness to Central and South America and its potential commercial proximity to the West Coast and the Asian markets could provide that charming port city with even more glorious days in the future.[13]

While the United States divided along geographic, economic, and political lines, Mexico experienced an equally dramatic split along economic, political, and social lines. Mexico of the 1840s and 1850s was bitterly divided into a conservative Church party and the Liberal party. The conservative party represented the world view

(New York, 1969), 6–14; Howard B. Schonberger, *Transportation to the Seaboard: The "Communications Revolution" and American Foreign Policy, 1860–1900* (Westport, Conn., 1971), 5, 239; and Brock, *Conflict and Transformation*, 15–17; Eric Foner, *Free Soil, Free Labor, Free Men: The Ideology of the Republican Party Before the Civil War* (New York, 1970), 9.

13. Rollin G. Osterweis, *Judah P. Benjamin: Statesman of the Lost Cause* (New York, 1933), 74–94; Robert Douthat Meade, *Judah P. Benjamin, Confederate Statesman* (New York, 1943), 73–75, 84, 121–23; Bray Hammond, *Banks and Politics in America from the Revolution to the Civil War* (Princeton, N.J., 1957), 680–85; Charles S. Sydnor, *The Development of Southern Sectionalism, 1819–1848* (Baton Rouge, 1948), 260–61; and Robert C. Reinders, *End of Era: New Orleans, 1850–1860* (New Orleans, 1964), 42–44. See also George D. Green, *Finance and Economic Development in the Old South: Louisiana Banking, 1804–1861* (Stanford, Calif., 1972), 57–58, 174–75, 179. For a contrary view, based entirely upon domestic considerations, however, see Merle E. Reed, *New Orleans and the Railroads: The Struggle for Commercial Empire, 1830–1860* (Baton Rouge, 1966), 63, 67, 68–75.

dominant among *creoles*, the army, the Catholic Church, particularly the higher clergy, and the large landowners. This world view centered upon preserving and continuing the *fueros*, special privileges of the clergy—including protection by church courts—and special privileges granted to the army and the wealthy. The conservative party wanted to continue the decentralized government which was so weak that it could be ignored or overthrown if it fell under control of the opposition and lacked the power to challenge the privileged groups. The conservatives would certainly continue to tolerate peonage, long since unconstitutional, but still common in Mexico, while opposing broader, non-church-sponsored education and resisting broader participation in politics.[14]

The liberals, mostly *mestizos* with a few Indians, were proponents of nineteenth-century liberalism. Their program favored free universal education under state control, the opening of political and economic life by removing *fueros* and other special privileges, and by redistributing corporate lands. The Mexican liberals also demanded a national education system, a national guaranty of freedom of religion, speech, and assembly, a national immigration policy, a national tariff policy (either free trade or low tariff and removal of interstate tariffs), a national system of weights and measures, a centrally controlled but small army, and subordination of the church to the national government.[15] They also pursued various projects aimed at facilitating national economic growth

14. In addition to the items in footnote 5, see Wilfred Hardy Callcott, *Liberalism in Mexico, 1857–1929* (Stanford, Calif., 1931); J. Lloyd Mecham, "The Origins of Federalism in Mexico," *Hispanic American Historical Review*, XVIII (May, 1938), 164–82; Ralph Roeder, *Juárez and His Mexico* (2 vols.; New York, 1947); Walter V. Scholes, *Mexican Politics During the Juárez Regime, 1855–1872* (Columbia, Mo., 1957); José Bravo Ugarte, *Historia de México* (Mexico, 1959) Vol. III, Pt. 2; Henry Bamford Parkes, *A History of Mexico* (3rd ed.; Boston, 1960); Frederick C. Turner, *The Dynamic of Mexican Nationalism* (Chapel Hill, 1968).

15. *El Siglo Diez y Nueve*, January 25, 1861; *El Monitor Republicano*, January 19, 21, 23, February 9, 10, 12, 24, 25, March 5, April 7, and July 4, 1861. The April 7 *El Monitor Republicano* is of special importance on the question of "Federación y centralismo." See also Raymond C. Wheat, "Francisco Zarco: The Liberal Spokesman of La Reforma" (Ph.D. dissertation, University of Texas, 1957); Juan O. Brom, "Las ideas políticas de Ignacio Ramírez," *Anuario de Historia*, VI–VII (1966–1967), 41–64; and Luis Cordova, "Protec-

through improvement of domestic and foreign communication and transportation systems.

The Mexican liberals shared with the Republican party in the United States a dislike of peonage/slavery, a desire for centralized government, a belief in national assistance for transportation development to aid the formation of a national market, a wider public land distribution, and broader education policy. The Republicans tended to favor a protective tariff policy because they had an immature industrial complex to protect. The liberals, in turn, favored a unified and simplified national tariff policy, eliminating the numerous state and local tax levies, in order to encourage foreign commerce and Mexico's internal economic growth. It was common then and later to envision shared ideas and institutions between liberal Mexico and republican United States.[16] The liberals' conflict with an organized and entrenched national church found no counterpart in the United States.[17]

Although the Mexican liberals were federalists in the sense that they opposed past abuses of central power to create dictatorship, the liberal goal of a strong national economy necessitated strengthening the central government and limiting state governmental powers. Their original opposition to the abuse of centralized power by *caudillos* like Santa Anna was first replaced by the argument that a strong congressional authority and strong state

cionismo y librecambio en el México Independiente (1821-1847)," *Cuadernos Americanos,* CLXXII (September-October, 1970), 135-53. Charles A. Hale, *Mexican Liberalism in the Age of Mora, 1821-1853* (New Haven, Conn., 1968), offers an excellent treatment of earlier Mexican liberal thought. Our differences regarding the role of centralism and federalism derive from the fact that he views earlier abstract liberal thought, whereas my judgments about Mexican liberalism are based upon later concrete actions, that is, what they did during the late 1850s and 1860s. For a recent synthesis describing liberalism's impact upon Europe, see W. E. Mosse, *Liberal Europe: The Age of Bourgeois Realism, 1848-1875* (London, 1974).

16. Richard N. Sinkin, "Modernization and Reform in Mexico, 1855-1876" (Ph.D. dissertation, University of Michigan, 1972), 368-69.

17. The antimasonic movement of the 1820s and 1830s, which attracted Thurlow Weed, Seward, Thaddeus Stevens, and other future leaders of the Republican party, was often associated with the defense of the liberal idea of a free, open society. However, while the liberals in Mexico opposed a powerful religious establishment, the antimasons opposed a myth, wrapped in a conspiracy. See Alice Felt Tyler, *Freedom's Ferment* (New York, 1962), 351-58; and Lee Benson, *The Concept of Jacksonian Democracy* (New York, 1969), 21-28.

governments might serve as a counterbalance to prevent the *caudillos*' abusing power. Later, however, this idea lost favor among the liberals when they realized that only a strong central authority could build the national economic, social, and political system they desired.[18]

The long Mexican-Texas crisis had convinced many liberals of the need for a strong central government. Whereas Mexican conservatives responded by looking for European support or a European monarch to stabilize the nation and generate the power necessary to halt Yankee expansionism, the liberals believed it possible to lessen the threat from the United States through a diplomacy of mutual accommodation, a course they followed, with only brief interruptions, with considerable success from 1858 until the present. For example, most liberals found no reason to blame the United States for the Mexican War. Charles Hale points out that "there was little display of *antiyanquismo* among the liberals; rather the war was generally discussed for what it revealed about Mexican social disorganization and political weakness." Edward H. Moseley adds that the liberals "blamed the archaic organization of the Mexican nation, and singled out the Church as the guilty part in its perpetuation."[19] The liberals interpreted the Mexican War as a sign of conservative decadence and chaos, while the conservatives blamed greedy, aggressive Anglo-Saxon Protestant society.

An often held but erroneous assumption is that the liberals "favored" or should have "favored" the *campesinos* and the *indígenas* of Mexico; but clearly liberalism was not an ideology rooted in rural values, nor particularly concerned with agricultural economic growth, but rather a system for justifying, organizing, and produc-

18. Hale, *Mexican Liberalism*, 34, 84–85, 92; Sinkin, "Modernization and Reform" 148–64, 182–202, 211, 235; and "Federación y centralismo," *El Monitor Republicano*, April 7, 1861, p. 1. See also Roberto Cortes Conde, *The First Stages of Modernization in Spanish America* (New York, 1974), 78–81.

19. Hale, *Mexican Liberalism*, 207; Edward H. Moseley, "The Religious Impact of the American Occupation of Mexico City, 1847–1848," in Eugene R. Huck and Edward H. Moseley (eds.), *Militarists, Merchants and Missionaries: United States Expansion in Middle America* (University, Ala., 1970), 46.

ing material progress in an industrial-commercial society.[20] The liberals were leading a bourgeoise revolution against the feudal remains of Spanish rule.

La guerra de la Reforma, 1857–1860, resulted in a permanent resolution of the internal conflict for political control of Mexico between the conservatives and liberals. The conservatives' defeat was so shattering that thereafter they could attempt to renew the conflict for the domination of Mexico only with the aid of a foreign ally, France.[21] From this and other interventions in Mexico, Gastón García Cantú drew the hypothesis that Mexico's foreign relations have reflected her internal struggles. Each internal battle for progress, if successful, produced foreign intervention, stemming from a conflict between foreign interests and Mexico's efforts to exercise national sovereignty. This foreign intervention was born in three centuries of Spanish feudal colonialism and has been sustained by Mexico's situation as part of the spoils of world imperialism.[22] Thus the internal struggle of the late 1850s was followed by an intervention inspired by the defeated conservative faction, with the principal intervening power, France, acting to protect its own economic access to Mexico and the rest of Latin America.

Meanwhile, during December, 1860, and January, 1861, the Mexican liberals took possession of a capital and a country exhausted by the long era of revolutions, revolts, and wars. Mexico

20. For the complaint about lack of liberal support for the "campesino" and "indígenas" see T. G. Powell, *El liberalismo y el campesinado en el centro de México, 1850–1876* (Mexico, 1974), 7, 71, 85–86. Powell (pp. 36, 127) complains that the Mexican campesinos' condition deteriorated after the conservatives lost power to the liberals, which is not surprising, however, since the conservative ideology was based upon agrarian values and agricultural economics while the liberal ideology developed with the industrial revolution. See also Tulio Halperin-Doughi, *The Aftermath of Revolution in Latin America*, trans. Josephine de Bunsen (New York, 1973), 30.

21. Richard N. Sinkin, "The Mexican Constitutional Congress, 1856–1857: A Statistical Analysis" (paper read at the 86th Annual Meeting of the American Historical Association, New York, December 1971), 17; Edward Maurice Caldwell, "The War of 'La Reforma' in Mexico, 1858–1861" (Ph.D. dissertation, University of Texas, 1935), 353; and Sinkin, "Modernization and Reform," 388.

22. Gastón García Cantú, "Las dos políticas exteriores de México," *Cuadernos Americanos*, año 18, CVI:5 (September-October, 1959), 41–55.

was at a low point in its economic and social history. Since 1810 the nation had experienced continual disorder, revolution, *pronunciamientos*, civil war, and banditry which sapped its economic strength and left it badly in need of recuperation. Mexico needed financial aid and a compassionate relaxation of demands from foreign powers regarding their claims against Mexico. With the beginning of the United States Civil War in 1861, Mexico found herself in a potentially advantageous situation. Both the Union and Confederate governments would compete for a favorable Mexican policy in regard to the international questions arising from political division and war in the United States.

II *The Contest for Position:*
  Corwin and Pickett, 1861–1862

THE PROSPECT for a mutually respectful relationship between Mexico and the United States appeared more promising in 1861 than at any time since 1821. The United States had been friendly, even if the friendliness was based on obvious self-interest, when President Benito Juárez' Liberal government had been without friends and in a desperate situation. When the Liberals entered Mexico City in late 1860, the nearly three years of American moral support were not forgotten. Moreover, other events and circumstances at the end of 1860 and beginning of 1861 combined to fortify these ties. Most Mexican officials interpreted the Republican victory in the 1860 presidential election as a sign that those southerners responsible for the rape of Mexican territory and wealth would no longer be in power, thereby creating a more cordial, relaxed atmosphere between the two countries.[1] During 1861 it became increasingly evident that the economic, cultural, and political goals of the Mexican Liberals were closer to those of the Republican party than those of the Confederate leadership.

Shortly after Juárez' government arrived in Mexico City, in a

1. Melchor Ocampo to Romero, December 22, 1860, in Romero (comp.), *Correspondencia*, I, 274.

series of editorials, *El Siglo Diez y Nueve* announced a policy of commercial liberalism and expressed its apprehensions concerning the developing split in the United States. The editor, Manual María Zamacona, later minister of foreign relations in Juárez' cabinet, argued that prohibitions, privileges, and monopolies in Mexico's commerce must be eliminated. Only by increasing exports could Mexico pay for necessary yet expanding imports which must be purchased "in the cheapest market." Zamacona also recognized the South's "mania" to acquire territory, which, through accident of geography, left Mexico a prime potential victim. While admitting annexationists existed in the North, he believed the Republican party under Lincoln sincerely sought to prevent southern expansionist projects. Although "the Northern states had served as a brake" on southern expansionism, Zamacona raised the question whether the most permanent hindrance to expansion might be permanent division since then the North and South would neutralize each other.[2] While later Zamacona's commercial policy, supported by Juárez and other liberals, received a sympathetic response from large numbers of United States businessmen, adventurers, and investors, his description of Mexico's position between northern and southern aspirations was immediately tested with the arrival of United States and Confederate States envoys.

During the first few months of the Lincoln administration, Buchanan appointee John B. Weller served as minister to Mexico. Weller's dispatches reflect the territorial expansionism common in the Buchanan administration's relations with Mexico. They also illustrate the traditional United States policy of using unsettled claims, alleged violated rights, and similar complaints to apply diplomatic pressure for imperialistic goals such as territorial cessions or grants of economic or transit privileges. Weller reported that his time had "been principally occupied in pressing the claims of American citizens," but that he saw "no prospect of recovering the claims due to Americans during the present generation accept [*sic*]

2. *El Siglo Diez y Nueve*, January 25, February 25, and March 29, 1861.

by a cession of territory." He also observed that it was an "auspicious period" to negotiate desirable treaties and guaranties against forced loans. Weller urged Foreign Minister Francisco Zarco to arrange a payment plan for all just claims, but realizing the state of affairs and wishing republican institutions success, he would not expect immediate payment.[3] Apparently Weller sought Mexican recognition of claims, which would become a powerful weapon if (when) the State Department decided to adopt a strong collection policy.

During the chaotic months of early 1861, while Weller maneuvered to obtain an advantageous position permitting later acquisition of Mexican territory, a sizable force of Mexicans and North Americans, under the command of a man named Moreno, entered Mexico from California. According to official reports received in Mexico City, this force had entered Mexico with the knowledge of the California authorities.[4]

Weller expressed disbelief when Francisco Zarco notified him that a raid had occurred. In response, Weller proposed that Mexico establish a policy encouraging United States citizens to colonize Mexico. Admitting that such immigrants must come as friends and not as lawless adventurers, Weller informed the Mexican government that "the hardy and enterprising citizens of the North would do much by the investment of their capital and labor to develop the vast and inexhaustible resources of this Republic." Finally, even if a

3. John B. Weller to the Secretary of State, March 18, 1861 and Weller to William H. Seward, April 11, 1861, in Diplomatic Dispatches, Mexico, in Record Group 59, National Archives. Microcopy numbers for National Archives materials are found in the bibliography.

4. Francisco Zarco to Benito Juárez, March 9, 1861, in Sucesos entre México y los Estados Unidos de América Relacionados con Texas y otros Estados Limítrofes, Archivo Histórico de la Secretaría de Relaciones Exteriores, H/200(72:73)/1., L-E-1097; Romero to Ministro de Relaciones Exteriores, February 22, 1861, March 17, 1861, and August 16, 1861; Zarco to Romero, March 13, 1861, enclosing Ministro de Governación U. Larsepas to Zarco, March 9, 1861, and Zarco to Juárez, March 11, 1861, in Romero (comp.), *Correspondencia*, I, 300, 318–319, 502–503, 765–68; Zorrilla, *Relaciones*, I, 418. See also Henry H. Goldman, "Southern Sympathy in Southern California, 1860–1865," *Journal of the West*, IV (October, 1965), 577–86.

raid had occurred, Weller could not believe that either "the Federal or State authorities have countenanced the movement."[5]

When word of the raid reached Washington, Secretary of State William H. Seward also doubted at first its occurrence and specifically denied Romero's charge that the authorities in California possessed prior knowledge. On April 6, Seward treated the matter briefly in his instructions to American minister to Mexico Thomas Corwin, stating that care would be taken first "to verify the facts . . . presented," then the neutrality laws would be applied against violations. Convinced that eventually Seward would receive trustworthy evidence of the Baja California filibuster, Juárez expressed his gratitude for Seward's reassurances.[6]

Shortly thereafter, Thomas Sprague, former commercial agent at La Paz, Baja California, supplied information, substantiated with further evidence from the Mexican government, which persuaded both Corwin and Seward that a raid had occurred. In early June, 1861, Seward appointed Joseph A. Nunes commercial agent at La Paz, instructing him to leave as soon as possible, since the State Department had "reliable information" regarding a Confederate plan to seize Baja California. If Nunes learned additional details of such a move he was to report to the United States naval and military commanders in that area, who would suppress it. At the same time, Seward had written Secretary of War Simon Cameron, requesting that the military forces in the Pacific area be prepared to offer aid to resist aggression against Mexico.

Assuring Mexico of United States disapproval of these violations of Mexican territory, Seward denied any responsibility for these acts or any desire for territorial aggrandizement. Never-

5. Zarco to Weller, March 12, 1861, and Weller to Zarco, March 16, 1861, in Sucesos entre México y los Estados Unidos de América Relacionados con Texas y otros Estados Limítrofes, Archivo Histórico de la Secretaría de Relaciones Exteriores.

6. Seward to Thomas Corwin, April 6, 1861, in Diplomatic Instructions, Mexico, in Record Group 59, National Archives; Thomas Sprague to Corwin, May 3, 1861, enclosed with Corwin to Seward, May 29, 1861, in Diplomatic Dispatches, Mexico, RG 59, NA; Romero to Ministro de Relaciones Exteriores, June 6, 1861, enclosing Romero to Seward, June 4, 1861, in Romero (comp.), *Correspondencia*, I, 413.

theless, rather than see Mexico forced into selling or losing by conquest all or any part of Baja California to the insurgents, the United States would be willing to consider a sale price from the Mexican government. This contingency was presented to the Juárez government carefully, emphasizing that the United States did not desire any Mexican territory, but was unwilling to see the Confederacy gain control of this valuable strategic and mining area. The Mexican government rejected the offer. While in the confusion of early 1861 other rumors of schemes circulated, the reality and rumors concerning Baja California provoked special concern because that area possessed significant value for the United States' future in the Pacific area.[7]

Lincoln and Seward considered the post of minister to Mexico one of the most important they had to assign. They hastened to fill the Mexican post, not, as has been claimed, because "of the armed intervention of England, France and Spain in Mexico," but rather precisely to prevent foreign involvement in Mexico. This intervention did not occur until nine months after Lincoln's inauguration.[8] Rather, the weakened condition of Mexico, foreshadowing possible European intervention or Confederate activity, prompted Lincoln and Seward to make an effort in early March, 1861, to head off an unwanted problem. Later, Corwin explained to Senator Charles Sumner that "the general and leading objects of my mission to Mexico were, first, to prevent the Southern Confederacy from obtaining any recognition here, and thus cut off the hope of augment-

7. Sprague to Seward, May 3, 1861 in *War of the Rebellion: Official Records of the Union and Confederate Armies* (128 vols.; Washington, 1880–1901), Series I, Volume L, Part 1, p. 475, hereinafter cited as *Official Records*. Unless otherwise indicated, all citations are to Series I. Seward to Joseph A. Nunes, June 3, 1861, in Consular Dispatches, La Paz, Record Group 59, National Archives; Seward to Simon Cameron, June 4, 1861, Cameron to Seward, June 8, 1861, in *Official Records*, Vol. L, Pt. 1, pp. 497, 504–505; and Seward to Corwin, June 3, 1861, in Diplomatic Instructions, Mexico, in RG 59, NA.

8. Harry J. Carman and Reinhard H. Luthin, *Lincoln and the Patronage* (New York, 1943), 79–80. Neither the French nor the British governments gave serious consideration to intervening in Mexico until July and August, 1861. The July 17 Mexican debt suspension law was the main motivating factor. See Carl Heinz Bock, "The Negotiation and Breakdown of the Tripartite Convention of London of 31 October 1861" (2 vols.; Ph.D. dissertation, Philipps-Universität, Marburg, Germany, 1961), I, 86–91.

ing the power of the South by acquisition, accompanied with slavery in Mexico or any of the Southern Spanish American Republics. Secondly, to use every proper means to prevent European power from gaining permanent hold upon this part of the American Continent." Corwin felt he had been successful in his first objective, but that the second posed considerable difficulties.[9]

The immediate foreign relations concern of the Lincoln administration involved avoiding an intertwining of the domestic rebellion with economically or strategically important foreign powers to which the Confederates would undoubtedly send agents. Primarily to prevent this latter possibility then, already on March 11 Lincoln pointed out to Seward that Britain, France, Spain, and Mexico were key posts which had to be immediately filled and suggested Corwin for Mexico. After consultation with his close advisor Thurlow Weed, Seward acted at once upon the Corwin appointment, which he laid before the Senate on March 13 for its advice and consent. This was too fast for Corwin, who insisted that the Senate delay consideration or he might have to reject the offer. Since he was immediately recognized as the ideal choice for a difficult post, his pending appointment found widespread approval. Soon withdrawing his reservations, Corwin had Senate approval. His post was considered so significant that he was ordered to depart at once for Mexico.[10]

Thomas Corwin, well remembered for his strong stand against the war with Mexico in 1847, was appointed minister to Mexico to

9. Lincoln to Seward, March 11, 1861, in Basler (ed.), *Works of Lincoln*, V, 281; and Corwin to Sumner, April 14, 1862, in Charles Sumner Papers, Houghton Library, Harvard University.

10. Lincoln to Seward, March 11, 1861, in Basler (ed.), *Works of Lincoln*, IV, 281; Corwin to Lincoln, March 13, 1861, in Lincoln Papers; Thurlow Weed to Seward, March 13, 1861, in William H. Seward Papers, University of Rochester; *New York Evening Post*, March 13, 20, 1861; *El Siglo Diez y Nueve*, March 24, 1861; *Harpers Weekly*, V (June 22, 1861), 386; John Jeffery Auer, "Tom Corwin: King of the Stump" (2 vols.; Ph.D. dissertation, University of Wisconsin, 1947), II, 499; and Seward to Corwin, April 6, 1861, in Diplomatic Instructions, Mexico, RG 59, NA. Romero claimed the United States would resort to a protectorate over Mexico to prevent Confederate influence from obtaining control of that country. Romero to Ministro de Relaciones Exteriores, March 9, 1861, in Correspondencia General con los Estados Unidos.

strengthen the Liberal government's belief that the new administration would not take advantage of Mexico's current weakness.[11] The new cordiality permitted the liberals to reinforce their own views of the past, which assigned less blame for the distrust, suspicion, and hostility which had dominated Mexican–United States relations to the United States government, and considerably more to the Mexican conservative forces—the church, the army, the *creole* aristocratic landowners, and to opportunistic national *caciques* like Santa Anna. Matías Romero observed that the conservatives wanted to sever all communications with the United States, "while the Liberal Party, which has the tie of similar political institutions with that country . . . and believes that the best means of impeding annexation is to open the country to the United States, conceeding [*sic*] them all reasonable privileges, with the objective of making annexation unnecessary and even undesirable."[12] Hence, initially, Mexican authorities generally welcomed Corwin's appointment. Manuel Durán, Mexican agent in New York City, described Corwin as "one of the most prominent men of this country." Although Romero also spoke highly of Corwin, he did inform his government that Corwin was a lawyer for the Sloo interests, one of the groups seeking Tehuantepec transit rights.[13]

Corwin, born in Kentucky, moved to Ohio at four years old. Sixty-seven in 1861, he had a full, active political life behind him. As general assemblyman and governor of Ohio, then congressman, senator, and secretary of the treasury, he had held public office for

11. Seward to Corwin, April 6, 1861, June 3, 1861, in Diplomatic Instructions, Mexico, RG 59, NA.
12. Matías Romero, *Estudio sobre la anexión de México a los Estados Unidos* (Mexico, 1890).
13. M. Duran to Ministro de Relaciones Exteriores, April 10, 1861, in Expediente Personal de Thomas Corwin, Archivo Histórico de la Secretaría de Relaciones Exteriores, H/323(73:72)/77, 24-23-40; Romero to Ministro de Relaciones Exteriores, March 13, 1861, in Romero (comp.), *Correspondencia*, I, 315–16. Romero reported on March 3, 1861, that Nathaniel Banks was the first choice for minister to Mexico and, if he refused, Corwin would be selected. Romero to Ministro de Relaciones Exteriores, March 3, 1861, in Romero (comp.), *Correspondencia*, I, 693–94. Corwin's relationship with the Sloo interests and the role of the latter group in the expansion of United States' economic interests into Mexico are discussed in Chapter IX.

about thirty years prior to his first diplomatic service. He was tall, stout, well dispositioned and charming. He used wit, anecdote, and satire to win office and to coddle or dominate men. Without previous diplomatic experience, he was nevertheless diplomatic in nature. A lifelong Whig, Corwin had opposed slavery in the territories, southern expansionism, and the Mexican War. That his opposition to expansionism derived from his antislavery views, was revealed during the negotiations in 1861 for a United States loan to Mexico, when Corwin then advocated territorial acquisition under a Republican administration.[14]

The large number of claims of United States citizens against Mexico appeared a likely threat to disrupt the existing good relations. Corwin's apparent lack of concern with the growing number and size of American claims can be better understood in the light of Secretary of State Seward's initial instructions to him. Noting that a lack of information in Washington made detailed directions difficult, Seward noted that the "archives here [are] full of complaints against the Mexican government," which it was his intention to defer until stability could be produced in Mexico, at which time they would be presented.[15] The Lincoln administration wanted to strengthen the Mexican Liberal government, which was sympathetic to the Republican ideology and suspicious toward the southern leadership.

Corwin's instructions permitted him to assume a position that appeared much more relaxed and friendly toward Mexico's turbu-

14. John Jeffery Auer, "Lincoln's Minister to Mexico," *Ohio Archeological and Historical Quarterly*, LIX (April, 1950), 115-28; Homer C. Hockett, "Thomas Corwin," *Dictionary of American Biography* (20 vols.; New York, 1946), IV, 457-58; William Y. Thompson, *Robert Toombs of Georgia* (Baton Rouge, 1966), 170-71. Two old, unsatisfactory collections of stories and anecdotes are Josiah Morrow, *Life and Speeches of Thomas Corwin* (n.p., 1896), and Addison P. Russell, *Thomas Corwin: A Brief Sketch* (Cincinnati, 1881). See also two dissertations which focus on Corwin's domestic career, Auer, "Tom Corwin: King of the Stump," and Darly Pendergraft, "The Public Career of Thomas Corwin" (Ph.D. dissertation, University of Iowa, 1943), and *Proceedings of a Meeting of Senators, Representatives, and Citizens, Held in the Reception Room of the United States Senate Chamber, in Memory of Hon. Thomas Corwin, Washington, D.C., December 19, 1866* (Washington, 1866).

15. Seward to Corwin, April 6, 1861, in Diplomatic Instructions, Mexico, RG 59, NA.

lent internal conditions. Moreover, he was the only diplomatic agent in Mexico City in mid-1861 who presented his credentials unconditionally. On May 9, 1861, in his address opening the Mexican Congress, Juárez underlined the very friendly relations with the United States, which he singled out as "most cordial and friendly," while merely indicating that diplomatic relations had been established with Great Britain, France, and Prussia.[16]

Nevertheless, personalities were not as important as ideologies. At the audience Juárez granted for the purpose of receiving Corwin's credentials, Corwin spoke of the shared values of the Liberals and Republicans. He noted the long battle in Mexico had resulted in the establishment of civil and religious liberty, and liberal social institutions and laws. Corwin's perception of Mexico's development was simply the reproduction of a model of the United States Constitution and political institutions. Mexico's achievement would be the liberal goals of "security of persons and property and the suppression of crime, harmonizing thus individual liberty with social progress and political tranquility." Corwin summarized his government's view of future relations in this manner: "I hope to be able to confirm our actual friendly relations with Mexico by extending even more our commercial exchanges, under mutually advantageous principles which justly unite the sister Republics with bonds of interest, in the same manner as the sympathy which naturally was born of the similarity of their respective political organizations."[17]

While Seward wished to give Mexico breathing space, the Mexican government soon discovered that where Corwin's friends or economic interests were concerned, the breathing space would be very thin. Corwin pressed several minor matters so hard that Ro-

16. Roeder, *Juárez and His Mexico*, I, 350–51; *Un Siglo de Relaciones Internacionales de México: A Través de los Mensajes Presidenciales*, No. 39, Archivo Histórico Diplomático Mexicano (Mexico, 1935), 94.

17. "Discurso de Thomas Corwin al presentar sus credenciales como Ministro de los Estados Unidos," May 21, 1861, in Jorge L. Tamayo (ed.), *Benito Juárez: Documentos, Discursos y Correspondencia* (14 vols.; Mexico, 1964–1970), V, 435–39, hereinafter cited as Tamayo (ed.), *Juárez Documentos*.

mero was finally instructed to have Seward direct Corwin "to raise his hand a little which had come to weigh so much in reclamations."[18] Even before Juárez' instructions arrived, Romero had approached Seward concerning the problem of Corwin and claims. While declining to issue new instructions, since he felt the existing ones were clear and precise, Seward agreed with Romero's interpretation of the instructions to Corwin.[19]

The Mexican disenchantment with Corwin intensified when he acted to sustain the French-Jecker loan. The Jecker loan, a dubious financial transaction between Jean Baptiste Jecker's financial house and the Mexican conservative government of Miguel Miramón, was a last-minute effort to prevent a Liberal victory in 1859. Later, after Jecker succeeded in interesting the Duke de Morny, Napoleon's illegitimate half-brother, in the loan, France pressed for its full payment. The Juárez government not only refused repayment, but noted that Miramón had collected just ten cents on the dollar of bonds issued.[20] In late 1861, Corwin unwisely joined several foreign representatives in urging the Mexican government not to carry out its threatened expulsion of Jecker. Initiating a technique which soon became his common weapon for bringing Mexico's case before the United States Congress and populace, Romero, without waiting for instructions, took a draft resolution censuring Corwin's conduct to Democratic Congressman Samuel S. Cox of Ohio, who introduced it in the House on December 15, 1862. A week later it passed the House.[21]

18. Juan Antonio de la Fuente to Romero, October 27, 1862, in Romero (comp.), *Correspondencia*, II, 802–803.

19. Romero to Ministro de Relaciones Exteriores, October 23, 1862, in Correspondencia General con los Estados Unidos.

20. Roeder, *Juárez and His Mexico*, I, 279–94; Bravo Ugarte, *Historia de México*, Vol. III, Pt. 2, p. 100–104; Rosalynd Pflaum, *The Emperor's Talisman: The Life of the Duc de Morny* (New York, 1968), 221–23; Bock, "Tripartite Convention of London," II, 343–49; Edgar Turlington, *Mexico and Her Foreign Creditors* (New York, 1930), 126–52; and Jan Bazant, *Historia de la deuda exterior de México, 1823–1946* (Mexico, 1968), 89–91. For the role played by British bondholders in the decision to intervene, see Philip J. Sheridan, "The Committee of Mexican Bondholders and European Intervention in 1861," *Mid-America*, XLII (January, 1960), 18–29.

21. Romero to Ministro de Relaciones Exteriores, December 22, 1862, in Correspondencia General con los Estados Unidos; Romero to Ministro de Relaciones Exteriores,

While Corwin's conduct in the Jecker affair drew criticism from Mexico and Congress, Seward sought to avoid further areas of disagreement between the two nations. Greatly concerned regarding the border area where Indians would now be able to move unrestrained due to the breakdown of American authority in a region where Mexican authority had been long prostrated, Seward instructed Corwin to draw Mexico's attention also to the dangers to the northern Mexican states from the neighboring secessionists. Since anarchy in Mexico would tempt the rebels to seek a strong position in northern Mexico, the United States influence was to be used to stabilize Mexico. While disclaiming any desire to aggrandize the United States territorially at the cost of Mexico, Corwin should warn the Mexican government that those American citizens in rebellion against the Washington government might attempt to take advantage of the situation for such purposes. Needless to say, Seward expected any effort by the rebels to obtain recognition from Mexico to be countered. Corwin should convince the Mexican government that the continuation of the Washington government "afford[ed] the surest guarantee Mexico [could] have that her integrity, union, and independence will be respected." Seward concluded that, although the Spanish American republics and the United States had not been as close as they should have been, due to the fault of all parties, they did have a mutual interest in supporting each other "against all disintegrating agencies within and all foreign influences or power without their borders." The result would be the triumph of the republican system in every American state. In this sense, Corwin was to convey President Lincoln's present and future lack of sympathy with European schemes to erect a

December 26, 1862, in Romero (comp.), *Correspondencia*, II, 743–46; Romero to Ministro de Relaciones Exteriores, February 6, 1863, in Romero (comp.), *Correspondencia*, III, 158–59; enclosure B. 1., October 3, 1862, in Corwin to Seward, October 27, 1862, in Diplomatic Dispatches, Mexico, RG 59, NA; and *Congressional Globe*, 37th Cong., 3rd Sess., 166. For Corwin's defense, see Corwin to Seward, January 8, 1863, in Diplomatic Dispatches, Mexico, RG 59, NA. For additional sources of conflict between Corwin and the Mexican government, see José de la Fuente to Corwin, September 27, 1862, April 13, 1863, and Corwin to de la Fuente, March 7, 1863, in Tamayo (ed.), *Juárez Documentos*, VIII, 58–59, 322–23.

protectorate over Mexico or to establish another form of government after overthrowing the present government.[22] As these words were written in April 1861, Seward may have been primarily concerned with obtaining Mexico's support against the Confederacy, a "disintegrating" agent within the United States. Later, however, after the French had intervened in Mexico, Romero would recall these words to Seward's attention.

In early May, 1861, following the formalities involved in Corwin's reception in Mexico, Seward requested permission from the Mexican government, via both Corwin and Romero, to land Union troops at Guaymas, Mexico, and move them into Arizona by the most direct route across Mexican territory.[23] Shortly thereafter, the Mexican Congress received the formal request.

Although the Mexican Congress met in secret, an unnamed friend presented Corwin with a memorandum of the proceedings, which can now be verified from the minutes of the Mexican Congress' secret sessions. After the Committee on Foreign Affairs reported unanimously in favor of the request and the president forwarded a favorable opinion, the Camara de Diputados then debated Seward's request at length in secret. Liberal leader José María Mata, supported by other deputies, expressed the opinion that Mexico would probably have to fight the South in the future in order to resist its efforts to conquer and extend slavery into Mexico. Hence, Mexico should take a stand at that time favorable to the North and against the South. One deputy indeed feared that if the South won, Mexico would eventually be drawn into a war to prevent Confederate filibustering. Other Mexican congressmen seriously considered calling for the United States to guarantee Mexico against slavery. Representative of a widely expressed view, the Speaker of the Camara considered the opportunity for an offensive and defensive alliance at hand, particularly since an agent of the South had just arrived seeking recognition. Since he also be-

22. Seward to Corwin, April 6, 1861, in Diplomatic Instructions, Mexico, RG 59, NA.
23. Seward to Corwin, May 9, 1861, *ibid.*

lieved Mexico would be forced to fight the South, the Speaker favored granting the permission Seward sought which could be the "first step towards the alliance . . . with the free states of the North." Mexico's desperate financial situation, coupled with Corwin's hints at a possible loan, undoubtedly warmed up some normally cool Mexican deputies who therefore supported the transit rights requested. In sum, the request received exceedingly friendly, very positive and amazingly fast action. Mexico's "liberal, prompt and magnanimous" approval of his request prompted Seward to assure the Mexican government of his deep appreciation for their action. Moreover, Seward assured them they would not "have cause to regret" the courtesy.[24]

Just as the United States government delighted over the permission it received to move troops across Mexico, Confederate agent John T. Pickett arrived in Mexico City. After the United States government had named its envoy to Mexico, the Confederate government felt some urgency in appointing an appropriate diplomatic agent to stymie Corwin's expected diplomatic offensive. During the early days of March, 1861, responding to the request of Confederate commissioner in Washington and former minister to Mexico John Forsyth to place his ideas on a proper Confederate policy on Mexico in writing, Pickett argued that the North would institute a commercial policy leading to control of Mexico's commerce and the exclusion of Confederate influence. Then using the leverage gained from commercial ties, the North would attempt to colonize the sugar and cotton lands of Mexico with free labor to give "a severe if not fatal blow to those great interests in our Confederacy." Pickett felt this policy would also fulfill a "long cherished design of surrounding African servitude by a cordon of flourishing free States." Here Pickett almost conceded the superiority of free labor, yet

24. A translated copy of the "memorandum of proceedings in the Mexican Congress with reference to the permission for transit of United States troops from Guaymas to Arizona" was enclosed in Corwin to Seward, June 29, 1861, in Diplomatic Dispatches, Mexico, RG 59, NA; Actas de las Sesiones Secretas, May 31, June 13, 17, and 20, 1861, Archivo de la Cámara de Diputados. See also Seward to Romero, August 27, 1861, in Correspondencia General con los Estados Unidos.

drew no rebuke from either Forsyth, Jefferson Davis, or any other high Confederate official who read his analysis of the Confederacy's Mexican problem. In Pickett's opinion, the ultimate purpose of United States policy was to block any future southern expansion southward. Evidence of the whole scheme was Corwin's appointment as minister to Mexico; after all, Corwin had fought southern expansion into Mexico during the Mexican War.[25]

At the same time, Virginian William M. Burwell warned the Confederate State Department of Yankee interest in Mexico and the significance of Corwin's appointment: "You will have observed that the first Diplomatic appointment of the new Administration has been conferred upon him who welcomed Americans with bloody hands to hospitable graves in Mexico. . . . Lincoln and Seward properly perceive that their main battle with the South is to be fought in Mexico. Hence they send the man who sided with Mexico in a war with his own country, to make interest for the free soil cause." Burwell then explained the necessity of impressing upon Mexicans how the common bonds of slavery/ peonage and an agricultural economy united the two countries. He suggested contacts with the leading Catholic authorities in Mexico to impress upon them that their institution would be safe within the Confederacy, but threatened in alliance with the United States. Finally, Burwell proposed reopening the question of transit rights between the Confederacy and the Liberals as agreed upon in the McLane-Ocampo treaty.[26] Both Burwell and Pickett analyzed the future struggle in Mexico and over Mexico in terms of competing systems, one of which they both defined as the "free soil" group. The other group consisted of their Confederacy allied with the Mexican conservative faction, which was Catholic, agriculturalist, in favor of peonage, and, to their understanding at least, willing to make concessions on transit rights, perhaps even willing to sell land to the Confederacy.

    25. Pickett to John Forsyth, March 13, 1861, in John T. Pickett Papers, Library of Congress.
    26. William M. Burwell to the Secretary of State (CSA), March 14, 1861, in Records of the Confederate States of America, Vol. IV, Library of Congress.

John Forsyth wrote Jefferson Davis on the day Corwin's nomination received Senate approval: "Mexican affairs have suddenly come to be very interesting to the Black Administration. Corwin... has been prevailed on to go to Mexico on account of the immense benefits it is supposed he will be able to confer on his government." Warning, as many others did, that Corwin's mission signaled an effort to undercut the South by strengthening abolition in Mexico and "to monopolize her markets as part compensation for the loss of those of the Southern States," Forsyth also warned, "We should not be behind them [the Lincoln government] in the field of diplomacy."[27] Corwin's mission was considered significant and a great threat to the Confederate future—which was "Southward to Destiny."

In April, 1861, Confederate Secretary of State Robert Toombs recommended sending agents at an early date to Mexico and the independent states of Central and South America, with instructions to establish a liberal commercial policy.[28] A successful Confederate agent could do much to outflank the Union blockade and establish important commercial ties with Mexico and the world. Nevertheless, despite a long mutual border along the Rio Grande which made Mexico a potentially valuable neighbor, the South acted less decisively in preparing a mission for Mexico than the Union government.

Sharp lines can be drawn to differentiate between the two agents, Corwin and Pickett, sent to Mexico in 1861. They were men of different generations as well as of differing backgrounds and personalities. Pickett was born into a prominent Kentucky family. He was a well-educated and, under agreeable circumstances, a pleasant man. His passion and temper were the ground for his often ill-mannered, even crude conduct. At one time a newspaper writer, Pickett possessed a certain flair for words which found vent in his

27. John Forsyth to Jefferson Davis, March 20, 1861, in Pickett Papers; "The South and Mexico," *New York Evening Post*, April 4, 1861.
28. Robert Toombs to Jefferson Davis, April 29, 1861, in Records of the Confederate States of America, Vol. LX.

dispatches and also in those parts of his instructions which he had been called upon to draft. More a man of action than words, however, he served many causes prior to 1861. Soldiering for Louis Kossuth in the Hungarian insurrection had earned him a general's commission. In 1850 he joined the López expedition to liberate Cuba, commanding against the Spanish during the battle of Cárdenas. Later, he was a filibusterer and comrade of William Walker. He retained much of the filibusterer's impetuousness and callous disregard for Latin Americans in his dealing with Mexican officials. His ample diplomatic credentials for the post of Confederate special agent near the Mexican government rested upon his service as United States consul at Turk's Island (Jamaica jurisdiction) from 1845 to 1849 and as consul at Veracruz from the mid-1850s until February, 1861. He also served as secretary to the Confederate commissioners sent to treat with the United States government in March and April of 1861.[29]

Pickett's commission, initial letter of instruction, and letter of introduction, all dated May 17, 1861, permit an insight into another problem of Confederate diplomacy, namely that their instructions to diplomats were at times contradictory, vague, and open to various interpretations. Confederate Secretary of State Robert Toombs instructed Pickett to seek persons interested in privateering, to issue them letters of marque and reprisal, to appoint consuls and prize agents, and, if recognition were extended to the Confederacy, to propose treaties of amity, commerce and navigation, and of extradition. This latter was to involve a new settlement of the border problems of Indians and bandit forays. Finally, Pickett was instructed on morals and social values. The Mexicans were corrupt, loved

29. Maisel, "The Origin of Mexican Antipathy," 259–64; Frank L. Owsley, *King Cotton Diplomacy* (rev. ed.; Chicago, 1959), 89. Pickett was not included in the *Dictionary of American Biography* and has not yet found a biographer. Perhaps his greatest contribution to history was the preservation of the bulk of the Confederate State Department archives which he later sold to the United States government for $75,000. See James Morton Callahan, *The Diplomatic History of the Southern Confederacy* (Baltimore, 1901), 11–24, for the history of the Confederate diplomatic archives.

grandeur, had contempt for parsimony, meanness, personal sloven-
liness and boorish manners, and more than anything were revolted
by drunkenness.

Many of his actions, including many that brought him criticism, were consistent with his instructions or with an ill-defined
Confederate policy toward Mexico. On the one hand, he was told
to proceed with convenient speed in order to place himself in contact with the government of the Republic of Mexico. On the other
hand, due to the independent nature of the sovereign states of the
Republic of Mexico, Pickett was not to hesitate to converse freely
with the local authorities at Veracruz, which he did. This states'
rights view demonstrated the Confederate State Department's failure to understand or accept the Liberal party's desire to establish an
effective central government.[30] Committed to states' rights domes-
tically, the Confederate foreign policy should have been able to adjust this view for export. Of course, it is possible that the Confederacy desired to encourage the states' rights faction in Mexico in order
to obtain a friendlier nation on its border. But contempt for Mexican authority apparently led the Confederate government to assume its actions would be either unnoticed or amendable, if necessary, through bribery.

Once at the seat of government of the republic and in contact
with the Mexican government, Pickett should waive form for substance. Neither his official reception nor official recognition of the
Confederacy was necessary.[31] As a basis for a friendly relationship,
Pickett was to point out that southern men and southern diplomats
had always been the best friends of Mexico, that both peoples, in-

30. Toombs to Pickett, May 17, 1861, and enclosure "Memorandum of Instructions for
Mr. John T. Pickett," in *War of the Rebellion: Official Records of the Union and Confederate Navies*
(30 vols.; Washington, 1894–1922), Ser. 2, Vol. III, 202–208; hereinafter cited as *Official
Records, Navies.*

31. Lucius Q. Washington, chief clerk in the Confederate State Department, claimed:
"The grand objective point of Confederate diplomacy for four years was to secure recognition as an independent Government for the Confederacy." See "The Confederate State Department," *Independent*, LIII (September, 1901), 2218–24.

volved in agriculture and mining, had similar commercial and trade interests in obtaining cheap foreign manufactured goods, that both societies were based upon similar labor systems, slavery and peonage. Pickett was then to impress upon the Mexican government the Confederacy's expectation of strictly neutral treatment in regard to commercial, political, or territorial concessions. In addition he was to make clear to the Mexican government that any grant of special advantage toward the Union would be regarded as evidence of an unfriendly disposition toward the Confederacy, which would be "deplored" and "protested" in the "promptest" and "most decided manner." Furthermore, observing the relationship between the United States representative and the Mexican government, he was to prevent any prejudicial treatment which would interrupt friendly, neighborly relations between Mexico and the Confederacy.[32]

Although his instructions had left much to interpretation, Pickett carried them out in a manner contemptuous of Mexico and Mexicans. His sarcasm and bitterness were often expressed directly to Mexicans. Pickett's only clear violation of his instructions occurred when he got drunk one evening, looked up a United States citizen named John A. Bennett who had spoken disparagingly of the Confederacy and physically assaulted him, for which he was placed under arrest.[33] On one occasion, when asked if he was in Mexico to seek recognition from the Mexican republic, Pickett replied he had been sent to recognize Mexico if he could find a government that would stand still long enough. On another occasion, responding to a comment about Mexican officers not on active duty going to serve in the Union army, Pickett wished the whole United States army would be officered by Mexicans, adding the warning that these Mexican officers should avoid capture or they would be

32. Toombs to Pickett, May 17, 1861, and enclosed "Memorandum," in *Official Records, Navies*, Ser. 2, Vol. III, 202–208.
33. *Ibid.*; Owsley, *King Cotton Diplomacy*, 92–109; and Maisel, "The Origin of Mexican Antipathy," 257–86.

forced to work for the first time in their life, hoeing corn or picking cotton. These incidents were repeated by Pickett in his official confidential correspondence, almost all of which was intercepted by Mexican or United States agents who reported the contents to Corwin and Juárez.[34] Since prior to Pickett's arrival in Mexico, Zarco had instructed Romero "to win the sympathy of the Union for making valid all the articles of the [Mexican] constitution against slavery, and to make it evident that Mexico will never consent to the extradition of slaves, on the contrary will offer asylum and protection to all colored races," the Liberals must have resented Pickett's reminder that vestiges of the illegal peonage system remained in Mexico.[35]

In addition to the nature of his instructions, Pickett's mission was handicapped by the burden of southern slave-state expansionism. The filibustering raids and rumors of 1860–1861 revealed to Mexico that expansionism was very much alive in southern minds. The Crittenden Plan, which included a proposal to preserve slavery in present territory "or future acquisitions" south of 36°30', spotlighted the latent expansionism. Romero considered Mexico, Cuba, and all of Central and South America jeopardized by the phrase "or future acquisitions." His view was supported by Congressmen John Sherman of Ohio and Charles Francis Adams of Massachusetts, who had spoken out against the same danger. Romero's warning found echo in an *El Siglo Diez y Nueve* story claiming the Confederate States intended to expand into all of Central America and the Caribbean, making the Gulf of Mexico a Confederate lake. To Romero and most liberals the leaders of the newly formed Confederacy were spokesmen for the expansionist plans to

---

34. Owsley, *King Cotton Diplomacy*, 99–101, and Maisel, "The Origin of Mexican Antipathy," 265–71, both quoting Pickett to Toombs, August 1 and 29, 1861, in Records of the Confederate States of America, Vol. XXVI, and Corwin to Seward, August 28 and September 7, 1861, in Diplomatic Dispatches, Mexico, in RG 59, NA.

35. Zarco to Romero, March 23 and April 10, 1861, and Romero to Ministro de Relaciones Exteriores, January 23, 1861, in Correspondencia General con los Estados Unidos.

be fulfilled by "future acquisitions," and Pickett represented these leaders.[36]

The Confederacy's policy toward Mexico was not influenced directly by "King Cotton," but rather by the geographical relationship. Mexico was beyond the Union blockade; thus it could supply the South, particularly the Trans-Mississippi Department, with metals, saltpeter, powder, sulphur, blankets and other textiles, and foodstuffs. Likewise cotton and other southern commodities could be exported safely. Some Rebel officials on the border noted the great potential for commerce with Europe through Mexico, although with less optimism when the Liberals commanded the frontier than later, when the French-Maximilian forces controlled the border.[37]

Furthermore, as "King Cotton" proved not to be the powerful weapon inducing European action to assure southern independence, a new Confederate policy developed which attempted to use Mexico as a pawn to be sacrificed in order to convince Napoleon III to abandon neutrality. The Confederacy was willing to overlook the Monroe Doctrine, to forego (or at least postpone) expansion into Mexico, to guarantee Napoleon's position in that country against

36. Maisel, "The Origins of Mexican Antipathy," iii–iv, 257–58; Durham, "American Expansionism into Mexico, 1848–1862"; Romero to Ministro de Relaciones Exteriores, February 9 and 21, 1861, in Correspondencia General con los Estados Unidos; *El Siglo Diez y Nueve*, February 25, 1861. Rembert W. Patrick, *Jefferson Davis and His Cabinet* (Baton Rouge, 1944), 94, claimed that since southern expansionism only aimed to maintain the power balance in the Union, with independence the South no longer needed to follow this course.

37. Hamilton P. Bee to the Confederate Secretary of War, October 12, 1861, and H. E. McCulloch to Samuel Cooper, October 17, 1861, in *Official Records*, IV, 118–19, 122–23. Use of Mexico for trade purposes can be traced in Gertrude Casebier, "Trade Relations Between the Confederacy and Mexico" (M.A. thesis, Vanderbilt University, 1931); William Diamond, "Imports of the Confederate Government from Europe and Mexico," *Journal of Southern History*, VI (November, 1946), 470–503; Robert W. Delaney, "Matamoros, Port of Texas During the Civil War," *Southwestern Historical Quarterly*, LVIII (April, 1955), 473–87; Consular Dispatches, Monterrey, and Consular Dispatches, Matamoros, in Record Group 59, NA; and Judith Anne Fenner, "Confederate Finances Abroad" (Ph. D. dissertation, Rice University, 1969). For an evaluation of Mexican participation in the border trade, see Blood to Seward, June 9, 1862, in Consular Dispatches, Monterrey, RG 59, NA.

the United States in return for French recognition which southern diplomats believed would result in French military intervention.[38]

Historian Donald Crook has suggested that the Confederate confidence that "ideological estrangement between aristocracy and democracy" would precipitate unfriendly displays against the United States "underrated the strength of the democrats in Western Europe." But the European "aristocracies did respond in a hostile way, if not hostile to democracy then hostile to growing United States power in the Caribbean, and Central and South America." And while the European powers may have wisely wished to avoid a confrontation, they gave numerous signs of their desire to clip the wings of the American eagle if it could be done while the eagle was distracted. The Confederacy allied itself with these interests when it adopted a warm and friendly attitude toward a European monarchy in Mexico and remained uncritical of Spanish restoration of power in Santo Domingo. European aristocratic efforts to counter the spread of liberalism in the New World cannot be gauged merely by the aggressive overt acts of Spain and France. Almost all the European monarchies immediately recognized the French puppet government in Mexico and sent accredited diplomatic agents, thereby opening up channels for financial and other forms of assistance, in addition to lending their moral and political support to Maximilian.[39]

The Confederacy would share land borders with only two countries—the United States and Mexico. Since Jefferson Davis' government would have no navy at the outbreak of hostilities, and since its harbors would be blockaded as effectively as northern ingenuity and energy would permit, desired war material could most

38. Owsley, *King Cotton Diplomacy*, 87–88, 507ff.
39. Donald P. Crook, *The North, the South, and the Powers, 1861–1865* (New York, 1974), 24; Burton J. Hendrick, *Statesmen of the Lost Cause: Jefferson Davis and His Cabinet* (New York, 1939), 115–16, 306–307; Arnold Blumberg, *The Diplomacy of the Mexican Empire, 1863–1867*, New Series, Vol. 61, Pt. 8 (1971) of *Transactions of the American Philosophical Society* (Philadelphia, 1971); and Alfred J. and Kathryn A. Hanna, *Napoleon III and Mexico: American Triumph over Monarchy* (Chapel Hill, 1971), especially Chaps. 1, 9, 12, 13, and 23.

safely enter through the Mexican-Texas border area, landing at the Mexican port of Matamoros and then going over the Rio Grande into Texas. Another secure possibility was overland trading with Monterrey, Saltillo, and Chihuahua, small Mexican interior mining, industrial, and agricultural centers which could and did supply the Confederacy with some war materials such as arms, lead, copper, saltpeter, and textiles. In sum, the question of whether the Confederacy would derive material benefit from trade with the world through Mexico and moral support from recognition by Mexico hung in the balance of the North-South diplomatic contest in Mexico.

As was so often true of Confederate-Union diplomatic battles around the world, the North had a lot to lose and little to gain. Northern diplomatic success would be measured in the negative objectives of restricting Confederate trade possibilities and denying it Mexican recognition. If the Yankees obtained a major success in their Mexican policy, both the immediate and long-range goals of southern expansion would be endangered. As Pickett suggested in early 1861, there were "immense advantages to accrue to the Confederate States in the future from the boundless agricultural and mineral resources of Mexico, as well as the possession of the invaluable inter-oceanic transit of the Isthmus of Tehuantepec."[40] Thus, not just possible future Confederate annexation, but also future commerce (if annexation did not take place for some reason), would be jeopardized by a successful, dominating United States policy in Mexico. Virginian politician William Burwell contended "that the development of Commerce upon your Gulf front constitutes one of the chief elements of your Confederate future prosperity." Burwell even saw immediate strategic benefits vis-à-vis the Union from a successful commercial policy with Mexico which could link trade between "the Gulf and the North Western States," serving as "a powerful inducement to the Manufacturing interests of Cincinnati

---

40. Pickett to Forsyth, March 13, 1861, and Forsyth to Jefferson Davis, March 20, 1861, in Pickett Papers.

and the provision trade of the North West to unite with" the Confederacy.[41]

Another person urging a more active policy, toward northern Mexico at least, was A. B. Bacon of Algiers, Louisiana, who wrote Jefferson Davis: "I believe it all important that we should have intimate and most friendly relations with the states of Tamaulipas and Nuevo León, irrespective of our having or not having a treaty with the central government at Mexico. . . . But I hope I have said enough to induce you to think it important to especially cultivate kindly relations with the authorities of Tamaulipas, by direct semi-diplomatic communications with them through your authorized agents, who should be constantly near them to do away with any false impressions made upon them, either by our enemies or our injudicious friends."[42]

Despite the council of various Confederate observers, the southern leadership, only vaguely perceiving the significance of the issue at stake, could not quite focus on the core of the matter. Pickett was not instructed to push for commercial ties or recognition. In the same manner, José Augustín Quintero, Confederate special agent sent to northern Mexico in June 1861, was instructed to obtain peace, stability, and order along the frontier, and only then, if the discussion was amicable, to seek closer and expanded trade.

Upon arriving at Veracruz en route to Mexico City, Pickett decided to take advantage of his contacts, stemming from prior years of residence in Veracruz as United States consul. He contacted Liberal leader José María Mata, assuring him that Mexico's resolution had much in common with the southern revolt against a strong central usurpation of power. He also reminded Mata of the favor shown by southern presidents toward Mexico, recalling that it was Yankee senators who had defeated the Forsyth and McLane treaties. Pickett postponed the continuation of his journey into the

41. Burwell to Secretary of State (CSA), March 14, 1861, in Records of the Confederate States of America, Vol. IV.

42. A. B. Bacon to Davis, November 18, 1861, in Records of the Confederate States of America, Vol. XXIV.

capital in order to discuss several matters, such as neutral rights, with his friend Ignacio de la Llave, who had just been elected governor of Veracruz. Desirous of treating Confederate ships on the same basis as United States vessels, de la Llave admitted that since neutrality was a national question, he would forward the matter to the national government. Nevertheless, Pickett assumed that de la Llave would govern correctly.[43]

At this time, hearing the rumor that the United States was proposing an offensive and defensive alliance to Mexico which would include a transit right for troops to move through Mexican soil and attack the Confederacy, Pickett sent a warning to the Mexican government via private persons and hastened to the capital. He arrived in Mexico City on July 4 and found public sentiment ranging from unfriendly to hostile toward the Confederacy. Meanwhile, Mata had written Pickett, suggesting his task would be difficult because Juárez' government would not act decisively on the United States–Confederate States question, to which Pickett replied that he did not expect decisive action, only respect for Confederate belligerent rights. Pickett judged the Juárez government very weak and unstable and scented revolution in the air.[44]

Soon after arriving in Mexico City, Pickett informed Minister of Foreign Affairs Zamacona that the Confederacy did not seek recognition, only friendly peaceful relations with Mexico, and of course, "the strictest neutrality" and full belligerent rights.[45] Although later charging that Mexicans lied to him, Pickett saw fit to assure Zamacona that "it is not the desire of the Confederate States to acquire more Mexican territory." When reporting this assurance to

43. Pickett to José María Mata, June 12, 1861, Pickett to Toombs, June 15, 1861, in Pickett Papers, Letterbook 1; Pickett to Toombs, June 27, 1861, in Records of the Confederate States of America, Vol. V; Franklin Chase to Frederick W. Seward, July 28, 1861, in Consular Dispatches, Tampico, RG 59, NA.

44. Pickett to Toombs, July 11, 1861, and enclosures, in Records of the Confederate States of America, Vol. V.

45. Pickett to John Cripps, July 19, 1861, Cripps to Pickett, July 20, 1861, and "Memorandum of J. T. Pickett of a conference with Zamacona, July 26, 1861," in Records of the Confederate States of America, Vol. IV.

the secretary of state, Pickett said: "It must not be supposed from the expression, in this capital, of the foregoing diplomatic language that I am not fully impressed with the fact that 'manifest destiny' may falsify the foregoing disclaimer. No one is more impressed than the writer with the great truth that, *Southward* the Star of Empire takes its way."[46] Pickett, sensing the need for "a new policy," wished to confront the Mexican government with a dilemma. Continued Mexican support of the Yankees might produce "the possible migration of our people, *en masse*," should the Confederacy be overrun on the northern borders. However, a policy of neutrality or friendliness toward the South could bring unexpected rewards, since Pickett offered "to transmit proposals for the retrocession to Mexico of a large portion of the territory hitherto acquired from her by the late United States."[47] Apparently, the Mexican government did not give special consideration to either Pickett's threat or his promise, since in the minds of most Mexican liberals the threat of southern advance upon northern Mexico would exist as long as the South existed. The prospect of retrocession was correctly perceived as an empty promise; the Confederacy was not offering to return Texas, which it could deliver, but rather California and Colorado, which it could not return to Mexico at that time, if ever.

Pickett's bluster and bluff did little more than annoy Liberal Mexican officials, while confirming their suspicions of the Confederacy. Pickett's difficulties in communicating with the Liberal government increased. Until late August, Pickett pursued a conciliatory policy toward the government in Mexico. He informed the Confederate secretary of state: "My mission here, if I rightly comprehend it, is to preserve the peace not to destroy it." Learned from a reliable source that the Liberal government had granted the United States permission to move troops across Mexican soil over Guaymas and into Arizona, a territory claimed by the Confeder-

46. Pickett to Toombs, August 1, 1861, in Records of the Confederate States of America, Vol. V.
47. Pickett to Toombs, August 1 and 16, September 28, 1861, *ibid.*

acy, Pickett nevertheless advocated a moderate but watchful policy of protest. He counseled that "although it behooves us to guard our flanks, I truly hope my conciliatory and even generous policy will be approved and sustained by my Government."[48] Soon he dramatically changed his attitude.

Having obtained an unofficial interview with Foreign Minister Zamacona, Pickett protested vigorously against the transit grant to the United States. Since New Mexico and Arizona had placed themselves under Confederate protection, he pointed out that the implementation of this permission could initiate warfare all along the northern frontier of Mexico. Pickett threatened that if the rumors alleging the transit grant were true, Mexico could expect "30,000 Confederate diplomats" to cross the Rio Grande. Pickett's tactlessness in this interview with Zamacona prompted the Mexican government to reconsider the privilege granted the Union government, but it also reinforced the Liberal view of an expansive slavocracy.[49]

In addition to Pickett's inquiry into the Guaymas transit permission, Confederate Brigadier General Henry H. Sibley, commanding in New Mexico, sent an unofficial diplomatic mission to Governors Luis Terrazas of Chihuahua and Ignacio Pesqueira of Sonora. Sibley wished to ascertain the reactions of these Mexican officials to the alleged transit grants. Sibley selected for this delicate task Colonel James Reily, whom Terrazas referred to as "a prudent man and a most accomplished gentleman." Specifically, Reily was to ascertain what course of action the Mexican governors contemplated if such a grant had or would be made. Sibley also sought a mutual agreement to permit crossing of the international border by troops of either nation when in pursuit of marauding Indians. Finally, Reily was instructed to explore the possibilities for a more active commercial exchange.[50]

---

48. Pickett to Toombs, August 28, 1861, *ibid.*
49. Maisel, "The Origins of Mexican Antipathy," 266, 270–71; Owsley, *King Cotton Diplomacy*, 99–101.
50. Henry H. Sibley to James Reily, December 31, 1861, Luis Terrazas to Sibley, January 11, 1862, and Reily to Sibley, January 20, 1862, in *Official Records*, IV, 167–68,

Although Reily rated the results of his meetings with Terrazas as a success, his objectives were poorly achieved. Terrazas denied notification of an agreement, "nor would my Government respect it," except if it met the necessary conditions of the Mexican constitution. Terrazas could not grant permission to troops of either nation—Union or Confederacy—to cross the border in pursuit of Indians. If this sort of cooperation appeared desirable, he would take steps to bring a proposal before the Mexican Congress. Finally, arguing that such action would violate Mexico's neutrality, Terrazas refused to initiate any official course toward facilitating trade. In spite of the extremely meager results, Reily, because he had worn his Confederate uniform and had been addressed as colonel of the Confederate States, concluded his mission had been exceedingly successful. His report terminated by congratulating Sibley for "having been instrumental in obtaining the first official recognition by a foreign government of the Confederate States of America."[51]

Although no more successful, Reily's meetings with Pesqueira succeeded in creating some consternation in the United States Southern California command. While returning to Texas through Arizona, Reily publicly announced his success with Pesqueira by alluding to receipt of permission for Confederate supplies to move "without let or hindrance" overland from Guaymas to Tucson. Suspecting an agreement binding Sonora to the Confederacy, Colonel James H. Carleton, commanding the District of Southern California, immediately wrote Pesqueira "to show Your Excellency how much you have been maligned." While awaiting Pesqueira's reply, Carleton suggested to the Pacific Coast commander that, if such were the case, the United States should "seize Sonora and hold it in good faith for our neighbor, to be given up whenever the Central Government of Mexico claims it." Pesqueira considered

171–74. Sibley's notes to Pesqueira and Terrazas were identical. See Sibley to Pesqueira, December 16, 1861, in *Official Records*, Vol. L, Pt. 1. pp. 766–68.

51. Reily to Sibley, January 20, 1862, in *Official Records*, IV, 171–74; and Reily to John H. Reagan, January 26, 1862, in *Official Records*, Vol. L, Pt. 1, pp. 825–26.

"the assertions circulated by Reily as exaggerated, or perhaps badly interpreted." Thanking Carleton for his "delicacy" in the matter, Pesqueira assured him that no agreement had been entered into, adding that in keeping with Juárez' circular announcing Mexican neutrality in the matter then disturbing the United States, only the rights of neutrals would be extended to Confederates.[52]

During the Guaymas transit grant crisis, Pickett's rasping activity produced at least a limited victory. However much ill will he had generated, he had also persuaded Zamacona to notify Romero that, based upon information unknown when the approval had been granted, Mexico now had grave reservations concerning the transit permission. Romero was to communicate to the United States government Mexico's strong desire to remain neutral in the Civil War, obviously implying that if the United States used the transit rights, Mexico might become involved in a conflict with the Confederacy. Since relations with the Lincoln administration were so good at that time, Romero proposed suspending the instructions until a relevant situation developed, rather than to convey the message at once.[53]

Achieving nothing satisfactorily in direct negotiations, in mid-August, 1861, Pickett initiated a personally conceived plan to extract advantage for the Confederacy from the Guaymas transit grant made to the United States. Although aware of the grant for several weeks, he chose not to inform his government because he "had deemed it judicious to permit the United States to make its preparations first, and then to make the counter demand," that permission be withdrawn or if not, the extension of an "equal right for the Confederate State troops with regard to all or any Mexican territory." Applying pressure for a withdrawl of the permission,

52. James H. Carleton to Pesqueira, May 2, 1862, Pesqueira to Carleton, June 2, 1862, Carleton to R. C. Drum, May 14, 1862, in *Official Records*, Vol. L, Pt. 1, pp. 1044–45, 1017–18; Pesqueira to George Wright, August 29, 1862, in *Official Records*, Vol. L, Pt. 2, p. 93.

53. Manuel María Zamacona to Romero, September 8, 1861, and Romero to Zamacona, October 1, 1861, in Correspondencia General con los Estados Unidos. See also Corwin to Seward, August 28 and September 7, 1861, in Diplomatic Dispatches, Mexico, RG 59, NA.

Pickett informed Zamacona that if the Confederacy received an inadequate response on this point, "the people of Texas would not be restrained from at once taking the initiative against Mexican soil."[54] In spite of earlier denials of aggressive intentions, on this as on so many other occasions, the slightest sign of disagreement in Mexican-Confederate relations produced a Confederate threat of aggression or annexation.

Finally, on September 27, 1861, Pickett was angered because the Mexican government had lied to him on paper, something "hitherto unseen in Mexican diplomacy." Although the precise point that he felt was a lie is not clear, he expressed his disappointment with the Mexicans: "Gratitude I did not hope for, but *neutrality* I certainly expected." Noting that he had attempted to "disabuse the Mexican mind in regard of the supposed aggressive policy of the Confederate States," he suspected that "an alliance offensive and defensive is being formed with the United States." Pickett proposed "the policy of *divide et impera*," to be pursued through the initiation of a policy of courting the conservatives and alienating the liberals. To achieve this goal, he urged supporting the conservative former president Zuloaga, the clergy, and the old army chiefs. He no longer considered a stable Mexican government possible; foreign intervention was necessary.[55] To alienate the Liberals, he purposely sent an official letter coded in Latin (an easily decipherable code for Spanish readers) which he wanted intercepted. His message was: "I have lost all hope of preserving peace. This Government will not retrace its steps. We should at once occupy a military position on the Rio Grande and march upon Monterrey.... I design, though hoping against hope, to remain here yet awhile, but within a short time to take my departure."[56] The letter's purpose

54. Pickett to Toombs, August 25, 1861, in Correspondencia General con los Estados Unidos; Pickett to Cripps, August 17, 1861, and "Cripps Memorandum," August 17, 1861, in Records of the Confederate States of America, Vol. IV.

55. Pickett to William Browne, September 27, 1861 (unofficial), Pickett to Toombs, September 28, 1861, in Records of the Confederate States of America, Box 6 and Vol. V.

56. Pickett to Browne, October 2, 1861 (enclosure C), with Pickett to Toombs, October 12, 1861, in Records of the Confederate States of America, Vol. V.

was to pressure the Mexicans into revoking the permission given the Yankees to move troops over Guaymas to Arizona, while compelling the Liberal government to quickly adopt a more conciliatory attitude towards the Confederacy or face the prospect of a Confederate invasion and Pickett's withdrawal. The plan lost its punch, however, when in late October Pickett advocated the same ideas— seizing Monterrey and rupturing the tenuous Mexican-Confederate relations—in an official dispatch not intended for Mexican eyes that was intercepted and brought immediately to Juárez' attention.[57]

After the drawn-out negotiations related to the Guaymas transit grant, fed by other disagreements over secondary matters, Pickett arrived at a further conclusion without consulting his superiors in the Confederate State Department. He decided he could best serve his government by becoming so involved with the Church party that he would be thrown out of Mexico. Pickett was convinced the Church party would soon come to power, at which time he would be able to return to Mexico.[58] Zamacona was not deceived by Pickett's plan to flirt with the conservative Church party. In mid-October, 1861, Zamacona observed that "the confidential agent of the Confederate States continues his intermittent correspondence with this government, and, not having quickly obtained the objectives of the correspondence, he begins to look elsewhere for support in some of the elements hostile to the nation and even in some members of the parliamentary opposition."[59]

At the end of October Pickett initiated a plan to sever Confederate-Mexican relations by sending an insulting dispatch to Foreign Minister Zamacona and by fighting with a northern sympathizer, John A. Bennett, at the latter's place of business. Pickett complained that Zamacona's replies to his notes constantly arrived

57. Pickett to Toombs, October 29, 1861, *ibid.*

58. Owsley, *King Cotton Diplomacy*, 105–108; Callahan, *Diplomatic History of the Confederacy*, 74–75. Callahan implies that Pickett arrived at his scheme to intrigue with the Church party in October. If this is so, he could have had no reliable information about a forthcoming foreign intervention.

59. Zamacona to de la Fuente, October 16, 1861, in Tamayo (ed.), *Juárez Documentos*, V, 127–28.

just before the mail departure, hence, *"after* the preparation of my despatches to my Government." Moreover, chiding the foreign minister for delaying his response to Pickett's September 16 note, the Confederate envoy hoped Zamacona would "find the time necessary to pay some attention to the unsatisfactory relations of Mexico with her nearest neighbor."[60]

Later the same day, Pickett and two friends appeared in Bennett's office. After a brief verbal exchange, Pickett began to strike Bennett, who, not expecting the attack, definitely got the worst in the encounter. Rumor quickly spread that Pickett was drunk and that the attack took place in a tavern. Although a friendly witness claimed Bennett had made no disparaging remarks about the Confederacy, Pickett never alleged it was Bennett's remarks to his face that angered him, but rather what Bennett was saying publicly about the Confederacy and the wives of Confederate officials (probably Jefferson Davis' wife). Then began the Confederate agent's plight. On the next day he was arrested, but allowed to retire to his hotel under arrest. Then a week later and again two weeks later, he was rearrested. Upon his third arrest, Pickett received an offer of release from detainment if he would pay an indemnity and apologize. Refusing the offer, he bribed an official for permission to pass his arrest in the house of Hungarian Gabor Naphegyi.[61]

Pickett regarded his ejection from Mexico after the Bennett incident as a clever, planned diplomatic victory: "It was my object to seize the occasion to fasten a diplomatic question on a Government which, whilst openly professing friendship and neutrality had at that time already clandestinely violated that neutrality, and was secretly intriguing against, and wholly unfriendly to and regardless of the rights, interests and honor of the Confederate States." Incon-

---

60. Pickett to Zamacona, October 30, 1861, in Correspondencia General con los Estados Unidos.

61. Edward H. Moseley, "A Witness for the Prosecution: the Pickett Incident," *Register of the Kentucky Historical Society,* LXVIII (April, 1970), 171–75, translating a letter from Archibald H. Gillespie, a witness to the fight, in *El Siglo Diez y Nueve,* November 22, 1861; *El Siglo Diez y Nueve,* November 19, 1861; Pickett to Toombs, November 29, 1861, and Pickett to Davis, January 11, 1864, in Pickett Papers.

sistently, given his claim to having sought expulsion, Pickett saw the United States minister behind the whole affair: "It is not a violent conclusion to suppose Mr. Corwin managed this entire business."[62] In this case and many others, Pickett's dispatches carry heavy post hoc explanations and evaluations, making the separation of reality and imagination nearly impossible.

After the incident leading to his arrest and expulsion, Pickett's policy recommendations regarding Mexico hardened. Now claiming to see real danger of northern expansion into Mexico, Pickett sought alliances with European countries or with internal Mexican factions to resist the Yankees' intrusions. The Confederate envoy warned the Mexicans that the Monroe Doctrine was dead, and they should not "delude themselves with the belief that North and South will combine together to resist this European Intervention in American affairs."[63] At the same time he repeatedly urged the Confederate government to approach Governor Santiago Vidaurri of Nuevo León and Tamaulipas, who allegedly was not very sympathetic to the Liberal government. Pickett argued that these northern states might readily be annexed, suggesting that "Governor Vidaurri may soon be disposed to meet us half way—but not in hostile array." In any event, Pickett requested that the Confederacy not adopt any policy without giving his ideas a full, careful study.[64]

Although ultimately Pickett departed Mexico in company with the French minister to Mexico, Count Dubois de Saligny, the Confederate agent's efforts to obtain political asylum from either de Saligny or Prussian Minister Baron Anton von Wagner proved unsuccessful. Once departed, Pickett turned his wrath on Zamacona, Juárez, Corwin, and Edward Lee Plumb (an American busi-

62. Pickett to Toombs, December 31, 1861, in Records of the Confederate States of America, Vol. V.

63. Pickett to Toombs, November 29, 1861, in Pickett Papers; Pickett to Cripps, December 27, 1861, Pickett to M. Taussig, January 19, 1862, in Pickett Papers, Letterbook 1.

64. Pickett to Toombs, January 31, 1862, and Pickett to Judah Benjamin, May 6, 1862, in Records of the Confederate States of America, Vol. V; Pickett to Davis, February 22, 1862 (unofficial), in Pickett Papers, Letterbook 1; and Pickett to William H. Browne, December 31, 1861, in Pickett Papers.

nessman serving Corwin as aide and courier) in a series of dis-patches written in late 1861 and early 1862, assigning them blame for his misfortunes.[65] Just prior to departing Veracruz, Pickett de-cided to leave Confederate citizens under the protection of the Prussian minister, but he could not even do this in a congenial manner. He informed Baron Anton von Wagner that notwithstand-ing Prussia's expressed hostility toward revolutionary movements and her statement that she would be the last to recognize the Con-federacy, he placed his "fellow-citizens... under your protec-tion."[66]

Declared *persona non grata* because of his drunken brawling rather than his relationship with the Church party, Pickett was not leaving behind the best image of the Confederacy. His trials and tribulations were not yet over, however. Before leaving, he ap-pointed South Carolinian John S. Cripps in Mexico City and Charles Rieken in Veracruz as "Acting Resident Agents" of the Confederacy, in both cases without authority from his government. Cripps reported soon after Pickett's departure that Mexico was full of animosity toward the Confederacy, a condition perhaps existing before Pickett's arrival, but in no way ameliorated by his presence.[67]

Pickett's return to the Confederacy was very slow. He stopped at Veracruz, Tampico, and Matamoros in order to discuss political matters with local Mexican leaders and to spread threatening gos-sip. While pausing in Tampico, he managed to make United States Consul Franklin Chase, who had been his colleague in the consular service in Mexico before the war, nervous and suspicious. Chase soon reported that William Yancey had met Pickett in Tampico and that they had jointly departed for Matamoros and Texas. Chase

65. Pickett to Toombs, November 29, 1961, December 31, 1861, in Records of Con-federate States of America, Vol. V. There is a large body of correspondence relative to the Bennett incident and its aftermath in Records of Confederate States of America, Vol. IV and V, and Box 6, and in Pickett Papers, Letterbook 1.
66. Pickett to Wagner, February 19, 1862, in Records of Confederate States of America, Box 6.
67. Callahan, *Evolution of Seward's Mexican Policy*, 26.

also claimed that one of Pickett's relatives, employed in the State Department, was supplying the Confederate agent with official information.[68] Upon his returning home, Pickett's mission dissolved into a series of disagreements with the Confederate government over improper accounts and expenses, and the unauthorized appointments of Cripps and Rieken, both rejected by Davis' government.[69]

Pickett never realized the total failure of his mission and continued to seek service in the diplomatic corps and to offer advice. In May, 1862, he wrote directly to President Davis, suggesting State Department administrative shortcomings fouled up his mission and if appointed assistant secretary of state, he offered to guarantee such errors would not recur.[70]

During his months in Mexico, Pickett was volatile, unthinking, imprudent, hasty, a heavy drinker, and much more that should have disqualified him for office. However, not just these personal characteristics, but also the guidelines for his activity, shaped by his instructions, destroyed his usefulness and produced failure in his mission. Moreover, his violent remonstrances about the Guaymas transit permission and other advantages given the United States could be interpreted as following the instructions given him, even if they were more spirited than necessary. A much calmer, abler agent, representing the conservative, proslavery, federalist views, would very likely have seen his mission fail, albeit with less friction and bitterness. With instructions which led him to repre-

68. *El Siglo Diez y Nueve*, December 6, 1861; Franklin Chase to Frederick W. Seward, March 7, 1862, and Chase to William H. Seward, March 11, 1862, in Consular Dispatches, Tampico, RG 59, NA.

69. Pickett to Rieken, February 26, 1862 (two letters), in Pickett Papers, Letterbook 1; Davis to Pickett, May 8 and 13, 1861, Comptroller of the Treasury to Pickett, May 20, 1862, in Pickett Papers; Pickett to Davis, May 9 and 12, 1862, Pickett to Comptroller of the Treasury, May 14, 1862, all in Pickett Papers, Letterbook 1; and Pickett to Toombs, February 4, 1862, in Records of Confederate States of America, Vol. V. According to the "Dates of Appointments" book in Records of Confederate States of America, Volume LX, neither Cripps nor Rieken ever received a formal appointment.

70. Pickett to Davis, May 6, 1862, in Pickett Papers, Letterbook 1. See also Pickett to Toombs, January 11, 1862, in Records of Confederate States of America, Vol. V.

sent the positive values of slavery, an agricultural economic system, and a decentralized state government system—while he used border problems as a threat—could only serve to show the Liberal government that its ties and future were more secure in association with the North if it wished to abolish peonage, centralize government authority, create a national economic structure, attract foreign trade and investment, and end filibustering. Pickett's outbursts revealed the expansionism of the southerner as Mexicans had always expected it from "gringos" in general, and southerners in particular.[71]

Unquestionably, Corwin was a much better choice than Pickett for the task of treating with the sensitive, cautious, and suspicious Mexican politicians. Part of the success of the Union policy, as well as the failure of the Confederate diplomacy in Mexico, is traceable to the respective selections of representatives. But the real choice for Juárez' Liberal government was between working with a neighbor who was a centralized, liberal democracy or a decentralized, restrictive, hierarchical government, which preached a policy of territorial expansion at Mexico's cost. Thus, the promise of friendly relations between Mexico and the United States was not seriously challenged by Confederate foreign policy, at least not as long as a liberal faction headed the Mexican government. The Mexican Liberals preferred cooperation with a government espousing a liberal ideology. Of immediate concern was the formalizing of the relations between Mexico and the United States. In 1861, the Mexican Liberals and the Republicans began negotiations in several areas.

---

71. Philip Van Doren Stern, *When the Guns Roared: World Aspects of the American Civil War* (Garden City, N.Y., 1965), 58, presents a devastating summary of the Pickett mission, calling Pickett "undoubtedly the poorest choice of all Confederate diplomats."

III Treaty Making: Attempts at Building a United States–Mexican Friendship, 1861–1862

During 1861 the need for machinery to adjust and regulate affairs between Mexico and the United States became evident. The Extradition Treaty of 1862 not only eased feelings between the two countries by adjusting the friction of the frontier, but also increased the confidence of American businessmen in the Mexican government, hence encouraging closer commercial ties. The Postal Convention of 1862 established regular and reliable mail communications, thereby aiding trade ties and economic activity between the two countries. The question of United States aid to Mexico to assist the latter in stabilizing its finances led to the negotiation of two precedent-setting loan treaties, both of which were rejected by the Senate. A fifth treaty concerning the commercial relations between the two countries, although advocated by many interested persons and groups from both countries, did not materialize at that time. Meanwhile, the Confederates, although dependent upon trade through Mexico to support their war effort, made no serious attempts to formalize trade relations with Mexico along the border area during the early years of the Civil War. Only in late 1864, in desperation, did the Confederacy seek more formal ties with Mexico, but then it turned to Maximilian's, not Juárez' Mexico.

The negotiation of postal and extradition treaties served as effective initiation into the field of diplomacy for Sebastián Lerdo de Tejada. Although he had served three months as ad interim secretary of foreign relations under President Ignacio Comonfort in 1857, not until late 1861, when Juárez selected him to negotiate with Corwin, did Lerdo de Tejada become permanently involved in diplomacy. Later, in 1863, because of his capable work on this earlier occasion, Juárez selected him as secretary of foreign relations.[1]

In early June, 1861, concerned about the need for faster, more frequent, and safer communication with his government, Romero suggested to Seward the need for the postal treaty.[2] New York businessman Edward E. Dunbar reminded Romero that regular steamship service initiated between Veracruz and New York, either directly or via Havana, would encourage trade. Desiring the negotiations of the postal convention conducted in Mexico City, Seward informed Romero that the necessary powers had been granted Corwin. Romero and Postmaster General Montgomery Blair, suspecting Corwin's personal interests were involved in this matter, decided to negotiate a postal treaty in Washington which they believed would be more acceptable than any drafted by Corwin. Since contrary instructions from the Mexican government arrived too late to halt Romero's negotiations with Blair, discussions for a postal treaty were conducted in both capitals. Ultimately the Romero-Blair draft treaty was rejected in favor of the Corwin-Lerdo de Tejada convention.[3]

The Corwin-Lerdo de Tejada treaty passed over the objection of Romero and Blair that it contained a provision to provide special

1. Frank A. Knapp, Jr., *The Life of Sebastian Lerdo de Tejada, 1823–1883* (Austin, 1951), 66. Knapp's solid study of Lerdo, unfortunately, criticizes Callahan, Rippy, and Thomas Nelson for confusing Sebastián and his brother Miguel Lerdo de Tejada while Knapp himself refers to Thomas Corwin as Charles Corwin.

2. Romero to Ministro de Relaciones Exteriores, June 1, 1861, in Correspondencia General con los Estados Unidos.

3. Romero to Ministro de Relaciones Exteriores, June 1 and 20, September 15, 1861, and February 10, 1862, *ibid.*

benefit to Corwin's friend, Edward E. Dunbar, whose ship line was to be granted the sole privilege of carrying the mails. In fact, Corwin had tried to satisfy either of two New York friends with the mail carrying privilege, Colonel Carlos Butterfield and Dunbar. Butterfield offered such poor terms, however, that the Mexican government summarily rejected his proposal. After Butterfield's proposal was rejected, Corwin voiced his doubts whether a regular mail service would ever be supported adequately by the United States government. In addition, Romero lent credence to the rumor spread by Senator Charles Sumner and other senators that Corwin pushed hard for the mail carrying provisions because he expected to make a "fortune" from it.[4]

After Butterfield's defeat, Corwin joined forces with Marshal O. Roberts, eastern steamship entrepreneur, and Dunbar. Although Dunbar was undoubtedly considering his own pocketbook, he had other motives for soliciting a postal contract. In mid-August, 1861, when Dunbar heard that Romero and Blair were negotiating a second postal treaty, he made it his business to discover the details. Fearing the concession might go to a crony of Seward's, a Mr. Schultz, thus placing his and Roberts' possibilities in jeopardy, Dunbar insisted that Corwin fight for a direct line connecting New York and Veracruz with liberty to touch at Havana. Romero's and Blair's draft treaty would permit a mere feeder line to run from New York to Havana, connecting with either the British or Spanish mail packets to Veracruz. Dunbar argued that this "arrangement would add nothing to existing facilities and effectually prevent the establishment of a national line which would prove of such immense advantage to both countries."[5]

4. Corwin to Anasa Mason, November 29, 1861, in Thomas Corwin Papers, Duke University Library; Romero to Ministro de Relaciones Exteriores, February 2 and July 1, 1862, in Correspondencia General con los Estados Unidos.

5. Corwin to Zamacona, September 25, 1861, in "El Sr. Corwin, remite ocurso relativa a una nueva prórroga para el establecimiento de una línea de vapores entre México y Nueva Orleans," in expediente 4-2-5624, Archivo Histórico de la Secretaría de Relaciones Ex-

At this time, three apparently separate projects for connecting Mexico with the outside world via steamers on the Pacific were being pressed, with Corwin involved in one of them. All claimed that the purpose was to develop the commerce and economic growth of the Pacific coast area. The three groups were the Pacific Mail Steamship Company, Holladay and Flint of San Francisco, and the Panama Railroad Company. Mexico's former president Ignacio Comonfort was secretly involved with the second group and Corwin supported the third. Later, the first two groups obtained grants, but the third was turned down.[6]

Although Romero and Blair preferred open bidding for the steam-line privileges, the United States Senate accepted the Corwin-Lerdo de Tejada Postal Convention without amendment. In the form finally submitted to the Senate, however, the postal treaty skirted the whole issue of favoritism in the mail steamship concession, but Dunbar's concern about a direct line was taken into consideration. The operative phrases in the treaty now stated: "So soon as steam or other mail packets, under the flag of either of the contracting parties [Mexico or the United States], shall have commenced running between their respective ports of entry" would the provisions of the treaty concerning mail subventions go into effect. Thus, only United States or Mexican vessels making direct contact could benefit from the mail subventions of the treaty. Despite his reservations, Romero expected that the closer communications provided for in this treaty "with the commercial emporium and indus-

teriores. (In spite of the file's title all the correspondence is related to a Veracruz-New York steamship line.) And Edward E. Dunbar to Corwin, August 14, 1861, in Edward Lee Plumb Papers, Library of Congress.

6. Contract between Juan Temple and the Pacific Mail Steamship Company, April 17, 1862, Francisco Azoy to Ignacio Comonfort, May 2, 1862, Comonfort to Azoy, June 21, 1862, Temple to Comonfort, December 19, 1862, all in Ignacio Comonfort Papers, Latin American Collection, University of Texas; *El Siglo Diez y Nueve*, August 25, 1861; Corwin to Zamacona, July 23, 1861, Zamacona to Ministro de Hacienda, August 2, 1861, "El Sr. Corwin, remite ocurso relativa a una nueva prórroga para el establecimiento de una línea de vapores entre México y Nueva Orleans," in expediente 4-2-5624.

trial metropolis of this continent" would produce important economic and commercial development for Mexico.[7]

The Corwin-Lerdo de Tejada Postal Convention was signed in Mexico City on December 11, 1861, approved by the Mexican Congress 102 to 0, and submitted to Juárez for ratification in January, 1862. Later, after United States Senate approval, it was ratified and returned to Mexico to have the ratifications exchanged and certified. After a brief delay, the postal treaty was finally proclaimed in June, 1862.[8]

The long history of bitter frontier strife—armed border crossings, cattle rustling, Indian forays, smuggling, racial incidents—pointed to the need for better means to reduce bloodshed and emotional outbursts along the Mexican-Texas border. By agreeing to extradite people charged with murder, assault with intent to commit murder, mutilation, piracy, arson, rape, kidnapping, forgery, counterfeiting, embezzlement of public funds, robbery, burglary, and larceny, defined to include cattle rustling or taking of goods or chattels valued at over twenty-five dollars if the act occurred within the frontier states or territories, it was hoped that an extradition treaty would supply a major contribution toward relaxing frontier tension.[9]

Before approving the extradition treaty, the Senate had insisted upon one minor amendment, the striking out of "theft and peculation" from Article III defining the crimes for which delivery of

7. George P. Sanger (ed.), *Treaties Concluded by the United States of America with Foreign Nations and Indian Tribes* (Boston, 1862), in *United States Statutes at Large*, 36–37th Congress, pp. 263–69, 266; Corwin to Seward, December 24, 1861, in Diplomatic Dispatches, Mexico, RG 59, NA; Romero to Ministro de Relaciones Exteriores, July 13, 1861, in Correspondencia General con los Estados Unidos.

8. The treaty text is found in Sanger (ed.), *Treaties;* Romero to Ministro de Relaciones Exteriores, December 6, 1861, in Romero (comp.), *Correspondencia,* I, 615; Seward to Corwin, April 10 and 16, 1862, in Diplomatic Instructions, Mexico, RG 59, NA; Corwin to Seward, December 24, 1861, in Diplomatic Dispatches, Mexico, RG 59, NA. The postal convention was apparently approved without discussion. See Actas de las Sesiones Secretas, December 13 and 15, 1861. See also *El Siglo Diez y Nueve,* June 1 and 2, 1862; Gideon Welles to W. W. McKean, April 16, 1862, Frederick W. Seward to Plumb, April 17, 1862, in Edward Lee Plumb Collection, Stanford University Library.

9. Sanger (ed.), *Treaties,* 257–61.

prisoners was to be made. Since the discussion was conducted in secret session, it is only possible to speculate about the reasons for striking them. Probably antislavery forces in the Senate wanted to make sure that fugitive slaves would not be extradited for running away with their clothes on, since legally slaves' clothes belonged to the master. Thus, Article II and parts of Article VI, insisted upon by the Mexican government, stated that no fugitive slave nor any-one committing a crime while in the condition of slavery would be extradited. Several United States newspapers criticized Corwin's negotiations after Mexico objected to the unclear wording which could lead to demands to return fugitive slaves. The *Chicago Tribune* charitably suspended judgment of Corwin until the treaty was pro-duced, secure in the conviction that Seward would not approve an ambiguous clause regarding the extradition of runaway slaves. Likewise, political prisoners and citizens of the country being asked to grant extradition would not be subject to the provisions of the treaty.[10]

The extradition treaty called for surrender of alleged criminals by means of requisitions made through the respective diplomatic agents. Exceptions were permitted in the case of frontier states or territories where extradition requests could be made by the chief civil officer of the state or territory, or by duly deputized civil or judicial officials, or, when civil authority in a border state or terri-tory was suspended, by the chief military officer in that area. Sur-render of persons would be to the executive of the nation, or, in the border areas, to the officials authorized to request extradition, with the requisitioning government bearing all expenses for the capture and delivery.[11]

It was hoped that the grant of broad extradition power to the authorities on the frontier, particularly in regard to the types of crimes they confronted daily, would allow for easier, more satisfac-

---

10. *Ibid.*; Romero to Ministro de Relaciones Exteriores, April 9, 1862, in Romero (comp.), *Correspondencia*, II, 123–24; "A New Light in Diplomacy," *Chicago Tribune*, November 7, 1861.
11. Sanger (ed.), *Treaties*, 257–61.

tory solutions to border problems. Criminal gangs, operating on both sides of the Rio Grande, followed a rough rule of using one side as a haven, where they committed few if any criminal acts, and the other side for robbing and plundering. The extradition treaty sought to eliminate the near certain immunity from social and legal responsibility that they found in their chosen haven area. It was to be hoped that border officials would institute a brisk series of arrests and extraditions, promoting law and order on the Mexican–United States border.[12] The more stable border conditions produced by the extradition treaty would serve to encourage United States commerce with and investment in the northern Mexican states.

An extradition treaty, signed in Mexico City on the same day as the postal convention, December 11, 1861, was approved by the Mexican Congress, 99 to 1. It followed an identical course through the treaty process, experiencing United States Senate approval by the narrowest possible margin, 27 to 13. Ratifications were exchanged in Mexico City on May 20, 1862, and the treaty was proclaimed in June, 1862.[13]

While the cordial exchange of views and the friendly negotiation of postal and extradition treaties between Mexico and the United States during 1861 and 1862 offer evidence of the developing closeness and friendship, the strongest examples of the increasing cooperation between the two powers grew out of the Mexican government's financial collapse following the assumption of power by the Liberals.

12. Zorrilla, *Relaciones*, I, 422; Barry M. Cohen, "The Texas-Mexico Border, 1858–1867: Along the Lower Rio Grande Valley during the Decade of the American Civil War and the French Intervention in Mexico," *Texana*, VI (July, 1968), 153–65; and the autograph manuscript of Francisco Mejía, "Épocas, Hechos y Acontecimientos de mi Vida y de los Que Fuí Actor y Testigo," written in 1878, Latin American Collection, University of Texas.

13. Seward to Corwin, April 10 and 16, 1862, in Diplomatic Instructions, Mexico, RG 59, NA; Corwin to Seward, December 24, 1861, in Diplomatic Dispatches, Mexico, RG 59, NA; Romero to Ministro de Relaciones Exteriores, April 9, 1862, in Romero (comp.), *Correspondencia*, II, 123–24. The extradition treaty was apparently approved without discussion. See Actas de las Sesiones Secretas, December 13 and 15, 1861; and *El Siglo Diez y Nueve*, June 1 and 2, 1862.

By 1861, the long *guerra de la Reforma*, only a final chapter in forty years of civil war and revolution, ended with a financially ruined Mexico. Corwin, observing the obvious sad state of Mexico's financial condition upon his arrival, proposed to aid Mexico financially even prior to the Mexican government's suspension of foreign debt payments. The great significance given to Mexican affairs is evident in Corwin's request and the Lincoln administration's decision to approve, for the first time, a direct United States government loan to sustain a friendly government. Juárez' Liberal government, threatened by internal disorder and external intervention, was considered essential for United States security and well-being. During the intervention crisis in late 1861 and early 1862, Corwin negotiated two loan treaties with Mexico: the Corwin-Zamacona treaty, signed in November 1861, and the Corwin-Doblado treaty, signed in April 1862. In the twentieth century, direct United States government loans to preserve "friendly" governments from internal and external threats are common; in the nineteenth century, these Mexican loan treaties stand alone, and although defeated in the Senate, both had administrative support and encouragement.

In his initial dispatches to the State Department concerning a loan to Mexico, Corwin suggested possible forms of securing the loan for the United States: first, he suggested the annexation of Baja California, because of its value to the Pacific trade, or alternatively, the Mexican tariff could be revised to give the United States a 50 percent lower duty than any other competitive power. Initially, in Corwin's mind the loan to alleviate Mexican financial difficulties was equated with United States commercial advantage. Later, on July 17, 1861, the Mexican government suspended payment of the foreign debt for two years. France and Britain reacted immediately by severing diplomatic relations with Mexico; Spanish relations with Mexico had been interrupted earlier.[14] Only later, after the threat of a French-Confederate alliance, did the main objective of a

---

14. Corwin to Seward, May 29 and June 29, 1861, in Diplomatic Dispatches, Mexico, RG 59, NA; Bravo Ugarte, *Historia de México*, Vol. III, Pt. 2, p. 95.

United States loan become the preservation of the political and territorial integrity of Juárez' Mexico. Thus, the basic motivation of the original loan proposal—to directly advance United States commercial interests—was forced into a secondary position behind a developing realization that liberal Mexico's territorial integrity was jeopardized by European intervention, thereby posing a different problem, now involving United States political and military security.

After Mexico suspended debt payments, Corwin immediately renewed his recommendation for financial assistance, advancing two new strong arguments. First, observing Mexico's reduced bargaining position, he saw an ideal opportunity for acquiring Baja California, Chihuahua, Sonora, and Sinaloa, since the public lands and mineral rights in these areas would most likely be used to secure the loans. Then, when Mexico could not pay, as seemed very probable, these areas would become United States possessions. Second, Corwin judged that the European powers had intervened in Mexico precisely because the secession crisis made it difficult for the United States to take positive counteraction. In spite of the embarrassing internal situation, Corwin wished the United States to fulfill its role as guardian of New World independence and civilization.[15]

Few of the scholars who have treated Mexican–United States relations during the Civil War or the Corwin loan negotiations have explained satisfactorily the apparent inconsistency of Thomas Corwin, arch-friend of Mexico and reputed defender of Mexican territorial integrity in 1847–1848, trying to persuade Seward to make a loan to Mexico with the expectation of foreclosing on a defaulting Mexican government, thereby obtaining several northern Mexican states for the United States. One historian, observing the inconsistency, suggested that perhaps Corwin assumed the

15. Corwin to Seward, July 29, 1861, in Diplomatic Dispatches, Mexico, RG 59, NA. Perhaps to encourage favorable action on his loan for lien proposal, in Corwin to Seward, August 28, 1861, Corwin referred positively to rumors of new mineral discoveries in Sonora and Chihuahua.

expansion-minded Seward would approve and lend his weight to a loan proposal only if couched in these terms.[16]

Quite obviously, Corwin's opposition to expansion derived from a judgment concerning who would benefit from the acquisition of new territory, the Democratic slave expansionists, or Republican free-soil expansionists. Corwin's dispatches to Seward reveal a believer in Manifest Destiny and a commercial expansionist. In late June, 1861, Corwin doubted that the Juárez government would sell any territory, except perhaps "little-valued" Baja California. Still, since this land was "much more valuable than is generally supposed in mineral resources," he believed it would be a good buy. One month later, the preliminary stages of his loan negotiations excited him because the United States might acquire sovereignty over Baja California, Chihuahua, Sonora, and Sinaloa. He tempered his annexationism by admitting he would not be anxious to add territory, other than Baja California, if Mexico were not threatened by European intervention. Still, he could not deny that "the United States are the only safe guardians of the independence and true civilization of this Continent. It is their mission and they should fulfill it."[17]

Corwin would prove a greedy expansionist. Although the loan proposals appeared to preserve Mexican sovereignty, Corwin, citing church property and unoccupied national lands as security, insisted upon and received as security for the Corwin-Zamacona loan not just a specific lien on public lands and mineral rights in the four north Mexican states cited by Seward, but in *all* of Mexico. As if to guarantee the ultimate absorption of Mexico into the United States, the whole of the nationalized Catholic Church property was also included in the description of security found in the treaty.[18]

16. Robert W. Frazer, "Matías Romero and the French Intervention in Mexico, 1861–1867" (Ph.D. dissertation, University of California, Los Angeles, 1941), 56.

17. Corwin to Seward, June 29, and July 29, 1861, in Diplomatic Dispatches, Mexico, RG 59, NA.

18. Corwin to Seward, July 29, 1861, *ibid.* A copy of the Corwin-Zamacona treaty was enclosed in Corwin to Seward, Mexico City, November 29, 1861.

Corwin's interest in Baja California, also, stemmed from his conception of future United States economic expansion. He desired the acquisition of Baja California because it might become "indispensable" to the Pacific coast states, and, because he recognized that area's "potential to harm United States Pacific trade" under foreign control.[19] Furthermore, his relationship to parties interested in a regular steamship line and his connection with the New York-based Sloo interests, a company involved in Tehuantepec transit rights, demonstrated Corwin's interest in certain commercial expansionist schemes.

An additional motive for offering Mexico financial aid at this time was to circumvent Confederate plans to exploit Mexico's weakened condition. Threatening aggressive action if Mexico did not adopt "correct" policies toward his government, Pickett tried to seduce Mexico to make the "right decision." In late 1861, to counteract Pickett's offer to return all Mexican lands, except for Texas, taken by the old United States government in return for free trade between Mexico and the Confederacy, Corwin contended the loan treaty would demonstrate the Union's willingness to take positive steps to aid Mexico in its time of need.[20]

Corwin's ambivalent position in regard to the most advantageous compensation for a United States loan found its counterpart within Lincoln's cabinet, an informant told Romero. In mid-July, 1861, Seward read Corwin's early dispatches calling for a loan to Mexico at a cabinet meeting. While Seward considered the acquisition of Baja California and other territory as the price, Montgomery Blair argued that the loan should be granted in exchange for commercial privileges.[21] No decision was reached, but soon rumors of a

19. Corwin to Seward, May 29 and July 29, 1861, *ibid*. Corwin's early dispatches contained his plans for territorial expansionism; increasingly thereafter he was concerned with commercial growth.
20. Callahan, *American Foreign Policy*, 283; Owsley, *King Cotton Diplomacy*, 101–102; Corwin to Seward, October 29, 1861, in Diplomatic Dispatches, Mexico, RG 59, NA.
21. Romero to Ministro de Relaciones Exteriores, July 17, 1861, in Tamayo (ed.), *Juárez Documentos*, IV, 592.

United States loan to Mexico in return for territorial or commercial concessions circulated in the United States, Mexico, and Europe.

The qualification in Corwin's instructions that any loan between Mexico and the United States must be acceptable to Britain and France very likely originated with or was strongly encouraged by opposition within the cabinet to Seward's proposal. At a cabinet meeting on August 27, 1861, in response to Seward's introduction of the question of a Mexican loan, Attorney General Edward Bates read a memorandum to the cabinet outlining four main objections to making a loan. First, the Republican party had opposed President Buchanan's efforts to establish a protectorate over Mexico; therefore consistency would dictate rejection of Corwin's proposal. Second, he was opposed to annexation since it would only weaken the United States. (Later in the memorandum, Bates acquiesced in the annexation of Baja California, which was "by obvious fact . . . different from the rest of Mexico.") Third, Bates argued that to follow the proposed policy would "alienate from us a large and influential class of the best people in Europe." This class was capable of deadlocking ministerial policy and altering international action. Fourth, the reaction of Britain and France might well lead them to aid the Confederacy. Bates believed these two countries desired to intervene in the Civil War, but lacked adequate justification. They might learn "our secret" (the expansionist nature of the loan) and, "putting us in the wrong," declare war on us. At the very least, Bates surmised, they would recognize the Confederacy. Whatever Seward may have thought of the soundness of such arguments, his respect for the political strength of Bates and others holding similar views might well have guided his hand, when five days later he instructed Corwin regarding the drafting of a loan treaty.[22]

Attorney General Bates had tellingly pointed out that the loan treaty would be inconsistent with past United States action, when

22. Howard K. Beale (ed.), *The Diary of Edward Bates, 1858–1866, American Historical Association, Annual Report, 1930* (Washington, 1933), IV, 188–93.

the Republican party leadership had successfully opposed such aggressive treaties during Buchanan's administration. Bates contended that the mere proposal of a loan would "disclose to the world our design upon Mexico—to dismember it at least, if not to absorb it altogether." He warned that "France and England will know, right well, how to deal with such facts," meaning as an excuse to intervene in the United States Civil War. He argued that even when at peace the United States should not act as "guardians of the crippled and insane nations round about us... but we are not in peace... we are in no condition to assume the guardianship of poor distracted Mexico." The United States could recklessly demonstrate its courage "by volunteering to thrust ourselves between united France and Britain and their interest or their ambition. But I am not brave enough to do it.... Already they are jealous of our growing power, and watching occasions to give us a crippling blow."[23]

In September, 1861, Seward authorized Corwin to open negotiations with Manuel Zamacona for a direct loan to Mexico. The United States would lend Mexico nine million dollars, a sum sufficient to pay 3 percent interest for five years retroactive to the July 17, 1861, decree on the funded Mexican debt of about sixty-two million pesos. Since Seward did not have confidence in Mexican financial ability, the interest would be paid in the United States. Mexico would repay the loan at 6 percent interest within six years of the date of the treaty. The loan would be secured by a specific lien on all public lands and mineral rights and the nationalized church property in Baja California, Chihuahua, Sonora, and Sinaloa. The treaty was conditioned upon Britain and France agreeing to forbear any hostile action against Mexico on account of nonpayment of interest during negotiations and as long thereafter as the interest was paid.[24]

23. *Ibid.*
24. Seward to Corwin, September 2, October 2, 1861, in Diplomatic Instructions, Mexico, RG 59, NA; and Corwin to Seward, November 29, 1861, in Diplomatic Dispatches, Mexico, RG 59, NA.

Mexican Minister Zamacona quickly perceived that the United States loan proposals sought to distance European intervention from the New World. Apparently the loan negotiations persuaded the Mexican Congress to expect strong United States support in its negotiations with European creditors, because in November, 1861, they voted overwhelmingly, 75 to 22, without discussion, to reject the pending and quite acceptable Wyke-Zamacona treaty, settling outstanding Mexican-British differences.[25] Paradoxically, Corwin's instructions permitted a loan to Mexico only if Britain and France would agree to forbear intervention under the conditions previously described. Thus, although the Corwin-Zamacona draft treaty had been forwarded to Washington, the Mexican rejection of the Wyke-Zamacona treaty compelled Corwin officially to withdraw his loan proposal.[26]

Lincoln first submitted Corwin's draft treaty to the Senate on December 17, 1861, shortly after a joint British, French, and Spanish expedition had landed on Mexican soil. Both Mexico and the United States desired to persuade these three powers to withdraw. Corwin's new instructions authorized him to negotiate a treaty which could be useful toward achieving this goal "if the occasion shall offer for Mexico to make a treaty with her invaders, and if Mexico shall...with a view to her aid in that emergency, apply... for some financial aid from the United States."[27] The Senate Foreign Relations Committee immediately began consideration, with at least one member approving of Corwin's draft, but the committee, troubled by threat of war with Great Britain over the seizure of the British Mail packet, the *Trent*, took no quick action. On January

25. Zamacona to Juan Antonio de la Fuente, October 16, 1861, in Tamayo (ed.), *Juárez Documentos*, V, 127–28; Peña y Ramírez resolution, Actas de las Sesiones Secretas, November 22, 1861.

26. George Wallace Malloy, "The United States and French Intervention in Mexico, 1861–1867" (Ph.D. dissertation, University of California, 1937), 76–77, and Robert Kenneth Lacrete, "Great Britain and Mexico in the Age of Juárez, 1854–1876" (Ph.D. dissertation, Case Western Reserve University, 1971), 154.

27. Seward to Corwin, February 15, 1862, in Diplomatic Instructions, Mexico, RG 59, NA.

24, 1862, Lincoln's second message requested early Senate action so Corwin could be given instructions which, fitting the new circumstances, would protect United States interests.

In early 1862, at the request of Sumner, businessman and future United States minister to Mexico Edward Lee Plumb prepared a long memorandum summarizing the arguments favoring a Mexican loan. Plumb's long association with Mexico and Mexican leaders through various investment projects and long sojourns in that country gave him the reputation, interest, and connections which involved him extensively in United States relations with Mexico during the 1860s. Plumb asserted that since the loan would revive and stimulate Mexican commerce by redirecting it away from European hands and into North American, it was "the true supplement to the Monroe Doctrine." Moreover, after replacing European influence in Mexico, "financial control of Spanish American affairs" would fall to the United States. Plumb added: "More important than all, by tranquilizing Mexico that country would cease to be a dangerous element in our own politics." Later, United States emigration into Mexico would increase until "in the course of time . . . the [Mexican] border states . . . will . . . segregate in due order of gravitation, peacefully into the American Union." More-over, desirous of maneuvering the European fleet out of the Gulf area, Charles Sumner, powerful chairman of the Senate Committee on Foreign Affairs, reported from his committee a resolution which recommended a treaty assuming interest on the Mexican debt and certain other liabilities, the sum to be held as small as possible, and the whole to be conditioned upon the British, French, and Spanish agreeing to withdraw.[28] This appeared a reasonable bargaining position.

Plumb's report for Sumner probably influenced the Foreign Re-

28. James D. Richardson (comp.), *A Compilation of the Messages and Papers of the Presidents, 1789–1897* (9 vols.; Washington, 1898), VI, 60, 63; Charles Sumner, "Report from the Committee for Foreign Relations upon the Draught of a Convention with Mexico, February 19, 1862," in George F. Hoar (ed.), *Charles Sumner: His Complete Works* (20 vols.; Boston, 1900), VI, 365–75. James G. Randall and Theodore C. Pease (eds.), *The Diary of Orville Hickman Browning* (2 vols.; Springfield, 1935), I, 516; and a memorandum dated 1862, enclosed with Plumb to Nathaniel P. Banks, May 9, 1866, in Plumb Papers.

lations Committee's favorable action toward a Mexican loan. The committee decided the anticipated advantages justified a moderate investment, which it defined as a $15 million maximum. The loan should have two conditions: 1) the assent of the allied powers and 2) ample security for the liabilities assumed. Regarding the security, the report suggested several possibilities, although admitting that perhaps Corwin, on the spot, should best be left the power of making the final decision. The security offered in the Corwin-Zamacona loan was considered adequate. Other possibilities included the right-of-way across Tehuantepec because of "its political and commercial value" and a 25 or more percent share of Mexican customs or other revenues. While insisting that the United States had no inclination to acquire Mexican territory, in discussing the value of Mexican public lands as security, the report noted that "the province of Lower California is unquestionably the territory of Mexico most interesting to the United States in a military and naval point of view."[29]

The whole Senate, faced with investigating the Ball's Bluff fiasco and organizing the Committee on the Conduct of the War, was determined, nevertheless, to reject this position. The Senate Radicals assigned priority to shaking up an army hierarchy and an administration whose loyalty and competence were questioned. McClellan's fabian tactics were producing distrust and lack of confidence among many political figures in Washington. Largely due to McClellan's strategy (or lack thereof) and the previous year's campaigns, the war, now entering its tenth month, was recognized as more than a brief affair. In addition, the *Trent* affair continued to unsettle relations with Britain.[30] The prospect of a longer war

---

29. Hoar (ed.), *Charles Sumner: His Complete Works*, VI, 365–75.

30. Malloy, "The United States and French Intervention in Mexico," 106–107. The British were also aware of the bind the United States was in because of the *Trent* affair and European intervention in Mexico occurring simultaneously. Lord Lyons, British minister to the United States, wrote: "I am told that the Senate is still more angry about the combined expedition against Mexico than about the *Trent* affair. They will hardly be so absurd as to manifest their displeasure in such a way as to add France and Spain to their adversaries." See Lord Lyons to Lord Russell, Washington, December 23, 1861, in Thomas W. Newton, *Lord Lyons, A Record of British Diplomacy* (2 vols.; London, 1913), I, 170.

meant difficult long-term financial measures would have to be undertaken just in order to finance the military machine. In sum, conditions during the winter of 1861–1862 presented an inopportune time to approach the Senate to adopt foreign obligation, entailing a large cash outlay.

In February 1862, the Senate, rejecting the Corwin-Zamacona loan treaty by a 28 to 8 vote, offered a brief substitute resolution: "Resolved, That in reply to the two several messages of the President with regard to a treaty with Mexico, the Senate expresses the opinion that it is not advisable to negotiate a treaty that will require the United States to assume any portion of the principal or interest of the debt of Mexico, or that will require the concurrence of European powers." This blunt and blanket rejection of financial aid to Mexico came too late, however, to end negotiations on this matter. Ten days earlier, Seward had instructed Corwin to negotiate, under certain circumstances, a new loan treaty. Since the first loan treaty, intervention, previously only a possibility which the United States and Mexican governments desired to avoid, had become a reality.[31]

Despite the unsettled condition of United States–Mexican relations in early February, 1862, Seward counseled Lincoln to nominate General Winfield Scott as "additional minister" to Mexico, thereby lending prestige and military authority to the United States position opposing foreign involvement in that country. Scott's illness, advanced age, and suspected inability to deal with the more wily foreign agents quickly generated sufficient senatorial opposition to block his nomination. Lincoln withdrew the nomination on

31. Hoar (ed.), *Charles Sumner: His Complete Works*, VI, 365–75, contains a copy of the report of the Senate Foreign Relations Committee, its proposed resolution, and the accepted substitute resolution. Unfortunately, the whole of the Senate discussion relative to the Corwin Mexican loan proposal was conducted in secret executive session. A set of Sumner-prepared draft amendments to a Mexican treaty appears to be misdated, 1861, in Lincoln Papers. They very likely refer to the 1859 McLane-Ocampo treaty. Romero reported the vote, 28–8, but due to the secrecy of the debate could learn no details. See Romero to Ministro de Relaciones Exteriores, February 26, 1862, in Romero (comp.), *Correspondencia*, II, 66–67.

February 27, citing Scott's infirmities as cause. Nevertheless, Scott's nomination prompted European countries to reevaluate the seriousness of Yankee interest in Mexico, and thus may have accomplished its underlying objective.[32]

European diplomats and political leaders interpreted the Corwin-Zamacona treaty as a sign of Yankee expansionism into Latin America, threatening their own economic, political, and cultural influence in that region. Gabriel García y Tassara, Spanish minister to the United States, confirmed in early 1862 that the early loan treaty actually prompted European powers to intervene in Mexico to protect their interests. Tassara observed that "if the United States assumes payment of the Mexican debt, it will be transferred from the allies to the Federal government and the influence which the allies now have over Mexico by virtue of said debts would be transferred also to this country, which is not in any manner agreeable to the European policy on this continent."[33] Tassara recognized clearly one key reason why the Lincoln administration quite readily agreed to negotiate the loan treaties, the desire to create financial power which could easily be converted into political power capable of influencing Mexican decision making.

To other Europeans Corwin's expansionistic loan proposal "guaranteed the aggression and legitimized the competition of the European Powers in Mexico," when a disinterested, generous policy would have been in the interest of the United States since its security was closely related to Mexico's. Mexico's desperate financial need and its expectation that the Corwin-Doblado loan treaty would be ratified, led the Juárez government to issue drafts upon the expected money, thus embarrassing Seward, particularly with the French. Naturally, the United States protested the drafts which

32. Lincoln to the Senate, February 27, 1862, in Basler (ed.), *Works of Lincoln*, V, 138; Romero to Ministro de Relaciones Exteriores, February 24, 1862, in Romero (comp.), *Correspondencia*, II, 63–65. See also Emily Balch to Joseph Swift, March 13, 1862, in Balch Family Papers, Box 2, University of Virginia Library; and *Manchester Guardian*, July 18, 1862.

33. Romero to de la Fuente, February 21, 1862, in Tamayo (ed.), *Juárez Documentos*, V, 780–81. See also Kinley J. Brauer, "Gabriel García y Tassara and the American Civil War: A Spanish Perspective," *Civil War History*, XXI (March, 1975), 5–12.

it had not authorized. England's Lord Palmerston also feared that the Corwin loan treaties were laying the groundwork for a United States foreclosure and hence saw some virtue in the French monarchical scheme.[34] The London *Times* claimed that United States policy had consistently interfered to prevent the "concerted action" necessary to make Mexico respectable and strong. From Great Britain it appeared the United States wished a weak Mexico which would eventually fall under United States domination. The three powers intervening in Mexico were interested in exploiting the troubles of the divided Union. Most damaging was the fact that "the lien on Mexican territory . . . reminded the world that American policy was manufactured in the interest of Springfield, Massachusetts, rather than of Springfield, Illinois."[35] Those aspects of the Corwin loan negotiations, aimed at obtaining closer control over mineral and agricultural producing areas in northern Mexico and greater commercial advantages with Mexico, suggest that the United States foreign policy served eastern manufacturing and commercial interests rather than midwestern agricultural interests.

In late January, 1862, Plumb informed Corwin about the treaty's prospects in the Senate and about Sumner's attitude toward it. Although evaluating general interest in Mexican affairs "much increased," Plumb thought that the Senate would not lend money directly to Mexico but might be persuaded to pay the interest on the debt. Plumb also relayed the conviction shared by Sumner and other senators that the imposing allied naval forces in the Gulf were waiting for the first convenient opportunity to operate against the Union; hence the Senate wished to undertake a course of action which would remove the fleets. One member of the Senate Foreign Relations Committee, Orville H. Browning, supported the Corwin-Zamacona loan of nine million dollars, if acceptable to

---

34. Seward to Dayton, August 23, 1862, Dayton to Seward, September 12, 1862, in U.S. Department of State, *Papers Relating to the Foreign Relations of the United States, 1862* (Washington, 1863), 377, 388; and Crook, *The North, the South*, 184.

35. Roeder, *Juárez and His Mexico*, I, 368; London *Times* editorial reprinted in the *Manchester Guardian*, August 31, 1861.

France and England, in order to get "them out of our waters until our domestic troubles were ended."[36]

Although appreciative of United States steps to encourage the withdrawal of foreign intervention, the Juárez government feared the response of the Mexican people if knowledge of its pledge of state lands as collateral for the United States loan were made known. Officially the Juárez government announced that the Corwin-Doblado loan would be made in return for granting the United States commercial privileges and passage for its troops across Mexican soil. In fact, it was claimed that the United States was making the loan offer "in order to maintain [Mexico's] territorial integrity." When, during the loan treaty negotiations, Edward L. Plumb arrived with the United States ratifications of the postal and extradition treaties, *El Siglo Diez y Nueve* published an extract from Seward's dispatch, which expressed concern over the possibility of a Confederate invasion of Baja California, while disclaiming any desire on the part of the Union government for Mexican territory. The same dispatch's offer to purchase Baja California rather than permit its seizure by Confederates was not published.[37] Obviously, the Liberal government could not risk renewing the traditional Mexican fear of United States territorial expansionism.

Despite the confusion and contradiction of receiving new instructions approving and the Senate's resolution of February, 1862, rejecting any United States financial aid to Mexico prior to writing his April, 1862, dispatch, Corwin forwarded the draft treaty he and Minister of Foreign Relations Manuel Doblado had signed on April 6, 1862. Corwin insisted his on-the-spot knowledge justified his action, arguing that it was necessary to help stabilize Mexico and to save the United States from future difficulties with the European powers. Corwin reported that following the negotiation of an agreement acceptable to both Mexico and Britain, Britain was terminating its intervention in Mexico. Since Spanish and French

---

36. Plumb to Corwin, January 29, 1862, in Plumb Papers; Randall and Pease (eds.), *Diary of Orville Hickman Browning*, I, 516.

37. *El Siglo Diez y Nueve*, March 9 and 14, and May 15, 1862.

claims were much smaller than British, Corwin assumed their settlement would present no major problem. Through financial aid, the United States could contribute toward terminating European intervention, bolstering Mexican independence and stability.[38]

In April, with the three European powers in disagreement, England and Spain were prepared to negotiate with Mexico and retire, after which Corwin believed France would also withdraw. When the French plenipotentiaries, Alphonse de Saligny and Admiral Jean de la Gravière Jurien, received notice of the Corwin-Doblado treaty, they immediately protested to Mexican officials, claiming the concessions granted the United States were within the lands, properties, and revenue held as security for the French debt. This claim the Mexican government vehemently denied.[39]

However, the Mexican government had pressed Corwin for a loan agreement in order to more quickly liberate their customs revenue from the demands of foreign creditors, thus permitting active campaigning against the guerrilla bands. The Mexicans contended that the loan would reveal United States friendship for Mexico and United States commitment to preventing forcible intervention in the New World. Corwin pointed out to Sumner the many safeguards he had written into the treaty and the concomitant protection to United States interests. To meet the domestic objection that the Civil War made money short, Corwin focused Sumner's attention on the section stating that Mexico would receive the proceeds from the sale of United States bonds, which Mexico must accept at par, absorbing any discount or commission, while repaying the par value of the bonds. To oversee the church property and national lands encompassed by the guaranty, which, despite Corwin's antiexpansionist reputation and the Juárez government's disclaimers of yankee greed, encompassed a lien on *all* public lands

38. Corwin to Seward, March 20, April 16, and May 5, 1862, in Diplomatic Dispatches, Mexico, RG 59, NA; José Fuentes Mares, *Juárez y la Intervención* (Mexico, 1962), 158–60.

39. Jean de la Gravière Jurien and Alfonse de Saligny to Doblado, April 15, 1862, Jesús Teran to Jurien and de Saligny, April 20, 1862, in *Le Trait d'Union*, April 23 and 24, 1862.

throughout Mexico, the treaty provided for a committee of five—three Mexicans and two North Americans. Through the United States members, Corwin intended to ensure "integrity and economy in the disposal of Mexico's lands and church property." Corwin also assumed didactic benefits from the participation of United States commissioners, who "would certainly attract purchasers from our country, who being dispersed among these people everywhere, would teach them lessons in morals, religion, and politics, which they have yet to learn, and which alone are wanting to make them proper citizens of a free Republic." Further, since our normal policy of warring with Mexico rather than displaying "neighborliness" left the United States with 10 percent of Mexico's trade while England had 75 percent, Corwin strongly implied that a redirection of policy toward more "neighborliness' might reverse the trade roles. Concluding his long letter to Sumner, Corwin reiterated his concern about European intrusion on this continent by emphasizing one important reason for fearing foreign power in Mexico: "A glance at the map is sufficient to warn us of the danger to our Pacific possessions, to be apprehended from an ambitious power in Mexico, with armies, navies, and money at command." The danger could be avoided by adopting his policy with the incumbent support of Spain and England. Moreover, to avoid this necessary step now would leave a European power in Mexico, which at some not distant day would have to be dislodged, at a much larger cost than eleven million dollars.[40]

Later, in May, 1862, with declining prospects that his loan treaty would be approved, Corwin made a final appeal to alter the apparent decision. Through A. C. Allen, former United States consul at Minatitlán, now involved in lobbying for the loan treaty in the United States, a Corwin letter reached Lincoln. Corwin pointed out that England had negotiated a treaty with Mexico which would give England control over church property and the unsold national lands if the Corwin-Doblado treaty were not

40. Corwin to Sumner, April 14, 1862, in Sumner Papers, Box 57.

ratified—a step which would join England's control over the major share of Mexico's trade with effective control over Mexico, including the Tehuantepec Isthmus. Yet, he advised, if the Corwin-Doblado treaty were ratified, "we have a hold in the future on Mexico, by settling all her immense vacant lands with our people and room enough in the tierra caliente for two millions of free negroes." On the one hand, by approving the loan treaty the United States would remove the prospect of English control of Mexico, retain a foothold in that country, win Mexico's "enduring friendship," and secure a home for freed blacks over many years to come. On the other hand, rejecting the treaty would not only produce the defeat of all these desirable prospects, but the United States would lose control over Tehuantepec and thereby forever "the control of the commerce of the East." Finally, Corwin asserted that the defeat of his treaty meant the Europeanization, not Americanization, of Mexico and the creation of a powerful, ambitious neighbor on the southern United States border, leading to wars and financial burdens in the future far higher than the sum he now proposed lending to Mexico.[41]

Not surprisingly, the Mexicans sought to induce the United States to accept the Corwin-Doblado loan. Aware from earlier Romero dispatches just how deeply committed the Lincoln administration was to locating a home for the freed blacks, preferably in the New World, and aware also that southern Mexico was an ideal site for a black settlement, Doblado used these two factors to pry support from Lincoln's administration for the loan. Doblado informed Corwin and Robert W. Shufeldt, United States consul at Havana on a special mission investigating possible black colonization sites in Mexico, that he could not make a contract to settle freed blacks in Mexico. If the United States agreed to the loan treaty, all unclaimed lands were under control of a joint Mexican–United States board, and if not, then they were under control of a joint Mexican–English board, so in no case could Mexico make the deci-

41. Corwin to Allen, May 18, 1862, in Lincoln Papers.

sion alone. To emphasize his position, Doblado issued a ministerial circular explaining where control of unclaimed lands rested.[42] The message was clear: if the United States was really interested in settling freed blacks in Mexico, it had only to approve the loan treaty. Corwin, following Doblado's lead, also applied pressure on Lincoln, stating that the administration's plan to colonize Negroes in Mexico would not succeed if the loan negotiations collapsed.[43]

In addition to the explanations in his official dispatches, Corwin sought privately to gain support for his loan treaties. In April, 1862, writing to Charles Sumner, Corwin noted that his mission had two purposes: to prevent Confederate recognition or annexation of Mexican soil, and to prevent European powers from gaining a foothold in the New World. Corwin observed that through various treaty arrangements, England—using very large claims against Mexico—and Spain and France—using much smaller claims—had collectively gained control of Mexico's customs revenues, thus greatly hindering United States attempts to obtain reduced duties. Since Mexico's customs revenues were pledged to repay European loans, the European countries would interpret any reduction granted to the United States as a violation of existing treaties disfavoring their own interests. Corwin reminded Sumner that before the three European powers arrived in Mexico he had proposed, negotiated, and submitted a loan treaty, the Corwin-Zamacona treaty, whose purpose was to pay the interest on the British loan and keep sufficient troops in the field to suppress the robber bands. Corwin claimed: "Congress rejected this treaty, and that act of folly has brought the three powers here." Corwin's serious concern was reflected in the more advantageous terms he now offered Mexico. The security—land and church property throughout Mexico—

---

42. *Ibid;* Romero to Ministro de Relaciones Exteriores, June 6, 1861, in Correspondencia General con los Estados Unidos; Romero to Ministro de Relaciones Exteriores, December 9, 1861, in Romero (comp.), *Correspondencia*, II, 32–34; Ponciano Arriaga to Jesús Terán, July 24, 1862, in Jesús Terán Correspondence, Latin American Collection, University of Texas.

43. Corwin to Seward, February 18, March 24 and 28, 1862, in Diplomatic Dispatches, Mexico, RG 59, NA; and Corwin to A. C. Allen, May 18, 1862, in Lincoln Papers.

remained the same, but Corwin now suggested a loan of eleven million dollars instead of nine million, with the two additional million to be paid immediately in one lump sum.[44]

Several observers in Mexico thought Corwin and his associates intended to profit from the loan treaty's financial arrangements. Suspicion of improper action focused on A. C. Allen, whom Corwin had selected to carry the Doblado loan treaty back to the United States. Even before Allen could depart Mexico, his hand-picked viceconsul, Bruno van Natzmer (who had been, incidentally, a filibuster with William Walker in Nicaragua), leveled serious charges against Allen. First, charging that Allen used the consulate as an adjunct to his business in Minatitlán, van Natzmer noted that his conduct of the office came under attack when he moved the consulate out of the building housing Allen's firm. Second, Allen allegedly became angry when van Natzmer forwarded the oath of allegiance for the consul's signature. Van Natzmer judged that Texan Allen's secessionist inclinations produced the angry reaction. Then, strangely, complaining to Corwin of Allen's action, van Natzmer was instantly dismissed from office. At the same time, an eastern businessman, Edward L. Plumb, also charged A. C. Allen with traitorous tendencies, based upon information obtained from an autographed Allen letter written to a party in the Confederacy, in which Allen stated, "he entertained the most supreme contempt for Mr. Lincoln and his whole cabinet." Plumb brought this matter directly to Seward's attention, only after learning that his confidential letter, communicating this information to Corwin, had been given to Allen.[45] Corwin's loyal support of Allen was probably due to their joint economic ventures.

While in Washington, Allen distributed a pamphlet, "Reasons

44. Corwin to Sumner, April 14, 1862, in Sumner Papers; and Corwin to Seward, March 24 and 28, 1862, in Diplomatic Dispatches, Mexico, RG 59, NA. The draft treaties discussed a loan in pesos; however, the dollar and the peso were equal in international exchange.

45. Pickett to Browne, January 27, 1862, in Pickett Papers, Letterbook 1; van Natzmer to Seward, April 8 and 26, and June 19, 1862, in Consular Dispatches, Minatitlan, RG 59, NA; and Plumb to Seward, May 4, 1862, in Seward Papers.

Why the Mexican Treaty Should be Accepted," which offered near identical reasoning to that contained in Corwin's April 14, 1862, letter to Sumner. Allen urged support for the Corwin-Doblado treaty "because it will give a virtual control and protectorate over that country; and which control in its results will enable us to monopolize its commerce and prevent all invasion of its soil by any foreign power." Not having seen a copy of the treaty, Romero could not decide how well founded and how precise the first "disadvantageous idea" of the Allen pamphlet was. Of course, the close relationship of Corwin and Allen involved more than winning approval for the treaty. Allen had arranged with his friend Manuel Doblado and the Mexican government that if the treaty were signed, Allen and his partners (one of whom was Corwin) would obtain a railroad concession in the Tehuantepec Isthmus. Thus, revealing in October, 1862, that approval of the treaty would confirm United States control over the Tehuantepec route and "ensure it against the schemes of Napoleon," Allen informed Seward that his railroad concession had no value if the loan treaty were not approved.[46]

In mid-June, 1862, when the Corwin-Doblado treaty was submitted to the Senate, Romero sought to persuade Senator Sumner that if the treaty were pending and not rejected, it would generate moral support for Mexico in its conflict with France. Similarly Corwin later suggested that his submission of an additional article to the rejected treaty would keep it alive. Sumner disagreed, however, convinced that the draft treaty was a diplomatic threat to France, which, if not permanently disposed of, could very well tempt that country to intervene in the Civil War. Romero attempted through friendly senators, unsuccessfully, to persuade the Senate that the loan treaty was not a threat to France, but Sumner's

46. "Reasons Why The Mexican Treaty Should Be Accepted," accompanying Corwin to Allen, May 18, 1862, in Lincoln Papers; Romero to Ministro de Relaciones Exteriores, June 23, 1862, in Tamayo (ed.), *Juárez Documentos,* VI, 670–71; Allen to Doblado, March 24, 1862 and April 22, 1862, in Manuel Doblado Correspondence, Latin American Collection, University of Texas; and Allen to Seward, October 8, 1862, in Seward Papers.

view prevailed. Despite Romero's efforts, the Corwin-Doblado treaty was rejected.[47]

Although formal negotiations for a commercial treaty never developed, the whole tenor of the interchange between the Liberal government and the Republican government encouraged increasing commercial ties. For example, during the loan negotiations in 1861–1862, Corwin had considered, then rejected the idea of demanding trade concessions as part payment for advancing money to Mexico. Upon presenting his credentials to Juárez, Corwin expressed the United States desire for a commercial treaty to formalize the trade ties that were so often mentioned in discussions of the future relations of the two countries. So it is not surprising that, when Mexico's congress began revising its tariff in late 1861, Corwin submitted to Zamacona a list of items whose downward rate modification would "stimulate and increase trade" between the two countries: "flour, salted meat, butter and cheese, tallow and lard, salted fish, manufactures of leather, manufactures of india rubber, and gutta pucha, floor oil cloth, carpets, brown cotton goods, printed cotton goods, casimeres [sic], crockery and glassware, cutlery, brushes and combs, machinery and mining and agricultural implements, printed books, paper, ready made clothing, rice and sugar." Corwin judged "these modifications...so important, and even vital, for the vast increase of commerce which should take place between the two countries" that he trusted he would "not be deemed to have departed from that line of strict deference to the internal policy of Mexico."[48] The bulk of the items to bear reduced duty or to be placed on a free list, favored midwestern agricultural and food processing interests and northwestern manufacturing interests. Among unprocessed agricultural items only rice and

47. Romero to Ministro de Relaciones Exteriores, July 1 and 8, 1862 in Correspondencia General con los Estados Unidos; Corwin to Seward, August 28, 1862, in Diplomatic Dispatches, Mexico, RG 59, NA. See also Romero to Ministro de Relaciones Exteriores, July 1, 1862, in Tamayo (ed.), *Juárez Documentos,* VI, 708–709; *El Siglo Diez y Nueve,* August 1, 5, and 28, 1862.

48. Corwin to Zamacona, November 22, 1861, in Plumb Papers.

sugar could enter under reduced duty, and neither seemed likely to become a major Mexican import, given that country's climate and capability to produce both products in sufficient quantities.

About the same time, Corwin also prepared a draft "Treaty of Friendship, Commerce and Transit." During the critical winter of 1861, with the Mexican Liberal government confronted by foreign intervention and the federal government mired in a civil war and facing the grave possibility of foreign intervention, Corwin's draft treaty proposed incorporating such objectives of liberalism as reciprocal religious freedom and a mutual pledge to oppose the establishment of slavery in Mexico, an article which would have been very useful to Juárez' government some years later when Maximilian permitted the sub-rosa reestablishment of slavery. Not unexpectedly, a perusal of the treaty reveals that the central elements concerned trade and commerce: United States acquisition of transit rights across Mexico; a preferential reduction of Mexico's tariff to expand United States commerce with Mexico; the opening up of Mexico's coastal trade to American vessels; the establishment of warehouse facilities for American merchants; and additional minor trade concessions. Mexico would agree not to subject United States citizens to forced loans or impositions, nor to dispose of any of its public domain to a foreign power. As compensation for these concessions the United States agreed to pay $10 million, out of which some $2 million would be held for payment of existing United States claims against Mexico.[49] The treaty would have produced vastly greater American influence in the Mexican economy. The greater United States economic stake in Mexico would have increased Mexico's security against an ominous external threat, since the economically involved "colossus of the North" would be less tolerant toward foreign intervention in that country.

Romero informed Juárez that someone close to Corwin had

49. "Treaty of Friendship, Commerce and Transits between the United States and the Mexican Republic," [n.d.-1861?], in Plumb Papers. Although the draft treaty bears no date, it was quite obviously written in 1861, since by 1862 Corwin knew that Mexico would not consider a tariff revision.

categorically stated that the United States was willing to pay up to $8 million for a commercial treaty. Allegedly, the New England merchants and manufacturers, seeking market compensation for the departed southern market, judged Mexico as an agricultural country to have the same needs as the South.[50] Still, given the pressing seriousness of domestic events in both countries, it is not surprising that negotiations for a commercial treaty were postponed. The joint Spanish-British-French expedition, planned and initiated in late 1861 and early 1862, broke down in April, 1862, with the Spanish and British forces withdrawing. Then in May the French forces attempted to march upon Mexico, force the overthrow of Juárez' government, and compel a favorable solution to Mexico's diplomatic and debt problems. The Mexican army defeated the French forces at Puebla on May 5, 1862, however, thus forcing the French to retreat and call for reenforcements under Marshall Achille Bazaine in order to correct the situation and save the French army's honor. In late May of 1863 the French finally entered Mexico City as the Liberal government fled north. During the next three years, the Liberals moved from San Luis Potosí to Monterrey, to Saltillo, to Chihuahua, and to El Paso del Norte in an effort to preserve their government in being. Additionally, after May, 1863, the Mexican Congress, which dissolved until after the French were defeated, granted Juárez special and extraordinary powers to combat the invaders. One condition of this grant restricted Juárez' treaty-making powers, hampering the negotiation of a commercial treaty.[51]

Since the Union cause rested at a particularly low and demoralizing point during late 1861 and early 1862, the Union government had to focus its attention on prosecuting the war, and the Radical Republicans focused their attention on defeating the power structure of the Lincoln administration in order to create support for their views on conducting the war. Thus, the Lincoln adminis-

---

50. Romero to Ministro de Relaciones Exteriores, June 8, 1861, Expediente Personal de Thomas Corwin.

51. Juárez' address to the first session of the 4th Mexican Congress, December 8, 1867, in *Un Siglo de Relaciones Internacionales de México,* 107.

tration found itself fighting the war, a Radical coup, very serious Confederate efforts to obtain British and French recognition, and, at the same time, attempting to turn back a European invasion of Mexico. Unable to handle all four problems, the Seward-Lincoln administration accepted the demise of the loan treaties. Still, the basic similarity of views and goals between the liberal regimes produced implemented treaties on postal affairs and extradition, two precedent-setting loan treaties which, despite an unfavorable situation, came close to success, and agreement in principle upon a commercial treaty, for which turbulent circumstances prevented negotiations. While Union relations with Juárez' government were quite friendly in the early years of the Civil War, Confederate relations with Liberal Mexico were markedly less smooth.

IV *Confederate Relations with Two Mexicos, 1862–1865*

IN THE period from 1862 to 1865, Confederate relations with Mexico were complicated by the uncertain, unstable situation in that country. As the early experiences of the Pickett mission in 1861 revealed, the Confederacy would not find a sympathetic response in Juárez' Mexico, but it might expect and demand a peaceful, orderly frontier relationship so that an additional trouble area would not plague the Richmond leadership. Moreover, the Confederacy would insist upon similar, equal, and neutral treatment from the Juárez government. The joint foreign intervention of 1862, which quickly became a unilateral French intervention, and the concurrent rumors of Maximilian's pending coronation as emperor of Mexico pleased and encouraged the Confederate leadership. They assumed that Maximilian's Mexico would be a friendly, sympathetic, and ideologically reliable neighbor. Recognition would be forthcoming; so might a military alliance, since the South was willing to bargain away the Monroe Doctrine for an alliance. But a victorious North would pose a threat to the new Mexican empire.

The years 1863 and 1864 seemed bursting with prospects of favorable action from the Confederate perspective. The Juárez government had conducted itself only within a marginally acceptable path from the Confederate viewpoint. It had revealed its favor for the North while maintaining an effort at formal neutrality. Admittedly, along the frontier the Juárez government's record was better; it had made no effort to block Confederate trade, although it had used the opportunity to increase the revenue it received from that trade. Nevertheless, the trade lines remained open. Still, the Confederacy had little reason not to welcome the change to the French-inspired Maximilian candidacy. Maximilian and French agents indicated that Maximilian indeed held a friendly, sympathetic trust in the Confederacy, and that he recognized its value as a buffer against the Union government, which continued to deny his right to assume the throne and issue unmistakable sounds and signs of displeasure. Still, despite the trials and tribulations of the Confederate effort to obtain the maximum desirable state of relations along the border, its chief difficulties did not lie in whether Juárez or Maximilian headed the Mexican nation, but rather within its own structure and outlook.

The Confederacy adopted a conservative diplomatic style, when a more liberal, revolutionary, dynamic approach was required in order to accomplish the strenuous, exhausting tasks that lay before the South. The Confederacy did not need the preservation of the international status quo. Its very claim to existence created a change. What it had to seek, then, was the most drastic favorable revision of international commerce and power that it could effect.[1] To achieve this goal, it required trading partners and the moral (and indirect material) support of recognition. Precisely these two items received low priority from the Confederate high command. In Mexico for example, both Pickett and José Augustín Quintero were instructed to be concerned primarily about other matters. They were to establish and maintain friendly relations, to seek Mexico's neutrality, and above all, to make it clear that the

---

1. On Confederate diplomacy see Henry Blumenthal, "Confederate Diplomacy: Popular Notions and International Realities," *Journal of Southern History*, XXXII (May, 1966), 151–71; Richard B. McCormack, "Los Estados Confederados y México," *Historia Mexicana*, IV (January–March, 1966), 337–57; Owsley, *King Cotton Diplomacy*; and Meade, *Judah Benjamin*.

Confederacy would not tolerate Mexico's granting special privileges to the United States. Only if other matters went smoothly were they to seek more formal trade ties.

Some Confederate citizens, experienced in frontier affairs, urged the Confederate government to seek closer relations with Mexico. Louisianian A. B. Bacon encouraged Jefferson Davis to develop "intimate and most friendly relations" with the Mexican border state authorities, which he maintained were quite independent of the central government. A Confederate agent could easily conduct the necessary "semi-diplomatic" negotiations to promote friendly relations. Aware of the desire among Texans to annex northern Mexico, Bacon argued, nevertheless, that annexation should not occur without the consent of the inhabitants. Alternatively, he suggested developing trade ties.[2]

The Union leadership, aware that use of the land border between Mexico and Texas could circumvent the blockade, sought to cut this avenue for Confederate trade with the outside world. Among several projects, the most serious was Seward's attempt to use Texas Unionist Lemuel Dale Evans to coordinate antisecessionist forces in Texas, aid them with federal resources, and extend the blockade of the Confederacy across the Rio Grande valley. Neither the Evans' project nor any other civilian-conceived plan accomplished the task of hindering Confederate trade through Mexico. Only General Nathaniel Banks's military invasion of the lower Rio Grande in 1863 disrupted border trade to any extent. Nevertheless, these early projects reveal an immediate awareness by Union leaders of the trade possibilities open to the Confederacy, trade possibilities which many Confederate leaders only slowly recognized.[3]

2. A. B. Bacon to Davis, November 18, 1861, in Records of the Confederate States of America, Vol. XXIV.

3. José Augustín Quintero to William Browne, March 22, and Quintero to Judah Benjamin, December 11, 1862, October 26, and November 9, 1863, in Records of the Confederate States of America, Vol. VIII; A. J. Hamilton to Juárez, April 9, 1864, Juárez to A. J. Hamilton, April 18 and May 22, 1864, in Correspondencia General con los Estados Unidos; and Thomas Schoonover, "Documents Concerning Lemuel Dale Evans' Plan to Keep Texas

Although Pickett, the chief Confederate agent in Mexico, never discussed border commerce with Mexican officials, the Rebel agent in northern Mexico, José Quintero, pushed for close mutual trade ties—but alas often went unrewarded because of his superiors' lack of interest. Quintero not only ably maintained friendly relations with Nuevo León Governor Santiago Vidaurri and other key figures in northern Mexico from 1861 until mid-1865, but he struggled and pleaded for expanding cotton trade and for purchasing military and medical supplies, and raw materials such as lead, saltpeter, and even food from across the border. Although cognizant of Vidaurri's assurances that trade would remain open to the Confederacy even if the central government ordered it closed, Benjamin discounted Vidaurri's assurances because of contrary reports "from too many quarters and in such authentic shape" that serious doubt was raised.[4] On numerous occasions Confederate or Texas agents, for petty, selfish reasons, stymied Quintero's efforts to maintain an open, friendly border trade. Frequently his appeals to the Texas governor or to the Confederate State Department to take action to facilitate trade went unheeded. Naturally, Quintero was not always ignored, but the relatively frequent total or partial closings of trade between Mexico and the Confederacy suggest that the Confederacy never clearly understood the essential value of its trade relations with Mexico.[5]

Quintero, recognizing that eventually the Confederacy would want access to the Pacific, and aware of the geography of the Mexican–United States border area, encouraged a project for a transcontinental railroad connecting Texas with Mazatlán on the Pacific. In the late summer of 1861, Quintero reported to the Con-

---

in the Union in 1861," *East Texas Historical Journal,* XII (Spring, 1974), 35–38. See also Romero to Ministro de Relaciones Exteriores, October 10, 1862, in Romero (comp.), *Correspondencia,* II, 573.

4. Pickett to Ochiltree, February 8, 1862, and Pickett to Davis, February 22, 1862, in Pickett Papers, Letterbook 1; and Benjamin to Quintero, April 30, 1862, in Records of the Confederate States of America, container 11.

5. Ronnie C. Tyler, *Santiago Vidaurri and the Southern Confederacy* ([Austin, Texas], 1973).

federate State Department that, while awaiting instructions in Texas, his friend General Hugh McLeod had suggested sounding out Governor Vidaurri relative to the topography from Texas to Mazatlán. McLeod argued a railroad through this country would bind northern Mexico to the Confederacy and would be the shortest route to the Pacific. Moreover, the railroad would service an area with a large agricultural population and at the same time an important mining area. Either the cool relations which existed between the Mexican Liberal government and the Confederacy after Pickett, or Confederate disinterest in the project prevented further action on this proposal at that time.[6]

Since the early days of his first mission to Mexico, Quintero had focused upon trade and commerce; however, he was seldom successful in awakening Richmond or the local Confederate authorities to its primacy. In particular, local Confederate agents gave Quintero great problems and little assistance. In early 1862, Colonel John Ford permitted José María Carvajal and his forces to rest and train on the Texas side of the Rio Grande, while conducting belligerent operations in northern Mexico. Mexican complaints reaching Ford were answered haughtily, causing Quintero to warn the State Department that "our *friendly relations with the Mexican frontier are fast dying away*. . . . I apprehend serious *difficulties*." Quintero reminded the State Department that Juárez' government was sympathetic to the Republican party, "yet we have . . . succeeded in securing the friendship of the Governors of the frontier states and now are on the eve of incurring their enmity, on account of the band of robbers who are permitted to abuse the hospitality of Texas."[7] However, Quintero, a mere subordinate, was not the individual responsible for the border area. Later in 1862, Quintero reported

6. Quintero to Robert M. T. Hunter, August 20, 1861; "Memorandum [addressed to Quintero] on the true route of the Pacific Rail Road for the Confederate States," n.d., signed by Hugh McLeod, in Records of the Confederate States of America, Vol. VIII.

7. Quintero to Browne, March 28, 1862, in Records of the Confederate States of America, Vol. VIII; Vidaurri to Juárez, January 21, 1863, in Tamayo (ed.), *Juárez Documentos*, VII, 286–87.

that as a consequence of Colonel Ford's favoritism towards Carvajal, Santiago Vidaurri, after contemplating pursuing Carvajal's forces onto the Texas side—an action which would have provoked widespread fighting—rejected the idea in favor of a two-cent-per-pound tax on cotton exported out of Mexico.[8] Thus Ford's ingenious scheme for law and order, an attempt to stop Mexican bandits from making forays into Texas by harboring and fostering the same sort of activity, led to unexpected and painful penalties for the Confederacy. Commerce was subordinated to law and order; the local interests predominated over the national necessity.

The diplomatic negotiations taking place in Mexico City also affected border relations. For example, in mid-1862, when Mexico desperately sought United States Senate approval of the Corwin-Doblado loan treaty, it naturally wished to demonstrate sympathy and cooperation with the United States government. Therefore, on June 6, 1862, Doblado instructed Vidaurri "to cut all relations with agents from the Confederate States." Vidaurri responded cleverly to this order. First, he pointed out that there were border factors unknown to the central government. Then, he forwarded a note from the United States consul in Monterrey, C. B. H. Blood, which suggested that the arms trade with the Confederacy was bad for both sides, yet which thanked Vidaurri for his generous "official and personal aid to Union refugees." From among the many vigorous complaints that Blood registered regarding the conduct of relations with the Confederate States, Vidaurri selected the only dispatch in which Blood had expressed gratitude for a generous act on Vidaurri's part.[9] Harboring no intention of breaking ties with the

---

8. Quintero to Browne, April 17, 1862, in Records of the Confederate States of America, Vol. VIII.

9. Doblado to Vidaurri, June 6, 1862, Vidaurri to Doblado, June 18, 1862, in Agentes de los EE Confederados del Sur de los EEUU de A., Archivo Histórico de la Secretaría de Relaciones Exteriores; C. B. H. Blood to Vidaurri, June 7, 1862, Vidaurri to Ministro de Relaciones Exteriores, June 18, 1862, in expediente 6-17-7, Archivo Histórico de la Secretaría de Relaciones Exteriores; and Quintero to Benjamin, July 5, 1862, in Records of the Confederate States of America, Vol. VIII.

Confederacy, if at all possible, Vidaurri sought both to maintain them and to avoid alienating the central government.

Quintero spent the next six months attempting to eliminate or reduce the two-cent-per-pound duty on cotton. By October, 1862, he had successfully negotiated its reduction down to one-half cent per pound, and border trade had picked up. Then another incident occurred, and the cotton export duty was back at two cents. Quintero was discouraged, to say the least.[10] Nevertheless, he did not lose faith in his ability to keep the trade moving, although in reduced quantities and with less advantage to the Confederacy because of the high cotton export tax.

Quintero's persistent and successful labors were attracting attention from the Confederate State Department and from Montgomery Blair of Lincoln's cabinet. In late July, 1862, Blair wrote Seward that "Franklin Chase now at Tampico ought to be made Consul General for Mexico, so that he may go to Vidaurri's dominions at once to counteract the intrigues of the Confederate commissioner José Antonio [sic] Quintero." While Congress actually entertained a resolution to elevate Chase's consulate to a consulate general, the resolution failed in 1862, but was finally successful in 1864.[11] In the fall of 1862, however, Blair's concern for northern Mexico influenced the decision to appoint a new consul at Monterrey to counteract Quintero's effectiveness. Confederate Secretary of State Judah Benjamin also recognized Quintero's outstanding effort. Expressing deep regrets for his inability to remove "the unjust and vexatious impediments thrown in the way of commerce between the Confederacy" and northern Mexico, Benjamin informed Quintero: "Your efforts to preserve amicable relations between our own and the Mexican authorities, and the zeal you have exhibited in the discharge of your duties have been noted by me with much satisfaction," clearly indicating that the faltering of rela-

---

10. Quintero to Benjamin, August 14, 1862, September 7, October 13, 1862, and enclosures, in Records of the Confederate States of America, Vol. VIII.

11. *Congressional Globe*, 37th Congress, 2nd Session, 1925.

tions between the two countries was in no way considered Quintero's responsibility.[12] Although the Confederate State Department could not readily control the action of local political or military men, it could protest major violations of neutrality by Confederate sources and obtain redress. Hence, when Colonel John R. Baylor invaded Mexican soil with regular Confederate troops, Benjamin sent an official apology.[13]

Early though fleeting signs that the Confederacy realized the key role that commerce could play in Mexican-Confederate relations occurred in late 1862 with the appointment of Bernard Avegno as commercial agent at Veracruz and Richard Fitzpatrick as commercial agent at Matamoros. However, Avegno was chiefly interested in a specific ship's cargo rather than the general commercial relations of Mexico and the Confederacy. Meanwhile Fitzpatrick worked to make the existing trade route operate smoothly, rather than to negotiate for more favorable trade terms and conditions for the Rio Grande route.[14] Serious commercial negotiations would require contact with a recognized authority, either the central government or Governor Santiago Vidaurri in Nuevo León and Tamaulipas. Pickett had not been instructed to open such negotiations and had not done so; Quintero attempted to alert Richmond of the value of this trade route, but with unsatisfactory results.

More amazing than the Confederate government's passing concern about trade and communications on this frontier is that its agents seemed inordinately concerned about stability and law and order on the frontier. Now, obviously the Confederacy had to be concerned about such matters. However, in the midst of a life-death struggle, where peace and order were plainly not prime concerns (destruction and death were more the order of the day),

12. Quintero to Benjamin, October 19, 1862, and Benjamin to Quintero, November 21, 1862, in Records of the Confederate States of America, Vols. VIII and XI; Blair to Seward, July 26, 1862, in Seward Papers.

13. Benjamin to Luis Terrazas, January 20, 1863, enclosed with Benjamin to Quintero, January 20, 1863, in Records of the Confederate States of America, Vol. XI.

14. For the dispatches from Avegno and Fitzpatrick, and instructions to them, see the Records of the Confederate States of America, Vols. VIII, XI, and LX.

supplies were vital to survival. One would normally expect trade matters to drive law and order issues into secondary consideration. Yet on the Texas border, peace and stability remained prime concerns.[15] Thus, when the Confederacy moved toward formal agreement with Mexican border officials, law and order, not trade issues, supplied the motivation.

In attempting to solve their mutual border problems, twice Confederate and Mexican officials came close to perfecting treaties which would have implied mutual recognition. Thus, in February, 1863, to prevent the border turmoil from producing a rupture of relations, Albino López, civil and military commandant of the state of Tamaulipas, and Brigadier General Hamilton H. Bee, Confederate commander of the West Sub-District of Texas, signed an agreement to extradite certain classes of criminals and to regulate other problems of mutual concern. Bee had initiated the negotiation by noting that he was "specially charged by my Government with the maintenance of friendly relations with the Republic of Mexico." A very satisfying aspect of the Bee-López agreement was the expressed willingness of Mexican officials to surrender counterfeiters. Operating through Matamoros, United States agents and "free enterprise" criminals had been slipping large amounts of counterfeit money across the border in order to discredit Confederate currency. Thanks to Bee, Quintero, and the cooperation of Mexican officials, this activity would now be punished.[16]

Although the Bee-López agreement was not a binding international treaty, it could easily have been converted into one. Throughout the unofficial negotiations Quintero acted as observer and advisor at the request of both Bee and López. Informed by Quintero's reports, the Confederate State Department followed the unofficial border diplomacy with considerable interest. At the same time, it clearly took the position that the Bee-López agreement was

15. Benjamin to Quintero, April 15, and December 22, 1863, in Records of the Confederate States of America, Vol. XI.

16. Benjamin to Quintero, April 15, 1863, *ibid.*

not a treaty. After the agreement was signed, Richmond cautioned Quintero to avoid demanding extradition, since "we have no right, in the absence of treaty stipulations, to demand the extradition."[17]

By mid-1863, the Union sea blockade was well established, prompting Secretary of the Navy Gideon Welles to campaign in the cabinet for a military expedition to close the Rio Grande trade route into the Confederacy. Welles contended: "Our blockade is rendered in a great degree ineffective because we cannot shut off traffic and mail facilities, or exclude commercial and postal intercourse with the Rebels via the Rio Grande." Welles observed that now "one or two hundred vessels" lie off the coast of Matamoros whereas before the war "there were never more than six or eight." Therefore he proposed a land operation to seize the left bank of the river, thereby preventing goods landed in Mexico from crossing into Texas. Later, in 1863, General Nathaniel P. Banks's command seized and held Brownsville for about four months. However, since it had not been decided that this mode of attacking the Confederacy deserved priority handling, when troops were needed elsewhere, most of Banks's command was withdrawn, leaving only a skeleton force at Brownsville. Since the force in Brownsville could not appreciably hinder the flow of trade over Matamoros to or from the Confederacy, in March of 1864 Welles renewed his call for action to cut the vital Confederate communications via the Rio Grande.[18]

In addition to the intrusion of Yankee troops in Texas, mid-1863 witnessed another potential disruptive change in power relationship on the Texas-Mexican border. Driven out of Mexico City by the French, Juárez headed north to San Luis Potosí, about half-

17. Hamilton H. Bee to Albino López, February 3, 18, 26, and March 1, 1863, and López to Bee, February 11, 22, 23, and 28, 1863, in *Official Records*, XV, 966–67, 975–78, 992–98, 1006–1007; and Quintero to Benjamin, November 2, 1862, January 30 and February 26, 1863, in the Records of the Confederate States of America, Vol. VIII.

18. Howard K. Beale (ed.), *Diary of Gideon Welles* (3 vols.; New York, 1960), I, 334–35; Welles to Seward, June 9, 1863, and March 5, 1864, in Gideon Welles Papers, Letterbooks 74 and 75, Library of Congress; Tyler, *Vidaurri and the Southern Confederacy*, 119–21; and Richard P. Weinert, "Confederate Border Troubles with Mexico," *Civil War Times Illustrated*, III (October, 1964), 41–43; Cohen, "The Texas-Mexico Border," 153–65.

way between Mexico City and Vidaurri's capital in Monterrey. Concerned about his future, Vidaurri attempted to persuade the Liberal government not to move further north, an impossible request in light of the French movements north to destroy or capture the Juárez government.[19]

During this confusing period, Quintero's able handling of the complex problems which developed on the border produced more praise from his superiors. Benjamin conveyed his "great satisfaction" with "the vigilance and discretion with which you supervise everything that can conduce to the public interests within the sphere of your duties." Benjamin added President Davis' wish "to express to you his own approval... of your conduct in the discharge of your functions."[20] Thus, late 1863 and early 1864 proved a confusing, fluid period along the border. While on the north bank the Union and Confederate forces vied for control, south of the Rio Grande imperial troops and Juárez' Liberal armies contested for control.

Quintero's ability to profit from altering situations did not fail him when Juárez expelled Vidaurri from Monterrey in the spring of 1864. Rekindling an old friendship with Juárez' son-in-law, Pedro Santacilia, Quintero made "private arrangements with the *President of the Republic*" prior to Vidaurri's loss of power. Projecting Vidaurri's fall and observing how "the old friendship of the Mexicans for the U.S. seems to have turned into cold indifference," Quintero arranged for Santacilia "to protect our trade." However, since Juárez depended upon duties from the trade with the Confederacy for his only reliable revenue, Quintero did not consider this maneuver a signal triumph. His foresight was immediately rewarded. The day after arriving in Monterrey, Juárez invited Quintero to dinner, introducing the Confederate agent to the cabinet.

19. Quintero to Benjamin, June 10, 1863, in Records of the Confederate States of America, Vol. VIII; Tyler, *Vidaurri and the Southern Confederacy*, 119, 134–41; Knapp, *Life of Lerdo de Tejada*, 80–81.
20. Benjamin to Quintero, December 22, 1863, in Records of the Confederate States of America, container 11.

Later, when the Union commander at Brownsville sought Quintero's arrest and extradition, Juárez personally informed Quintero that since Mexico had always exempted political offenders from extradition, no Confederate in Mexico would be extradited.[21]

Confederate leaders assessed the French invasion of Mexico in various manners. In March, 1862, Matthew F. Maury suggested to James Orr, chairman of the Confederacy's Senate committee on foreign relations, that the South should offer France economic advantages in order to bring the two countries closer together. To ensure that the French obtained the same ideas, Maury wrote to a ranking naval acquaintance in Paris describing the political and commercial advantages of a French-Confederate alliance. In early 1863, the *Charleston Mercury* found no reason to be dismayed by the joint maneuver into Mexico and, indeed, very enthusiastically received the rumor that the French had conquered Matamoros, which the *Mercury* interpreted as an opportunity for the Confederacy to reverse a previously unimaginative and poorly directed foreign policy. Arguing that with the Rio Grande under joint French and Confederate control cotton and other southern exports would find ready, unhindered world markets, and manufactured goods and war materials from Europe's industrial centers would flow into the Confederacy, the *Mercury* was reacting effervescently, but alas precipitately, to a rumor.[22]

A Confederate agent in Europe stated his government was not opposed to monarchical government. James Williams' pamphlet *The Rise and Fall of "The Model Republic"* allowed that, while it is proper for the North American region to practice republican freedom, "it cannot be denied that in almost every other part of the American continent the experiment of democratic institutions has ended in

21. Quintero to Pedro Santacilia, January 29, 1864, in Archivo Juárez; Quintero to Benjamin, February 1 and 28, April 3 and 7, 1864, in Records of the Confederate States of America, Vol. VIII.
22. Maury to James Orr, March 6, 1862, Maury to de la Marche, March 15, 1862, in Matthew F. Maury Papers, Library of Congress; Charleston *Mercury*, January 4 and 14, 1863.

complete and hopeless failure." He suggested that "Mexicans may well hail the establishment of different political institutions, founded upon a properly organized monarchy, as the turning point in their destiny—the full stop in their downward career, the harbinger of a great future for the Nation."[23]

In late 1862, Napoleon discussed with Sichele de Vere, a University of Virginia professor, the possible linking of Confederate and French destinies as the result of the French expedition in Mexico. De Vere reported that Napoleon sought compensation in Mexico for the loss of the West Indies. As de Vere understood the conversation, France required a foothold on the Florida coast, "un autre Gibraltar," to protect its Gulf commerce, and Napoleon also hinted at recovering at least a foothold in Louisiana. De Vere's revelation of these ambitious schemes did not seem to alarm the Confederate State Department. Perhaps the reported conversation was discounted as speculative or exploratory. Or perhaps France's increasing problems in Europe, such as the Polish uprising, reduced Confederate concern with her "grand design."[24] When the European crisis, stemming from the Polish uprising, appeared on the eve of solution in September, 1863, James Mason, Confederate agent in England, requested specific new instructions for himself and Slidell regarding the southern policy toward a monarchy in Mexico. Realizing that when peace came between the states, "a licentious and irresponsible mob Government" would rule in the North, Mason pondered the advantages to the Confederacy of having a friendly French-sponsored government in Mexico.[25]

In late 1863, Maury sought to persuade his friend Maximilian of the closely intertwined destiny of the Confederacy and Maximilian's future empire. Admitting that a few years ago the southern states would have protested Maximilian's claim to Mexico, Maury now encouraged Maximilian by hinting that California and the

23. James Williams, *The Rise and Fall of "The Model Republic"* (London, 1863).
24. Sichele de Vere to Benjamin, January 23, 1863, Benjamin to de Vere, January 27, 1863, in Records of the Confederate States of America, Vols. LXII and LXIII; and Mason to Benjamin, March 19, 1863, in James M. Mason Papers, Library of Congress.
25. Mason to Benjamin, September 4, 1863, in Mason Papers.

Pacific coast area would soon separate from, thereby weakening, the Union. Maury informed a well-placed friend in France of the golden opportunity for the French to execute their policy of surrounding Mexico with weak states. The Confederacy would be weak when the Civil War ended, and with the Union divided the North would be also. To increase imperial Mexican security, Maury suggested to Maximilian obtaining a few French ironclads to rule the Pacific coast area, thereby further dividing and weakening the United States. Maximilian took the proposal under consideration, while thanking Maury for his service in communicating southern opinions, his personal advice, and his offer to resign from the Confederate navy to serve in Maximilian's.[26]

As Maximilian prepared to depart for Mexico, James Williams and famed Confederate spy Rose Greenhow privately and independently sought to spark an alliance between the empire and the Confederacy. Williams offered to serve as an intermediator for informal contact between the archduke and Jefferson Davis. Williams hoped to increase Confederate sympathy for Maximilian. Greenhow proposed a similar course directly to Maximilian. In addition, Williams endeavored to persuade James Mason to accompany Maximilian to the New World. Conscious of the desirability of direct contact with Maximilian, the Davis government instructed Mason to cross to the continent and contact him, issuing Mason a blank commission to be filled out as he found necessary. Dishearteningly for the Confederacy, sometime during early 1864 the emperor revised his evaluation of a Confederate alliance. In March, 1864, Mason reported Maximilian's refusal to see Slidell in Paris.[27]

26. Maury to Maximilian, October 8, November 10 and 25, 1863, Maximilian to Maury, October 24, 1863, Maury to J. de Chabannes, October 24, 1863, in Maury Papers.

27. James Williams to Maury, January 22, 1864, in Maury Papers; Williams to Mason, December 18, 1863, January 15 and 22, February 5, 1864, Benjamin to Mason, January 25, 1864, and Mason to Benjamin, March 16, April 12, 1864, all in Mason Papers; Williams to [?], November 15, 1863, Rose Greenhow to Maximilian, January 30, 1864, in Archiv Maximilian von Mexiko, folders 52 and 83, Haus- Hof- und Staatsarchiv, Austrian Staatsarchiv. See also James Williams to [?], December 23, 1863, Matthew F. Maury to Williams, December 19, 1863, Leopold to Maximilian [January, 1864?], in Archiv Maximilian von Mexiko, folder 60.

As the Confederate situation deteriorated, southern politician George Henry suggested the abolition of slavery might make recognition more palatable to France. Henry noted that military success had made the Mexican invasion, at first viewed unfavorably, popular in France. Now the French people were impatient with the United States for not recognizing the new empire, but the French liberals continued to remind the nation of southern slavery. Moreover, Austria's natural inclination in favor of the Mexican venture had been reinforced by the sympathy northern congressmen expressed for Hungarian independence. But, thankful for support for her rule found in the Confederate Congress, Austria urged Napoleon to recognize the Confederacy. Henry was convinced that abolishing slavery should make it easier for Napoleon to submit to Austrian urging.[28]

Another critic of Confederate foreign policy, Paul Pecquet du Bellet, proposed that the strongest policy available to Davis' government would intertwine the destinies of the South and Mexico with the commercial aspirations and strategic interests of France. Du Bellet suggested: 1) French recognition of the Confederate States of America (C.S.A.); 2) a treaty ceding Mexico to the C.S.A. after the war on terms similar to the Louisiana cession; 3) the C.S.A. assuming a $1 billion obligation to France to be paid from the profits extracted from Mexican lands and mines; 4) a C.S.A. commercial treaty granting France special privileges over all other European countries, such as free entrance, free trade, and free exportation of cotton; and 5) the C.S.A. agreeing to bear all costs should French recognition lead to war between France and the United States.[29] Although recognizing the intertwined fate of Mexico and the Confederacy, du Bellet's proposal was unlikely to

28. George Henry to Davis, February 25, 1865, in Jefferson Davis Papers, Duke University.

29. Paul Pecquet du Bellet, *The Diplomacy of the Confederate Cabinet of Richmond and its Agents Abroad: Being Memorandum Notes Taken in Paris during the Rebellion of the Southern States from 1861 to 1865*, No. 23, Confederate Centennial Studies Series (Tuscaloosa, Ala., 1963), 96–97.

be attractive to Napoleon even in a revised form since it offered France the large risk of a major war for uncertain future profit.

Richmond first learned of the Mexican regency's interest in relations with the Confederacy from an early November, 1863, Quintero report. Quintero described a conversation with Señor A. Vignau, confidential agent of General Juan Nepomuceno Almonte, imperial regent of Mexico, which revealed the friendly disposition of Mexico toward the South. Vignau claimed that Mexico would recognize the Confederacy "upon the arrival of Maximilian." However, there was no request for a Confederate agent, nor promise that he would be received if he did appear in Mexico City. Despite Vignau's guarded language, the Davis government decided to send a minister to Mexico.[30]

Maximilian's acceptance of the Mexican imperial title pleased Jefferson Davis' government, renewing its hope for closer ties with Mexico. Naturally, Rebel sympathizers tried to convince Maximilian, just as Confederate agents in France tried to convince Napoleon that the South and Mexico should, indeed must, unite for mutual protection against Yankee aggression. Observing the relationship between Confederate and Mexican affairs, King Leopold of Belgium informed Maximilian just prior to his departure for Mexico that Belgium could not guarantee the Mexican empire, because Britain had not recognized the Confederacy. John Slidell had unofficially assured the southern government that Maximilian had made recognition of the Confederate States one condition of his accepting the Mexican crown.

In December, 1863, learning of the decision to send a second mission to Mexico, Pickett considered himself slighted because he had not been consulted. Submitting a long letter of gratuitous advice to Davis to be passed on to William Preston, head of the new mission, Pickett focused on the Mexican character, the superiority of slavery over peonage, and the need to correct misconceptions

30. Quintero to Benjamin, November 4, 1863, Benjamin to Quintero, December 22, 1863, in Records of the Confederate States of America, Vols. VIII and XI.

regarding the historical friendliness of Yankees and southerners in past relations between Mexico and the United States.[31]

In January, 1864, President Jefferson Davis appointed William Preston "Envoy Extraordinary and Minister Plenipotentiary" to the imperial government of Mexico. The desperation of the South required them to make this bold move for recognition, an effort not in keeping with normal Confederate caution in diplomatic matters. Preston was even instructed to pursue more active trade ties. The only significant initiative Preston took during this mission occurred in June, 1864, five months after his receiving instructions and one week after Maximilian finally arrived in Mexico. Taking advantage of the recent Henry Winter Davis resolution and of his friendship with General Almonte and the Marquis de Montholon, Preston attempted to hasten his reception. Pointing to the threatening Henry Winter Davis resolution, Preston warned that even though Lincoln and Seward would try to explain it away at this time, the United States was committed to the Monroe Doctrine and the preservation of democratic government in the western world. He predicted that after such a unanimous expression of popular will the United States government could not long resist taking the necessary action, suggesting that the emperor should turn at once to the Confederacy for friendship and a barrier against the North. His appeal won no ground in Mexico and earned him a rebuke from Richmond. Preston had stated in his letter to Montholon that he was ready "to lay before the Emperor the evidence of our right to recognition." Finding this form of pleading undignified, Benjamin sharply reminded him that his instructions only authorized him to recognize the new empire.[32] Preston was again reminded that if his mission were not immediately successful, he should return to the Confederacy.

31. Pickett to Davis, January 11, 1864, in Pickett Papers; Benjamin to Davis, December 28, 1863, Davis to the Confederate Senate, December 28, 1863, in Records of the Confederate States of America, Vol. XX.

32. William Preston to Juan N. Almonte, June 6, 1864, Preston to Marquis de Montholon, June 8, 1864, Preston to Benjamin, June 29, 1864, and Benjamin to Preston, July 22, 1864, all in Records of the Confederate States of America, Vol. VII, Pt. 1, and Vol. XVII.

Preston's mission never reached Mexico. After a series of delays and hesitations, Maximilian refused to meet even informally with a Confederate agent. With the Mexican refusal to meet with Preston, Confederate hopes for recognition from Mexico collapsed. Finally in mid-January, 1865, the mission was canceled. Only in July, 1865, did a defeated Preston land in Mexico—"I have drifted in the general wreck into this remote corner of the world"—prior to heading to Canada or Europe.[33]

The irony in Maximilian's rejection of the Preston mission was that for the first time the Confederacy sent an agent to Mexico with instructions which adequately recognized the realities of the Confederate position. The touchy question of recognition was set to one side by declaring that formal recognition was not required, that public reception of its minister would be equivalent to recognition. But Preston was instructed to pursue the matters which should have been of prime concern to the Confederacy all along: a military alliance and commercial privileges, especially along the frontier, although Preston was to propose that eventually a most-favored-nation treaty should govern Mexican-Confederate commercial relations.[34]

The William Preston mission in 1864 and negotiations in late 1864 on the Mexican-Texas border indicate that the Confederacy eventually realized that recognition could be valuable. The Preston

33. Follow Preston's correspondence in Records of the Confederate States of America, Vol. VII, Pt. 1; Preston to Adolfo [?], July 6, 1865, in Alexander Caldwell Jones Papers, Virginia Historical Society; John Slidell to Benjamin, December 3, 1863, *Official Records, Navies*, Series 2, III, 968–70; José Fuentes Mores, *Juárez y el Imperio* (Mexico, 1963), 122–23; and Kathryn A. Hanna, "The Roles of the South in the French Intervention in Mexico," *Journal of Southern History*, XX (February, 1954), 15.

34. Davis to Preston, January 7, 1864, and four letters to accompany Preston on his mission, *Official Records, Navies*, Series 2, II, 154–55, 988–90; and Benjamin to Preston, January 7, 1864, in Records of the Confederate States of America, Box 17. The Davis administration wisely rejected the suggestion of several members of the Senate Foreign Relations Committee to merely authorize Preston to accept a Mexican alliance proposed rather than risk a rebuff by proposing such an agreement. See A. E. Maxwell to Benjamin, January 6, 1864, in Records of the Confederate States of America, Vol. LXII. J. Frederick Dorman, "General William Preston," *The Filson Club History Quarterly*, XLIII (October, 1969), 301–310, is a brief biographical sketch of Preston.

mission was a desperate attempt, apparently doomed before it left the South. The Mexican-Texas border negotiations came close to achieving a de facto recognition for the South, but once again, interestingly enough, not the vital trade concerns of that border area, but the secondary problems of law and order led the Confederacy to seek a more formal agreement with its Mexican neighbors.

Late in 1864, the occupation of Matamoros by French and Mexican imperial forces under the command of General Tomás Mejía nullified the Bee-López agreement. During General Tomás Mejía's command in Matamoros relations along the border entered their warmest stages. Quintero waxed mellow after contacting Mejía and his subordinates, claiming, "Should our Government desire to make any arrangements calculated to favor our cause either in a political or commercial point of view, I have no doubt that they could be effected through the authorities here."[35] Yet, then more than any earlier time, the frontier was subjected to disorder and crime because the Liberal government's authority in Tamaulipas had been declining for over a year, and, on the other side, Confederate authority was likewise weakening as the Civil War dragged on and appeared to be a losing cause. Neither the empire nor the Confederacy benefited from the disorder which acted as a restriction to trade and tax revenues. More importantly, the Confederate and imperial leaders on the border shared political sympathy and believed that their governments mutually sought recognition. Unfortunately for the Confederacy, this atmosphere could only be enjoyed a few short months before the collapse.

In December, 1864, therefore, General James E. Slaughter, Confederate commander of the West Sub-District of Texas replacing Bee, and General Tomás Mejía signed an extradition agreement of seven articles, which quite closely followed the provisions of the 1862 extradition treaty between the Republic of Mexico and the

---

35. Quintero to Benjamin, November 5, 1864, and enclosure A, Quintero to E. Kirby Smith, October 21, 1864, in Records of the Confederate States of America, Vol. VIII; Dayton to Mejía, September 28, 1864, Mejía to Dayton, September 28, 1864, Slaughter to Mejía, December 2, 1864, in Tamayo (ed.), *Juárez Documents*, IX, 400–402.

United States. The last article of the Slaughter-Mejía agreement expressed the mutual expectation of a formal diplomatic act: "Notwithstanding . . .the probability, the parties making them have, that in due time, they will be formally accepted by their respective Governments, elevating them to solemn treaties, the present, therefore, has no official character, but [is] made purely in confidence between the undersigned commanders."[36] United States Generals Edward R. S. Canby and William A. Vile, receiving creditable reports that Slaughter and Mejía had reached some agreement on the mutual return of deserters, were very upset and disturbed by this sort of collusion between the Rebels and the imperial forces.[37]

Although not technically treaties, both the Bee-López and Slaughter-Mejía pacts had the effect of international agreements since they were enforced equally upon all citizens of both nations. The Mejía-Slaughter extradition agreement might well have become the basis for a political understanding between the Confederates and imperial Mexico, had not the Confederacy collapsed only a few months later. The Bee-López and Slaughter-Mejía agreements obtain significance not only because they indicate the seriousness with which both Confederate and Mexican officials treated border problems, but also because they are instances when the Confederate government nearly obtained recognition via a back door. While growing out of law and order problems, both agreements represent first steps toward an implicit recognition. Noteworthy in both, the more important matter of Confederate trade along the frontier was relegated to a secondary position.

In mid-1864, a final emissary, Émile la Sère, was appointed commercial agent of the Confederate States at Veracruz. Whereas Avegno had acted as a mixture of purchasing agent and expediter, la Sère was instructed to concentrate entirely upon the expediting

36. Slaughter-Mejía agreement, in *Official Records*, Vol. XLVIII, Pt. 1, pp. 1329–30; Mejía to Etchison, January 10, 1865, in Consular Dispatches, Matamoros, RG 59, NA.

37. Edward R. S. Canby to Edwin Stanton, January 27, 1865, and William A. Vile to George B. Drake, January 12, 1865, enclosed in Seward to Bigelow, February 21, 1865, in U.S. Department of State, *Foreign Relations of the United States, 1865*, Pt. 3, pp. 371–72.

of material purchased in Europe by other agents. La Sère went quickly to Mexico City, where in addition to his work as commercial agent, he also sent reports of public and official sentiment in the empire toward the Confederacy. In August, 1864, he reported progress in making the arrangements for commercial ventures. He also warned of popular rejection of Maximilian and the Confederacy: "No one here—Mexican or foreigner—thinks that Maximilian would remain one month in the throne if the French Army was withdrawn . . . a large majority of the Mexicans are against us. . . . They say . . . the North has always been their friend—the South the enemy— . . . the French on the contrary are to a man for us." La Sère's mission, begun too late to alleviate the Confederates' trade problems, could only serve to report the erosion of respect for the South in Mexico.[38]

The worsening war situation and the defeat of Confederate diplomatic plans in Europe and Mexico, particularly Maximilian's rejection of the Preston mission, also eroded southern respect for imperial Mexico. Then, a political movement developed in the South to reassert the Monroe Doctrine, perhaps even in conjunction with the federal government. Although Francis Gerrity, an authority on southern newspaper editorial opinion, stated that "to the bitter end the Confederate press appeared unreconciled to the Monroe Doctrine," the Monroe Doctrine was not entirely ignored in the Confederacy. Rebel desire for French recognition prevented expression of concern about French intervention in Mexico until after the rejection of the William Preston mission. On November 7, 1864, Congressman John P. Murray of Tennessee rose in the Confederate House to introduce a series of joint resolutions which declared a lack of sympathy with the monarchical government in the New World. Several weeks later, Henry Stuart Foote of Tennessee offered resolutions in the House, asserting that the people of the

38. La Sère's dispatches are found in Records of the Confederate States of America, Volume 9, and Pickett Papers, Volume 2; and instructions to La Sère are found in Records of the Confederate States of America, box 11.

Confederacy adhered to the principles of the Monroe Doctrine.[39] Rather than summarily rejecting the Monroe Doctrine, perhaps, the South believed all along that it had been offering to trade the Monroe Doctrine for something it desired more—independence.

In January, 1865, responding to the Francis P. Blair mission proposing a joint Union-Confederate campaign to expel the French, and, perhaps, to the rejection of the Preston mission, Virginian Congressman Daniel C. De Jarnette introduced a resolution in the House to pave the way for a joint military combination to clear foreign troops from Mexico. In a confused, linguistically ludicrous resolution De Jarnette asserted that the Confederate States might unite with someone to put an end to all "seeming violations" of the Monroe Doctrine.[40] This latter-day concern for the Monroe Doctrine could produce nothing of value for the Confederacy, however. It had long since passed its opportunity in foreign relations.

Often dismissing the Confederate diplomatic failure in Mexico in terms of Pickett's personality, historians overlook the broader aspects and avoid the valuable analysis which can be derived from studying his, Quintero's, or Preston's instructions. Certainly the situation was fraught with difficulties. Many Mexicans distrusted the South, and more able diplomats might have quieted the fears somewhat and stabilized relations. But the instructions of the Confederate diplomats and the conservative world view behind them were the key Confederate problems. These instructions demonstrated the inability of the South to understand the times, its own neighbors, or world currents. To instruct an agent going to the Liberal government in Mexico to emphasize mutually shared interest in slavery/peonage, in agriculture, in states rights, and their long friendship, is shocking in light of the decade-long Mexican civil war

39. Francis X. Gerrity, "American Editorial Opinion of French Intervention in Mexico, 1861–1867" (Ph.D. dissertation, Georgetown University, 1952), 149; Confederate States of America, "Proceedings of the Confederate Congress," *Southern Historical Society Papers* (New Series, Volumes 6–14; Richmond, Va., 1923–1959), N.S. XIII, No. LI (1958), 269, 387, 398.

40. *Ibid.*, 260.

during which the Liberals had fought to abolish peonage, establish a centralist government, create the basis to convert their economy to an industrial-commercial economy, and to destroy an agrarian, aristocratic elite. Furthermore, for the Confederate leadership to refuse to draw maximum material advantages from the Texas-Mexican border, but rather for years to be more concerned about international law matters reflects a mentality which was woefully out of place in the industrializing nineteenth century. Moreover, the Liberals had constantly claimed it was southerners who threatened their country with dismemberment and annexation and the reestablishment of slavery. In sum, the South was badly out of tune with its times, very clearly in relation to Mexico, but very likely elsewhere also. Fortunately for the Confederacy, the divisive impact of the Civil War and the European challenge to the New World produced internal and external stresses for the Union which prevented a more effective policy to counter faltering Confederate relations with Mexico.

V United States Domestic Politics and the Deterioration of Relations with Mexico, 1862–1865

E VENTS transpiring during the years 1862–1865, cataclysmic in their effects upon each nation, produced strains and tensions which tore the fabric of mutual cooperation, woven with considerable difficulty between 1858–1862. To a large extent, Matías Romero's attitude paralleled the shifting policy of the Lincoln administration toward Liberal Mexico. The Mexican government's attitude toward the United States, however, followed Romero's lead quite faithfully. As the Civil War dragged on, United States attention focused more urgently on domestic affairs and away from projects of assistance for Mexico. Romero responded by intensifying his activity, increasing his contacts with the opposition factions, and often doggedly opposing the Lincoln administration's policy toward the Mexican muddle.

Although some asserted that Romero was not mature enough or of sufficient stature to manage the key United States post during the crisis of foreign invasion, ultimately he was considered an excellent agent. The Mexican Congress, determined to send a prestigious person as minister to Washington, appointed several well-known figures. Fortunately for Mexico, no one arrived to replace Romero who remained as chargé until his elevation to minister in the fall of 1863. Juárez had such confidence in Romero that for a time he was Mexico's only diplomatic agent abroad responsible for keeping his government informed on European and New World developments. Later, even with other agents active in Europe, Romero functioned as the center for external information, receiving and forwarding dispatches en route to Mexico, and being informed of foreign developments in separate dispatches from the European agents. Hence, Romero was the key diplomat, occupying the key diplomatic position in Mexico's struggle against foreign aggression.[1]

Some of the strains upon Mexican–United States relations in the early 1860s, developing from the outbreak of the war, were of a kind that one would expect between neutral and belligerent powers. Following the presidential blockade proclamations of April 19 and 27, 1861, a series of incidents occurred involving alleged attempts by Mexican-registered ships to run the Union blockade. New Orleans was the site of the first incidents involving Mexican-owned vessels. The *Alfonsina*, attempting to leave New Orleans for Tampico shortly after the blockade began, was stopped and burned. The *Brillante*, in the same port when the blockade began, was given four days to leave. Departing later for Key West carrying contraband of war, the *Brillante* was seized and declared a legal prize by a United States admiralty court. The *Oriente*, seized attempting to enter the port of New Orleans after it fell to Union forces, but prior to official termination of the blockade, was later placed at liberty without indemnification, and Seward postponed adjudication. The *Soledad Cos*, seized off Galveston despite a thinly veiled attempt by means of a shadow sale to pass off the Confederate vessel as Mexican, was condemned as a fair prize in 1866.[2] De-

---

1. Actas de las Sesiones Secretas, July 18, 23, 1861; and *El Siglo Diez y Nueve*, January 21, April 3, 1862.
2. Zorrilla, *Relaciones*, I, 423–25. The exchange of notes concerning the *Brillante* and *Oriente* can be followed in Romero (comp.), *Correspondencia*, II, 89–91, 119, 304–306, 327–28, 384–86, 590–91, 741–42. The extensive exchange of correspondence on the *Soledad Cos* or *Anna Taylor* can be followed in Correspondencia General con los Estados Unidos. Romero to Ministro de Relaciones Exteriores, April 17, 1866, in Romero (comp.), *Correspondencia*, VII, 426–27, reports the condemning of the *Soledad Cos*.

spite the ambiguity of maritime law and the slow dissemination of Lincoln's blockade notification, Mexico and the United States avoided a serious disagreement over alleged violations of the Union blockade.[3]

In 1863, a maritime case of greater interest, complexity, and difficulty occurred. Irascible Acting Rear-Admiral Charles Wilkes of *Trent* notoriety forcibly seized the vessels *Noc-Daquy* (previously the *Virginia*) and *Pepita* while they were under the custody of Mexican officials for violation of Mexico's international agreement on slave trading. Romero protested that Wilkes' seizure of both ships violated Mexico's sovereignty. The State Department answered Romero's protest by forwarding a copy of Wilkes' dispatch stating that his seizure of the *Noc-Daquy* occurred in international waters. A letter from J. H. Stevens, who resided in Mérida, implied, however, that the seizure had occurred in Mexican waters. More to the point, the captain of the *Noc-Daquy* affirmed the State Department's contention that this ship was a Confederate vessel preparing to run arms and munitions into Mobile. The *Pepita* was seized because it had a "particular relationship" with the *Noc-Daquy*. In the following years, Mexico's persistent wish for active United States aid against the French reduced the lingering *Noc-Daquy* incident to unimportance.[4] Not a significant naval power, Mexico had no intention of pressing a maritime disagreement strongly enough to endanger Mexican–United States relations. Nevertheless, Romero

3. While Mexico and the United States avoided major conflict regarding maritime law, Britain and the United States disagreed in a major way over trade routes between Europe and the Confederacy via Matamoros. See Stuart L. Bernath, *Squall Across the Atlantic: American Civil War Prize Cases and Diplomacy* (Berkeley, 1970), 34–84, 166–68.

4. Romero to Ministro de Relaciones Exteriores, February 23 and March 13, 1863, in Romero (comp.), *Correspondencia*, III, 227–29, 273–79; Statement of Charles Wilkes, December 29, 1862, and [J?] H. Stevens to Governor of Yucatán, January 12, 1863, in Archivo Histórico de Matías Romero, Banco de México; and correspondence relative to the steamer *Virginia*, alias *Noc-Daquy*, in *Official Records, Navies*, II, 40–44. The Mexican government seized the slaver *Saint John* in the fall of 1861 with no apparent protest or reaction by the United States government. See the exchange of correspondence in "El Ministro de Relaciones participa haber sido apresada en Campeche la barca americana negrera 'Saint-John'," Archivo Histórico de la Secretaría de Relaciones Exteriores; and Zorrilla, *Relaciones*, I, 424–25.

registered Mexico's maritime complaints to be pursued after current graver problems were resolved.

During 1861–1862, Mexico's apprehension arose concerning a proposal to colonize freed blacks in Mexico. In June, 1861, Montgomery Blair first approached Romero about the possibility of moving a large number of black freedmen to the island of Cozumel, off the southeastern coast of Yucatán, or elsewhere in Mexico. Blair believed the lands called *tierra caliente* would be suitable for Negro habitation. Romero observed that labor was not needed in the *tierra caliente* regions, yet he assured Blair that Mexicans were without color prejudice and desired immigrants. In reporting this incident, Romero added his impression that Blair's proposal originated in the cabinet.[5]

Beyond a few questions from Seward in December concerning Yucatán, Romero engaged in no further conversation regarding black colonization until February 1, 1862, when Blair again broached the subject of colonizing Negroes in Mexico. Blair now suggested that the United States wanted to purchase the island of Cozumel. Without rejecting Cozumel as a possible colonization location, Romero assured Blair that Juárez would not permit the alienation of another inch of national territory. Blair claimed the Negroes would only go if allowed to retain their United States citizenship and enjoy the protection of the United States. Romero pointed out that, recently, the laws of Mexico had been revised to permit foreigners to own real property. Despite Blair's disclaimer that the United States desired no new Mexican territory, when reporting this conversation, Romero could not help conjuring up the image of the United States colonizing Cozumel in order to create a demand for Yucatán's annexation to the Union à la Texas of 1820–1836.[6]

5. Romero to Ministro de Relaciones Exteriores, June 6, 1861, in Correspondencia General con los Estados Unidos. See V. Jacques Voegeli, *Free but not Equal: The Midwest and the Negro During the Civil War* (Chicago, 1968), 23–25, 45, 127, for the contemporary justification and criticism of black colonization.

6. Romero to Ministro de Relaciones Exteriores, December 9, 1861, and February 1, 1862, in Romero (comp.), *Correspondencia*, I, 640–41 and II, 32–34.

Remarks by Secretary of the Treasury Salmon Portland Chase sustained Romero's fears. Regarding black colonization plans for Central America, Chase wrote that "except as a means of getting a foothold in Central America" he did not approve it. The use of black colonization to initiate either a commercial or territorial expansionist policy was a very real possibility.[7]

Aware of the Lincoln administration's desire to colonize blacks in Mexico, Robert W. Shufeldt, United States consul at Havana, traveled to Mexico City to solicit Mexican approval of his specific plan for settling the blacks in Tehuantepec. Shufeldt argued that Tehuantepec, besides being an ideal home for the freed blacks, offered immense commercial and strategic value for future United States trade with Asia and the Pacific area. In 1862, both Corwin and Doblado used Lincoln's known commitment to colonization to apply pressure in favor of the Corwin-Doblado loan, arguing that without the loan the land would be pledged to Britain and therefore unavailable for United States freedmen.[8]

The chief advocates and organizers of colonization schemes viewed their projects in various lights. Colonization would supply a foothold upon key areas necessary for controlling trade with the Pacific area and Asia; it would also play a significant role in the contest between imperialism (foreign rule) and republicanism (self-rule). The black colonists would be planted at crucial points such as Tehuantepec, or the Panamanian Isthmus, thus giving the United States control over the key transit areas. By freeing the slaves and

---

7. David Donald (ed.), *Inside Lincoln's Cabinet: The Civil War Diaries of Salmon P. Chase* (New York, 1954), 156–57. See also F. Parraga to Ambrose W. Thompson, September 26, 1862, enclosed in Romero to Ministro de Relaciones Exteriores, November 12, 1862, September 20, October 31, 1862, in Romero (comp.), *Correspondencia*, II, 581–85, 397, 567; and the concluding chapter of Nícia Vilela Luz, *A Amazônia para os Negros Americanos* (Rio de Janeiro, 1968). The best study of black colonization is Willis Boyd, "Negro Colonization in the National Crisis, 1860–1870" (Ph.D. dissertation, University of California at Los Angeles, 1953), which gives some notice to imperialist notions in colonization schemes.

8. Corwin to A. C. Allen, May 18, 1862, in Lincoln Papers; Robert W. Shufeldt to Frederick W. Seward, January 16, 1862, in *Official Records*, Series 3, I, 871; and Shufeldt to Sumner, January 17, 1862, in Sumner Papers, Volume 56. For Shufeldt's interest in black colonization in general, see Boyd, "Negro Colonization in the National Crisis," 415–16.

destroying the privileged class in the United States, potential New World aristocratic allies of European despotism would be eliminated, while the black colonies would occupy areas which were the prime targets for European imperialist ambition.[9]

Arguing that its territory was the objective of French imperialism, the Mexican government sought material aid and assistance as well as moral support from the Lincoln administration, which, however, engaged in suppressing a widespread revolution, could offer little more than moral support. For several reasons the United States government refused to allow exportation of arms, munitions, and other war materials. First, in the early years of the war, 1861–1863, war supplies were needed for the Union army and the state militia. Second, the United States government feared that the supplies might intentionally or accidentally fall into Confederate hands. Third, the Lincoln-Seward administration refused to antagonize France during the years 1862–1865 when the French threat of recognition of the Confederacy appeared real and potentially disastrous. An incident verifying the soundness of administration fears occurred in early 1863, when arms shipped out of New York for Liberal troops arrived at Matamoros. Lacking sufficient cash to purchase the shipment, the Liberals made a deal with Confederate officials, permitting them to acquire whatever supplies the Liberals could not pay for.[10] The Lincoln administration's neutrality policy intended to prevent precisely this kind of misuse of its neutrality.

Since recognition of a state of war between Mexico and France would destroy the geographical advantages Mexico derived from being close to the United States, by severely restricting the legal flow of American money, material, or men to Juárez' government, the Union government avoided this step, maintaining instead neu-

9. James Mitchell to Lincoln, May 18, 1862, "Important Considerations for Congress," with Ninian W. Edwards to Lincoln, August 9, 1861, in Lincoln Papers; F. P. Blair, Sr. to Lincoln, November 16, 1861, in Blair Family Papers, box 1, Library of Congress; Shufeldt to Seward, November 21, 1861, in Consular Dispatches, Havana, RG 59, NA; Ambrose Thompson to Seward, March 30, 1863, in Seward Papers.

10. Bee to J. Bankhead Magruder, February 15, 1863, in *Official Records*, XV, 979–81; Quintero to Benjamin, March 1, 1863, in *Official Records*, Series 2, Vol. V, 842.

trality.[11] Already in November of 1861 Romero had suspected that Seward would do little or nothing to aid Mexico. Describing Seward's attitude as cold and reserved, Romero cynically assumed that, only if Seward could turn a profit for the United States from Mexico's troubles, would the United States become involved, but not simply to aid in sustaining Mexican nationality and liberty.[12]

Perhaps Romero never fully realized the problems facing Seward. During the course of the Civil War, Seward's first duties were to prevent recognition of the Confederacy, to sustain in international law the blockade of the South, and to avoid serious diplomatic problems that could lead to a foreign war. The *Trent* affair and the French intervention presented theoretically similar difficulties for Seward. With imprudent handling, either event could have involved the United States in a major foreign war, something Seward and Lincoln intended to avoid. That the Republic of Mexico might have ceased to exist if the United States had been drawn into a war with either France or England never adequately entered Romero's consideration. Not viewing the international situation as broadly as Seward, he never appreciated Seward's adroit handling of the United States foreign relations.[13]

11. Romero to Ministro de Relaciones Exteriores, October 9 and December 22, 1861, June 5, 1862, in Romero (comp.), *Correspondencia*, I, 553–57, 659–60, II, 226–27; Romero to Ministro de Relaciones Exteriores, September 18, 1862, in Correspondencia General con los Estados Unidos; Philip W. Kennedy, "Union and Confederate Relations with Mexico," *Duquesne Review*, XI (Spring, 1966), 48–51; Robert R. Miller, "Matías Romero: Mexican Minister to the United States during the Juárez-Maximilian Era," *Hispanic American Historical Review*, XLV (May, 1965), 233–35.

12. Romero to Ministro de Relaciones Exteriores, November 23, 1861, in Correspondencia General con los Estados Unidos; Callahan, *American Policy*, 289; Miller, "Matías Romero," 234–35.

13. Glyndon G. Van Deusen, *William Henry Seward* (New York: Oxford University Press, 1967), 288–375, 486–96. In 1867 Seward prepared tables revealing the quantity of his correspondence with foreign governments during the years 1861–1865. Moderately low total and yearly average statistics for State Department correspondence with the United States minister in Mexico resulted in part from Thomas Corwin's departure from that country in early 1864. Nevertheless, the strong exchange maintained between Seward and Romero permitted Mexico to occupy fifth place among all nations in the number of communications made with Seward over that five-year period, a quantitative indicator of the importance of Mexican relations to the United States. See Miscellaneous Public Papers, 1861–1869, box 62, folder 13, in Seward Papers.

One of Romero's superiors appreciated the quandry for Seward and the Lincoln administration posed by the French intervention in Mexico during the Civil War. Juan Antonio de la Fuente, former Mexican minister of foreign relations, was recalled to his old post for eight days during an August, 1862, cabinet reorganization. In words recognizing the United States' dilemma regarding French intervention extremely well, de la Fuente observed, "We ought to expect nothing of the United States while they are engaged in their Civil War and fear to compromise themselves with France. In my exchanges with Mr. [Manuel] Doblado, I always told him . . . that the only occasion in which we could count on the aid of the Washington government, would be if France should recognize the South."[14] De la Fuente's argument apparently did not convince Romero.

Lincoln's neutrality upset Romero and the Mexican government, particularly when they found out they would not receive the war materials they needed because they were judged to be contraband goods. The French obtained food, mules, and other supplies from New Orleans, New York, and San Francisco, while Mexico was denied the arms and munitions necessary to resist the French. In 1862 and early 1863, Seward and Romero held several heated interviews over this controversial neutrality interpretation. Ugly rumors spread regarding Seward's catering to the French intervention in Mexico. One repeated by Attorney General Bates claimed that Seward had presented French minister Mercier with maps, charts, and related materials deposited by General Scott in the public archives. Making no headway with Seward, in late January of 1863 Romero and McDougall tried to embarrass the administration by exposing the unfairness of this neutrality policy. Passed unanimously, McDougall's resolution requested the president to inform the Senate concerning the general prohibition against exporting war material and "the orders which have been

14. Juan Antonio de la Fuente to Romero, August 27, 1862, in Tamayo (ed.), *Juárez Documentos*, VI, 818–19.

given in respect to the exportation of war contraband for the use of the French army invading Mexico."[15]

Although convinced that the United States was violating its own neutrality law, the Mexican Liberals could not coax any other course out of the Lincoln administration. Francisco Zarco contended the United States policy was unwisely self-defeating: "Whatever American aid is given France, will later be a weapon against the United States itself, against the Monroe Doctrine, and will serve to foment the rebellion and the Civil War, and to encourage Bonaparte in his intention of intervening throughout the American continents." In July, 1865, Romero informed Seward that the Mexican liberals were without arms, the ability to manufacture arms, or revenue to purchase arms or war materials, adding that "with arms and means we can terminate in a few months the war which France is waging against us; and without these elements, we shall be obliged to limit ourselves to resisting the French, who will be enabled to remain in Mexico for an indefinite period, with great danger to the peace of this continent, until they find themselves compelled to quit that country through weariness." Romero assured Seward that Mexico could solve the problem all by itself in a short period if only permitted to negotiate a public loan and to purchase and export arms from the United States.[16]

Conversely, neither Seward, the Lincoln administration, nor most United States historians have fully recognized the problems facing Mexico after 1861. In this small nation, economically bankrupt as the result of decades of internal disorder, including the long, bitter, recently ended *guerra de la Reforma*, the victorious liberals were facing a still sizable domestic minority faction—the conservatives—sustained by one of the most powerful European nations, France. Nor have United States historians given due atten-

---

15. Beale (ed.), *Diary of Edward Bates*, 311–12; Washington *Daily Globe*, February 1, 1863, enclosed with Romero to Ministro de Relaciones Exteriores, February 3, 1863, in Romero (comp.), *Correspondencia*, III, 162, and Basler (ed.), *Works of Lincoln*, VI, 66–67.

16. Francisco Zarco, "Violación de las obligaciones de neutralidad," *El Siglo Diez y Nueve*, February 22, 1863; and Romero to Seward, July 23, 1865, in U.S. Department of State, *Foreign Relations of the United States, 1865*, Pt. 3, pp. 638–40.

tion to the claim of Mexican historians that the Mexican defeat of the French army at Puebla, on May 5, 1862, saved the United States from dismemberment. Since this defeat delayed the French advance one year, Mexican historians claim that if the French army had reached the Texas frontier in late 1863 instead of late 1864, the outcome of the Civil War might have been reversed.[17] The hypothesis that the Mexican republic might have ceased to exist if the United States had been drawn into a war with France, or, the contention that the Civil War might have permanently dismembered the United States if the French and Confederate forces had established contact earlier in the war, both point out ways in which historians and participants have suggested the close interrelationship of the two conflicts. From many important perspectives the French intervention and the Civil War were parts of the same struggle.

Seward faced an embarrassing problem relative to recognition when in early 1863 the United States consul at Manzanillo, John Xantus, one of the United States' foremost naturalists, conceded that his consular power was derived from Tobáz, the local *cacique*, and not from the Juárez government's exequatur. The *cacique* was extracting fines from a United States viceconsul for alleged violations of the public order, and, at times, jailing the viceconsul. Primarily concerned with a biological and botanical examination of western Mexican natural life, Xantus found this unofficial arrangement the one best assuring that his work would not be continually disturbed. Seward's immediate, summary dismissal of Xantus probably saved the United States from a reproach by the Mexican government.[18] Xantus' action undermined Seward's policy of not recognizing revolutionary, military, non-democratically

17. Daniel Moreno, "Mr. E. L. Plumb en México y la acción en las cumbres de Acultzingo 1862," *Boletín del Archivo General de la Nación*, 2ª Serie, III (1962), 175–98; Alfonso Teja Zabre, *Historia de México* (Mexico, 1935), 343.

18. The archives of the Secretaría de Relaciones Exteriores contain individual files for United States consuls. The Xantus file contains much intriguing information on the incident. One letter from Ramón de la Vega, governor of Colima, while protesting Xantus' innocence, urged a hearing for Xantus, who otherwise threatened to publish "all" correspondence on the

approved authorities as illustrated in the United States position regarding the Confederacy, and the General José Antonio Páez regime in Colombia. While seeking his exoneration and restoration to his post and continuing his botanical work, Xantus remained near Manzanillo, creating problems for his successors. It was to no avail, however, as he was not reappointed to the consular post.[19]

Another embarrassing problem, involving territorial integrity, confronted Juárez as well as Seward in 1863. In mid-September, 1863, José Domingo Cortes, claiming to be governor of Sonora and representative of a separatist movement in Sonora, Sinaloa, Chihuahua, Durango, and Baja California, arrived in Havana bearing a note from Corwin stating he "appeared to be a gentleman." Approaching the United States consul in Havana, Thomas Savage, with Corwin's note, Cortes parlayed it into a letter introducing him to Seward. Savage correctly assumed Cortes would present Seward with a plan from the governors of the northern Mexican states to detach these states from the central government and annex them to the United States. Hearing of Cortes' venture, Plumb, knowledgeable of Mexico's politicians, cautioned Frederick Seward that he had never heard of Cortes, who he assumed was not a prominent Liberal. Plumb also passed on to the State Department information from the Mexican consul in New York, Navarro, alleging that Cortes had once been in Santa Anna's army and later expelled from Puebla by General Ignacion Zaragoza. Plumb warned that Cortes' "objectives are purely personal, if not illegitimate."[20] To further discredit Cortes, Romero forwarded to Seward letters from Governor Luis Terrazas of Chihuahua and General F. García Morales,

matter, in Expediente Personal de John Xantus y D. L. Lane, Archivo Histórico de la Secretaría de Relaciones Exteriores. See also Xantus to Seward, May 14 and August 1, 1863, and Xantus to Charles H. Poor, April 8, 1863, in Consular Dispatches, Manzanillo, RG 59, NA.

19. See Nathan L. Ferris, "The Relations of the United States with South America during the American Civil War," *Hispanic American Historical Review*, XXI (February, 1941), 59–64; John S. Blake to Seward, January 31, 1864, in Consular Dispatches, Manzanillo, RG 59, NA.

20. Thomas Savage to Seward, September 11 and 12, 1863, Plumb to Frederick Seward, September 21, 1863, in Seward Papers.

governor and military commandant of Sinaloa—the former denying knowledge of Cortes, and the latter characterizing Cortes as a
Spanish intriguer, but both agreeing that Cortes had never held
high office on the west coast of Mexico.[21]

In a second interview, Seward informed Cortes that the United
States would not act upon his request. After his plans were rejected, Cortes pleaded with Seward for return passage to Sonora via
Panama, promising to repay the sum and to report to Seward regularly in the future. Assuming the French would publicly interpret
Cortes' mission as proof of Mexican dissatisfaction towards Juárez,
Romero urged the Liberal government to take countermeasures. He
recommended public denunciation of Cortes and popular demon-
strations in Mexico's Pacific states. Other than issuing an order to
expel Cortes from Mexican territory, however, the Mexican government apparently decided that ignoring his activities would best
keep them unknown.[22] Perhaps José Cortes did not return to Sonora, however, since a year and a half later, a "Cortes" published
stories in New York City maintaining that twice Juárez had tried to
sell Sonora to the United States. If Cortes were an opportunist, the
New York stories were natural employment, since Jesús González
Ortega, pretender to the presidency of Mexico, would have paid
well for anti-Juárez propaganda at this time.[23]

By 1864, the bleak outlook for the Liberal government had

21. Romero to Seward, July 9, 1864, enclosing Luis Terrazas to Romero, January 11,
1864, and F. García Morales to Romero, January 24, 1864, in U.S. Department of State,
Foreign Relations of the United States, 1865, Pt. 3, pp. 576–78.

22. Romero to Ministro de Relaciones Exteriores, November 20, 1863, Correspondencia General con los Estados Unidos; Lerdo de Tejada to Manuel Ruiz, January 16,
1864, in *Official Records*, Vol. XXXIV, Pt. 2, pp. 216–17.

23. Cortes to Seward, September 30, 1863, in Seward Papers; Romero to Plumb, May
2, 1865, in Plumb Collection. In December, 1862, Plácido Vega had ordered a "Franco
Cortez," a local Sonoran political figure, to travel to San Francisco to purchase arms. José
Domingo Cortes claimed that his mission had originally been to go to San Francisco. Possibly a small-time politician, given some travel money and a few letters of introduction, attempted to extract great material advantage from the situation, and when the situation deteriorated, he just stuck around, serving whoever might pay. See Vega to Carlos E. Norton,
December 8, 1862, in Plácido Vega Papers, Stanford University; and Savage to Seward,
September 11 and 12, 1863, in Seward Papers.

reopened the possibility of the alienation of Mexican territory. Between the collapse of the Corwin loan negotiations in mid-1862 and late 1864, the Liberals had not discussed possible territorial cession. During 1861 and 1862, while a member of the Mexican Congress, Lerdo de Tejada, a nationalist, had strongly disapproved of the proposed territorial lien. Thus, Lerdo de Tejada's association with the government made territorial cession appear less likely. However, in 1857 Lerdo had advocated granting all "terrenos baldíos" in the Isthmus of Tehuantepec to Jecker and Company in order to attract foreign colonists. Lerdo de Tejada's earlier proposal suggests that he had not always been so unsympathetic to foreigners, nor incapable of risking foreign control over Mexican territory. Still, after the Liberal government had been driven back to Chihuahua, Lerdo de Tejada insisted upon instructing Romero that "the integrity and independence of the national territory" would be preserved.[24]

When, influenced by the northern flight of the Liberal government and by rumors of Maximilian's transfer of land to Napoleon, Romero approached Seward regarding the possibility of exchanging Baja California in return for aid to Mexico, the proposition leaked out. While the opposition publicized the affair to influence nationalists against the Liberals, Lerdo de Tejada immediately rebuked Romero for violating his trust and bringing discredit on the Liberal government. Again Lerdo de Tejada reasserted the Liberal government's unwillingness to condone the loss of any territory.[25] The stakes in the contest between the empire and the Liberals would be all of Mexico or none.

---

24. Knapp, *Life of Lerdo de Tejada*, 105–108; and Lerdo de Tejada to Romero, December 30, 1864, in Romero (comp.), *Correspondencia*, IV, 565–67; Sebastián Lerdo de Tejada to the Mexican Minister to Great Britain, September 15, 1857, in Documentos Varios, legajo 22, Archivo Histórico, Museo Nacional de Antropología y Historia. Some historians, Roeder for example, claim Juárez "preserved" Mexico intact. But, Juárez had been ready in the McLane-Ocampo treaty and during the Corwin loan negotiations to seriously jeopardize ownership of parts of Mexico. Lerdo de Tejada had strongly opposed both.

25. Romero to Ministro de Relaciones Exteriores, November 24, 1864, and Lerdo de Tejada to Romero, January 26, 1865, in Correspondencia General con los Estados Unidos.

During the early years of the United States Civil War, Romero confronted not only an inactive administration but also an indifferent Congress. Prior to late 1863, only Senator James A. McDougall of California spoke out continuously and vigorously against French intervention. Elected to the Senate in early 1861 after William Gwin resigned, McDougall defeated a former minister to Mexico, John B. Weller. Probably reflecting California's geographic and cultural position, McDougall immediately became interested in the Mexican situation. An early sympathetic cooperation between Romero and McDougall gave Romero access to Senate gossip and furnished him with a willing outlet to inform the Senate of Mexican affairs. As early as January, 1862, a McDougall resolution brought to the attention of the Senate and nation the dangers and consequences of the French intervention in Mexico. The McDougall tie was particularly useful between 1861 and 1864 when Romero attempted to establish himself in the diplomatic, congressional, and politically influential circles of Washington.[26]

More important than relations with McDougall was Romero's contact with the powerful Charles Sumner, chairman of the Senate Foreign Relations Committee. In 1861 and early 1862 Romero and Sumner had amiable relations. After the Senate Foreign Relations Committee's recommendation to accept the Corwin loan treaty in principle was rejected, Sumner altered his attitude. He often agreed with Romero in principle, but they usually disagreed over the most appropriate method of objecting to French intervention in Mexico. Sumner feared any demanding action might produce an undesired French reaction—undesired by the United States at least while the Civil War continued. Mexico would have to wait until the domestic problem was solved. Naturally, Romero did not agree with this attitude. Beginning in early 1862, Seward and Sumner

26. Russell Buchanan, "James A. McDougall: A Forgotten Senator," *California History Society Quarterly*, XV (September, 1936), 199–212; and Marvin Goldwert, "Matías Romero and Congressional Opposition to Seward's Policy Toward the French Intervention in Mexico," *The Americas*, XXII (July, 1965), 23–26. For examples of McDougall's efforts, see *Congressional Globe*, 38th Cong. 1st Sess., 145, 1227, 3496, and 3499–3500.

usually agreed on broad foreign policy issues in relation to Mexico and foreign intervention in that country. The combined Sumner-Seward influence in the Senate was impossible to combat successfully.[27]

Long prior to the foreign intervention, Romero had considered a propaganda network in the United States a desirable tool for obtaining Liberal goals such as attracting investment capital, or, later, generating United States pressure to sustain a firm policy of opposition to the French intervention. Romero's initial effort to launch a propaganda machine occurred in June, 1861, when he sought to have Edward E. Dunbar serve as confidential agent for two hundred dollars monthly. Dunbar would have placed Mexican documents and news stories in newspapers and forwarded the principal United States papers to Mexico. Despite the Mexican government's rejection of the proposal because of the lack of funds, Dunbar became a loyal propagandist for the Mexican republic.[28] Romero soon discovered alternative publication routes. Often receiving no other reward than the necessary funds to publish their tracts, Edward Lee Plumb, Robert Dale Owen, George Church of the New York *Tribune*, and New York businessman James Beeckman, as well as the Associated Press agent in Washington, worked for Romero as propagandists. Various congressmen introduced requests for information in order to print it at government expense, or sought materials and advice from Romero regarding their speeches on Mexican affairs. Romero was making slow but shaky progress toward creating a large, effective propaganda machine in the United States.

Former attorney general Edward Bates of Missouri refused to

27. David Donald, *Charles Sumner and the Rights of Man* (New York, 1970), 36, 101–103; Van Deusen, *William Henry Seward*, 316, 367; Romero to Ministro de Relaciones Exteriores, June 23, 1864, in Romero (comp.), *Correspondencia*, IV, 237–238.
28. Romero to Ministro de Relaciones Exteriores, June 8, 1861, and Manuel María Zamacona to Romero, September 11, 1861, in Correspondencia General con los Estados Unidos; Romero to Plumb, April 17, 1862, and February 17, 23, 27, 1864, in Plumb Collection; and Romero to Ministro de Relaciones Exteriores, March 5, 1862, in Tamayo (ed.), *Juárez Documentos*, VI, 42–43.

accept the radical contention that Mexico's troubles were part of the war of the rebellion:

These Radicals are extremely anxious to have the war continued as long as possible, for without a pretense of war, they may find it hard to continue much longer, the use of *martial law*, and hitherto that has been their only dependence for carrying out their tyranny in Missouri. That shift may last the Radicals sometime yet- It is a pretty conception—say they. The Empire in Mexico is part of the rebellion, and until it is put down the war continues; and so long as we are at war, we must have martial law, q.e.d. This chimes in exactly with Thad. Stevens' doctrine that in time of war the constitution is inoperative.[29]

Bates considered the radicals' argument asserting a tie between the rebellion and the French intervention a political ploy to permit firm control of the South.

The Radical failure to unseat Seward in December, 1862, and Romero's own inability to obtain his objectives from the Lincoln administration so disheartened Romero that he raised the question of suspending relations with the United States. A short time later, in May, 1863, Romero did resign, creating a de facto suspension until October, 1863. Romero resigned as Mexican chargé d'affaires because he no longer wished to struggle against Seward's obstructionist policy and because he was without salary or funds needed to maintain an effective congressional lobby.[30]

While the Mexican government was not responsible for Seward's blindness, it was for the nonpayment of Romero's salary and for the lack of funds to maintain the necessary information services. Romero agreed to return to Washington in the fall of 1863 as Mexican minister only after receiving assurances of an adequate salary, paid regularly, and an expense allowance sufficient to permit him to lobby effectively among congressmen. Romero immediately ran

29. Beale (ed.), *Diary of Edward Bates*, 523.

30. Emma Cosío Villegas (ed.), *Diario personal de Matías Romero, 1855–1865* (Mexico, 1960), 557–76; and Romero to Ministro de Relaciones Exteriores, February 26, 1863, in Correspondencia General con los Estados Unidos; Romero to Ministro de Relaciones Exteriores, January 19, 1863, January 21 and 29, 1864, in Romero (comp.), *Correspondencia*, III, 124–25, and IV, 10, 13–15.

into a road block. After his presenting his credentials to President Lincoln, the customary speeches were made. Although Lincoln spoke warmly and sympathetically of Romero personally, nothing significant was said in either speech. As Romero reported, "Seward forbade any allusion to the present condition of affairs and so I made none."[31] Romero recalled the hopelessness of trying to get Seward to consider Mexican problems in the proper light.

The grossly negligent, inadequate recognition of Mexico's difficulties by the United States government, as interpreted by Romero, frustrated and angered the Mexican minister. So from late 1862 through the presidential election of 1864 Romero aided the anti-Seward and anti-Lincoln movements. Moreover, although informed of this course, his government did not instruct Romero to curtail his consultations with the Radical opponents of the Lincoln administration, his sympathizing with them, and his passing of information to them. (Romero often permitted them to read his official correspondence with Seward.) For example, Romero wished the Radicals well in their unsuccessful maneuver to force Seward out of the Lincoln administration in late 1862. During the crisis of mid-December, 1862, Romero's act of drafting a note in anticipation of Seward's resignation was indicative of how strongly he hoped for Seward's dismissal. Without direct evidence revealing how Romero obtained the information that Seward might be forced to resign, it can only be speculated that his Radical friends were keeping him informed. Romero shared the Radical Republicans' tendency to assign Seward almost full responsibility for the Lincoln administration's foreign policy toward Mexico.

In great part the cooperation of Romero and the Radicals rested upon a shared view of the intimate relationship between the French intervention and the southern rebellion. While on numerous occasions after 1862 Romero asserted that the French intervention and the United States Civil War were part of a united effort to destroy

31. Romero to Plumb, October 28, 30, and November 11 and 18, 1863, in Plumb Collection.

republicanism, the Radical leaders were slower in publicly pro-
nouncing a similar view. However, in early 1863, prompted by the
French mediation offer in the United States Civil War, Thaddeus
Stevens spoke out on the indivisibility of the Union with the argument that France, long obstructing Mexico's right to decide its own
governmental form, was now threatening to meddle in United
States problems. Thaddeus Stevens revealed why the French conducted themselves so despicably:

I know very well where the sympathies of the monarchies of Europe tend.
There is nothing they so much dread as a prosperous, mighty republic on
this continent. It would be a school in which their subjects would learn the
value of democratic principles, would gradually accept the idea of universal liberty, would learn to govern themselves, and dispense with thrones
and nobilities. In a few years, if we remain united, we would become a
match for any or all the despots of Europe. If this nation were broken into
fragments, and two or three republics were to arise upon its ruins, we
should be a feeble people, incapable of self-defense. The Old World
would shape our institutions, regulate our commerce, and control all our
interests. Free trade would bring with it the destruction of our manufactures, the prostration of our commerce, and finally dictate the rulers who
should sit upon our thrones. The fate of Greece, of Italy, and I fear the
approaching fate of Mexico, should be our warning.

Stevens knew that Napoleon III had established himself in Mexico
in order to "strike this Republic now in our troubles; and hereafter
if his aristrocratic allies, the Confederate States, shall become a nation." Noting that France's avowed purpose in Mexico was to
"obstruct the progress of this Republic on this continent," Stevens
considered the French occupation of Guaymas preparation for a
future attack on California. Finally, aiming at a favorite Radical
target, Stevens warned that United States inaction was contemptible because of "the moral cowardice of the Foreign Department. . . .
May God renovate our strength, and give strength and energy to
the Cabinet!"[32]

32. *Congressional Globe*, 37th Cong. 3rd Sess. 1417–19. See also Thaddeus Stevens to
Simon Stevens, November 17, December 21, 1862, in Thaddeus Stevens Papers, Library of
Congress; Mary Elizabeth Noyes to Benjamin Wade, February 4, 1863, in Benjamin F.

Long convinced that he could not achieve meaningful aid to Mexico through Seward and the normal diplomatic channels, Romero, immediately upon his return, searched for a house in which he could entertain the influential of Washington at formal dinners. Just before Christmas, after a long, frustrating search, he rented a house, spent the next month furnishing it, acquiring and training a staff, and giving trial dinners to work out any problems that might exist. Finally, on the evening of January 21, 1864, Romero earnestly began to eat his way into Washington's inner political and diplomatic circles. In less than sixty days he gave sixteen formal dinner parties, thirteen of them aimed primarily at the cabinet, the Senate, and the House. Every cabinet member and most of the Senate and House leaders—some fifty congressmen in all, including Charles Sumner, John Sherman, Lyman Trumbull, Benjamin Wade, Schuyler Colfax, Thaddeus Stevens, Zachariah Chandler, Reverdy Johnson, and Henry Winter Davis were guests at his table. Vice-President Hannibal Hamlin and Supreme Court Justices Samuel F. Miller and Stephen J. Field were also Romero's guests. The dinners continued unabatingly after the initial sixty-day period; only now Romero began to repeat invitations to certain guests, something he had rarely done during the first two months.[33]

Even during the initial phase of his intensive and certainly expensive lobbying campaign, Romero collected dividends. On the evening of January 18, 1864, Congressman John Kasson of Iowa called on Romero with some resolutions on Mexican affairs, hostile toward France, which Kasson assured Romero would pass unanimously when presented to the House. Confident they would pass, but wanting to assure their success, Romero decided to put his full

---

Wade Papers, Library of Congress; Wade to Chandler, October 2, 1864, Chandler to his wife, February 17 and 27, 1865, in Zachariah Chandler Papers, Library of Congress.

33. Cosío Villegas (ed.), *Diario de Matías Romero*, 576–88; and Romero to Plumb, March 15, 1864, in Plumb Collection. See Cosío Villegas (ed.), *Diario de Matías Romero*, 585–615, for the frequency of his contact with anti-administration politicians. See also Romero to Ministro de Relaciones Exteriores, December 27, 1862, January 19, 1863, January 21, 1864, in Romero (comp.), *Correspondencia*, II, 743–46, III, 124–25, and IV, 10; and Romero to Chandler, April 19, 1867, February 9, 1869, in Zachariah Chandler Papers.

influence behind them, while letting up on an alternate set of resolutions McDougall had introduced in the Senate.[34]

After consulting with Romero, Kasson read his revised resolutions on January 28. A short time later, Chairman of the House Committee on Foreign Affairs Henry Winter Davis visited Romero to discuss Mexican affairs. Again Romero discovered a friend of Mexico. Although Davis had not read Kasson's resolution, he was preparing resolutions on the same matter; but if Kasson's were similar in tone, he would have them treated as emanating from the Foreign Affairs Committee.[35]

Several weeks later Romero inquired about the resolutions' progress. The two congressmen believed the French government was tired of the intervention and wished to leave Mexico. Romero cited the debates of the *Corps Législatif* as reported in the *Moniteur*, Napoleon's official newspaper, to convince Davis that additional pressure was needed. In early March, 1864, the House asked the executive for the correspondence on Mexico, a first step toward building up pressure for a strong course of action.[36]

Nothing quite so stirred Romero to action between 1862 and 1865 as the chance to do battle with Seward. So when he learned that Seward had called the members of the House Foreign Affairs Committee into his office and pressured them not to act upon the Kasson or Davis resolutions, Romero prepared for action. Meeting with Davis in mid-March, Romero argued that the resolutions would make the French expedition unpopular in France, would

34. Cosío Villegas (ed.), *Diario de Matías Romero*, 575; and Romero to Ministro de Relaciones Exteriores, January 19, 1864, in Correspondencia General con los Estados Unidos. Edward Younger, *John A. Kasson: Politics and Diplomacy from Lincoln to McKinley* (Iowa City, 1955), contains no mention at all of any relationship between Kasson and Romero, or Mexico, or the French intervention.

35. Cosío Villegas (ed.), *Diario de Matías Romero*, 577–79; Romero to Ministro de Relaciones Exteriores, January 30 and 31, 1864, in Correspondencia General con los Estados Unidos.

36. Cosío Villegas (ed.), *Diario de Matías Romero*, 585, Romero to Ministro de Relaciones Exteriores, March 2, 1864, enclosing Romero to Henry Winter Davis, February 27, 1864, and Davis to Romero, March 1, 1864 (mistakenly dated May 1, 1864), in Correspondencia General con los Estados Unidos.

cause Maximilian to reconsider accepting the crown, and would inspire the Mexican people to greater resistance. He insisted that these results were possible without increasing the danger, feared by both Seward and Davis, of a strong French reaction. Contending this joint resolution would never pass the Seward-Sumner Senate alliance which controlled United States–Mexican policy, Romero saw no danger. His passionate, glowing presentation evoked Davis' offer to take action at the next House Foreign Affairs Committee meeting. Soon Davis' committee recommended a substitute for Kasson's two resolutions which incorporated their intent in one stinging resolution declaring,

The Congress of the United States are unwilling by silence to leave the nations of the world under the impression that they are indifferent spectators of the deplorable events now transpiring in the republic of Mexico, and that they therefore think fit to declare that it does not accord with the policy of the United States to acknowledge any monarchical Government erected on the ruins of any republican Government in America under the auspices of any European Power.[37]

Thus, on April 4, Romero's new political campaign for Mexico won its first major victory with the House's unanimous acceptance, 109 to 0, of Davis' resolution against French intervention in Mexico, and, of course, indirectly against the Seward-Lincoln conduct of foreign relations. Neither the conviction that the war was about to end nor partisan politics seems adequate to explain the unanimous vote for Davis' resolution. The best answer must give considerable credit to aroused and concerned influence groups such as editors, businessmen, and local politicians. Although Romero was responsible for marshaling many of these influence groups, the popular awareness of the new level of danger encompassed in Maximilian's arrival was evident. Despite the incisiveness of Davis' resolution, Romero was convinced that somehow Seward had per-

37. Cosío Villegas (ed.), *Diario de Matías Romero*, 589; Romero to Ministro de Relaciones Exteriores, March 16, 23, 1864, in Correspondencia General con los Estados Unidos; *Congressional Globe*, 38th Cong. 1st Sess., 1408.

suaded Davis to soften the resolution.[38] The Spanish government "supposed that the attitude assumed by the House will produce complications with France, and may lead to a war." However, when Dayton faced Drouyn de Lhuys after the Davis resolution, he rebuffed the French foreign minister's query, "Do you bring us peace, or bring us war?" with the observation that these resolutions "embodied nothing more than had been constantly held out to the French government from the beginning."[39]

Since they conceded the resolution could not pass the Sumner-Seward forces in the Senate, Romero and Davis expected only propaganda and moral gains from their action, until Seward committed a *faux pas* which prolonged and intensified the effect of the April resolution. Seward sought to soften the impact of the House action by explaining to the French that foreign policy was an executive responsibility and by pointing out that the House-passed joint resolution was not even a binding expression of congressional opinion until the Senate concurred. Again Romero played a major role in aid of anti-administration forces when he convinced Davis that Seward had offered an explanation even before the French solicited one, thus inciting Davis to have the House request an explanation from the president. Seward had played directly into the hands of the administration's opponents. While Davis probably had various reasons for urging his resolution, certainly central was his desire to prevent Lincoln's renomination. The next day Lincoln submitted copies of Seward's correspondence with Dayton on this matter, which Davis had printed in the *Congressional Globe* and separately as a House document in an effort to embarrass the Lincoln administration. Although Davis' maneuvers did not prevent Lincoln's renomination, they did temporarily open up the possibility that

38. Romero to Ministro de Relaciones Exteriores, April 6, 1864, in Romero (comp.), *Correspondencia*, IV, 122–23. In fact the vote reached more than 109 to 0 since on the following day, April 5, two more congressmen, Morrill and Pendleton, obtained permission to register their votes in the affirmative, a privilege extended to all who were absent on April 4. *Congressional Globe*, 38th Cong., 1st Sess., 1408, 1426–27.

39. Koerner to Seward, April 2, 1864, Dayton to Seward, April 22, 1864 in U.S. Department of State, *Foreign Relations of the United States, 1864*, Pt. 4, p. 16, Pt. 3, p. 76.

Lincoln might be forced to withdraw. A second National Union convention was planned for September. In the meantime, Davis and the Radical faction devised a two-pronged attack: the Wade-Davis reconstruction bill to embarrass Lincoln's reconstruction policy, and another Davis resolution asserting congressional authority over foreign policy to pointedly embarrass the Lincoln administration's conduct of foreign affairs. However, since this latter resolution openly attacked the president during an election year, many Republicans refused to suspend House rules in order to discuss it. Following the prolonged administration-Radical debate growing out of the April 4 resolution, the imperial newspaper, *Eco del Comercio*, interpreted Congress' lack of action as an indicator that Maximilian's government had nothing to fear from the United States.[40]

Davis' final efforts to get political mileage out of this were to be delayed until the winter of 1864–1865, due to the recess of Congress at the beginning of July. In late 1864, Davis' resolution from the preceding June was defeated in the House. Davis requested to be relieved from his position as chairman of the Foreign Relations Committee, prompting a long, enlightening debate. Whereas Davis had intended to chastise Lincoln, preventing his renomination, now many Radicals preferred taking aim at Seward. The resolution read:

Resolved, That Congress has a constitutional right to an authoritative voice in declaring and prescribing the foreign policy of the United States, as well as in the recognition of new powers as in other matters; and it is the constitutional duty of the President to respect that policy not less in diplomatic negotiations than in the use of the national force when authorized by law; and the property of any declaration of foreign policy by Congress is sufficiently proved by the vote which pronounces it; and such proposition while pending and undetermined is not a fit topic of diplomatic explanation with any foreign Power.

40. *Congressional Globe*, 39th Cong. 1st Sess., 2427, 2475, 3309; Romero to Ministro de Relaciones Exteriores, May 26, 1864, in Romero (comp.), *Correspondencia*, IV, 183–84; Basler (ed.), *Works of Lincoln*, VII, 359; Milton Lyman Henry, Jr., "Henry Winter Davis and the Radical Republican Use of Foreign Policy" (paper presented at the OAH Convention, April, 1973); and *Eco del Comercio*, May 10, 12, and 17, July 5, 1864.

Debate, centering upon the phrase "duty of the President," revealed that many congressmen wanted to alter the resolution to attack Seward. Thaddeus Stevens claimed, "Not the President... but one branch of the Executive Government took upon it to rebuke" the House, "and to inform foreign nations that we were an impertinent set of intermeddlers." Stevens insisted "the President does not interfere with the Foreign Minister in his policy. He is allowed to carry it on himself, and to be responsible for it." Stevens announced his intention to amend Davis' resolution, placing the burden where it belonged. George S. Boutwell, Republican congressman from Massachusetts, likewise excused Lincoln while finding fault with Seward. Since the Senate had not approved the resolution, the president had not disobeyed his constitutional duty, but Boutwell believed "the manner in which the Secretary of State expressed his opinion as to the rights of the House in respect to foreign affairs was not agreeable to me; I should be glad, in some proper way, to protest against it." Republican Eldridge Gerry Spaulding of New York also considered that "the action, perhaps, of one member of the Cabinet was uncalled for, when he reflected in a measure upon the action of this House... but I could not vote for it impugning the conduct of the President or any [other] member of his cabinet."[41]

Probably with varied reasons for wishing the Seward-Lincoln administration to fall, Romero and Davis used Seward's political blunder of belittling Congress' foreign-policy role for their ends. Believing that Congress was the agent of popularly expressed will, Davis charged Seward and Lincoln with obstructing the implementation of the national will regarding French involvement in Mexico. Behind Davis' theory of the source of sovereignty was the Radicals' central problem: how to obtain and exercise more power and greater control over wartime and postwar reconstruction policy.[42]

41. *Congressional Globe*, 38th Cong., 2nd Sess., 48–53.
42. Cosío Villegas (ed.), *Diario de Matías Romero*, 600; Goldwert, "Matías Romero," 30–33; and Bernard C. Steiner, *Henry W. Davis* (Baltimore, 1916), 316–19. Eric L. McKitrick, *Andrew Johnson and Reconstruction* (Chicago, 1960), 93–119, and T. Harry Williams,

Romero, on the other hand, convinced Seward was following a policy friendly to France and unfriendly to Mexico, believed that as long as Lincoln remained president, Seward would continue as architect of foreign policy.

While engaged in persuading Davis to use his power and influence for Mexico's cause, Romero revealed his views on the forthcoming presidential race. Writing early in the campaign, he speculated there would be four candidates: Lincoln for the moderate Republicans; John C. Frémont for the abolitionists; Salmon P. Chase for the Radical Republicans; and General George B. McClellan for the Democrats, who might also split into factions. Romero was convinced that if Lincoln won reelection, Seward would continue as secretary of state; hence, "for us, then, the election of any of the other candidates would be suitable." Already in March, 1864, as a step to accomplish his desired end, Romero sought to encourage both Frémont and McClellan to speak out on Mexican affairs. Several weeks later, Romero discussed the administration's Mexican policy with Frémont in New York.[43]

Following Romero's dinner campaign, other politicians began speaking out on the Mexican problem. Republican Congressman William B. Allison of Iowa compared the landed, aristocratic structure of Mexico under the Church party with southern elitist society. Noting that both societies were oppressive of the masses, he was convinced that free schools, free churches, freedmen, and access to the land would create conditions permitting social progress in the South. He surmised that such a program would also be acceptable to the Mexican Liberal party. He speculated that "the fate of Mexico shows how impossible it is to maintain a permanent republican Government over the few selfish, proud aristocrats who

Lincoln and the Radicals (Madison, 1960), 324–25, describe various Radical theories of Congress' role in the United States government. Monographs on the foreign policy of Republican and Democratic parties and the political factions are urgently needed.

43. Romero to Ministro de Relaciones Exteriores, March 18, 1864, in Correspondencia General con los Estados Unidos; Romero to Ministro de Relaciones Exteriores, April 9, 1864, in Romero (comp.), *Correspondencia*, IV, 126.

own the soil and wealth of the country, even without the demoralizing and aggravating evils of slavery."[44]

Even Fernando Wood, acknowledged Confederate sympathizer in the United States Congress, accepted the interrelationship of Mexican affairs and the Civil War. Wood feared that "while this struggle is going on, an empire is planted in Mexico. If the war continues, the consequence will be not only perpetual disunion and the South a desolation, but an empire will be so firmly rooted on American-Mexican soil that the battle-wasted population and exhausted resources of the American 'nation' cannot uproot it." Aware that if the war continued "republicanism will stand alone on this as on the old continent," Wood believed a restored Union would produce the immediate demise of the empire, while a long war would secure its existence. This dilemma Wood described as "the crisis of the fate of the Union."[45]

Other congressmen spoke out for an aggressive stand on Mexican affairs. During the debate on abolishing slavery, Godlove Orth noted that slavery was being sustained in part by foreign forces among which he singled out the French. He wailed against Napoleon III, who, "seized with the Quixotic idea that it was his mission on earth to be the chosen protector of the Latin races, with all their bigotry and superstition, and to extend them wheresoever the French eagle would enable him to accomplish his desires, introduced French intrigue, French diplomacy, French arms into the neighboring republic of Mexico for the purpose of subverting her Government, destroying the rights of her people, and inaugurating on this continent a political system antagonistic to our own, and which should sooner or later threaten to destroy our peace or endanger our safety." Convinced that Napoleon's Mexican adventure occurred only because of the rebellion, Orth found it natural that "in the first glimmering of success to our arms the minds of our people are instinctively turned to Mexico." He presumed that

44. *Congressional Globe*, 38th Cong., 1st Sess., 2115.
45. *Ibid.*, 2943.

"among the first of our duties growing out of this rebellion will be to declare" Maximilian a "temporary Emperor." Orth concluded that the day had arrived when "we no longer needed to submit to indignities."[46]

Encouraged by his lobbying successes, in early 1865 Romero complained about Corwin's conduct favorable to Maximilian and the fact that the United States government was acting less energetically toward the French intervention than public opinion in North America called for. Again reiterating the relationship of the Confederacy with Maximilian's empire, the Liberals lamented that "Mexico has been the first victim of that combination, monstrous abortion of European machiavelliansim and of the treason of American conservatives."[47]

As the Civil War ended, Romero observed: "[Since] the indications are that for the present the Government would not like to be immediately involved in a contest with France, a treaty of alliance by which Mexico could obtain some aid from the United States, is not feasible under the present condition of things. This being the case, it remains for us to obtain from private citizens what we cannot expect from the government." Cleverly, Romero argued the wisdom of borrowing money "from citizens of the United States, with the object, among others of giving them a direct interest in the stability of the national government of Mexico and the development of the national resources."[48] Thus, a private loan would accomplish the prime Mexican Liberal goals of committing the United States to the Mexican Republic's national security, and at the same time attracting United States interest to the growth and development of the Mexican economy.

The Liberals also complained about an alleged United States–French agreement permitting Napoleon free hand in Mexico in re-

46. *Congressional Globe*, 38th Cong., 2nd Sess., 143.

47. "La Cuestión estranjera," *Periódico Oficial del Gobierno Constitucional de la República Mexicana*, January 17, 1865; Romero to Frederick W. Seward, March 30, 1865, in Seward Papers.

48. Romero to Plumb, May 2, 1865 (confidential), in Plumb Collection.

turn for his noninterference in the Civil War. Although disappointed with Lincoln's passivity toward the French intervention in Mexico, when word of his assassination arrived Mexico proclaimed official mourning, calling attention to his eminent personal qualities and to the friendly relations existing between Mexico and the United States during his administration. Romero hoped that following Lincoln's assassination, "if we are successful in preventing Seward's continuation in the Cabinet," Johnson's much more acceptable Mexican policy would prevail. Although open to various interpretations, Romero's "we" might well have referred to Romero's Radical friends in Congress. While the official response to Lincoln's death reflected a natural reaction to a tragedy, it also demonstrated another truth about the Liberal attitude toward the United States. However depressed and bitter the Liberals became toward United States policy, they invariably sought to maintain an external show of comradeship between the two New World liberal powers. The Mexican leaders reasoned that a persistent show of solidarity would continually cause the French to pause and reevaluate their position, whereas an open feud with the United States would only hearten the French.[49]

To overcome the obvious coolness of the United States government, beginning in mid-1863 the Mexican government sent special agents to float loans, buy war materials, and encourage stronger support from the Union. Although often proposed with confidence, arms purchasing projects seldom advanced beyond the planning stage. Of those that did, only a couple contributed significant material or financial support to the Liberals. In late 1862, Manuel Doblado proposed to raise at least a million dollars in arms and cash in California or elsewhere in the United States, if he could guarantee the transaction with Mexican government lands in Chihuahua, Durango, and Sonora. To ensure success, Doblado sought "a spe-

---

49. Teran to Lerdo de Tejada, April 24, 1865, in Jesús Teran Correspondence; Romero to Juárez, April 27, 1865, in Archivo Juárez; Circular signed by Lerdo de Tejada, May 16, 1865, in *Colección de leyes, decretos, y circulares expedidas por el Supremo Gobierno de la República* (3 vols.; Mexico, 1867), II, 239.

cial authorization from the Supreme Government, so broad that there would be no obstructing the negotiations in their essentials."[50] Failure to obtain authorization ended his plan. Often the optimistic estimates of funds and arms available in the United States depended upon delegating vast, broad powers to an individual of questionable integrity. Occasionally proposals came from United States citizens who figured to gain a financial or other material advantage from the transaction. In mid-1863 Jacob Leese, prime mover of a development project in Baja California, offered to supply arms, men, and war materials to the Liberals to aid in expelling the French, provided the Mexican government would cede public lands in Sinaloa, Sonora, and Chihuahua in payment.[51] Most successful projects began during the final stages of the Civil War or in the immediate postwar months.

The first major Liberal mission, directed to secure men and supplies in the United States, departed Mexico in mid-1863 under the direction of former governor of Sinaloa General Plácido Vega. Authorized to purchase rifles, rifle-making machines, rifled cannon, gunpowder, and munitions, Vega and a fellow Mexican purchasing agent in California, General Gaspar Sánchez Ochoa, also acted as propaganda agents. They founded and developed the Mexican Clubs (by Vega), primarily Spanish-speaking, and the Monroe League (by Ochoa), primarily English-speaking. The Mexican Clubs and Monroe League marshaled public sentiment in support of Juárez' government and the Monroe Doctrine and against the French intervention. Vega was authorized to borrow up to $260,000 against Mazatlán and Guaymas customhouse receipts, to dispose of certain Mexican islands and other national property, and to sell mining and exploitation concessions. Funds from these sources plus gifts and loans from sympathizers permitted him to disperse some $620,000 over the slightly more than two years he was engaged in purchasing activity. Ultimately he forwarded to Mexico about 22,000 rifles,

50. Doblado to Juárez, December 30, 1862, in Archivo Juárez.
51. Leese to Charles Murray, August 6, 1863, in Seward Papers.

plus gunpowder, ammunition, other war materials, and perhaps a hundred or more volunteers. Returning in late 1866 as head of a volunteer expedition, instead of being welcomed, Vega was accused of misappropriating funds and arrested.[52]

Another major mission was entrusted to the twenty-eight-year-old Ochoa who, while serving as military commandant and governor of Sinaloa, had announced that funds could be raised in San Francisco with Mexican bonds. Commissioned in December, 1864, he arrived in San Francisco six months later, accompanied by various United States advisers. Ochoa's commission allowed him to issue $10 million in bonds only for sale in California, bearing about 6 percent interest and secured by Sinaloa and Sonora mining taxes and customs revenue. He was authorized to purchase up to six shops, 60,000 rifles, artillery, cavalry arms, and munitions, to recruit and organize foreign volunteers, including the appointment of their officers, and to purchase ships, including the appointment of their captains. Ochoa so mismanaged the loan negotiations that in the end he mortgaged the entire $10 million bond issue for a cash advance of $30,000 in gold from San Francisco financier Samuel Brannan. In late 1865, acting contrary to his instructions, Ochoa moved to New York where his bond issue conflicted with a major bond project initiated by General José María Carvajal, forcing Romero to enter the picture to prevent the two Mexican loan issues from competing with each other. In return for keeping his bonds off the market, Ochoa was promised a share of the larger issue. Hearing discrediting rumors of Ochoa's activities, the Mexican government at first merely subordinated his contract negotiations to Ro-

52. Robert R. Miller, "Plácido Vega: A Mexican Secret Agent in the United States," *The Americas*, XIX (October, 1962), 137–48; Robert R. Miller, "Gaspar Sanchez Ochoa: A Mexican Secret Agent in the United States," *The Historian*, XXIII (May, 1961), 318–19; Miller, "Matías Romero," 228–34. See also "Club Mexicano en Nueva York," expediente 2-2-2084, Archivo Histórico de la Secretaría de Relaciones Exteriores; Zarco to Romero, November 3, 1864, in Archivo Matías Romero; E. George Squier to Banks, December 4, 1865, in Nathaniel A. Banks Papers, box 61, Library of Congress; Romualdo Pacheco to Vega, October 14, 1864, in Vega Papers; Dexter Perkins, *The Monroe Doctrine, 1826–1867* (Baltimore, 1933), 448–49.

mero's supervision, then suspended his commission, and voided his last agreement with Brannan. Ochoa refused to obey Lerdo de Tejada's instructions to return to Mexico.[53]

Ochoa apparently fell under the spell of General John C. Frémont, who vaguely offered aid in the bond sale in exchange for economic concessions in Mexico. In trouble with the Liberal government, Ochoa bargained his recognition of self-exiled Jesús González Ortega as president of Mexico, for Ortega's approval of the Frémont-Ochoa agreements. Later, after Ortega's return to Mexico ended in immediate capture and imprisonment, Ochoa recognized the impossibility of his situation. Following several interviews with Romero at the Mexican Legation in Washington, Ochoa requested amnesty and rehabilitation in return for turning over information about the Frémont contracts. In June, 1867, Ochoa left New York for Mexico after Romero had paid his hotel bill and his ship passage.[54]

As the Civil War drew to a close, Francis P. Blair, Sr., formerly a member of Andrew Jackson's "Kitchen Cabinet" and father of Lincoln's postmaster general, Montgomery Blair, developed a scheme aimed to end the Civil War and to expel the French in one stroke. Just after Christmas Day in 1864, Blair wrote to Jefferson Davis, expressing a desire to relate certain views in person. Permission was granted and, with a safe-conduct pass from Lincoln, Blair met with Davis in early January, 1865. Following a general amnesty and a secret armistice, Blair suggested that Davis would be made temporary Mexican dictator by Juárez, taking command of a Confederate-Union-Mexican army to free Mexico of the French. The avowed purpose of the expedition would be the preservation of

53. Sebastián Lerdo de Tejada to Romero, October 9, 1865 (two letters), January 16, 1866, in Romero (comp.), *Correspondencia*, VI, 307–11, 436–38. See also Miller, "Gaspar Sanchez Ochoa," 316–28; Robert W. Frazer, "The Ochoa Bond Negotiations of 1865–1867," *Pacific Historical Review*, XI (December, 1942), 397–410.

54. Miller, "Gaspar Sanchez Ochoa," 321–28; Frazer, "The Ochoa Bond Negotiations," 401–10; and Sheridan to Commanding Officer at Brazos Santiago, Texas, October 25, 1866, in Jesús Gonzáles Ortega Correspondence, Latin American Collection, University of Texas.

the Monroe Doctrine. Implicit in the proposal was reunion of the two sections without slavery.

In his discussion with Davis, Blair depicted an unreliable France as a possible oppressor of the South. After all, Blair argued, the South stood to suffer from the Napoleonic concept of making the "Latin race" supreme in the southern section of the North American continent. This idea originated with Napoleon I, who, as part of his plan for building a New World empire, proposed to stir up rebellion among the blacks in the southern states in order to use black revolution to facilitate his conquest. Blair urged Davis to use his power to prevent the subordination of the southern people to the Latin race. Blair projected:

Suppose secret preliminaries to armistice enable President Davis to transfer such portions of his army as he may deem proper for his purpose to Texas... suppose this force on the banks of the Rio Grande, armed, equipped and provided, and Juárez propitiated and rallying the Liberals of Mexico to give it welcome and support, could it not enter Mexico in full confidence of expelling the invaders, who taking advantage of the distractions of our own Republic, have overthrown that of Mexico and established a foreign despotism to rule that land and spread its power over ours? I know Romero, the able patriotic minister who represents the Republic of Mexico near our Government. He is intimate with my son Montgomery, who is persuaded that he could induce Juárez to devolve all the power he can command on President Davis—a dictatorship if necessary, to restore the rights of Mexico and her people and provide for the stability of its Government....But if more force were wanted than these, Mexican recruits, and the army of the South would supply, would not multitudes of the army of the North, officers and men, be found ready to embark in an enterprize, vital to the interests of our whole Republic?[55]

With plenty of troops and sufficient authority, the Monroe Doctrine could be defended and the Anglo-Saxon interests preserved in face of a Latin threat. Blair offered a final inducement: "If in delivering Mexico, [Davis] should model its states in form and principle to adapt them to our Union and add a new Southern Constellation

---

55. Memorandum to President Lincoln: "Suggestions submitted to Jefferson Davis," [early 1865], in Blair Family Papers, box 2.

to its benignant sky while rounding off our possession on the continent at the Isthmus and opening the way to blending the waters of the Atlantic and Pacific surrounding our Republic with the walls of the Ocean, he would complete the work of Jefferson, who first set one foot of our colossal Government on the Pacific." Blair informed Lincoln that Davis doubted Napoleon's interest in Mexico was permanent. Rather, Davis judged Napoleon's goal to be limited to a naval base on this continent. From the tenor and content of his conversation with the Confederate leader, Blair conjectured that Davis supported republicanism on this continent, but faced strong opposition from determined secessionists. Later, Davis also recalled that the joint Mexican mission was the chief matter discussed with Blair.[56]

Another old Jacksonian politician, Duff Green, wrote Jefferson Davis on December 29, 1864, surveying the world power struggle for control of trade and commerce in a manner implying support for Blair's project. Noting that France's success in Mexico would give them preeminence in the area of the isthmus as well as on the Pacific coast of North America, and observing also that the population and territorial extension of Asia made control of the Pacific a key to wealth and power in the future, Green concluded: "The Confederate States are no less interested than the United States in preventing the occupation of Mexico and the Pacific States by France or G. Britain, and hence it would seem that our common interests require that we should terminate the present war upon the basis of a cooperation for the maintenance of the Monroe Doctrine." Green pointed out that such a proposal would strengthen

---

56. *Ibid.*; Blair to Lincoln, February 8, 1865, in Blair Family Papers; John G. Nicolay and John Hay, "Abraham Lincoln: A History; Blair's Mexican Project; the Hampton Road's Conference; the XIIIth Amendment," *Century Magazine*, New Series, XVI (October, 1889), 839–43; Romero to Ministro de Relaciones Exteriores, February 4, 1865, in Romero (comp.), *Correspondencia*, V, 42–45; and Jefferson Davis, *The Rise and Fall of the Confederate Government* (2 vols.; New York, 1958), II, 613–14. "The Blair Mission," *Chicago Tribune*, January 13, 1865, is very critical of Blair's effort, referring to "self-appointed diplomats" and "busybodies . . . bringing their country into disrepute," reflecting the general Radical dislike for the Blair family.

the peace forces in the North and if it failed would facilitate an agreement with England and France to divide the occupation of the Pacific states and control of the Pacific trade. Perhaps in part due to Green's prodding, Blair's mission led to the Hampton Roads conference in February, 1865.[57]

Not surprisingly, Mexican affairs and the possibility of joint action against French intervention in Mexico were central discussion topics at Hampton Roads. While Seward and R. M. T. Hunter wished to explore the idea more deeply and Alexander Stephens spoke strongly in favor of the plan in principle, Confederate Commissioner John Campbell was skeptical. Lincoln, however, was unsympathetic, unless the question of reunion was resolved first.[58]

When the Hampton Roads conference failed to unite the sections, both sides tried to use the Blair project to discredit the other, thus gaining support in Europe. The Confederate agents in Europe pointed out that the Yankee plan considered the possibility of war against France and/or England. Meanwhile, United States diplomats informed the European powers that coincidental with Confederate requests for recognition and perhaps intervention on the part of France and England, the South was contemplating possible military action against those same countries, a highly inconsistent position.[59]

While historians have dismissed the Blair mission quite lightly, Romero considered the proposal both serious and significant. So apparently did the Union and Confederate governments. Although the Mexican Liberals had been attempting for some time to obtain individual volunteers, in coordination with Blair's scheme, Romero drafted and submitted to his government an agreement permitting two corps of United States and Confederate veterans, commanded

57. Duff Green to Davis, December 29, 1864 (confidential), Jefferson Davis Papers.

58. "Memoranda of the conversation at the conference in Hampton Roads," March 13, 1865, by John A. Campbell, in Robert M. T. Hunter Papers, University of Virginia; and R. M. T. Hunter to James M. Mason, September 19, 1870, in Fitzhugh Lee, "The Failure of the Hampton Conference," *Century Magazine*, LII (July, 1896), 476–78.

59. Mason to Benjamin, March 31, 1865, and enclosure, "Minutes of a Conversation held with Lord Palmerston at Cambridge House, March 14, 1865," in Mason Papers.

by North Americans, to enter Mexico to join the Liberal army in fighting the French. Blair proposed that Davis would be offered the overall command, with Robert E. Lee and U. S. Grant as his corps commanders.[60] In March, 1865, Juárez' government authorized Romero to name a general-in-chief and in conjunction with this general to name subordinate commanders and staff officers to command a joint military force to enter Mexico and cooperate with the Liberal army against the French. Juárez assumed the United States would guarantee that any force sent to Mexico would not interfere in the domestic political struggle, attempt to annex Mexican territory, subvert republican institutions, or undermine the recognized government of Mexico. Even though the time-consuming communications system connecting Romero and the Juárez government prevented receipt of the final authorization until after the Confederacy had surrendered, the Liberal government accepted, in principle, Blair's scheme to unite the North and South and preserve the Monroe Doctrine through military action against the French in Mexico.[61]

Based upon the possibility of Union-Confederate cooperation, General Lew Wallace's plan had a definite basis in political reality. It represented an effort by anti-Blair forces to undercut Francis P. Blair, Sr.'s discussions with Jefferson Davis. Wallace sold his idea to Grant on a bet in January, 1865: "While Blair and Singleton are in Richmond, let me . . . invite the commandant of Brownsville to an interview. . . . I'll wager you a month's pay that I win and that Blair and company lose."[62] Both were to fail.

60. Romero to Ministro de Relaciones Exteriores, February 4, 1865, and enclosures, in Romero (comp.), *Correspondencia*, V, 42–45; Juan José Baz to Romero, June 14, 1865, in Archivo Matías Romero; "La Emigración de los Estados-Unidos," *Periódico Oficial*, July 18, 1865; Juárez to Romero, August 25, 1865, and Enrique A. Mejía to Romero, September 20, 1865, in Archivo Juárez; Romero to Juárez, August 22, 1865, in Tamayo (ed.), *Juárez Documentos*, X, 176–77; and decrees signed by Juárez, August 11, 1864, and September 28, 1866, *Colección de leyes, decretos y circulares expedidas*, II, 91–93, and III, 94–95.

61. Lerdo de Tejada to Romero, March 29, 1865 (three letters), Romero (comp.), *Correspondencia*, VI, 121–25. See also Arthur Shaff to Frank Blair, July 6, 1865, in John M. Schofield Papers, box 8, Library of Congress.

62. Lew Wallace to Grant, January 14, 1865, *Official Records*, Vol. XLVII, Part 1, p. 512.

Lew Wallace credited Lincoln with a significant role in the early development of his plan to aid the Mexican republic: "It was well known that Mr. Lincoln, in the midst of all his troubles, was anxious to help his neighbor, President Juárez, if he could without portending the forthcoming Rebel collapse, feared many Confedermit to him a plan for that purpose. After consideration, he sent me to Gen. Grant, then at City Point besieging Richmond." Grant, portending the forthcoming rebel collapse, feared many Confederate soldiers would pass to Maximilian and form the nucleus of a new fighting force, which might cost the United States thousands of lives to defeat again. In the first instance, the Wallace-Grant plan of early 1865 called for uniting Federal and Confederate troops to defend the Monroe Doctrine by ousting the French from Mexico. Wallace approached the Confederate leaders in Texas, but they rejected any cooperative military ventures without instructions from Richmond. Wallace recalled that Grant also desired to make the Mexican Liberals more effective by making arms available to them in their struggle with the imperial forces. So, another objective in sending Wallace to the Rio Grande to establish contact with the Liberals was to determine their attitude toward the Rebels entering their territory and to inquire what material assistance they needed to prevent the armed Rebels from crossing into Mexico. Then Wallace was to devise ways to procure and deliver the requested material to the Liberals, without, however, involving the United States government. Soon after arriving at Brownsville, Wallace met General José María Carvajal, Liberal governor of Tamaulipas, whom Wallace annexed to his scheme, apparently intending to use Carvajal as the channel for funneling arms into Mexico.[63]

Carvajal, fluent in English, favorably impressed Wallace, as did a document from Juárez granting Carvajal powers for one year, beginning in November, 1864, to purchase rifles and munitions, to enlist volunteers, and to negotiate a foreign loan. After settling de-

63. Extract, Wallace to [?], in Lew Wallace Papers, Indiana Historical Society; and Robert R. Miller, "Lew Wallace and the French Intervention in Mexico," *Indiana Magazine of History*, LIX (March, 1963), 31–50.

tails, including Wallace's compensation for assistance in negotiating the arms purchases and the loan, Carvajal agreed to accompany Wallace back to Washington.[64]

Although Wallace functioned as Carvajal's advisor, his most beneficial action was introducing Carvajal to General Herman Sturm, unquestionably the hardest working and most successful Mexican agent in the United States with the sole exception of Romero. Commissioned a brigadier general in the Mexican army, Sturm was named purchasing agent for the Mexican government in the United States and empowered to raise and forward United States citizens to Mexico as volunteers. At Mexico's bleakest moment, Sturm gave Carvajal $4,600 in return for 50 acres of mining land and 4,440 acres of agricultural land in Tamaulipas. Sturm also recognized Daniel Woodhouse's United States, European, and West Virginia Land and Mining Company as a swindle, saving Mexico money and misspent effort.[65]

Later, Sturm arranged a meeting between Carvajal and Jonathan N. Tifft, a partner in the respectable New York firm of Corlies and Company, which led to the floating of a Mexican bond issue. Finally, Sturm's greatest service involved persuading munitions firms and dealers to accept the stagnant Mexican bonds in payment for needed war materials at sixty cents on the dollar. Ultimately this coterie, largely through Sturm's labor, was responsible for sending more aid than all other Mexican agents combined: over two million dollars worth of munitions, arms, and other war materials, several ships, and hundreds of United States volunteers to Mexico. Furthermore, they produced considerable domestic pressure for official action against the French intervention. This popular domestic pressure reinforced the more subtle backroom

64. Robert R. Miller, "Herman Sturm: Hoosier Secret Agent for Mexico," *Indiana Magazine of History*, LVIII (March, 1962), 1-3, 15; Irving McKee, *"Ben Hur" Wallace: The Life of General Lew Wallace* (Berkeley, 1947), 91-95.

65. Miller, "Herman Sturm," 1-15; Wallace to Carvajal, May 5, 1865, in Wallace Papers; and Robert W. Frazer, "The United States, European and West Virginia Land and Mining Company," *Pacific Historical Review*, XIII (March, 1944), 28-40.

political intrigues in which Romero and those friendly to Mexico (or unfriendly to the Lincoln-Seward leadership) were involved.[66]

The most audacious step taken by this coterie was the formation of a military force. When Wallace was offered command of the troops to be sent to Mexico, Grant, who had been advising Wallace, almost parted company with this scheme. Grant judged either General William T. Sherman or General John Schofield would make a more competent commander. Temporarily, Grant may even have entertained the idea of going himself. However, Romero, on intimate terms with Grant since they discovered in early 1865 that they shared a mutual desire to force the French out of Mexico, urged the general to let Wallace continue with the organizational labors, implying he could be gently nudged out later. Romero, overwhelmed by Grant's commitment to the cause of Mexico, characterized it for Juárez: "The favors which Grant does us, exceed our expectations; he would hardly be able to do more if he were Mexican." Later, Schofield was selected to command the combined ex-Confederate–ex-Union volunteer force. Meanwhile, Wallace continued with the necessary organizational work, preparing a force which would guide interest away from internal affairs and focus attention in the United States upon Mexican relations.[67]

Thus, during the Civil War years, the Liberal government found themselves in no position to block Mexican-Confederate trade. This was true even when Juárez' government was forced into the northern regions along the Texas border. On the other hand, the Mexicans could, with considerable justice, claim that the United States followed a policy of "neutrality" which favored the French intervention. This policy of "neutrality" so angered Romero that he participated in various anti-Seward, anti-Lincoln maneuvers during the years 1862–1865. However, the necessity of sur-

---

66. Miller, "Herman Sturm," 1–15; and Bazant, *Historia de la deuda exterior de México*, 95.
67. Miller, "Lew Wallace," 37–39; Miller, "Herman Sturm," 3–4; Romero to Juárez, June 20, 1865, in Archivo Juárez. See also Margarita Juárez to Juárez, April 7, 1866, and Romero to Juárez, July 28, 1866.

vival compelled both governments to subordinate their desires for economic growth, social progress, and political reform to defeating the domestic enemy. After Lincoln's death and the end of the Civil War, with the various Mexican agents productively at work, with a softening of United States policy towards movement of men and material into Mexico, with Johnson and Grant demonstrating friendly postures toward Mexico, the attitude of Romero mellowed and his hostility toward Seward quieted. Moreover, while the Romero and Seward viewpoints differed markedly in how to resolve the tangled problems arising from the French intervention and United States Civil War, they shared a similar conception of the central issue at stake—the conservative, aristocratic, monarchical Old World's challenge to the liberal, republican system of the New World.

VI The Tangle of Two Wars: French Intervention in Mexico During the United States Civil War, 1861–1865

DURING the 1860s, the issues at stake between the French-Maximilian and United States–Liberal position were not just governmental form—republicanism versus monarchy—or social objectives—freedom versus oppression—but rather a clash involving fundamentally different views of how the western hemisphere should be constituted. Although the fact of foreign intervention in Mexico initially did not provoke a great deal of excitement in the United States, the accompanying rumors of possible Spanish or French efforts to reestablish the monarchical form of government did elicit considerable concern.[1] By the time the Spanish and the British withdrew in April, 1862, the French scheme to build an empire for the glory and grandeur of Napoleonic France and, more than incidentally, to stop the Anglo-Saxon expansion into Latin America was well known. The key document revealing French in-

---

1. Francis X. Gerrity, "American Editorial Opinion of the French Intervention in Mexico, 1861–1867" (Ph.D. dissertation, Georgetown University, 1952), 34, 43–44, 334. On Spanish diplomacy, see Bock, "Tripartite Convention of London"; Brauer, "Gabriel García y Tassara and the American Civil War," 15–19; LeRoy H. Fischer and B. J. Chandler, "United States-Spanish Relations during the American Civil War," *Lincoln Herald*, LXXV (1973), 134–47. On Franco-Austrian relations regarding Mexico, see Nancy Nichols Barker, "France, Austria, and the Mexican Venture, 1861–1864," *French Historical Studies*, III (Fall, 1963), 224–45.

tentions towards Mexico and the United States is Napoleon III's letter of July 3, 1862, instructing General Elie Forey on French policy in the New World. After establishing a set of guidelines for Forey's mission, Napoleon wanted a joint French-Mexican process to select the future governing institutions for Mexico: "The object to be attained is not to impose on the Mexicans a form of government which would be obnoxious, but to assist them in their efforts to establish, according to their own wishes, a government which may have a chance of stability, and can secure to France the settlement of the injuries of which she has to complain." Not really permitted a free choice, the Mexicans had to choose a stable government which would satisfactorily settle French claims. Revealingly, however, one half of the letter to Forey discussed not Mexican affairs, but rather France's future in the New World.[2]

Realizing some people might inquire why France invested manpower and money to stabilize the Mexican government, Napoleon proposed to reply: "The prosperity of America is not a matter of indifference to Europe, for it is that country which feeds our manufactories and gives an impulse to our commerce. We have an interest in the republic of the United States being powerful and prosperous but not that she should take possession of the whole of the Gulf of Mexico, thence command the Antilles as well as South America, and be the only dispenser of the products of the New World." Perhaps Napoleon was disturbed by the United States threat to gain domination over Mexico as posed in the Corwin loan treaties, thus placing French industry at the mercy of United States allocation of Mexico's raw materials. Moreover, Napoleon contended that France, by helping Mexico to remain independent, "shall have restored to the Latin race on the other side of the Atlantic all its strength and its prestige; we shall have guaranteed security to our West India colonies and to those of Spain; we shall have established our friendly influence in the center of America; and that

2. Napoleon to Elie F. Forey, July 3, 1862, in *Senate Executive Documents,* 38th Cong., 2nd Sess., No. 11, pp. 190–91.

influence, by creating immense markets for our commerce, will procure us the raw materials indispensible for our manufactures." Napoleon's conclusion revealed the reality of his commercial concern and the hollowness of his interest in presenting Mexico a free political choice. He concluded that "military honor," "necessities of policy," and the "interests of our industry and commerce" compel France "to boldly plant our flag there, and to establish either a monarchy, if not incompatible with the national feeling," or some government offering greater prospects of stability.[3]

Napoleon's whole scheme, labeled the "Grand Design," sought to create a strong French interest in Spanish America by emphasizing the shared Latin origins. Contrasting catholicism with protestantism, Napoleon warned of the threatening cultural shock of increasing Anglo-Saxon influence.[4] The phrase *Latin America*, a core element in his propaganda effort dating back into the 1840s, intrigued Napoleon. In addition to the older, culturally oriented view, events of the 1860s, such as the Mexican suspension of payments, the United States Civil War, and the Corwin loan treaties, influenced Napoleon's decision making. Nevertheless, the seed idea was long buried in Napoleon's mind, merely awaiting germination. His instructions to Comte de Flahault, French ambassador to England, in October of 1861 demonstrate that his letter to Forey was not merely a reaction to current developments. All the ideas later incorporated in the Forey letter were presented to Flahault nine months previously. The Flahault letter even indicated that he already had Maximilian's name in mind for emperor of Mexico,

3. *Ibid.*

4. John Leddy Phelan, "Pan-Latinism, French Intervention in Mexico (1861–1867) and the Genesis of the Idea of Latin America," in *Conciencia y Autenticidad Históricas* (Mexico, 1968), 279–98; Hanna and Hanna, *Napoleon III and Mexico*, particularly Chaps. 1 and 7; Henry Blumenthal, *A Reappraisal of Franco-American Relations, 1830–1871* (Chapel Hill, 1959), 168; Henry Blumenthal, *France and the United States: Their Diplomatic Relations, 1789–1914* (Chapel Hill, 1970), vii; and Crook, *The North, the South*, 90–91. For a similar Spanish view, see *La Epoca* (Madrid), March 13, 1862, clipping enclosed in Horatio Perry to Seward, March 15, 1862, in U.S. Department of State, *Foreign Relations of the United States, 1862*, 486–87. On French information regarding United States policy and attitudes toward Mexico, see Daniel B. Carroll, *Henri Mercier and the American Civil War* (Princeton, 1971), 275–303.

which refutes the alleged intention to permit the Mexicans to decide their political fate.[5]

A defender and later historian of the French intervention, Abbe Emmanuel Domenech, contended that "the success of our expedition concerns not merely our national self-love, the honor of our flag, but above everything else, our commerce.... Latin America... Mexico, Central and South America, would become to France what Asia is to England—*its vast market*." The *Atlantic Monthly* likewise interpreted French aggression in Mexico as part of a French scheme for world empire with posts girdling the earth from France to Martinique, Veracruz, Acapulco, Tahiti, Saigon, ports on the Red Sea, Algiers, and back to France again.[6] Later, Napoleon asserted that a central motive for the expedition, beyond the reestablishment of order in Mexico and the redress of legitimate complaints, was "to open to our commerce vast outlets."[7] To this extent at least, Napoleon's project was in deep conflict with United States goals and aspirations to play a significant economic role in Mexico and the New World.

Auguste Billault, minister without portfolio in Napoleon's government, justified before the French legislature the intervention as a means to halt United States expansion. In response, José María Iglesias, Mexican congressman and future minister of public works (*Fomento*) in Juárez' cabinet, pointed out that, while the United

5. Napoleon to Comte de Flahault, October, 1861, in Mexiko, carton 11, Politisches Archiv, Austrian Staatsarchiv.

6. Quoted in Gorham D. Abbot, *Mexico and the United States: Their Mutual Relations and Common Interests* (New York, 1869), 225–26; and G. Reynolds, "Mexico," *Atlantic Monthly*, XIV (July, 1864), 51–63. Britain saw its interests being served by the French involvement in Mexico. Lacrete, "Great Britain and Mexico," 195. See also *El Siglo Diez y Nueve*, January 12, 1862; E. Lefefre, *Documentos Oficiales recogidos en la Secretaría privada de Maximiliano: Historia de la intervención francesa en México* (2 vols.; Brussels and London, 1869), 91; Richard Eugene Bailey, "The French in Mexico in the Nineteenth Century: The Franco-Mexican Political and Commercial Contacts; French Influence on Society," *Mexican Review*, IV (Winter, 1943–Summer, 1944), 15–23; and Memorandum, "Mexico, England, France and Spain" [1865?], Justin Lot Morrill Papers, container 8, Library of Congress.

7. John A. Dix to Seward, February 15, 1867, in U.S. Department of State, *Foreign Relations of the United States, 1867*, Part 1, p. 252, enclosing an English translation of Napoleon's address to the Corps Législatif of February 14, 1867.

States had followed a policy of absorption, no one had labeled this policy "good, just or worthy of imitation" as the French seemed to believe. Nevertheless, if France attacked Mexico, *El Siglo Diez y Nueve* saw no other recourse than to request United States protection. Since the northern neighbor had constantly cast a longing glance at Mexican territory, it was conceded that Mexico might lose some of its territory as the price of such assistance.[8]

After the French conquest of Mexico City and the subsequent creation of a satellite regime in Mexico under the Archduke Ferdinand Maximilian of Austria, the Juárez government maintained a precarious existence in El Paso del Norte and Chihuahua. Although the Liberal army dwindled to only a few thousand troops near the government and its revenue had shrunk, Juárez and his cabinet hung on stubbornly. In Europe and Mexico City during 1863 and early 1864, the first act of a drama was unfolding as Maximilian was persuaded that the Mexican people sought his leadership. He was induced to accept a title and authority which never attracted popular support in Mexico, nor even the very enthusiastic support of large elements of the church hierarchy and the landed elite. Maximilian's client status was indicated by both his financial dependence upon France and the fact that the only reliable military force in Mexico, the French expeditionary force, remained under the complete command of Marshall Bazaine.

In mid-1862 Seward also recognized conflicting systems, describing conservatism as the European political system and republicanism as the New World system. Informing Dayton of the nature of the problem, Seward explained why the European powers decided to take advantage of current United States troubles. Seward knew that the European politicians were "judging us by European, not American, standards, and under the influence of European, not American, interests and sentiments":

---

8. José María Iglesias, *Refutación del Discurso pronunciado por Mr. Billault Ministro sin Cartera en el Cuerpo Legislativo Francés sobre la política del Emperador en México* (Mexico, 1862), 4. See also *El Siglo Diez y Nueve*, November 5, 1861.

Republicanism and federalism are, to European statesmen, if not unintelligible, at least impracticable, principles; and durable power on the American continent is, in their esteem, a mere chimera. To them monarchy seems, if not the most beneficial system of government which could be devised, at least the only one which could assure the preservation of national sovereignty, and guarantee public tranquility and peace.

But Seward did not fear, since he believed that "this nation is conscious that it possesses a government the most indestructible that has ever been reared among men, because its foundations are laid in common political, commercial, and social necessities, as broad as its domain, while the machinery of that government is kept in vigorous and constant activity, because the power which moves it is perennially derived from the suffrages of a free, happy, and grateful people."[9] If the New World system could be protected, Seward possessed faith in Mexico's future as a liberal society.

Early in the course of French intervention, Seward clearly evaluated Mexico's potential for material progress and political democracy:

Difficult as the exercise of self-government there has proved to be, it is, nevertheless, quite certain that the attempt to maintain foreign authority there would encounter insurmountable embarrassment. The country possesses immense, practically inexhaustible, resources. They invite foreign labor and capital from all foreign countries to become naturalized and incorporated with the resources of the country and of the continent, while all attempts to acquire them by force must meet with the most annoying and injurious hindrance and resistance. This is equally true of Mexico and of every portion of the American continent. It is more than a hundred years since any foreign state has successfully planted a new colony in America, or even strengthened its hold upon any one previously existing here. Through all the social disturbances which attend a change from the colonial state to independence, and the substitution of the democratic for the monarchical system of government, it still seems to us that the Spanish-American states are steadily advancing towards the establishment of permanent institutions of self-government. It is the interest of the United States to favor this progress, and to commend it to the patronage of

9. Seward to Dayton, June 20, 1862, in U.S. Department of State, *Foreign Relations of the United States, 1862*, 351–54.

other nations. It is equally the interest of all other nations, if, as we confidently believe, this progress offers to mankind the speediest and surest means of rendering available to them the natural treasures of America.[10]

Seward argued that material as well as moral development and progress would best be served for the whole world if Europe left the liberal governments of the New World to their own devices. During the course of the French intervention, despite analyzing the New World clash with the Old World similarly to the Mexican liberals, Seward seldom considered using his influence to compel forceful action to prevent European interference in New World governments.

Later, in recognizing Juárez' yeomen service for liberalism, Seward ventured an estimate of Mexico's future for Señora Juárez as she prepared to return to her country: "If as I trust, Republican institutions are ultimately to become permanent and universal, you and your consort will have a distinguished place in the history of those who labored and suffered most for the establishment of the system of self government."[11] Soon many Mexicans and some North Americans adopted a radically different estimation of the threat posed by Old World intervention and became disillusioned with Seward's course of moderation.

Many key United States diplomats interpreted the foreign intervention into Mexico in terms similar to liberal opinion in Mexico and the United States, that is, as part of conflict between two world views which encompassed the divergent political institutional forms of republicanism and monarchy, but went much beyond these limitations. During the early, indecisive years of the United States Civil War, most United States diplomatic agents advocated a policy of registering complaints with the foreign intervention in Mexico, but postponing any confrontation until after the South was defeated. In Austria, J. Lothrop Motley left no doubt that the United States objected to the foreign intervention in Mexico, particularly

10. Seward to Dayton, April 24, 1863, in *Foreign Relations of the United States, 1863*, Pt. 1, pp. 662–63.
11. Seward to Margarita Maza de Juárez, November 6, 1867, in Seward Papers.

since it appeared that this foreign intervention seemed bent upon transforming the government form in Mexico from a republic to a monarchy. James E. Harvey, United States minister in Portugal, also analyzed the conflict in Mexico in terms of a conflict between "liberal institutions and constitutional government" and "despotic rulers and champions of absolutism." In May, 1864, responding to Charles F. Adams, United States minister in Britain, Seward agreed that the European nations were jealous of United States advancement—"their great prosperity and progress have necessarily provoked this political antagonism"—suggesting the unified attack of European conservatives upon New World successful experiments in liberalism. Yet, Seward pointed out that "foreign and remote dangers can scarcely be expected to gain serious attention, when the immediate domestic perils of the conflict absorb the popular mind." Writer Gorham Abbot also was convinced that the conflict over Mexico concerned more than just political institutions, but also involved civil and religious freedom, and commercial progress. His analysis, suggesting the many facets of a worldwide confrontation of liberalism versus conservatism, saw much more than merely republican or monarchical institutions to be at stake.[12]

The United States Civil War has often been evaluated within the framework of conflicting world views. Richard Cobden agreed with Sumner that "you [the Union] are fighting the battles of liberalism in Europe as well as the battle of freedom in America.— It is only necessary to observe who are your friends and who your opponents in the old world to be satisfied that great principles are at stake in your terrible conflict."[13] The *New York Evening Post* claimed that "on the successful maintenance of the Constitution and Union depends the progress of liberal governments all over the

12. James E. Harvey to Seward, October 17, 1863, and George G. Fogg to Seward, October 2, 1863, Motley to Seward, November 24, 1863, in U.S. Department of State, *Foreign Relations of the United States, 1864*, Pt. 4, pp. 120–21, 273–74, 389; Motley to Seward, February 12, 1862, in *Foreign Relations of the United States, 1862*, 563–64; Seward to Adams, May 3, 1864, in *Foreign Relations of the United States, 1864*, Pt. 1, pp. 723–74; and Abbot, *Mexico and the United States*, 147, 193–94, 374, 383–84, 390–91.

13. Cobden to Sumner, January 11, 1865, in Sumner Papers, Volume 140.

civilized world. Our failure would be hailed by the tories of Europe as a conclusive proof of the innate weakness and insecurity of popular government." It described the Mexican liberals' destiny in similar terms. Their success offered that country a new future: "Instead of bigotry, ignorance and despotism, that fair country will be characterized by free suffrage, freedom of religion, freedom of the Press, free trade, trial by jury, the right of public assembling, the right of petition, and indeed, all those privileges which in the present age the most civilized peoples require."[14] Some historians, among them A. R. Tyrner-Tyrnauer, David Potter, and Raimundo Luraghi, have recognized the international setting of the American Civil War in terms of its relationship to the worldwide rise of liberalism, nationalism, and industrialization in the nineteenth century.[15]

Presented with a fuzzy, largely unrecognized problem in identifying the factors which prompted their resistance, the Liberals resorted to a long list of issues at stake or they referred to the conflict of the New World or Republican "systems with the Old World or Monarchical system." In examining their views, it becomes quite clear that a liberal world view, a mix of nationalism and democracy, all bound together by an ideolog involving political, economic, and social elements, were contrasted with remnants of several old orders—feudalism, mercantilism, aristocracy, and monarchy—

14. New York *Evening Post*, March 7, 1861, May 28, 1861; James G. Blaine, *Twenty Years of Congress: From Lincoln to Garfield* (2 vols.; Norwich, Conn., 1884–1886), I, 597–98; L. Maria Child to George Julian, June 16, 1862, March 27, 1864, in Giddings-Julian Papers, boxes 1 and 2, Library of Congress.

15. A. R. Tyrner-Tyrnauer, *Lincoln and the Emperors* (London, 1962), 7, 11–12, 29, 127–28; David M. Potter, "Civil War," in C. Vann Woodward, *The Comparative Approach to American History* (New York, 1968); Raimundo Luraghi, "The Civil War and the Modernization of American Society: Social Structure and Industrial Revolution in the Old South before and during the War," *Civil War History*, XVIII (September, 1972), 230–50. See also William A. Williams, *The Contours of American History* (Chicago, 1966); Martín Quirarte, *Historiografía sobre el Imperio Maximiliano* (Mexico, 1970), 215; Egon Caesar Corti, *Maximilian and Carlotta in Mexico*, trans. Catherine Alison Phillips (2 vols.; New York, 1928), II, 443–45; Hanna and Hanna, *Napoleon III and Mexico*, 185–90; Robert W. Frazer, "Latin American Projects to Aid Mexico during the French Intervention," *Hispanic American Historical Review*, XXVIII (August, 1948), 385–86; and *Manchester Guardian*, March 28, 1865.

which formed the conservative world view. Matías Romero, who continually claimed that the French intervention and the Civil War were two halves of a whole, enumerated the matters at stake as "liberty, equality, self-government, progress and civilization."[16]

The Liberals' desire not only to retain their political, social, and economic gains, but to institute further progress in these areas produced a reaction against French-Mexican conservative intervention which, to a certain extent, temporarily overcame any cultural or racial objections to the Anglos. Other Latin American countries, feeling threatened by European monarchies, likewise claimed brotherhood with the United States based upon shared constitutional and political forms and shared liberal ideology. Francisco Zarco, in a long editorial in *El Siglo Diez y Nueve*, argued that the Juárez government came to power as a result of a free expression of the national will and was following popular ends. He praised United States policy, "whose objective was to restore peace, save order, and give protection to all the interests." Warning that "our enemies...are also yours," Zarco believed the United States would respond to Mexico's call for aid, "because they should consider that an attack on Mexico is a prelude, very surely, to an attack against the whole American continent."[17]

An important Mexican liberal newspaper, *El Monitor Republicano*, sensed a "spirit of the epoch" at work, which consisted of doubt and revolution against error and restriction. *El Monitor* asserted that, while Catholicism impeded the moral development of the nation, monarchy, calling upon divine right, enslaved mankind. Democracy would help free the people imbued with the "spirit of the epoch." Yet, in a later editorial, *El Monitor* stressed the complexity of differences between the liberal and the conservative Weltanschauungen. Although the editorial compared repub-

16. Romero to James R. Doolittle, September 9, 1862 (confidential), in Duane Mowry (ed.), "Doolittle Correspondence," *Publications of the Southern History Association*, IX (July, 1905), 242–43.
17. Francisco Zarco's editorial "Sobre los asuntos de México," *El Siglo Diez y Nueve*, January 6, 1862.

licanism and monarchy as opposites, clearly these terms, understood only in a political sense, were too restrictive. *El Monitor* saw monarchy sustained by despotism, military force, and divine rights; republicanism by reason, popular will, and human rights. The monarchy established classes and privileges; a republic accorded human equality. Monarchy removed human dignity; the republic elevated it. Monarchy supported fanaticism; republics combatted it. Monarchy milked the people to sustain luxury; republican government was much less onerous. Monarchy imposed; republics deliberated. Monarchy encouraged pompous show which stratified society; republics were simple and unified. Monarchs ruled by caprice, republics by popular reason. Monarchy weakened and opposed the principal tendency of man, namely liberty, whereas the republic developed and consolidated it. *El Monitor* concluded that Europe—the center of monarchical forms—could triumph temporarily, but that ultimately progress, democracy, and republicanism would triumph.[18] Some Mexican liberals were suspicious of European liberals, thus further separating the New World from the Old World, even when both professed similar ideological beliefs.[19]

In mid-1864, the Mexican Liberal government's official newspaper published a lengthy analysis of the worldwide struggle of liberalism and republicanism against their enemies:

The entire world crosses in the present one of the most tremendous and dangerous crises. The American [continent] has come to be the grand theater in which the destiny of humanity is at stake, since, in great proportion the great principles of liberty and retrogression which are pulling modern societies in contrary directions are being debated in it [the American continent]... the times of a universal renovation approach, in which,

18. "El Espíritu de la Epoca," and "La Europa y la América," *El Monitor Republicano,* August 10 and 11, 1862, and October 29, 1862. See also "La Aristocracia en México," *La Bandera Nacional,* July 16, 1864, which discusses aristocracy in Mexico by touching religion, the army, wealth and economic power, and a number of social questions, hence indicating that to the liberals the term "aristocracy" described a particular type of society.

19. Jesús Camarena to Juárez, June 6, 1862, in *El Siglo Diez y Nueve,* June 19, 1862.

throughout the world, the hopes will be realized, that, like a divine prom-ise, will protect the disinherited classes from the depths of their misery.

Scarcely had the desolate war in the United States broken out ... when the governments of old Europe believed the moment had arrived to carry into effect their ambitious views, suffocating the liberty which, from the New World, had risen up as a menace to their corrupt traditions. [Santa Domingo, Mexico, and Peru] ... have revealed the common danger which menaces the nationality of the Americas. Since they are not able to be considered like isolated events which affect secondary or purely local interests, but rather as the expression of deliberate thought, of a fixed plan, whose final consequence would be the eradication of the beginning of liberty in the New World, substituting in its place the poisoned shoot of European aristocracies and monarchies ... we raise our voices in order to maintain, finally, sufficiently high, the banner of progress, the future, and the union of free America.[20]

Here was a shrill protest against the threat to Mexico and the New World republics embodied in the arrival of Maximilian in Mexico as emperor by the grace of Napoleon III.

In 1865, Jesús Terán, Mexican minister to Great Britain, suc-cinctly stated Mexican liberal assumptions about the unity of interests and ideology between Mexico and the United States. "I disapprove of the conduct which the Washington government is ob-serving, because it is offensive to American brotherhood, to democ-racy, and to liberal things in general."[21] Since monarchy and empire were undesirable governmental forms in the New World, clearly, all sister liberal republics should oppose their reinstitution.

Considerable liberal opinion in Latin America shared Romero's and Seward's analysis. Articles from *El Comercio* of Lima, Peru, and *La Voz de Chile* advocated similar analyses. European powers inter-vened or planned to intervene because of the embarrassed position of the United States. "Latin or Saxon, the New World recognizes the same fundamental principles in its political organization; this

20. Editorial from *El Nuevo Mundo*, reprinted in *Periódico Oficial* (Monterrey, Mexico), July 12, 1864, in Archivo Histórico, legajo 19, ff12, Museo de Antropología y Historia, Mexico City.
21. Jesús Terán to Juárez, October 12, 1865, in Archivo Juárez.

idea is that of democracy." The European powers wanted to "liquidate the republican institutions in all the New World." One major European power, England, was an exception. Although England had participated in the Mexican intervention, she was not considered as basically an enemy. On the contrary, *El Comercio* contended that "our interests and our institutions make it advisable to maintain good relations with England, which definitely is the free and liberal power in Europe, and intimate relations with the United States, if this is possible, conforming to the basis of equality."[22] The French invasion prompted many New World liberals to respond sympathetically to Mexico's plight, often calling for a Pan-American meeting to coalesce joint action to aid Mexico and prevent the extension of the monarchical system.

Many Spanish-American spokesmen called for joint action in light of European intrusions in the New World. Francisco María Iglesias, Costa Rican minister of foreign relations, also considered whether to support a continental league. The Costa Rican government, convinced that without United States participation the league would not be effective in preventing the European dangers, sought guaranties against filibustering or annexation on the part of the United States before agreeing to support a continental league.[23]

During the fall of 1862, the Chilean foreign minister clearly expressed the concept that shared liberal institutions in the New World would lead to the greatest mutual material growth, although he recognized the limitation of language and culture:

Notwithstanding the diversity of origin and of language, the United States and the Spanish American republics are mutually united by the strong

22. "Peligro del Nuevo-Mundo," from *El Comercio* (Lima, Perú), in *El Siglo Diez y Nueve*, June 2, 1862; and "Democracia americana y absolutismo europeo," from *La Voz de Chile*, in *El Siglo Diez y Nueve*, June 22, 1862.

23. Emeterio S. Santovenia, *Lincoln: El Precursor de la Buena Vecindad* (La Habana, 1951), 27, 168–69, 190; *El Siglo Diez y Nueve*, July 21, August 10, and September 2, 1862; Eugenio Amunategui to Romero, February 28, 1862, Blas Bruzual to Romero, June 13 and 17, 1864, in Archivo Romero; M. Murillo to Romero, March 21, 1863, in Tamayo (ed.), *Juárez Documentos*, III, 452–53; *Manchester Guardian*, September 21, 1863; and Francisco María Iglesias to Ministro de Relaciones Exteriores of Colombia, July 11, 1862, in Archivo Romero.

bond of analogous political institutions, in whose development they found the home of a growing prosperity, which must, of necessity, cause each to view the fate of the others as of an interest not foreign but their own. . . . The sincere union of all the republics of the American continent, whatever be their historical antecedents, will be a fact pregnant with great and profitable results, since it must cooperate not only to the security of republican institutions, but, also, to the moral and material progress of these states, and even to the preservation of friendly relations with European nations, while Chili, as well as the United States, desires to cultivate and foment.[24]

Chile, like most other South and Central American republics, was seriously disturbed by European threats to the New World.

For a brief period it appeared as if the United States might even act in a manner encouraging European involvement in New World problems. In late 1862 the United States proposed joint action with Britain and France to preserve the security of passage across the Isthmus of Panama as the result of political events in New Granada. When the publication of the *Foreign Relations of the United States* volume for 1862 revealed this offer, Romero immediately called upon Seward and urged upon him the dangerous precedent of that course. It amounted to foreign intervention in the internal affairs of an American state, similar to France's conduct in Mexico, and naturally a course which Mexico could not approve of. Romero believed that the United States did not approve of such action either, let alone initiate and participate in it.[25]

With the crisis of foreign intervention in Santo Domingo, Mexico, and elsewhere in Latin America, some New World countries proposed an agreement with the United States creating a hemisphere Monroe Doctrine with an inter-American military force to sustain it. Originating in mid-1861, this movement lasted until the beginning of 1863 without any more success than similar earlier

24. Manuel A. Tocornal to Thomas H. Nelson, September 13, 1862, in U.S. Department of State, *Foreign Relations of the United States, 1863*, Pt. 2, pp. 1186–88.
25. Romero to Seward, March 21, May 19, 1863, in Romero (comp.), *Correspondencia*, III, 318–20.

Latin American efforts to convert the Monroe Doctrine into a Pan-American doctrine.[26]

Peru took the lead, issuing a call for a uniform policy by Spanish American republics in November, 1861. Federico L. Barreda, Peru's consul in New York City, was elevated to the rank of minister and instructed to work for a Pan-American organization against foreign intervention in the New World. The response was weak and mixed. At this stage, before foreign troops actually landed in Mexico, some Latin American republics saw no serious danger, and others felt Mexico was responsible for the intervention. The appointment of Doctor Manuel Nicolas Corpancho as Peruvian minister to Mexico with instructions to go to Mexico via Washington reinforced Peru's commitment to action against foreign intervention. Corpancho, remaining in the United States only a short time, conferred indefatigably with Romero in early January, 1862, and announced that Peru would supply five or six thousand men for a joint venture to aid Mexico.[27]

After Barreda's and Corpancho's initial suggestion met with an unfavorable response following intensive consultation with Romero during the spring of 1862, Barreda aired a second Peruvian proposal. Committing those nations that signed to affirm that the Civil War was only an insurrection, to promise not to recognize the independence of the Confederate States, and to deny the right of the Confederacy to issue letters of marque and reprisal or to use their harbors, this second proposal dangled tempting bait before Seward if he would sign an inter-American pact. In return all signators would mutually guarantee each others' boundaries and independence. Barreda, representing Peru, arranged a meeting with Chile, Mexico, New Granada, and two agents representing the five Central American republics to consider a pact; however, Seward's re-

26. Frazer, "Latin-American Projects," 377–88.
27. *Ibid.*; Cosío Villegas (ed.), *Diario de Matías Romero*, 437–38. For Corpancho's ideas on Latin American unity, see Corpancho to Doblado, November 20, 1862, and José V. de la Cadena to Doblado, November 22, 1862, in Doblado Papers.

fusal to include the United States as a signatory doomed the convention. Only Peru and Costa Rica signed Barreda's proposal.[28]

In mid-1862, arguing that liberty and peace were dependent conditions, Corpancho defined peace: "Peace is industry, agriculture, commerce, work, credit, education." From an "American Federation," he continued, would come "the force to turn back foreign attacks and peace to develop internal interests. The American continent will be for the foreigner only one grand, rich flourishing nation." Asserting the New World was superior to the Old, Corpancho maintained, "Our superiority consists in progress, and all our actions are inspired by these two ideas: liberty and the Americas."[29] These ideals motivated Corpancho and others to an ongoing effort to create an American Union.

In late 1862 Corpancho again proposed a continental treaty in a further effort to gain United States support for Latin America. Emanating from New Granada, a call went out to gather for a Pan-American conference at Panama on January 1, 1863. In September, 1862, Seward informed Romero that the United States viewed the proposed Panama conference and all Latin American projects to band together to preserve their independence with approval. The United States would not attend, however, and the conference, whose chief purpose was to obtain United States aid for Mexico and United States cooperation in guaranteeing Latin American independence, never came about. Seward feared that United States participation might offend France, prompting her recognition of the Confederacy. Naturally, a subsequent Mexican Foreign Ministry suggestion for an inter-American congress to solve mutual problems met with a cool response in Washington.[30]

28. Romero to Ministro de Relaciones Exteriores, April 4, April 27, and November 29, 1862, in Romero (comp.), *Correspondencia*, II, 119–22, 153–55, 640–41, and Cosío Villegas (ed.), *Diario de Matías Romero*, 427–61.

29. "Paz perpetua en América ó federación americana," *El Siglo Diez y Nueve*, May 9, 1862.

30. Frazer, "Latin-American Projects," 383–84; Romero to Ministro de Relaciones Exteriores, September 18, 1862, in Correspondencia General con los Estados Unidos; Fuente to

For over a year after early 1863 all maneuvers to incorporate the United States into a Pan-American movement to prevent or remove foreign intervention in the New World ceased. For example, the United States was not invited to the Second Congress of Lima, which met from November 14, 1864, until March 13, 1865, during which eight Latin American nations signed three treaties. Nevertheless, despite the ostensible, public reason for omitting the United States—its ongoing civil war—several Latin American countries objected to not inviting the United States, since the prime purpose of the meeting was defense against actual and threatening European intervention in Santo Domingo, Mexico, Colombia, Ecuador, and Peru. Obviously, to counteract European aggression, United States cooperation was necessary. In March, 1865, Blaz Bruzual, Venezuelan minister to the United States, judging the Civil War was approaching an end, consulted with Romero, Asta Buruaga (Chilean chargé d'affaires), General Eustorgio Salgar (Colombian minister), and General Tomás Cipriano de Mosquera, also of Colombia, regarding Pan-American cooperation. Later, while interviewing Seward, Bruzual asked if the United States would unite itself to a formal request, made by Venezuela, Chile, and perhaps other Latin American states, for the French to withdraw from Mexico. Pointing to the exhausted physical and financial state of the nation, Seward responded that, since the United States could not afford any foreign complications at that time, it would have to decline.[31]

Seward rejected Pan-Americanism as a means to counter French or other European influence because it was contrary to the

---

Romero, October 27, 1862, and Romero to Ministro de Relaciones Exteriores, November 29, 1862, in Romero (comp.), *Correspondencia*, II, 640–41, 804; and "Congreso Americano," from *Mercurio* (Valparaiso, Chile), in *El Siglo Diez y Nueve*, August 15, 1862. On the inter-American idea, see Gordon Connell-Smith, *The Inter-American System* (London, 1966). For early attempts at an American Union excluding the United States, see G. A. Nuermberger, "The Continental Treaties of 1856: An American Union Exclusive of the United States," *Hispanic American Historical Review*, XX (February, 1940), 32–55.

31. Romero to Ministro de Relaciones Exteriores, March 8, 1865, in Correspondencia General con los Estados Unidos.

traditional United States policy of no entangling alliances. When the Civil War ended, United States power was free to be applied to the French in Mexico, but Seward believed they had to be removed with diplomacy rather than force.[32] After the Civil War, the exhausted state of the nation made peace highly desirable. The idea of creating an inter-American union, perhaps without United States participation, lived on in spite of Seward's repeated rejections. In 1867, Carlos Butterfield traveled to South America on various matters, one of which was to generate support for an alliance of the Spanish American republics.[33]

From the earliest stage of foreign intervention, Seward sought to make clear that the United States would frown upon any political interference in the New World. This message was transmitted to the French through various direct and indirect channels. Early in 1862, Seward clarified the United States position on foreign intervention in Mexico during a conversation with Baron Frederick von Gerolt, Prussian minister to the United States, when he warned that "the erection of a monarchy in the Mexican Republic must lead to serious consequences and without doubt, sooner or later, to serious conflict between the powers taking part in that act and the United States." Since Seward did not request his remarks be kept confidential, he intended to signal France and the other participating powers. To make sure that his views were clearly expressed to France, Seward informed United States minister to France William Dayton, "We do not desire to suppress the fact that our sympathies are with Mexico...nor do we in any sense, for any purpose, disapprove of her present form of government, or distrust her administration." Moreover, Seward justified the Corwin loan projects as an effort to circumvent the portending confrontation between the intervening powers and the United States.[34]

32. Joseph G. Whelan, "William Henry Seward: Expansionist" (Ph.D. dissertation, University of Rochester, 1959), 82–83.

33. Carlos Butterfield to Romero, March 22 and April 22, 1867, in Archivo Romero.

34. Baron von Gerolt to Prussian Foreign Minister, March 5, 1862, in Mexiko, carton 11, Politisches Archiv; and Seward to Dayton, June 21, 1862, in U.S Department of State, *Foreign Relations of the United States, 1862*, 254–55.

Despite his assertion that the United States did "not desire an annexation of Mexico, or any part of it; nor do they desire any special interest, control, or influence there, but they are deeply interested in the reestablishment of unity, peace, and order in the neighboring republic," Seward had ambiguous thoughts on the matter. Only five days later he fondly recalled that the United States had served as protector of the New World. Seward reminded France: "It is well understood that through a long period, closing in 1860, the manifest strength of this nation was sufficient protection, for itself and for Mexico, against all foreign states. That power was broken down and shattered in 1861 by faction." Warning France that its course was ill considered in the eyes of the United States public opinion, Seward pointed out that the Union government believed that "their own safety and the cheerful destiny to which they aspire are intimately dependent on the continuance of free republican institutions throughout America." A French policy other than the decision to withdraw, "would probably scatter seeds which would be fruitful of jealousies, which might ultimately ripen into collision between France and the United States and other American republics."[35] This was one of the few instances when Seward seemed to approve possible inter-American alliance or military cooperation.

In early 1862, Edward Plumb warned Seward that Mexico might be maneuvered into appearing to favor the establishment of a European monarchy. Manuel Doblado, not a very scrupulous man in Plumb's judgment, had inexplicably agreed to permit the allied forces to leave the unhealthy area of Veracruz for the healthier highlands, thereby bypassing all the strong mountain passes which offered the best chance of resisting an allied military advance. Plumb was suspicious. Juárez might well reject the agreement, splitting the Liberal party and leaving Doblado with the support of the foreign elements, the church, the conservative party, and some

35. Seward to Dayton, September 26, 1863, and Seward to Motley, October 9, 1863, in U.S. Department of State, *Foreign Relations of the United States, 1863*, Pt. 2, pp. 936–38.

of the moderate liberals who preferred peace. Doblado would first replace Juárez and then later reach a personally rewarding understanding with the monarchists. Plumb concluded that the United States must keep an eye on developments in Mexico.[36] Later, Plumb cautioned Sumner that the French were using the Jecker claims to gain a foothold in Mexico after which the South might be recognized, putting "a different face... on our struggle." Plumb pointed out that the United States had potential allies, Spain and England, who were dissatisfied with France's course. The thrust of Plumb's argument was that French activity in Mexico stemmed from hostility toward the United States.[37] At this stage Plumb was undoubtedly trying to convince Sumner, whose position as chairman of the Senate Foreign Relations Committee made him a central figure in the fate of the loan treaties, that the Corwin loan treaties furthered United States interests.

Various congressional and press responses criticized the allied intervention. An early congressional resolution calling for information on allied activity in Mexico was penned by Ohio Congressman Clement L. Vallandigham, southern sympathizer and alleged Copperhead leader, thus provoking concern whether Confederate interests sought to embroil the Union in trouble with the allies. Suspicion increased when Vallandigham not only insisted upon this resolution which inquired about the Corwin loan treaties, but expanded it into an examination of other possible areas of conflict with the allied powers. In March and April, 1862, Congress received several additional resolutions of inquiry regarding Mexican affairs. Although merely asking for information, these resolutions indicated a persistent congressional interest in the Mexican imbroglio.[38] Meanwhile, in March, 1862, the *Chicago Tribune* informed the European powers that the United States had the ability "to first

36. Plumb to Seward, March 7, 1862, in Seward Papers.

37. Plumb to Sumner, April 29, 1862, in Sumner Papers, box 58. See also Plumb to Sumner, January 26, 1864, in Plumb Papers.

38. *Congressional Globe*, 37th Cong., 2nd Sess., December 4, 1861, March 3, 1862, April 15 and 21, 1862, pp. 15, 1041, 1677, and 1754.

crush out rebellion at home and then turn its attention to the maintenance of continental questions not abandoned, but only temporarily held in abeyance by our national difficulties."[39] Congress and
the press warned Europe early in the Civil War that, although suspended, United States interests in Mexico were permanent.

Napoleon's offer to mediate in the United States Civil War produced repercussions in the United States which he probably did
not expect. Charles Sumner, a voice of caution in regard to the
French intervention in Mexico since early 1862, reacting to Napoleon's intrusion into American affairs, hinted at strong action in
Mexico as a possible countermove. Although John Bright wrote to
Sumner trying to temper his response, Sumner prepared a near
endless speech, "Our Foreign Relations; Showing Present Perils
from England and France," to vent his anger. After noting Napoleon's intentions at limiting or excluding United States influence in
Latin America as expressed in the Forey letter, and at keeping the
continent open to additional foreign influence, Sumner observed
that Napoleon was not satisfied "with stirring against us the Gulf of
Mexico, the Antilles, and the Latin race," but sought to divide the
Union with his offer of mediation. Sumner detected an intimate
relationship between the Mexican and domestic conflicts; "The
throne of Mexico is offered to an Austrian archduke. The desire to
recognize the independence of Rebel Slavery is openly declared.
These two incidents together are complements of each other." The
French ruler loomed as the archenemy of republican government:
"Trampler upon the Republic of France, trampler upon the Republican Mexico, it remains to be seen if the French Emperor can prevail as trampler upon this Republic."[40]

Since official word arrived confirming the European interven-

39. "The Mexican Question," *Chicago Tribune*, March 6, 1862.
40. Charles Sumner, "Our Foreign Relations: Showing Present Perils from England
and France . . . at the Cooper Institute, September 10, 1863," in Hoar (ed.), *Charles Sumner:
His Complete Works*, VII, 368–69, 372–73; and Bright to Sumner, January 30, 1863, in
Sumner Papers, bMS Am 1.19; Adam Gurowski, *Diary* (3 vols.; Boston, 1862–1866), II, 18;
and Seward to Dayton, December 29, 1862, in U.S. Department of State, *Foreign Relations of
the United States, 1863*, Pt. 1, p. 639.

tion in Mexico, northern opinion speculated whether any of the intervening powers intended to use their location in Mexico to recognize or otherwise aid the Confederacy. Another point disturbing Sumner was the persistent rumor of French intentions to annex Texas, perhaps as a concession from the Confederacy in return for recognition. Lincoln also seemed anxious, writing General Nathaniel Banks that events in Mexico "render early action in Texas more important than ever." Lincoln's concern was sharpened by a telegram from General-in-Chief Halleck the following day. Then several days later, Lincoln wrote to General Ulysses Grant that recent events in Mexico underlined "the importance of reestablishing the national authority in Western Texas as soon as possible."[41]

With Union fortunes on the field of battle faring badly during the summer, fall, and winter of 1862, even continual rumors from Europe that Napoleon intended to make a monarchy out of Mexico could not arouse vigorous United States support for an aggressive Mexican policy. Finally, in the first half of 1863, certain developments rekindled United States interest. Reacting to his own personal political needs to defend California's interests, his ideals, and to the rumors of impending monarchy, California's Senator McDougall introduced a resolution strongly critical of French continuance in Mexico. This resolution labeled the French attempt to subjugate Mexico as "not merely unfriendly to this Republic, but to free institutions everywhere; and that it is regarded by this Republic as not only unfriendly, but as hostile . . . further . . . it is the duty of the Republic to require of the Government of France that her

---

41. Lincoln to Banks, August 5, 1863, Halleck to Banks, August 6, 1863, and Lincoln to Grant, August 9, 1863, in Basler (ed.), *Works of Lincoln*, VI, 364–65, 374–75. See also "The French Emperor's Policy in America," "The French in Mexico," and "France in Mexico," *Harper's Weekly*, VII (February 14, 1863), 98, VIII (June 11, 1864), 371, and IX (February 11, 1865), 82; *Manchester Guardian*, September 14, 1863; Crook, *The North, the South*, 52–55, 62–63, 90–91, 184, 267–68, 282, 355; Edward E. Dunbar, *The Mexican Papers* (New York, 1860–1861), No. 5 (April, 1861), 278; Corwin to Manuel Doblado, December 12, 1861, in Tamayo (ed.), *Juárez Documentos*, V, 349; and Paul H. Reuter, Jr., "United States–French Relations Regarding French Intervention in Mexico: From the Tripartite Treaty to Queretaro," *Southern Quarterly*, VI (July, 1968), 469–75.

armed forces be withdrawn from the territories of Mexico." Indicative of growing sentiment against France, even in the bleak period of earlier 1863, Sumner's impassioned plea not to take up consideration of the resolution which he feared would give aid and comfort to the rebellion by threatening to embroil the United States in a war with France, lost 29 to 16. Then, Sumner delivered a longer speech, urging that the rebellion must remain the prime United States concern, while leaving open the possibility of future action in Mexican affairs. Cognizant of the need to clear the French from Mexico, Sumner merely pondered the best time and method to accomplish that goal. "Let the Rebellion be overcome, and this whole continent will fall naturally, peacefully, and tranquilly under the irresistible influence of American institutions."[42]

In September of 1863 United States minister to Holland James Shepherd Pike evaluated for Maine Senator William Pitt Fessenden European views on the continuation of the French army in Mexico and on the recent announcement that Maximilian would become emperor. Europeans were amazed at the United States tone "of submission to the act as a thing with which we have nothing to do. This is not what is expected of us in Europe and is not becoming." Pike denied past United States boasting was sufficient reason "why we should in the present emergency run into pusillanimity of behavior when a case arises which menaces both our doctrine of govt. and our national safety." He then explained that the European balance of power concept made every nation concerned with what a powerful nation did with a weaker one, and he felt that concept should apply to the United States, France, and Mexico. Pike reminded Fessenden that "remonstrance is the first weapon, if that does not answer, they apply force." Recognizing the restraining role of the Civil War, Pike conceded: "We are in a position when we must necessarily be prudent, but I suppose we are not so reduced yet that we must withhold the temperate though clear and firm expression of our opinion upon a subject of great national impor-

42. Hoar (ed.), *Charles Sumner: His Complete Works*, VII, 257–61.

tance." Pike concluded that "if nothing hostile is meant we shall not suffer from a manly and dignified protest"; so, he hoped "Congress will not omit to act promptly on the subject, though of course with prudence." Pike decided that the gathering of French power for the Mexican intervention projected a coming conflict in the Gulf between the United States and France, hence making New Orleans a "key to our empire." The empire obviously was the one to be achieved by economic growth and domination of the Latin American states bordering the Gulf.[43]

At the end of the Civil War, Plumb, in a memorandum and a journal article, delineated past and present problems regarding the French and United States policy clash over Mexico. In the memorandum, apparently recalling the Corwin loan treaties and other forms of material and moral support, he argued that

Seward gave birth to a principle of policy, on the part of the United States, as wise and farsighted and as important as the Monroe Doctrine itself, and vitally related to that doctrine because its necessary complement. It was . . . the principle that while we will not allow any European Power to intervene in the internal affairs of the Nations upon this Continent, we will ourselves, aid those Nations when, for their own and our safety and well being, assistance in the form of pecuniary and moral aid to maintain their independence and enable them to attain a stable and prosperous condition may be properly rendered or may become necessary.

Then in a discussion, presaging the later Roosevelt corollary, Plumb indicated that the European countries had a reasonable complaint when Spanish American governments were unstable and disruptive of commerce. Yet when they attempted to redress their grievances and to establish stable governments, they ran into the Monroe Doctrine and a United States government which would neither act nor permit others to act against the reigning anarchy. Plumb interpreted Seward's policy of taking Mexico under wing as the first sign that the United States was willing to see Mexico be-

43. Pike to Fessenden, September 3, 1863, in James Shepherd Pike Papers, Library of Congress; and Pike to Seward, August 19, 1863, in U.S. Department of State, *Foreign Relations of the United States, 1863*, Pt. 2, p. 824.

come an independent and prosperous power. Plumb reaffirmed that the United States desired no further annexation, except for "a slight change in the existing boundary so as to give us access from our present interior possessions of Arizona and Utah to the Gulf of California, and the control of the Peninsular of Lower California for military and naval considerations." Many "antiexpansionists" made this exception because of the excellent harbor facility at Magdalena Bay and the valuable strategic position of Lower California in regard to the Panama-California route. California Governor Frederick L. Low relayed his concern and fear that Napoleon would receive Sonora and Sinaloa as payment for the Mexican debt to France, reminding Seward that "the Mexican question is one that is of especial importance to the people of this State."[44]

Since "an Empire in Mexico under any circumstance is impossible [and] only Republican institutions can be allowed to prevail," Plumb concluded that "the matter of placing a loan in the United States to aid the Republic of Mexico must be considered." Recognizing that France would withdraw quickest under "honorable conditions," Plumb questioned whether the United States government could not use its good offices to persuade Mexican Liberals to recognize some of the imperial debt—that owed to France—and whether the interest on this debt could not then be paid out of the proceeds of the United States loan. Plumb urged quick action because "every day's delay only renders [France's] position worse and her withdrawal more delicate by reason of the plain, outspoken character of the remarks of our public men, while the debate in the coming Congress, it is probable, will assure almost the character of open threats." Although recognizing that such a policy would transfer "these Diplomatic claims from Europe to America," Plumb concluded that the European bondholders would probably favor such a settlement since their paper, which had depreciated so sharply, would appreciate as a result of the loan.[45]

44. "France, Mexico and the United States," September 27, 1865, in Plumb Collection; and Frederick Low to Seward, July 18, 1864, in U.S. Department of State, *Foreign Relations of the United States, 1864,* Pt. 3, pp. 136–37.

45. "France, Mexico and the United States," September 27, 1865, in Plumb Collection.

About mid-1865, Plumb's periodical article summarized his view of the conflict over Mexico during the preceding decade:

Through long years of struggle in which progress and republicanism have contended with retrogression and the institutions of the past, European influence, both commercial and diplomatic, in Mexico has uniformly and constantly placed itself upon the side of retrogression. That influence in the past has been active and potent, and it has largely contributed to keep the country in the state of turmoil and disorder always attendant upon a contest which can only be terminated by the decisive triumph of one or the other of the antagonistic principles involved.

During the pre-Civil War years, the United States had only served as an example, not actively intervening to support the Liberal party, while the conservatives were always sustained by the monarchical governments of Europe. Plumb interpreted United States recognition of Juárez in 1859 as signaling a new policy for the United States "to throw the weight of our influence and power into the scale to decide once and forever the question that the countries of this continent who have adopted republican institutions shall be aided to maintain those institutions and that such institutions are definitely adopted as the form of government that is to be maintained upon this continent." Plumb claimed that "our recognition of the Constitutional government of President Juárez, in opposition to the government of Miramon recognized by the European powers, turned the scale in favor of republican principles in Mexico and the contest terminated soon after." But then the Civil War gave European rulers, especially Louis Napoleon, another try at destroying republican institutions in Mexico. Since the whole intervention was based upon the false assumption of the permanent division of the United States, Plumb concluded that because of the intensity of feeling among American people on this matter, "nothing but the speedy withdrawal of Maximilian and of the European troops can prevent open hostility against France being forced upon the administration."[46]

46. "The United States and France: Our Diplomatic position upon the Mexican question" [1865?], in Plumb Collection.

Naturally, just as the liberal governments sought to increase their security by denying monarchical, aristocratic systems access to the New World, the Mexican empire sought to secure itself by extending its political system. Central America, because of its proximity to Mexico, immediately aroused the interest of Maximilian. Soon after assuming the Cactus Throne in mid-1864, he issued a proclamation incorporating several areas claimed by British Honduras into his new realm, thereby reinforcing rumors which indicated that he had an eye for expanding into Central America. Maximilian's decree prompted the British governor of British Honduras to inform Charles A. Leas, United States commercial agent in Belize, "that Great Britain would never relinquish the colony to Mexico; that the opinion is gaining popularity in England that it is not politic to hold so many dependencies at so great a distance; . . . and intimated, as he once before plainly observed, that the United States would be more suited to exercise jurisdiction in Central America than Mexico." Although aware that the governor may have been sounding out United States ambition in Central America, Leas personally stated his belief that the United States would "lend its full moral support" to fix the Central American countries with "good stable governments of a republican character."[47] The Mexican imperialists also made contact with the conservatives grouped around Guatemalan President Rafael Carrera, prompting them to dispatch known monarchist Felipe Nerí del Barrio as Guatemalan minister to Mexico and to indicate their willingness to cooperate with the conservative forces of Mexico.[48]

Not surprisingly, the liberal parties in Mexico and Central America instituted an exchange of ideas and information to counteract the conservative initiative. Eventually they speculated re-

47. Charles A. Leas to F. W. Seward, November 12, 1864, in U.S. Department of State, *Foreign Relations of the United States, 1865*, 65–67.
48. Hanna and Hanna, *Napoleon III and Mexico*, 186–89. See also "La Cuestión Estranjera," *Periódico Oficial*, January 17, 1865; and Mariano Degollado to Mexican Imperial Minister de Negocios Exteriores, July 15, 1865, in Luis García Pimental Collection, CONDUMEX, VII-1, 2–4, #134, Centro de Estudios de la Historia de México.

garding joint, developing proposals to overthrow conservative rule. In former president of El Salvador Gerardo Barrios' opinion, the only reasons Carrera had not proclaimed for the Mexican empire and joined Guatemala to Mexico were Maximilian's inability to assert his authority over all of Mexico and the fact that Oaxaca and other southern Mexican states near Guatemala remained firmly loyal to Juárez. Barrios feared that "only the termination of the United States Civil War can guarantee our institutions."[49]

After the Civil War, Barrios suggested to Romero using Central America as a point supporting the Oaxacan liberals with men, arms, and a refuge in their war on Maximilian. He proposed acquiring arms, ships, and a few men in the United States in order to overthrow Carrera's successors in Guatemala, then to use Guatemala as the base for sustaining the Liberals in southern Mexico. Romero responded that such an enterprise required money that he could not supply at that time. Then in late May, 1865, word arrived that El Salvador had experienced a popular rising against conservative President Dueñas. Convinced that the liberal majorities in El Salvador, Honduras, and Nicaragua favored him, Barrios decided to try to unite liberal Central America. The resulting triumph of the liberal party "would be beneficial for the United States since the Central American conservatives had favored granting a transit concession in Nicaragua to a Captain Pim, an English engineer." Likewise, the Mexican liberals should rejoice at the forthcoming liberal victory in Central America, since it might "save the independence of [their] country." Barrios proclaimed that "peace in the United States had saved Mexican independence, and will assure republican institutions on the whole continent."[50] Time and time again, Central American, Mexican, or other Latin American liberals were compelled to recall to the United States its role in defending the liberal New World institutions from Old World attack, a call that often referred to the Monroe Doctrine.

49. Gerardo Barrios to Romero, February 10, 1865, in Archivo Romero; and *La Gaceta del Salvador*, January 4, and March 29, 1862.
50. Barrios to Romero, May 3 and 30, 1865, in Archivo Romero.

Much attention has been given to the detail of whether Seward used the words *Monroe Doctrine* in his French correspondence. He apparently avoided the label, but did set out to protect the central objective of that doctrine. There are logical explanations as to why Seward chose not to assert the Monroe Doctrine principles under their proper name. Nothing could be gained in using terminology known to provoke anger and hostility among the French. Not only unnecessary, it would generate patriotic, unifying support for Napoleon III at a time when internal opposition to his Mexican policy was growing. Furthermore, Seward must have realized that the Monroe Doctrine was merely a statement of United States policy to protect certain vital interests, with no basis in international law. The policies expressed therein would be maintained or ignored according to United States ability to compel respect through the use or threat of use of force. On one hand, the Civil War limited United States ability to threaten with force. On the other, since the French experiment in empire was interpreted as a threat to vital United States interests, no doctrine or name was needed.[51] In any event, the goal of the Monroe Doctrine, preservation of the New World for United States expansion, was defended in the 1860s.

Rumors of French imperial designs initiated a serious discussion of the meaning and significance of the Monroe Doctrine, which had an active, popular domestic following in the United States. True, Seward did not mention it by name in his exchanges with foreign countries, but he did on numerous occasions affirm United States commitment to the principles of the doctrine. Used during the 1850s as a partisan statement for advancement of slavery, the Monroe Doctrine emerged from the Civil War, in the words of one historian, "immensely strengthened, and firmly anchored in the thought of the American people and in the policy of their government." By 1866, United States newspapers considered the Monroe Doctrine an inviolable keystone in the arch of American diplo-

---

51. Jordan Donaldson and Edwin J. Pratt, *Europe and the American Civil War* (Boston and New York, 1931), 242; Van Deusen, *Seward*, 367; Frederic Bancroft, "The French in Mexico and the Monroe Doctrine," *Political Science Quarterly*, XI (March, 1896), 35–43.

macy.[52] It was, however, to undergo a subtle change as its emphasis was expanded from preserving territorial integrity to enlarging and securing commercial opportunities for United States merchants, investors, and adventurers.[53]

What of the applicability of the doctrine to the situation in Mexico? Its principles were relevant. The question is when were they violated? Not in 1862, as has been claimed.[54] Given the chronic violation of the rights of foreigners and their property and Mexico's inability to comply with her international obligations, Seward correctly recognized the right of the British, French, and Spanish to declare war to protect the rights of their citizens and to obtain satisfaction for their claims. Juárez, however, contended that the physical fact of intervention violated the Monroe Doctrine. A violation of the Monroe Doctrine would occur in Seward's eyes when France tried to convert a war to secure its rights into one to secure a friendly French-controlled government. Seward was primarily interested in checking the spread of European influence and resulting commercial advantage throughout Latin America.[55] From the beginning of the French intervention, Seward's general policy and attitude had developed appropriately to the ever-increasing commitment of the intervention. At first the State Department merely objected to the projected intervention as unnecessary under the circumstances. Then it refused to associate with the intervening powers. Finally, its protests against the establishment of monarchical government culminated in the near ultimatum of late 1865. Viewed in this manner, the unfolding of Seward's policy seemed reasoned and fitting.[56]

52. Perkins, *The Monroe Doctrine*, 420–21; Gerrity, "American Editorial Opinion," 335.

53. Richard W. Van Alstyne, *The Rising American Empire* (Chicago, 1965), 98–99, 149–51, 160–62; Ernest Paolino, *Foundations of the American Empire: William Henry Seward and U.S. Foreign Policy* (Ithaca, N.Y., 1973), 29; Williams, *The Roots of the American Empire*, 121–22; Perkins, *Monroe Doctrine*, 545–48.

54. Bancroft, "The French in Mexico," 42–43.

55. Whelan, "William Henry Seward: Expansionist," 82–83; *El Siglo Diez y Nueve*, November 10, 1861, January 16, 20, 1862; and Juárez to Plácido Vega, April 3, 1862, in Vega Papers.

56. Hector Petin, *Les Etats-Unis et la Doctrine de Monroe* (Paris, 1900), 194, 199–200; and Bancroft, "The French in Mexico," 41.

In 1863, Joshua Leavitt, abolitionist and defender of the Monroe Doctrine, observed that the conflict was not just between monarchy and republican government, or freedom and slavery; nor was the European intervention in Mexico just a matter of taking advantage of the circumstance of the Civil War. Leavitt, reviewing the evidence and arguments for a planned operation by the European powers, singled out for special emphasis two factors: "money Power, and papal Power," both of which exercised nefarious influence in this matter in his judgment. Leavitt contended that "we must rather believe that there was, somewhere, a preexisting concert of design, to help the rebellion into full being, and thus make an opportunity, while our government was embarrassed, to overthrow the Monroe Doctrine, and get at once a firm footing on this continent for the political system of Europe."[57]

In early 1865 Henry Winter Davis of Maryland, speaking in Chicago on the "Lessons of the War," analyzed the Civil War, foreign intervention in Mexico, and Europe's role in both. Davis defined the opposing sides as the United States and Latin American nations on one side, and Europe, to which he assigned "imperialism," "aristocracy," and "hereditary thrones," on the other. Davis was convinced that the European powers, daring to act only because the United States was split by the Civil War, had destroyed "the most free and liberal government" Mexico had ever had. He rejected the repeated European criticism that anarchy ruled in Mexico, replying, "let them leave Mexico, if they don't like the state of anarchy which prevails there." Davis wanted Mexico to be free to work out its own salvation; the New World must have freedom from "here to Cape Horn." These factors were what Davis called "the first results," or the chief lesson of the war.[58]

In 1865 Iowa politician and diplomat John Kasson interpreted the French intervention in Mexico as a step taken not just for

57. Joshua Leavitt, *The Monroe Doctrine* (New York, 1863), 35–46.
58. "Lessons of the War. Security for the Future, and Self-Government by Law, with Liberty Guarded by Power," in Henry Winter Davis, *Speeches and Addresses Delivered in the Congress of the United States and on Several Public Occasions* (New York, 1867), 571–73.

"commercial advantages, but to discredit the republican system." Grouping all European intervention in the New World during this period together, Kasson saw a European "system" at work. Kasson concluded by affirming "that the underlying motive of the non-colonization principle [of the Monroe Doctrine] was and is the danger which European dominions in America offer to our material interests, both in peace and in war. It means a flanking position, a military and naval rendezvous in time of war, and an exclusive commercial position in time of peace."[59]

It was not just the embarrassing internal situation of the United States that held Seward back from a stronger stand on the principles of the Monroe Doctrine. He had to wait beyond the rumor, the boast, even the official dispatch, for the fact of French violation of the doctrine. A physical act had to occur. Maximilian's arrival and assumption of power in Mexico was the act. Anything short of such a physical act warranted no more concern than Seward gave to the French intervention, namely, statements of United States concern about certain courses of conduct and restatements of United States principles regarding the establishment of foreign monarchies in the New World.

When Maximilian departed for Mexico, Seward recognized the possibility that "new embarrassment" might develop with France. Reaffirming his belief in a special relationship between the United States and Mexico, he stated that, despite Maximilian's assumption of authority, the United States would "not forego the assertion of any of our national rights." He remained "now firm, as heretofore, in the opinion that the destinies of the American continent are not to be permanently controlled by any political arrangements that can be made in the capitals of Europe."[60]

In mid-1864, Senator Orville Browning described some of the

59. John Kasson, *Evolution of the Constitution of the United States of America and History of the Monroe Doctrine* (Boston, 1904), 258–59. See also Plumb to Sumner, January 26, 1864, in Plumb Papers.

60. Seward to Dayton, April 30, 1864, in U.S. Department of State, *Foreign Relations of the United Staves*, 1864, Pt. 3, p. 80.

disturbing rumors, reports, and tension prevalent in Washington. At a meeting of the Senate Foreign Relations Committee, Sumner drew upon his "secret agents" in Europe, whom he trusted more than the State Department officials, to report that Napoleon was friendly toward the United States and had no intention of permanently occupying Mexico. Yet, Sumner also announced that respected businessman-inventor Cyrus W. Field, just back from Europe, confirmed that Napoleon had inquired about laying a telegraph line from France to Mexico. Other reports to the committee included one of a French agent in London purchasing rails for a Veracruz to Mexico City railroad—all in all not signs which were consistent with the expressed desire of the French to withdraw.[61]

During the last half of 1864, Monroe Doctrine supporters under various organizational names developed into a significant popular pressure group. A few clubs may have existed previously, but only at this point did they grow, multiply, and become a national force. These clubs represented a further indicator of public reaction to Maximilian's arrival, occasionally producing friction in French–United States relations.[62] Precisely this type of organized, popular, vocal, and monied associations best influenced politicians, even those least sensitive to public opinion.

The Monroe Doctrine came under consideration in the 1864 national political conventions. The National Union party passed a set of eleven resolutions, introduced by New York newspaper magnate and Republican party chairman Henry J. Raymond. An old friend and political ally of Seward, his eleventh resolution restated Seward's policy towards French intervention in Mexico up to mid-1864, naturally not mentioning the Monroe Doctrine. Raymond's resolution revealed the fear of some Lincoln supporters

61. Randall and Pease (eds.), *Diary of Orville Hickman Browning*, I, 613–14.

62. Perkins, *The Monroe Doctrine*, 448; Robert R. Miller, "The American Legion of Honor in Mexico," *Pacific Historical Review*, XXX (August, 1961), 231–32; Miller, "Plácido Vega," 143–44; Gerrity, "American Editorial Opinion," 334; French Minister L. de Geofroy to Seward, April 26, 1864, and Seward to Geofroy, May 28, June 22, 1864, in U.S. Department of State, *Foreign Relations of the United States, 1864*, Pt. 3, pp. 216–17, 219–22.

that, unless active steps were taken to rally support around the administration's Mexican policy, the president might lose the election. The Illinois state convention, although sending delegates to the National Union convention pledged to Lincoln, demonstrated the perhaps unconscious thought pattern linking the rebellion with foreign intervention in its resolution that "the nation will have to sustain [the Monroe] doctrine so long until its authority is vindicated and the rebellion conquered."[63]

The Democratic convention, nominating General McClellan on a platform emphasizing war weariness, could not approve a Monroe Doctrine plank which might produce war with France. Nevertheless, on the first day of the convention, it had to maneuver quickly to prevent acceptance of two resolutions by a Mr. Allricks of Pennsylvania. One read in part: "We cannot view with indifference the open repudiation and violation of the Monroe Doctrine." An immediate move for adjournment after the reading of this resolution prevented its consideration and possible acceptance.[64]

During the Civil War, newspapers, pamphlets, and public speeches in the North and South ceaselessly discussed the Monroe Doctrine and the French intervention. Through Romero the Mexican Liberal government got a jump in propagandizing its positions and building firm, organized support for its views. A late starter, the Maximilian government nevertheless sent a large number of more adequately financed agents to the United States to influence public opinion.

Responding to the new, aggressive United States position indicated in the Davis resolution of April 4, 1864, Edouard Drouyn de Lhuys used the Marquis Adolphe de Chambrun's trip to the United States in December, 1864, to obtain a report on the progress of the Civil War and to learn the truth about United States sentiments on

63. Republican Party, *Proceedings of the National Union Convention Held in Baltimore, Md., June 7th and 8th, 1864* (New York, 1864), 57–58; and Romero to Ministro de Relaciones Exteriores, June 12, 1864, in Correspondencia General con los Estados Unidos.

64. Democratic Party, *Official Proceedings of the Democratic National Convention, Held in 1864 at Chicago* (Chicago, 1864), 10–11, 27–28.

the Mexican venture. In February, 1865, de Chambrun met with Sumner, who expressed a desire not to send United States troops to Mexico, but conceded "certain rowdy elements" could "get out of hand." Sumner also wanted to avoid recognizing French imperial claims. After the first weeks in the United States, de Chambrun accurately reported, "It is certain that no one wants war in Mexico, but they will go pretty far to insist on this theory: the entire Continent must be under American control." Further, de Chambrun warned that United States trade access to Mexico was a potentially significant issue: "[If] American indignation should be aroused at the expulsion of commercial representatives, things might turn very badly in Mexico." But several months later, with the war terminated, de Chambrun noticed a tougher line developing, first with the sending of Sheridan to command a hundred thousand men on the frontier, and then, with public opinion beginning to clamour for action "to oust the French and enforce the Monroe Doctrine." [65]

Observing that northern politicians were urging ever-stronger action regarding Mexico on the Lincoln administration, Maximilian apparently assigned credit for this shift of northern attitudes to the techniques of Mexican Liberals' propaganda rather than to more fundamental ideological and material grounds. To counteract the bad press, Maximilian named Luis de Arroyo consul general for the Mexican empire in New York. Arroyo's principal task was to pursue United States recognition directly rather than, as in the past, via Napoleon's diplomatic representative. To arrange a meeting with Seward, Arroyo contacted Thomas Corwin, now a silent sympathizer of the empire. [66]

Corwin's relationship with the Liberal government and the empire has not been properly interpreted. One Corwin biographer claimed Mexico's friendship with the Union resulted from Corwin's

65. Charles Adolphe de Chambrun, *Impressions of Lincoln and the Civil War: A Foreigner's Account*, trans. Adelbert de Chambrun (New York, 1952), vii, 19, 47–48, 142–43, 167–68.

66. Robert W. Frazer, "Maximilian's Propaganda Activities in the United States," *Hispanic American Historical Review*, XXIV (February, 1944), 4–9; Zorrilla, *Relaciones*, I, 459–60; and Luis Arroyo to Corwin, March 2, 1865, forwarded by Corwin to Seward, in *House Executive Documents*, 39th Cong., 1st Session, No. 73, p. 573.

sympathy with the Liberal party, while another pointed out that Corwin maintained friendly relations with both the French provisional government and the Liberals, but asserted that Corwin's sympathies were entirely with the Liberals. Although Corwin favored the Liberal government from 1861 until mid-1863, sometime after May, 1863, when Corwin decided not to move north with Juárez' government as it fled from the French invaders, his opinion changed. By the winter of 1863–1864 it was rumored that he was partial to the empire, and his dispatches to Seward began to reflect an ambivalent position on domestic Mexican politics. In the spring of 1864, John S. Cripps, unofficial Confederate agent in Mexico City, informed the Confederate State Department that "an effect of the cordiality now prevailing between the United States Minister and the Mexican [imperial] Cabinet is to be noted in the animosity heretofore spent upon the American Union now concentrated in single intensity upon the Southern Confederacy."[67] In June, 1864, after interviewing Corwin, a Washington reporter affirmed a New York newspaper story asserting Corwin now favored Maximilian and monarchy for Mexico. Then, in August, 1864, alarmed because Corwin and his son William were working for United States recognition of the empire, Lerdo de Tejada admonished Romero to neutralize any damage Corwin might do to Mexico in the United States. After Romero officially notified Lerdo de Tejada in September, 1864, that Corwin's resignation had been accepted, Lerdo de Tejada expressed great relief. Now Corwin's opinions favorable to the empire would be less threatening. In fact, Romero claimed his investigations revealed that Corwin's open sympathy with the intervention forced his resignation.[68]

67. Auer, "Tom Corwin," II, 502; Pendergraft, "Public Career of Thomas Corwin," 735–36; Corwin to Seward, January 27, March 28, 1864, in Diplomatic Dispatches, Mexico, RG 59, NA; and Cripps to Confederate Secretary of State, April 22, 1864, in Records of the Confederate States of America, Vol. VII, Pt. 1.
68. Romero to Ministro de Relaciones Exteriores, June 9, September 28, October 2, 1864, in Correspondencia General con los Estados Unidos, pp. 542–43, 603, 628; Lerdo de Tejada to Romero, August 13, 1864, January 10, 1865, in Romero (comp.), *Correspondencia*, IV, 538, and VI, 12.

Romero's report on Corwin's activity in early 1865 confirmed earlier Liberal suspicions of Corwin's conversion to the empire. Corwin had attempted to arrange a meeting for imperial agents Luis de Arroyo and Mariano Degollado with Seward and offered Degollado advice when called upon. Later, upon the first anniversary of Corwin's death, Seward excused Corwin's conduct during his last year and a half, by declaring that what concerned Corwin at this time was "to prevent the dismemberment of his own country."[69] Subsequent evaluations of Corwin's career as minister to Mexico by historians suggest that Seward successfully covered Corwin's tracks.

Maximilian's agents sought support in the United States from the business community and the press, by retaining the legal services of Clarence Seward, nephew of the secretary of state, and finally by bribing key politicians. All their efforts failed in achieving the ultimate goal, recognition. Maximilian's propaganda effort, although adequately subsidized, began too late and had to overcome a strong hostile environment, which was continually nurtured by Romero and his friends. While Maximilian's propaganda effort had too many chiefs and too little organization and coordination, the comparatively greater success awarded Romero's efforts was undoubtedly due to the favorable reception they found.[70]

From its inception, the European intervention in Mexico raised serious questions regarding its motivation and objectives. Understood as a French (European) maneuver to undercut United States cultural, economic, and political influence not only in Mexico but throughout Latin America, the intervention was also viewed as a

69. "Unos Mejicanos," "Desaire de los Estados Unidos a Maximiliano," March 20, 1865, in Reforma, Intervención y Imperio Colección, XXVIII-1, folder 6-7, Centro de Estudios de la Historia de México; "Estados Unidos," *Periódico Oficial del Gobierno Constitucional de la República Mexicana*, February 22, 1866; Degollado to Ministro de Negocios Exteriores, July 21, 1865, Luis García Pimental Papers, VII-1, folder 2-4, Centro de Estudios de Historia de México; and *Proceedings of a Meeting in Memory of Hon. Thomas Corwin*, 15-16.

70. For a full account of Maximilian's agents, see Frazer, "Maximilian's Propaganda Activities," 4-28. See also Romero to Ministro de Relaciones Exteriores, October 17, 1865, in Romero (comp.), *Correspondencia*, V, 700-703.

means of aiding the ideologically conservative Confederacy and of posing a general threat to liberal, republican governmental forms everywhere in the New World. While United States government leaders, the domestic opposition, and many Latin American leaders agreed that the French intervention must not be unchallenged, they often disagreed regarding the best means of challenging. Under Seward's leadership the United States refused to participate in any Pan-American movement, the countermove most favored by the Latin American states. Likewise, the Lincoln administration rejected any strong assertion of the Monroe Doctrine by name, insisting, however, that its principles would be maintained. The creation of numerous Monroe Doctrine leagues, or Mexican clubs, which succeeded in sending some material aid to Mexico, were also very successful in arousing public opinion in favor of a strong United States policy to remove the French and Maximilian. Upon assuming the throne in Mexico, Maximilian decided that the negative reaction to him in the United States was the product of a Juárez-government-sponsored press campaign. His counter-publicity campaign, although adequately funded, proved unavailing, suggesting that public sentiment was indeed overwhelmingly opposed to foreign intervention and/or monarchy in Mexico. The swelling anti-interventionist sentiment in the United States complicated the early Reconstruction years by intertwining a major but controversial foreign relations problem with the serious domestic disagreements.

VII *Untangling Two Wars: French Intervention During the Early Reconstruction Years, 1865–1867*

M OST HISTORIANS of the middle period view the French intervention in Mexico as a disruptive action, which Seward solved more or less smoothly and satisfactorily by removing the matter from contemporary domestic consideration, thus preventing a rupture in the domestic political system. For example, Hans Trefousse in his excellent book on the radicals asserted,

During the post-war years, the radicals' difference about foreign policy constituted a serious obstacle to Republican unity. The problems of Mexico, where the French had taken advantage of the disturbed conditions in North America to set up a puppet empire, might have caused a serious rift because of Winter Davis's and other extremists' insistence on strong measures had not Seward's skillful diplomacy contributed to Napoleon III's withdrawal from the Western Hemisphere. This left the Mexican liberals under Benito Juárez free to overthrow the Emperor Maximilian, so that further involvement in the republic's affairs became unnecessary.[1]

Still, many historians have noted that not all prewar expansionists were southern slaveholders; some were northern expansionists who looked to develop spheres of influence for American manufacturers

---

1. Hans L. Trefousse, *The Radical Republicans: Lincoln's Vanguard for Racial Justice* (New York, 1969), 451–52.

and traders in Mexico, Central America, and elsewhere. Walter LaFeber and Ernest Paolino have argued that Seward revealed a compelling interest in Mexico and Central America, derived from his desire to control the transit rights which were so vital to his vision of commercial empire with Asia. "Further involvement" in Mexico may have been "unnecessary," but it did occur in political, ideological, and economic matters.[2]

In mid-1865, after Lincoln's assassination, political factors suggested that Mexico's problems would receive prompt, friendly attention. First, Congressman John Conness of California, previously a vocal opponent of strong action toward France, announced his intention to support Romero. More important, however, Romero expected that President Johnson would favor active support for the Liberals. In July, 1865, with illness limiting his personal contacts, Johnson met with Romero. After discussing the whole range of problems relevant to French intervention in Mexico, Romero, deeply impressed, summarized his "deep satisfaction" with Johnson's remarks as follows: "He will not approve Seward's policy. Seward will have to change his conduct, submitting himself to Johnson's ideas which will be, no doubt, the genuine defense of the Monroe Doctrine."[3] This was to prove a false hope.

Romero's personal interviews with the president occurred so frequently and without the secretary of state's official knowledge that on July 26, 1865, Seward found it necessary to chastise Romero's action in a circular to the Diplomatic Corps. Calling attention in the "Romero" circular to certain "irregularities," Seward

---

2. Rembert W. Patrick, *Reconstruction of the Nation* (New York, 1967), 202–203; Paolino, *Foundations of the American Empire*, 20–21, 29, 105, 128–29, 145, 204–205; Walter LaFeber, *The New Empire: An Interpretation of American Expansion, 1860–1898* (Ithaca, N.Y., 1963), 1–59; Williams, *Roots of the American Empire*; van Alstyne, *The Rising American Empire*; Michael Webster, "Texan Manifest Destiny and the Mexican Border Conflict, 1865–1880" (Ph.D. dissertation, Indiana University, 1972); and David M. Pletcher, *Rails, Mines, and Progress: Seven American Promoters in Mexico, 1867–1911* (Ithaca, N.Y., 1958).

3. Romero to Ministro de Relaciones Exteriores, May 2, 1865, in Romero (comp.), *Correspondencia*, V, 328–29; Romero to Ministro de Relaciones Exteriores, July 8, 1865, in Correspondencia General con los Estados Unidos; and Perkins, *Monroe Doctrine*, 471, quoting from Johnson's Nashville address of June 10, 1864.

suggested that foreign diplomats accredited to the United States observe the same regulations and courtesies that United States diplomats observe in their countries. Seward pointed out that the president would receive diplomats accredited to him only on ceremonial occasions, and that diplomats not accredited to the president should conduct their negotiations with the secretary of state. Romero observed that the circular "appears to be directed exclusively at me."[4]

Although Seward left no record of further dissatisfaction over Romero's conduct, Romero continued to meet Johnson privately, if perhaps more discreetly. Indeed, the "Romero" circular appeared when Seward was uncertain that he could prevent the Grant-Romero-Schofield plan from committing the United States to action in Mexico which might produce war with France. Possibly, Seward became so assured of his dominance relative to United States policy that he no longer viewed the continued meetings as a threat. Long convinced that Seward would not permit Mexico the assistance which Romero believed it rightfully could expect, in September, 1865, Romero thought he detected a change in Seward's mind. Perhaps the secretary would adjust his position in order to justify his Mexican stand before an increasingly restless Congress and public opinion. Soon thereafter, when Seward defeated the Schofield mission to Mexico, Romero reverted to his earlier judgment of Seward, reporting that, since Johnson was under the influence of Seward, Mexico could expect no change in policy.[5]

While the administration saw no need for urgent, strong action in Mexico, plainly other leaders in the United States saw danger in the French intervention, often speculating upon the need for United States intervention. In mid-1865 elder statesman Francis P. Blair, Sr., expressed to President Johnson his concern about the "fate of Republican Institutions throughout the continent and pos-

4. State Department Circular, July 26, 1865, and Romero to Ministro de Relaciones Exteriores, July 30, 1865, in Correspondencia General con los Estados Unidos.

5. Romero to Ministro de Relaciones Exteriores, September 21, 1865, in Correspondencia General con los Estados Unidos; Romero to Juárez, November 30, 1865, in Archivo Juárez.

sibly beyond it." Of three great problems, Blair considered the "policy of permitting the potentates of Europe to plant a monarchy in the midst of our continent, to hold the key to the Isthmus—to open or shut the gate to the Ocean between our Atlantic and Pacific possessions and to array a great military power on both flanks of our Republic wielded by a despot," most serious for the United States' future.[6]

George Bancroft, addressing a joint meeting of the House and Senate on the anniversary of Lincoln's birthday in 1866, characterized Napoleon III's intervention in Mexico as a continual harassment to Lincoln and as more than merely a conflict between monarchy and republicanism. Focusing upon the tie between the Confederacy and the Mexican conservatives and the Republicans and the Mexican liberals, Bancroft designated the sources of conflict as "the bigoted system which was the legacy of monarchy" and "republican institutions." While problems stemming from slavery, monarchy, and the Catholic Church were elements of the conflict between systems, Bancroft located the root of disagreement much deeper in the systems. Bancroft explained:

It was seen that Mexico could not, with all its wealth of land, compete in cereal products with our Northwest, nor, in tropical products, with Cuba: nor could it, under a disputed dynasty, attract capital, or create public works, or develop mines, or borrow money; so that the imperial system of Mexico, which was forced at once to recognize the wisdom of the policy of the republic by adopting it, could prove only an unremunerating drain on the French treasury for the support of an Austrian adventurer.

Bancroft knew that the monarchical system could not provide the "progress" for Mexico which the laissez-faire liberal system of the Republican party or Juárez' party could.[7]

While recognizing that Napoleon III's conduct during the rebellion did not inspire confidence either in his wisdom or integrity, The *North American Review* argued that neither war with France nor

6. Blair to Johnson, July 28, 1865, in Blair Family Papers, box 2.
7. George Bancroft, "Speech to the Joint Session of Congress on Abraham Lincoln's Birthday," in *Congressional Globe*, 39th Cong., 1st Sess., 802–805.

American annexation of Mexico was a desired outcome of the intervention. Nevertheless, the editors could "not but feel how important it is to the interest and welfare of America to perpetuate democratic institutions on this continent, and to maintain a community of republics, united in principle and feeling. The advantages, not so apparent to this generation, are for the millions yet unborn." Since democracy and monarchy cannot grow together, at stake in the conflict were "Democratic institutions" and "principle and feeling."[8]

Hugh McCulloch, hopeful that the United States could avoid war with France over Mexico, feared that the army on the Rio Grande under Grant's orders might do something "imprudent." To McCulloch the acquisition of a protectorate would be a near calamity for the United States. Salmon Chase, pondering the French intervention in Mexico, wondered why "the French Emperor [has] anymore right to espouse one side of this purely Mexican quarrel than the American Republic has to espouse the other side? What objection then to sending fifty thousand American soldiers into Mexico, & say to Napoleon hands off on both sides! We won't interfere for Juárez if you don't interfere for Maximilian."[9]

Republican leader James G. Blaine also clearly recognized the conflict in world views brought out by Napoleon's invasion of Mexico. After all,

The success of the establishment of a Foreign Empire in Mexico would have been fatal to all that the United States cherished, to all that it hoped peacefully to achieve... it threatened the United States upon the most vital questions. It was at war with all our institutions and our habits of political life, for it would have introduced into a great country on this continent, capable of unlimited development, that curious and mischievous form of government, that perplexing mixture of absolutism and

8. Review of *Documents Relating to Mexican Affairs*, in *North American Review*, CII (April, 1866), 459, 469.

9. McCulloch to J. M. Forbes, February 1, 1866, in Hugh McCulloch Papers, Library of Congress; Hugh McCulloch, *Men and Measures of Half a Century: Sketches and Comments* (New York, 1889), 387; and Chase to Nettie Chase, May 19, 1866, in Salmon P. Chase Papers, Library of Congress.

democracy—imperial power supported by universal suffrage,—which seems certain to produce aggression abroad and corruption at home.

Blaine hypothesized that this bastard system "would have spread through Central America to the Isthmus, controlling all canal communications between the two oceans which are the boundaries of the Union, while its growth upon the Pacific Coast would have been in direct rivalry with the natural and increasing power of the United States." Blaine believed this rival power would have been not only a "constant menace to American Republics but a source of endless war and confusion between the great Powers of the world."[10] Firm, clearly conceived policy would avoid these dreadful future complications.

George E. Rush described the ideological nature of the Mexican conflict to Senator Sumner as "the great battle of Republicanism vs Imperialism." Noting that Mexico had been fighting this battle unaided for five years, Rush wanted the United States to offer a helping hand immediately. After the French withdrawal was announced, Democratic leader Samuel Cox expressed his hope that Mexico faced a bright future, to which Romero responded that "it would be both creditable and profitable" for the United States to lend aid to Mexico to brighten the future. Later, when word of the special Campbell-Sherman mission arrived in Veracruz, the United States consul in Constantinople, Edward Joy Morris, described the "great interest" and the "universal approbation" in the local press concerning the establishment of a United States protectorate in Mexico.[11]

After Maximilian's infamous October, 1865, decree condemning all who continued to resist the empire to immediate execution upon capture, Plumb, pointing out the barbarity of this decree, queried Sumner whether "many of us may have been mistaken in believing that Louis Napoleon would voluntarily withdraw from

10. Blaine, *Twenty Years of Congress*, I, 597–98.
11. George E. Rush to Sumner, January 29, 1867, in Sumner Papers; Romero to Cox, October 31, 1866, in Samuel S. Cox Papers, Brown University Library; and Morris to Seward, November 17, 1866, in Seward Papers.

Mexico." Although sharing Sumner's desire to avoid another war, Plumb wondered if strong action in support of besieged Latin American countries might not be the best way to avoid war:

Has not in fact the time come when in behalf of our own dignity as the great exemplar of free government and for the protection of our weaker sister Republics who have remained faithful to us through our long and difficult struggle and who would at any time have joined us as our allies, who are now menaced Mexico by France, and Peru and Chile by Spain under the inspiration of Louis Napoleon, has not the time come for us to rise up and say in all our dignity and strength these things shall no longer be? The Republics of this Continent shall no longer be interfered with by the Powers of Europe? In fine is not such immediate and *determined* self assertion the *surest* means of avoiding war? [12]

Plumb developed the comparative thesis that, since the South wrongly took up arms to defeat Lincoln, and since the conservatives and their European allies improperly took up arms to defeat Juárez, it was as necessary for the United States to insist upon recognizing only the constitutional authority of Juárez in Mexico, as to insist that the South recognize the constitutional authority of Lincoln. [13]

Plumb, interpreting the whole past conflict within Spanish American society as an ideological battle, found that "all Spanish America, free from that curse [slavery] long before we were, ranged themselves on the side of the Union and held out their hands in a grasp of fraternal sympathy with the great republican party of the North. . . . The whole struggle in these Spanish American countries since their independence instead of being chronic anarchy has been, I believe, simply the one great issue of progress battling for its advance with retrogression holding it back, of liberty under republicanism seeking to establish itself in place of the institutions and moral despotism of the past." [14] Thus, in mid-1866, Plumb strongly supported a loan to Juárez' government because it would

12. Plumb to Sumner, October 26, 1865, in Plumb Papers. See also Ramsey to Seward, November 14, 1865, in Seward Papers.
13. Plumb to Sumner (same to Banks), January 3, 1866, in Plumb Papers.
14. Plumb to Sumner, July 26, 1867, in Plumb Papers.

be used to pay foreign and United States claims against Mexico, it would revive commerce diverting it from European to United States hands, and it would maneuver financial control of Spanish-American affairs toward the United States, and, finally, by encouraging peace south of the Rio Grande, it would remove Mexican affairs as "a dangerous element in our own politics."[15] The loan would free Mexico from foreign influences and open it to United States activity.

In a mid-1866 editorial series written for the New York *Herald*, later collected and published as a pamphlet, George Church speculated that Napoleon intended to unite the aristocratic South with his newly constructed monarchical Mexico. Since the French intervention in Mexico was related to the southern rebellion, Church noted that the interlacing of Mexican and southern fate would grant France access to its own cotton supply and a near monopoly of the world's cotton supply. Monarchical Europe's constant scheming to weaken republican governments provided a basic motive of self interest to justify United States intervention. However, Church also found positive reasons to encourage United States intervention in favor of the Liberals, even to the point of war: "The nation that lives entirely for itself can make but a poor mark in the history of the world, and the jingle of its money bags will scarcely throw its echoes so far into the future as would the broad policy of protection to human progress." Having fought long and hard to preserve New World liberal institutions, Mexican Liberals, in Church's opinion, deserved United States aid now.[16] Later, with the French withdrawn and Maximilian executed, Church advocated a United States policy to encourage Mexico's progress, but otherwise a course which would "let her alone."[17]

Viewing the contest as more than one of conflicting governmental forms, the *Chicago Tribune* observed religion's role in

15. Memorandum, enclosed in Plumb to Banks, May 9, 1866, in Plumb Papers.

16. George E. Church, *Mexico: Its Revolutions; Are They Evidence of Retrogression or of Progress?* (New York, 1866), 70–84.

17. Church to Banks, July 27, 1867, in Banks Papers.

Mexico, concluding that "with him [Maximilian] falls the influence and power of the priesthood in Mexico—an influence and power that have been steadily used to degrade the people, and to keep them in a condition of the most abject ignorance and superstition. It may be that the prospect of the progress of Mexico under any government is sufficiently dubious—under that of her priesthood it would be hopeless." Insisting upon the inter-relationship of the French intervention in Mexico to the southern rebellion, the *Chicago Tribune* further asserted that if the rebellion had succeeded, so would Napoleon's venture in Mexico. When the rebellion failed, "Napoleon would be compelled to abandon his undertaking, for he well knew that with the Union restored, the United States would never consent to see a monarchy set up by foreign bayonets, on this continent."[18] Despite the bravado, North Americans recognized the danger inherent in a combination of refugee Rebel and Franco-Mexican power.

Beginning in 1864, several colonization schemes attracted southerners to Mexico, generating friction between the Union government and the Franco-Mexican empire and encouraging the belief in a tie between the Confederacy and Maximilian's empire. The first and most prominent project was developed in 1862 by Dr. William Gwin for colonizing the northern and western states of Sonora, Sinaloa, and Baja California. After previously approaching Napoleon, Gwin submitted his plan to Maximilian's consideration in January, 1864. Anticipating Maximilian's approval, Gwin left Paris for Mexico in mid-1864. Stopping in Havana, he discussed his plans and goals at length with Confederate minister to Mexico William Preston, alleging considerable support from Napoleon. From Mexico, Confederate agent Émile la Sère reported that the success of Gwin's plan depended upon attracting a sizable immigration of southern sympathizers from California and upon instituting "our system," implying some variation of slavery.[19]

18. "Maximilian and the Rebellion," *Chicago Tribune*, June 13, 1867.
19. Gwin to Maximilian, January 5, 1864, in Archiv Maximilian, reel 10; Preston to Davis, June 28, 1864 (private), in Records of the Confederate States of America, Vol. VII,

In mid-1865 Romero furnished the Union government with some intercepted Gwin correspondence in an effort to persuade the Johnson cabinet to apply force in Mexico. Romero was overly optimistic, however. At the June 16, 1865, cabinet meeting, Grant's suggestion to take "decisive measures," received little support. Seward opposed such action vigorously, prompting Welles to remark in his diary, "Seward acts from intelligence, Grant from impulse."[20] Seward speculated that Gwin's activities in Sonora "forebode even more inconvenience to whatever government may exist in Mexico than of ultimate harm to our own country."[21]

After several meetings, the cabinet decided that the United States minister to France should inform the French government that Gwin's plan was "a danger or, at least, a menace to the United States." Furthermore, "the President of the United States sees himself obliged to deduce that His Majesty, the Emperor of the French, follows in these Mexican matters a policy which is materially in disaccordance with the neutrality that he promised to observe at the beginning of the war with regard to the political institutions of that country." Finally, the United States minister should assure the French government that, having defeated the insurgents north of the Rio Grande, the United States did not care to see them "reorganizing in the condition of military and political enemies of the Union, on the opposite bank." Since the charge was based upon unofficial documents of doubtful character, the French refused to respond, only repeating the previous declaration of maintaining a scrupulous and impartial neutrality in regard to all questions which might agitate or divide the United States.[22]

Pt. 1; and La Sère to Benjamin, July 22, 1864, in Pickett Papers. For a different view of Gwin's role, see Joseph A. Stout, Jr., "The Last Years of Manifest Destiny: Filibustering in Northwestern Mexico, 1848–1862" (Ph.D. dissertation, Oklahoma State University, 1971), 165, 171–73, 180, 184–86.

20. Romero to Juárez, June 26, 1865, in Archivo Juárez; Beale (ed.), *Diary of Gideon Welles*, II, 317; McCulloch, *Men and Measures of Half a Century*, 387–88.

21. Seward to Dayton, September 15, 1864, in U.S. Department of State, *Foreign Relations of the United States, 1864*, Pt. 3, p. 146.

22. Romero to Ministro de Relaciones Exteriores, November 16, 1861, in Romero (comp.), *Correspondencia*, I, 597–98; Callahan, *American Policy in Mexican Relations*, 298–99,

Although many judged Gwin's plan to be a Confederate or a French plot, the plan never obtained the official approval of the French government; nor was it ever officially submitted to the South. Napoleon III contemplated acquiring those northern areas of Mexico as part payment of the debt Maximilian owed to France. The French scheme called for encouraging discharged French or foreign soldiers to settle and exploit Mexico's northern states, thus forming a solid military wall blocking possible United States aggression against Maximilian. Correctly judging that any alienation of Mexican territory would destroy his chances of ever being accepted by a majority of the Mexican people, Maximilian refused to coalesce with Napoleon's plan.[23] Rumors of Napoleon's plan to acquire northern Mexico naturally disturbed North American opinion.

Other schemes for colonizing in Mexico developed among the defeated Confederates. Matthew F. Maury was appointed imperial commissioner of colonization, with Sterling Price, Isham Harris, John Perkins, and W. T. Hardeman as his subordinates. Although the various former Confederate agricultural settlements were allegedly conceived to aid Maximilian against possible United States aggression, or to form a base for eventual reinvasion of the South, Maximilian denied both allegations. Normally, Maximilian refused to accept former Confederates in the imperial army, although the settlements were permitted small self-defense militia units. For the most part, the ex-Confederates quickly accepted Maximilian's decision. Other rumored projects involving southerners indicated that they might acquire control of key areas in Mexico, such as

305–306; J. Fred Rippy, "Mexican Projects of the Confederates," *Southwestern Historical Quarterly*, XXII (April, 1919), 312–15; John Bigelow to Edward Drouyn de Lhuys, August 1, 1865, in Tamayo (ed.), *Juárez Documentos*, X, 62–63; and Drouyn de Lhuys to Bigelow, August 7, 1865, in Luis Orozco (ed.), *Maximiliano y la restitución de la esclavitud en México* (Mexico: Secretaría de Relaciones Exteriores, 1961), XIII, 78–79. For the objections of one of Maximilian's agents, see José Hidalgo to the Ministro de Estado, April 30, 1864, in Tamayo (ed.), *Juárez Documentos*, VIII, 810–11.

23. William Corwin to Seward, August 29, 1864, July 11, 1865, and July 22, 1865 (confidential), in Diplomatic Dispatches, Mexico, RG 59, NA; and Romero to Ministro de Relaciones Exteriores, June 24, 1865, in Romero (comp.), *Correspondencia*, V, 401–408.

the Tehuantepec Isthmus, or the silver mining area around Zacatecas.[24] The instability of Maximilian's regime, the difficulty of financing the trip to Mexico, the scarcity of reliable information about the Mexican settlements, the weariness after four years at war, the dislike for the French venture (many southerners believed in a rather strong interpretation of the Monroe Doctrine) explained the lack of interest shown by southerners in these former Confederate settlements.[25]

In the early postwar months, many Confederates wanted to believe that the United States and the Franco-Mexican or British forces would clash, thereby offering the South either a chance to rise again or to bargain for a more acceptable peace settlement. Plumb alerted Banks in January, 1866, that "in Mexico rebel traitors in concert with foreign enemies have taken up arms to resist and expel Benito Juárez the Constitutionally elected President of the whole Republic," pointing out the similarity between this southern plan and their earlier efforts to oust Lincoln. An imperial report on a colony of former Confederates near Durango, Mexico, observed that they were well armed and mounted and "in a case of emergency, would be very useful to the Government of the Department." Some former Confederates like Jubal Early, a lieutenant-general in Robert E. Lee's army, journeyed to Mexico after the Civil War ended "to ascertain if there was any prospect of a war between Mexico and France on the one side and the United States on the other, and to go into it if there was." However, discovering Maximilian's weak support among Mexicans, and the empire's dependence upon French troops to survive, Early immediately recognized no prospect for war existed and departed. After arriving in Havana, he wrote an open letter warning other

24. Blumberg, *The Diplomacy of the Mexican Empire*, 76–79; Hanna and Hanna, *Napoleon III and Mexico*, 221–35; Sheridan to Steele, July 24, 1865, in Philip H. Sheridan Papers, box 2, Library of Congress; and Arturo Suarez Farrens to M. F. Maury, February 6, 1865, in Maury Papers.

25. Hanna, "The South in Mexico," 16–21; Zorrilla, *Relaciones*, I, 441–45; Jack Aubrey Dabbs, *The French Army in Mexico, 1861–1867* (The Hague, 1963), 135–42; William Corwin to Seward, August 25, 1865, in Diplomatic Dispatches, Mexico, RG 59, NA.

unreconciled Rebels that Mexico was not the starting point for a continuation of the contest. Although hopes and rumors persisted for a long time, within a year most Rebels realized that the conflict would not be reopened.[26]

Nevertheless, the United States government, aware that the hostile exiles were potential allies for the French and Maximilian, announced that it would hold those authorities permitting the entrance of Confederate refugees into Mexico responsible for their action. Since the Rebels might join the imperial forces to make war upon the United States, the Johnson administration was naturally concerned about having enough troops near the border. In November, 1865, Seward requested information on the number of troops that could be transferred west of the Mississippi in an emergency. To prevent hostilities with the United States while avoiding conflict with the defeated Rebels, both the Juárez government and the French-Maximilian authorities permitted former Confederates entrance into the country, provided they disarmed and followed a peaceful course.[27]

Although neither the military dreams nor the colonizing effort of the Confederates proved successful, in late 1866 Mexican land was transferred to the long-term occupation of the United States. The course of the Rio Grande changed, moving the Chamizal district, previously part of Paso del Norte, to the Texas side of the river, while also shifting a small piece of Texas to the Mexican side. Both areas were claimed and defended by Texans. For over one hundred years, however, the Chamizal remained Texas territory until returned to Mexico in 1968.[28]

26. Plumb to Banks, January 3, 1866, in Banks Papers, box 62; "Conway's Report on the Palacio Colony" [early 1866], in Maury Papers; Early to Goode, June 8, 1866, and Early to J. C. Reynolds, December 11, 1867, in Jubal A. Early Papers, Duke University; and James Spence to Mason, June 16, 1865, in Mason Papers. See also Sheridan to Grant, February 7, 1866, in Sheridan Papers, box 4.

27. A. H. Cañedo to P. J. Osterhaus, June 4, 1865, Grant to Johnson, June 19, 1865, in *Official Records*, Vol. XLVIII, Pt. 2, pp. 771, 923–24; Grant to Seward, November 10, 1865, in *Official Records*, Series 3, V, 489–90.

28. Luis Terrazas to Lerdo de Tejada, October 31, 1866, enclosed with Lerdo de Tejada to Romero, December 5, 1866, in Correspondencia General con los Estados Unidos;

Mexican imperial expansionism, aimed at Central America, also attracted United States diplomatic attention. In 1866, a Liberal Mexican agent in Central America reported that conservative agents in Guatemala were attempting to create support among the municipalities in favor of the Mexican empire and in favor of annexation by that regime, but with only limited success due to internal Guatemalan opposition. In early 1868, to crown the defeat of the conservative ideology, Lorenzo Montúfar, one of the most renowned nineteenth-century Central American liberal thinkers, publicists, and politicians, proposed combining the forces of dissident, separatist regions within Guatemala, the liberal followers of the recently executed former president of El Salvador, Gerardo Barrios, liberal Minister of State Tomás Ayón's followers in Nicaragua, and Mexico's victorious Liberal army. Montúfar's conclusion revealed the strength of his attachment to liberalism, as he suggested that Mexico might annex his country, Guatemala, afterwards, but he pleaded: "Do not call me a traitor for suggesting this idea. I am not. Mexico is not a foreign country for me, and I much rather desire that my country form a part of Mexico than to see it submitted to the Jesuits and managed by foreigners. The Neapolitans were not traitors in uniting themselves to the great Kingdom of Italy. Neither were the Romans who wished that their birth place be united to Italy and not a victim of the Pope and the French."[29] In response to internal conservative factions and Maximilian's influence, victorious Mexican Liberals and some Central American liberals considered a joint Mexican–Central American attack upon the remaining entrenched power center of conser-

Caleb Cushing to Robert MacClelland, November 11, 1866, Seward to Romero, February 5, 1867, Romero to Seward, February 6, 1867, all enclosed with Romero to Ministro de Relaciones Exteriores, February 6, 1867, in Correspondencia General con los Estados Unidos. See the New York *Times*, October 29, 1968, for a full story of the transfer of El Chamizal region back to Mexico.

29. Luis Abela to Romero, May 7, 1866, October 4, 1866, in Archivo Romero; Fitz Henry Warren to Seward, August 16, 1867, in U.S. Department of State, *Foreign Relations of the United States, 1867*, Pt. 2, p. 290; Lorenzo Montúfar to Romero, February 10, 1868, in Archivo Romero; and Plumb to Seward, May 10, 1867, in Plumb Collection.

vatism, Guatemala. At times, the overriding attraction of the total liberal world view submerged the subordinate nationalism.

While United States diplomats followed rumors of Maximilian's expansion into Central America closely, the United States–French tension in the post–Civil War years derived primarily from the aggressive, vigorous actions of the United States military along the Rio Grande border. The United States forces, strongly opposed to the French intervention, often called for direct military action against the French. Many generals calling for action were citizen-soldiers, such as John Logan, Lewis Wallace, and Frank Blair, Jr. However, key figures among the professional army high command, such as Ulysses S. Grant, Philip Sheridan, John Schofield, and Winfield Scott Hancock, all possessing national if not international reputation as soldiers, also condemned the continued presence of a large French force in Mexico.

Seward asked United States Minister to France John Bigelow to enlighten the French government regarding the dangers inherent in the United States–French confrontation along the border. Since "owing to the popular character of our government, our national policy is not adopted from the choice of any President or any particular administration," Seward wanted the French to understand that "every important or cardinal policy is a result of the determination of the national will." Moreover, Seward asserted that policy formed in this manner "has been found to be essential to the safety and welfare of the Union." Since the Civil War, popular opinion had turned strongly to Mexican affairs and insisted upon the termination of foreign intervention, a disturbing development in the light of the "military forces of the two nations, sometimes confronting each other across the border."[30] Here was a clear, pointed indica-

---

30. Seward to Bigelow, September 6, 1865, in U.S. Department of State, *Foreign Relations of the United States, 1865*, Pt. 3, pp. 412–14; and Charles Byron Blackburn, "Military Opposition to Official State Department Policy Concerning the Mexican Intervention, 1862–1867" (Ph.D. dissertation, Ball State University, 1969). On suspicion of French reliability, see Joseph A. Wright to Seward, November 15, 1865, in *Foreign Relations of the United States, 1865*, Pt. 1, pp. 67–68.

tion to the French that the border problems would bode ill for future United States–French relations.

General Grant was, perhaps, the most outspoken among the soldier-critics. But *Harper's Weekly*, noting the spreading unrest and dissatisfaction with the French presence in the months after the Civil War, cautioned against the strong aggressive stance proposed by Grant and others who argued that if France did not voluntarily withdraw it should be forced out. *Harper's Weekly* editors feared Grant's stand offered the Rebels an opportunity to revive opposition, adding that the presence of a European power in Mexico was not such a serious matter, since after all, the British were in Jamaica and Canada and the Spanish in Cuba.[31]

Interpreting the French intervention as part of the rebellion and as an act of war by France against the United States, Grant argued that as soon as the rebellion terminated north of the Rio Grande, the United States army should move south to finish the other half of the conflict. Grant proposed notifying Napoleon that if he did not immediately withdraw his forces, United States troops would aid the Liberals in ousting the French and their allies from Mexico. In July, 1865, Grant wrote President Johnson that viewing "the French occupation of Mexico as part and parcel of the late rebellion in the United States, and a necessary part of it to be suppressed before entire peace can be assured," a general officer should be given leave to serve in Mexico. In other correspondence Grant detailed the record of cooperation and coordination between the French and the Confederacy and sketched the future dangers threatening the United States, if it did not immediately compel the French to depart.[32] Grant ordered General Schofield on a mission to the border area, ostensibly to inspect troops but in reality to prepare for leading a private army of former Union and Confeder-

---

31. "Our Continental Duty," and "Our French Relations," *Harper's Weekly*, IX (August 26 and November 18, 1865), 530, 722; *Chicago Tribune*, December 1, 1865; and Blackburn, "Military Opposition."

32. Grant to Johnson, June 19 and July 15, 1865, and September 1, 1865, in *Official Records*, Vol. XLVIII, Pt. 2, pp. 923–24, 1080–81, and 1221.

ate soldiers to Juárez' aid. Although admitting he would prefer to avoid war altogether if possible, Grant preferred fighting now rather than in the future.[33]

Desirous of achieving French withdrawal from Mexico by diplomatic pressure, and aware that influential people opposed his course of action, Seward acted circumspectly and skillfully in separating Schofield from the Wallace-Romero-Grant plan for joint United States–Mexican military expedition against the French. Possibly Seward's persuasive arguments in the cabinet more tellingly undermined the plan to send a volunteer force to Mexico than his diversion of Schofield to Paris. Willing to accept a volunteer force only with the official approval of the United States government, the Mexican government insisted upon a guaranty of its independence, democratic institutions, and republican form of government.[34] Thus, when Seward successfully persuaded the cabinet to reject Grant's suggestion for forceful action, the possibility of large-scale troop movements to Mexico became remote. Not unexpectedly, Romero, Grant, and their allies continued their search for ways to compel a forceful United States policy.

After Seward offered him the diplomatic mission, Schofield considered himself faced with "the responsibility of deciding the momentous question of future friendship or enmity between my own country and our ancient ally and friend." Closer to the truth, Schofield's account also reflects something he never understood clearly—the struggle for power that was taking place around him.

33. Grant to Sheridan, July 25, 1865, in Sheridan Papers, box 64. See also the "Field Dispatch and Telegram Book, 1864–1871," and Sheridan to Grant, November 5, 1865, in Sheridan Papers, boxes 55 and 39. On Austrian concern about possible United States–Mexican imperial conflict, see Wydenbruck to Comte Mensdorff, October 30 and November 2, 1866, in Vereinigte Staaten, carton 21, Politisches Archiv, Haus-, Hof- und Staatsarchiv, Austrian Staatsarchiv; Lago to Comte Mensdorff, November 28, 1866, Lago to Baron de Beust, December 28, 1866, and Baron von Magnus to Graf Otto von Bismarck, March 17, and 28, 1867, in Mexiko, carton 11, Politisches Archiv.

34. Lerdo de Tejada to Romero, March 29, 1865, in Romero (comp.), *Correspondencia*, VI, 121–23; Romero to Juárez, April 27, 1865, in Archivo Juárez; John M. Schofield, "The Withdrawal of the French from Mexico," *Century Illustrated Magazine*, New Series XXXII (May-October, 1897), 128–37; Romero to Ministro de Relaciones Exteriores, August 4, 1865, in Correspondencia General con los Estados Unidos; and Van Deusen, *Seward*, 489–90.

Romero and Grant wanted Schofield to accept a field command to oust the French, while Seward preferred as an alternative solution for Schofield to accept the diplomatic mission so that the military project could be sidetracked.[35] Seward's plan carried the day.

Nevertheless, to persuade Napoleon of the seriousness of the United States attitude toward the unsettled Mexican conflict, Grant ordered General Sheridan and nearly 100,000 men to move to the Texas-Mexican border. Acting without specific instructions from the president, Grant communicated his directions to Sheridan in both written and verbal forms, with the verbal instructions best revealing his purpose behind sending the troops to the border. Desiring to oust the French if they did not withdraw on their own, and unwilling to risk a reversal in policy, Grant urged Sheridan's command to move to the Rio Grande "before they could be stopped." Once the troops arrived they would act under secret, verbal instructions rather than written, public orders.[36]

After learning about projects of former Confederates to attract immigrants to Mexico, Grant's fellow soldier and subordinate Major General Philip H. Sheridan argued: "I have for some time believed that we never can have a fully restored Union, and give a total and final blow to all malcontents, until the French leave Mexico." Sheridan summed up well his and Grant's views when he wrote: "I sometimes think there is still an understanding between the rebels of the Southern States and Louis Napoleon. That such understanding did exist before the surrender of Lee there is no doubt. The contest in this country for the last four years was the old contest between absolutism and liberalism, and Louis Napoleon saw it, and acted on it, but waited too long."[37] Part of the mutual

35. John Schofield, *Forty-Six Years in the Army* (New York, 1897), 382–83.

36. Ulysses S. Grant, *Personal Memoirs* (2 vols.; New York, 1892), II, 545–46; Philip H. Sheridan, *Personal Memoirs of P. H. Sheridan: General United States Army* (2 vols.; New York, 1888), II, 210–28; Charles A. Dana and James H. Wilson, *The Life of Ulysses S. Grant, General of the Armies of the United States* (Springfield, Mass., 1868), 377–78; and *Chicago Tribune*, December 1, 1865.

37. Sheridan to Grant, November 5 and 26, 1865, in *Official Records*, Vol. XLVIII, Pt. 2, pp. 1252–53, 1258. See also Sheridan to Grant, August 1, 1865, in *Official Records*, Vol. XLVIII, Pt. 2, pp. 1147–48.

attractiveness between Grant and Sheridan on one hand, and the radicals on the other, was their similarity of analysis on the broad significance and implications of France's Mexican policy.

Shortly after arriving at the border, Sheridan began to gather specific charges against the imperial forces in Mexico. After the surrender of Confederate commander E. Kirby Smith, all remaining Rebel war material in Texas became United States government property. Nevertheless, some of this material found its way into Mexico, and Sheridan knew who was responsible: "There is no doubt in my mind that the representatives of the Imperial Government along the Rio Grande have encouraged this wholesale plunder of property belonging to the U.S. Govt. and that it will only be given up when we go and take it." Additionally, his subordinates reported the French as being "saucy and insulting" to Americans. Scrupulously returning any material from Mexican Liberals that improperly fell into his hands, Sheridan clearly wanted to harass the "French-Mexicans" as much as possible short of war. For example, Sheridan instructed General Frederick Steele, commander at Brownsville, to "annoy the French authorities as much as you can through others without provoking actual hostilities or without making it too apparent." On another occasion he warned Steele: "Don't come to any actual hostilities but annoy those people—I mean the Franco-Mexicans, as their present manner and their past conduct in their dealing with and assistance to the rebels is and has been infamous."[38] Sheridan was slowly gathering information which would justify future military action against the empire.

In early July, 1865, Sheridan, disturbed by the state of affairs along the Mexican border, ordered troops placed in condition for active service. Sheridan's constant aggressive posture toward the Franco-imperialist forces perhaps prompted a subordinate, General Weitzel, to inquire in late 1865: "Am I authorized to commence

38. Sheridan to Grant, June 28, 1865, in Banks Papers, box 60; and Sheridan to Steele, July 7 and 13, 1865, and Steele to Sheridan, July 14, 1865, in Sheridan Papers, box 2.

hostilities in case force is attempted to be used with American citizens?" Weitzel was disturbed when a forced loan was levied among North Americans to sustain French interests. Sheridan decided other solutions than war were available.[39]

Throughout the summer of 1865, Sheridan maintained that Seward's policy weakened Juárez' legitimate government in Mexico, while strengthening Maximilian's illegitimate government. On several occasions, Sheridan privately expressed his fear that the United States was about to extend recognition to Maximilian's government just when the Liberals were "in better condition than at any other period since the advent of Maximilian." Certainly the improved condition of the Liberals was not due to Seward's policy, but rather to the policy of Grant and Sheridan. To counter Seward's policy and apply psychological pressure upon the French in Mexico, Sheridan stopped at San Antonio to review and prepare troops as if about to undertake a campaign; then he headed for the border escorted by a cavalry regiment. While on the border, he opened communications with Juárez, "taking care not to do this in the dark, and the news, spreading like wildfire, the greatest significance was ascribed to my action." Sheridan encouraged the rumors that he intended to cross the Rio Grande and aid the Liberals by openly inquiring about forage and food in northern Mexico and by ordering a pontoon train moved to Brownsville. In coordination with his action near San Antonio, Sheridan renewed complaints and threats near Brownsville. Using the alleged mistreatment of a black United States citizen near Matamoros, Sheridan ordered steps taken which could be interpreted either as a reaction to the mistreatment of Americans or as preparations for a campaign. No courtesies were to be exchanged with General Mejía's forces, no supplies of any kind were to cross to Matamoros, and Sheridan warned Mejía "that if this occurs again I will not accept excuses for

39. Sheridan to Merritt, July 5, 1865 (confidential), Weitzel to C. H. Whillesey, December 27, 1865, and Sheridan to H. G. Wright, January 19, 1866, in Sheridan Papers, box 4. See also Enrique Mejía to Romero, December 21, 1865, in Ulysses S. Grant Papers, Library of Congress.

such conduct; that he [Mejía] will not be permitted to commit acts against the United States which are no accident and expect our government to accept personal apologies for his bad faith." Sheridan sought to encourage and sustain Juárez by conveniently leaving surplus arms and munitions where Liberals could find them. When the French fell back toward Monterrey, Sheridan assumed his ominous activity had compelled the retreat.[40] Thus, Sheridan implemented a hostile policy toward the French-Mexican imperialists which he, Grant, and many other professional soldiers considered appropriate, indeed obligatory.

In the fall of 1865, Sheridan described for Grant the relationship between the rebellion and Napoleon's conduct as a conflict between "Absolutism and Liberalism." Responding to a query from another friend, Sheridan denied that the Mexican matter was a hobby of his; rather he reiterated his conviction that

We never will have a restored union till the French leave Mexico and I have considered this so important that I have thought the government should have demanded their withdrawal. The occupation of Mexico was a blow at republican institutions, a blow at our country, and if they are allowed to remain the malcontents of the South who love any flag better than the old flag, will be an element of strength for France in our midst, which will be more dangerous than the Copperheads of the North during the struggle just gone by. . . . it is not their [Mexico's Liberals'] quarrel alone but ours too. Not their safety but ours also in time to come.

Claiming four years of fighting was enough, Sheridan nevertheless cautioned against allowing the United States to "waver until the Rebellion is ended."[41] For Sheridan, as for Grant, the French intervention was intertwined with the rebellion.

Sheridan not only despised Seward's handling of the Mexican question but felt a deep sense of frustration at the course of events. Writing to a subordinate officer in late 1866, Sheridan acknowl-

40. Sheridan, *Memoirs*, II, 214–17; Sheridan to Grant, September 26 and 28, 1865 (private) in Sheridan Papers, box 3; and Blackburn, "Military Opposition," 117–19, 169–70.
41. Sheridan to Grant, November 5, December 23, 1865, Sheridan to Weitzel, December 23, 1865, and Sheridan to Nesmith, December 14, 1865, in Sheridan Papers, boxes 3 and 39; and Sheridan, *Memoirs*, II, 217.

edged that he had been impatiently urging a hard policy toward French intervention in Mexico for eighteen months. Disgusted, Sheridan noted that "Seward . . . perhaps saw the same thing but wanted to get some diplomatic glory and entered into an understanding with Louis Napoleon" to withdraw the French forces in installments. Sheridan found the State Department methods very slow: "In truth, it was often very difficult to restrain officers and men from crossing the Rio Grande with hostile purpose."[42]

In the fall of 1866, his patience worn thin, Sheridan informed General Sedgwick, commander at Brownsville, that the United States must not only support the legitimate government in Mexico, the Liberals, but most also warn the usurping governments not to violate the neutrality between the United States and Mexico. Sheridan insisted that his instructions would be "enforced against the adherents of the Imperial Buccaneer representing the so-called Imperial Government of Mexico, and also against Ortega, Santa Anna and other factions." The publication of this Sheridan letter prompted Grant to recompose his letter of October 9, 1866, authorizing Sheridan's instructions to Sedgwick. Except for the word *Buccaneer* used to describe Maximilian, which Grant considered perhaps unnecessary since the French and Maximilian had decided to withdraw, Grant approved of Sheridan's letter.[43] During this fall crisis, Sheridan revealed his awareness of the commercial value of United States–Mexican border commerce. Hoping the government would support him in "restoring peace to our border and trade and commerce to our people," Sheridan estimated that trade would reach twelve million dollars yearly as soon as peace was restored.[44]

When several weeks later General Sedgwick ordered troops into Matamoros to protect American lives and property and to assist the

42. Sheridan, *Memoirs*, II, 215–17; Sheridan to Newhall, November 20, 1866, in Sheridan Papers, box 39.

43. Sheridan to Thomas W. Sedgwick, October 23, 1866, and Grant to Sheridan, October 31, 1866, in Sheridan Papers, box 39.

44. Sheridan to George K. Leet, November 14, 1866 (telegram), in Andrew Johnson Papers, Library of Congress.

Liberals, General Mariano Escobedo, Juárez commander in the area, interpreted Sedgwick's intrusion as unfriendly to Mexican Liberals. To ease the tension, Sheridan appeared in Brownsville a few days later to personally reassure Escobedo. Removing the offending general, Sheridan explained to Escobedo that he had ordered Sedgwick "to aid the legitimate authorities in case they solicited aid," which satisfied the Mexican general.[45] Until the French withdrew, Sheridan and Grant did all in their power to intimidate the Franco-Mexican forces and to aid the Juárez government. But other military groups in the United States were also organizing support for the Mexican Liberals.

Another projected military venture, involving the plan by Wallace, Romero, Johnson, and Grant to organize a corps under General Schofield's command, was undermined when Schofield decided to undertake Seward's proffered diplomatic mission in Paris in late 1865. Still, Wallace, Romero, and Grant continued privately to raise a military force to aid the Liberals. Wallace, Carvajal, and Sturm suggested a plan to send military colonists from the United States to Mexico, without causing an international incident. Land would be offered to United States settler-volunteers on the same basis that it was being offered to Mexican soldiers. Once over the border, carrying personal weapons and ammunition of course, these legitimate settler-volunteers would be organized to fight the French without technically violating United States neutrality. Then, when Schofield finally returned from Paris, an army would be in place along the Rio Grande, equipped, trained, and ready to move. General R. Clay Crawford was appointed to organize and drill the troops arriving in the Rio Grande valley. Acting indiscreetly, Crawford openly proclaimed his mission, hence attracting unwanted attention, generating rumors, and arousing suspicion. He also announced that General Grant and President Johnson had

45. Escobedo to Romero, December 1, 1866, in Archivo Romero; Escobedo to Juárez, December 6, 1866 (confidential), in Archivo Juárez; Sheridan to Grant, November 27, 1866 (telegram), and Stanton to Sheridan, November 30, 1866, in U.S. Department of State, *Foreign Relations of the United States, 1866*, Pt. 3, pp. 422–23.

ordered him to the frontier. Although Grant had approved of the private military force in principle, the publicity compelled him to declare that Crawford's activity was purely private in nature. On January 5, 1866, Crawford and nearly one thousand of his men crossed the Rio Grande, sacked the Mexican port of Bagdad, and were returned to Brownsville amidst a barrage of complaints regarding violated neutrality. Despite Crawford's indiscretions and his raid on Bagdad, the imperial newspapers reacted mildly to Crawford's frontier escapades. *El Mexicano*, pointing out that Crawford was a low character and a former Walker filibuster, avoided using his raid to excite a strong feeling against the United States.[46] Imperial policy towards Crawford's raid seems a good indication that the aggressive posture of Sheridan, Grant, and other United States military leaders had generated an attitude of respectful concern in French Marshal Bazaine's and Maximilian's governing councils.

Repudiated by the Romero-Grant group after his raid upon Bagdad, Crawford continued his planning and boasting for over a year, attempting on several occasions to raise a force to move into Mexico. But, since Crawford now operated without any contact with Romero's agents, issuing his proclamations anonymously, he was nearly impossible to control. At this time, Carvajal returned to the Rio Grande to assume command over the border volunteers and to establish a firm base for future operation. In the summer of 1866, Wallace made his way to Mexico with a shipload of military supplies, which was lost in part when his arrival at Matamoros coincided with a revolt against Carvajal. Persevering, nevertheless, Wallace went into the interior of Mexico in search of Juárez and his government. Finally locating Juárez, Wallace and a companion, sometime New York *Herald* correspondent George E. Church, negotiated for mining and land grants without success. Although

---

46. Miller, "Lew Wallace," 37–38, 41; and Wallace to Romero, November 24, 1865, in Wallace Papers; Lawrence Kip to Sheridan, January 21, 1866, in Sheridan Papers, box 4; and *El Mexicano*, January 28, 1866, p. 55.

Wallace was unsuccessful in his investment and exploitation ventures, the continued flow of arms into Mexico helped maintain a high level of tension between the United States and the Franco-Mexicans.[47]

In 1866 and 1867 the long pent-up reaction against French violation of the New World found expression in Congress. A simple proposal to lend limited financial support to United States manufacturers who wished to show at the Paris Exposition of 1867 met with a critical reaction in the Senate. Republican Senator James W. Grimes of Iowa proposed to amend the resolution requesting government funds and assistance so that no aid would be available until France assured the United States that all French troops would be withdrawn "from the just territorial jurisdiction of the Republic of Mexico." Senators Wade, Howard, and McDougall spoke strongly in favor of Grimes's amendment. Both Wade and McDougall based their objections in part upon the familiar framework of the worldwide contest, conservatism versus liberalism. McDougall, claiming to see the Holy Alliance at work behind France's action, clearly discerned "certain forces in Europe [determined] to subjugate Spanish America." Only after the French assured their eminent withdrawal could the influential commercial and manufacturing interests easily acquire sizable sums of government money and other assistance to support their attendance at the exposition.[48] Hostility to France was intense.

Seeking to relax the strains on United States–French relations, Seward frustrated and angered Romero by blocking any official or semiofficial aid to the Liberals. He further annoyed the Mexican minister when he carelessly became associated with an intrigue involving Santa Anna which appeared to be unfriendly to Juárez'

---

47. Navarro to Romero, April 2, 1867, in Archivo Romero; Miller, "Lew Wallace," 40–50; McKee, *"Ben-Hur" Wallace*, 100–113.
48. *Congressional Globe*, 39th Cong., 1st Sess. 3155–62 for the Senate debate referred to. But see also *Congressional Globe*, 39th Cong., 1st Sess., 126, 160–61, 187–88, 286, 359, 1371–75, 1390–1406, 3137–39, 3182–85, 3302, 3304–3306, 3521, and 39th Cong., 2nd Sess., 323–24.

government. This intriguing private plan to force the French out involved negotiations between Santa Anna and a leader of the Fenian movement, William Roberts. With Mexican agents following the various Santa Anna–Fenian meetings as closely as possible, Juan Baz, Mexican agent in New York, concluded that the Fenians would send ten thousand armed men to Mexico, if they could acquire a few thousand dollars. Juan Navarro, however, took the affair lightly, suggesting that it was a plan to fleece Santa Anna.[49]

Cruising through the Caribbean in January, 1866, to recover his strength after the strain of the Civil War and the near fatal attack upon him in April, 1865, Seward visited Santa Anna at St. Thomas. This brief visit complicated United States–Mexican relations in the summer of 1866, when Santa Anna came to the United States, allegedly at the request of Seward. Clearheaded observers warned the Johnson administration that, lacking authorization to speak for any faction in Mexico, Santa Anna and his secretary Gabor Naphegyi spoke for their own private interests. Santa Anna attempted to counter these denunciations with a personal letter to President Johnson explaining that although invited by "a distinguished member of Your Exs. Cabinet," his services had been refused by the representative of Republican Mexico. Then, while preparing to return to St. Thomas, three special invitations had arrived inviting him to mediate in Mexico's troubles. The invitations were "first, from the Clergy and conservative party... second from the Chief Military leaders that serve now under the Archduke Maximilian... and 3dly they come even from the Archduke himself." Preferring to return to St. Thomas rather than pursue a course which the United States did not approve of,

---

49. Romero to Juárez, March 3 and April 12, 1866, in Archivo Juárez; Romero to James W. Beekman, January 19, 1867, in James W. Beekman Papers, New York Historical Society; Juan Baz to Romero, September 26, 1866, Juan Navarro to Romero, September 27, 1866, in Archivo Romero; and Charles F. Adams to Seward, December 1, 1865, in U.S. Department of State, *Foreign Relations of the United States, 1866,* Pt. 1, p. 25. Brian Jenkins, *Fenians and Anglo-American Relations during Reconstruction* (Ithaca, N.Y., 1968), makes no mention of any Fenian relations with Santa Anna.

he sought United States advice regarding his response to these offers.[50]

Interestingly, the Santa Anna–Naphegyi scheme involved the appointment of John T. Pickett, former Confederate agent to Mexico, as general of division and Santa Anna's chief of staff. In return for $25,000 in bonds, $5,000 in gold before departing for Mexico, and $500 per month in paper currency, Pickett agreed to serve as political advisor, provided that Santa Anna "would receive the reins of Government from Maximilian," make a commercial treaty with the United States, and then cede Lower California and Sonora to the United States. Moreover, during this period, Pickett insisted that no alliances with European powers were to be negotiated and after the cession of territory, a constitutional convention would be called, followed by free elections, "it being distinctly provided that no attempt shall be made to establish the monarchical form of government." Before departing, Santa Anna proclaimed that he was being accompanied by "a responsible person who could at all times remind me of the views and wishes of the United States," and that his mission would advance "the interests of both the United States and Mexico."[51] The Santa Anna mission ended in failure. Compelled to leave the Veracruz area, Santa Anna sojourned to Sisal in the Yucatán peninsula, where Mexican agents seized him, apparently from a United States vessel. A stormy United States reaction was abated upon learning that no violation of the United States flag had occurred and that Santa Anna would not be shot but merely expelled from Mexico after serving a brief period in prison.

Whatever President Johnson's original point of view, he became convinced of a need for greater information regarding Mexican af-

50. Plumb to Caleb Cushing, October 1, 1866, in Caleb Cushing Papers, Library of Congress; Grant to Sheridan, October 9, 1866 (confidential), in Sheridan Papers, box 39; Henry Ward Poole to Seward, October 19, 1866, in Seward Papers; Santa Anna to Johnson, November 30, 1866, in Johnson Papers; and Oakah L. Jones, Jr., *Santa Anna* (New York, 1968), 144 ff.

51. Jones, *Santa Anna*, 144ff; a large body of documentation, in Pickett Papers, Volume 2, 9870–9942; and Manuel María de Meja to Romero, April 20, 1867, in Archivo Romero.

fairs. In late 1866, Johnson sent former Indiana governor Oliver Morton on a secret mission to "intimate informally to Louis Napoleon that it would be impossible for the administration to withstand the pressure of public opinion in America for the expulsion of these troops if their withdrawal was postponed much longer." Morton was to point out advantages of voluntarily withdrawing rather than facing an official demand. This message was not entrusted to either the United States minister in Paris or the French minister in Washington because it was designed to avoid possible embarrassment to the French government.[52]

In mid-1866, Johnson attempted to appoint Lewis D. Campbell of Ohio minister to Mexico. A friend of the president's, Campbell was selected primarily because of his support of Johnson's domestic politics. In addition, Campbell had occasionally expressed views on United States policy toward Mexico that were similar to Johnson's. In regard to Mexico, Campbell advised allowing Juárez to draw upon United States financial assistance for aid in ejecting Maximilian. Only if this course failed should the United States serve notice upon Napoleon to withdraw his troops. The United States needed a respite to reunite itself and gather its strength.[53] Although Campbell claimed the office was thrust upon him, already in April, 1866, he had requested Senator James Doolittle to take action to move his nomination through the Senate, or, at least, to have his nomination rejected for specific reasons.[54] From the beginning of his service Campbell gave numerous indications that his private affairs and his domestic obligations (illness in his family) might prevent his leaving the country.

Learning that Campbell had received instructions to depart for Mexico, Edward Lee Plumb sought Caleb Cushing's influence to help him win the post of secretary of legation. Successful in his

52. William Dudley Foulke, *Life of Oliver P. Morton* (2 vols.; Indianapolis, 1899), II, 457–58.

53. Campbell to Johnson, May 8, 1865, in Johnson Papers.

54. Campbell to Doolittle, April 25, 1866, in James Rood Doolittle Papers, Library of Congress.

effort, Plumb was commissioned on November 5, 1866, receiving instructions several days later directly from Seward in an interview, which, suggestive of the significance of Mexican affairs, was attended by General Grant, Attorney General Stansbury, Caleb Cushing, and General Thomas Ewing. Finally, in November, 1866, Campbell, Plumb, and General William T. Sherman were ready to depart on an important special mission intended to reestablish contact with Juárez' government, to oversee the promised partial withdrawal of French forces, and to impress the French with the seriousness with which the United States viewed Mexican matters. During the voyage to Mexico, Plumb conversed at length with Sherman. The general's assertion that "a Monarchy would have been better for Mexico" prompted Plumb to supply Sherman with several propaganda tracts regarding Maximilian's disruptive role in Mexico. Over the next few days, Plumb's paper bombardment directed toward converting Sherman continued with undetermined effect.[55]

Arriving at Veracruz in late November, 1866, after learning that Maximilian, rejecting abdication, had decided to return to Mexico City and fight for his throne even without the aid of the withdrawing French forces, the mission remained only three days before proceeding to Tampico. At Tampico Campbell and Sherman conversed with Consul General Franklin Chase, and Campbell attempted to communicate with the Mexican secretary of foreign relations via a letter entrusted to the Mexican commander, General Gómez. Then, the *Susquehanna*'s party departed for Brazos Santiago, at the mouth of the Rio Grande.[56]

After communicating with General Escobedo on December 8 and 9, "it was agreed upon by Mr. C. & myself [Plumb] should proceed as soon as we could get our baggage from the *Susquehanna*, to Monterey, where Genl. Escobedo said he thought Prest. Juárez would be willing to come if Mr. C. would go there. Genl. E. also

55. Campbell to Johnson, July 17, 1866, in Johnson Papers; Plumb to Cushing, October 6, 1866, in Cushing Papers; and Campbell mission diary, in Plumb Collection.

56. Campbell mission diary, and Plumb to R. S. Chew, December 7, 1866, in Plumb Collection.

promised to wait for us until Thursday when we would accompany him to Monterey." Plumb, eager to establish contact with Juárez in central Mexico, assumed that Campbell and Sherman would accept General Escobedo's suggestion. However, week-long bad weather made it impossible to unload the baggage or re-land Campbell and Plumb, forcing Escobedo to inform them on December 17 that, while he had to depart for Monterrey, he would leave a proper escort for them in Matamoros. Then on December 18 a Dr. Quin, claiming to have departed recently from Juárez' headquarters in Chihuahua, contended that Juárez was still in that city with no intention of moving to Monterrey. This disheartening information, along with the rumored activity of Mexican bandits Canales and Cortinas between Matamoros and Monterrey and Campbell's growing homesickness, prompted him to order the party's return to New Orleans. The sudden announcement of Campbell's new decision startled Plumb, who "tried to dissuade him, or at least to allow me to remain here, so that the appearance at least of not altogether backing out could be avoided. But all was of no use- Had either to make a personal issue or go with him." Over Plumb's objection that the early withdrawal would be interpreted as the mission's failure and that Campbell's quick departure from Mexican waters "deeply offended the Mexican government and people," the Campbell mission immediately began its return to the United States.[57]

In New Orleans, the conflict between the Radicals and Johnson over Mexican policy overtook the Mexican legation, producing a disagreement between Plumb and Campbell which quickly terminated their official relationship. Plumb's bitter reaction to Campbell's insistence that he return with the mission from Brazos Santiago to New Orleans was an early sign of the souring relationship between them. Then, Campbell's refusal to permit Plumb to see Seward's dispatch which instructed the minister to remain in New Orleans until further orders persuaded Plumb that the dispatch censured Campbell.[58]

57. Campbell mission diary, in Plumb Collection.
58. Plumb to Robert S. Chew, January 2 and 31, 1867, in Johnson Papers; and Campbell mission diary, in Plumb Collection.

In early January, 1867, the break between Campbell and Plumb became manifest, almost public. General Sheridan openly referred to Campbell as "a damn fool," and Plumb, known to be furious over Campbell's inability to do anything, complained to State Department employee Robert S. Chew and to Caleb Cushing about Campbell's inactivity and his excessive, incapacitating drinking. Additionally, Plumb stressed the urgency of sending an energetic mission into Mexico. Chew contributed to the declining reputation of the Campbell mission by passing on Plumb's negative views on Campbell's course of action (or inaction). Since his position in the State Department might lead a listener to assume that Seward had spoken critically of Campbell's course, Chew's criticism probably had a double impact. Meanwhile, expressing his desire to return to Ohio, Campbell described his continuation at his post as martyred service. Throughout the spring of 1867, Plumb continued to complain of Campbell's inaction and his excessive drinking, specifying exact dates and incidents, and suggesting that additional information regarding Campbell's conduct could be obtained from General Sheridan or his aide Colonel Crosby.[59]

Only on April 10 did Campbell launch his counterattack to Plumb's campaign to discredit him. Writing directly to President Johnson, Campbell stressed Plumb's dubious connection with the New York speculators, who had suggested Plumb as secretary of legation. Campbell admitted he had been taken in "through the cunning management of crafty speculators." Noting Plumb's continual reference to the "large individual interests in Mexico that needed his attention," Campbell judged that private economic rather than public interests motivated Plumb. Furthermore, Campbell alleged that Plumb was not a friend of Johnson's policy, since "he associates here with radicals of the most violent class." Campbell admitted that upon arrival in New Orleans he began to

59. F. D. Macin to Romero, January 7, 1867, in Archivo Romero; Plumb to Chew, January 2 and 31, 1867, in Johnson Papers; Plumb to Cushing, January 7, 1867, in Cushing Papers; Campbell to Banks, January 5, 1867, in Banks Papers; and Plumb to W. T. Sherman, January 28, 1867, in Plumb Papers. See also James Mackie to Plumb, February 8, 1867, and Church to Plumb, March 3, 1867, in Plumb Collection.

act as his own secretary, withholding information from Plumb. While acknowledging that the public interest demanded harmony in the legation, Campbell declared it impossible under the current circumstances. Finally, although he had gone over Seward's head, writing confidentially and directly to the president, the minister wished his confidential letters be shown to the secretary of state. The conflict ended in mid-June, 1867, after Plumb wrote three more letters detailing Campbell's associations and drinking habits. Campbell was forced to resign several days later.[60]

In the final months of the French intervention, just as he had consistently and continuously done in the earlier years, Juárez expressed the idea that Mexico must look to itself for salvation, even though he would not reject proper United States assistance. He simply did not believe United States aid was forthcoming. Juárez conveyed his doubts in direct language and sometimes in vivid metaphors: "There is little, then, to expect from the powerful, because they respect each other, because they fear each other"; "I know that the rich and powerful nations neither feel nor even less seek remedies for the misfortunes of the poor"; "wolves do not bite each other, they respect each other." Certain the United States would not go to war with France over Mexico, Juárez only expected United States involvement which would not lead to war.[61] In early 1866, although some Mexican Liberals saw indications of forthcoming American intervention, Juárez continued to expect only indirect support. Still, the supportive moral pressure and potential physical presence of the neighboring United States limited France's choices. Juárez knew that France would only deceive weak powers, "but not those, who, like the United States, can reclaim and punish such a fault."[62] Juárez was aware that United States assistance would be

---

60. Campbell to Johnson, April 10, 1867 (private), in Seward Papers; and Plumb to Chew, June 10, 11, and 12, 1867, in Diplomatic Dispatches, Mexico, RG 59, NA.

61. Juárez to Pedro Santacilia, August 25, 1865, January 12, 19, and February 2, April 13, 1866, in Archivo Juárez.

62. Juárez to Pedro Santacilia, March 9, 1866, Juan José Baz to Juárez, April 26, 1866, José Godoy to Juárez, February 12, 1866, Regino Chavez to Auretiano River, June 7, 1866, all in Archivo Juárez; and Juárez to Berardo Revilla, April 24, 1866, in Tamayo (ed.), *Juárez Documentos*, X, 869–70.

limited to whatever could be done without causing a United States–French war.

The idea soon spread, nevertheless, that the United States was responsible for compelling the French to leave, along with the related idea that the United States Civil War and the French intervention were related events. Francisco Zarco, former editor of the official Liberal newspaper *El Siglo Diez y Nueve* countered these ideas with a disclaimer:

I believe that it will always suit us to be in good relations with the United States, but also that it will suit us to tell the truth and not attribute the fall of the empire and the retirement of Napoleon to this country. Grant's and Sheridan's idea that the invasion of Mexico was part of the Southern rebellion, and that the defeat of the South was our salvation is not more than Yankee fantasy. What saved us is the resistance of our people and your perseverance, and we have nothing to thank this nation for.

United States friendly intervention to save Maximilian's life and assertions by North American newspapers that the United States had played a major role in saving the Mexican Republic prompted countercharges from Mexican nationalists, who pointed out that Mexico had saved itself from the French through six long years of resistance.[63]

Some Mexicans were willing to concede a significant United States role in aid to the Liberals. When the Mexican Congress met after Maximilian's fall, Romero, recently returned to Mexico, reported to Seward that Juárez and Ezequial Montes, president of the Congress, "both spoke very kindly of the United States, acknowledging the fact that we had their sympathy and moral support during our war with France, and how much we are indebted to them for this. Since Señor Montes could speak more freely about this than President Juárez, he was, naturally, more explicit." But both were content with past United States action and looked forward to

---

63. Zarco to Juárez, September 14, 1866, in Archivo Juárez; *El Boletín Republicano*, July 9, 1867; Roberto A. Esteva, "La Unión Latino-Americana," *El Boletín Republicano*, November 5, 1867; and Ignacio Altamirano, *La Nota de Campbell* (Toluca, 1867), 3–8.

future American cooperation in the restructuring and modernizing of Mexico's economy and society.[64]

The years 1864–1867 witnessed a rising United States interest in Mexican affairs at all levels from the administration and Congress down through local newspapers to Mexican-friendship or Monroe Doctrine clubs. The Preston mission, the ex-Confederate colonization schemes, and the Monroe Doctrine supplied the great body of material for public discussion. The Monroe Doctrine was reaffirmed, although not without considerable popular and congressional pressure, urging forward the Lincoln and Johnson administrations. Romero continued to support the Radicals in the domestic struggle with the Johnson administration because he shared their dislike for Seward's policies. But Romero's role in the domestic political fray merely focuses attention on the international as well as national basis of that internal conflict. In spite of Corwin's assistance, Napoleon's best efforts to obtain United States support for Maximilian's government failed. Finally, none of the various colonization schemes achieved a level of success sufficient to menace United States predominance in the New World. The Radical Weltanschauung demanded impatiently the immediate removal of conservative, Old World threats to the progress of the New World liberal social, political, and economic system, which, created in the image of the United States, would also assure its future prosperity and security. But clearly the disagreement with the United States among factions regarding the proper means of protecting the New World and the assigning of priorities to Mexican and other external problems brought foreign affairs into the domestic political struggle.

64. Romero to Seward, December 9, 1867, in Seward Papers.

VIII *Mexico and United States Postwar Politics*

MANY HISTORIANS insist that the Reconstruction era focuses upon the racial-social or political-economic role of blacks in a white man's society and upon the political and economic relationship between the South and the rest of the nation, the North, and the West.[1] Other historians have demonstrated that the disagreement between North and South did not solely involve specific domestic political-economic matters, but also conflicting views of the United States role in the world.[2] Most attention has been paid to purely domestic examinations of these conflicting world views. However, since a successful French intervention meant severe limitation, perhaps elimination, of United States influence south of the Rio Grande, the French intervention in Mexico did affect United States domestic political division in 1865–1867.

Certainly, winning the Civil War and reconstructing the nation were more urgently pressing matters than preserving unrestricted access to Latin America. However, with the United States econ-

---

1. See the recent syntheses: Roy F. Nichols, *The Stakes of Power, 1845–1877* (New York, 1961); Weisberger, *The New Industrial Society;* and Brock, *Conflict and Transformation.*
2. See for example, Williams, *Contours of American History;* LaFeber, *The New Empire;* Williams, *Roots of the Modern American Empire;* Milton Plesur, *America's Outward Thrust: Approaches to Foreign Affairs, 1865–1890* (DeKalb, Ill., 1971); and Paolino, *Foundations of the American Empire.*

omy growing, with the implementation of an expansive laissez-faire program during the Civil War, and with leaders of the economy optimistic about future growth, it would have been a mistake to assume that United States policy vis-à-vis the curtailment of its future expansion into Latin America was so secondary a matter as to be insignificant. On the contrary, access to Mexico and other Latin American areas, particularly for investment and raw materials, but also markets, was of constant worrisome concern to many American politicians and businessmen during the 1860s and increasingly so after the Civil war ended, permitting greater attention to external concerns.[3]

While there was broad agreement in the 1860s on the importance of Latin America for future United States development, there were conceptual differences regarding how and when it would be valuable to future expansion. Some, such as General Ulysses Grant, General Lew Wallace, Congressman Nathaniel Banks, Senators James McDougall and Benjamin Wade, lawyer-investor Benjamin Cheever, and businessman-diplomat Edward Lee Plumb considered Mexico and the rest of Latin America excellent locations for acquiring raw materials, investing surplus capital, or exporting technology, if conditions were favorable. Favorable conditions meant the end of a French involvement in Mexico, with the corre-

---

3. See Chapter IX. On French–Mexican–U.S. relations in the 1860s, see Perkins, *The Monroe Doctrine;* Van Deusen, *Seward;* Lynn Case and Warren Spencer, *The United States and France: Civil War Diplomacy* (Philadelphia, 1970); and Blumenthal, *France and the United States.* From July 1, 1865, until June 30, 1867, a period usually considered as concerned with intensive domestic developments, the *Chicago Tribune* devoted eighty-eight editorials exclusively to United States foreign relations. This total excluded a large number of editorials which dealt with the tariff, domestic developments in foreign countries, and war and diplomacy between foreign nations. Significantly, thirty of the eighty-eight editorials centered on the Mexican question. Nor did the *Chicago Tribune* ignore the interrelationship between foreign policy and the domestic political division; various editorials pointed out that domestic factions differed importantly on foreign as well as domestic issues. For a general description of the rapidly expanding economic productivity and export trade during the mid-nineteenth century, see North, *Growth and Welfare in the American Past*, 75–85; Williams, *Roots of the Modern American Empire*, 6–14; Edward Chase Kirkland, *Industry Comes of Age: Business, Labor and Public Policy, 1860–1897* (Chicago, 1967), 278–305; Hans Ulrich Wehler, *Der Aufstieg des amerikanischen Imperialismus: Studien zur Entwicklung des Imperium Americanum, 1865–1900* (Göttingen, Germany, 1974), 19–37.

sponding threat to the whole of Middle America—from Mexico down to the Panamanian isthmus—and the Caribbean.

In general, the Radicals, who had long disagreed with the Mexican policy of President Lincoln and Secretary of State Seward, became spokesmen for those interests which sought to develop a firm, active, and insistent policy which would compel the French to leave Mexico. They intended to assert and to uphold the Monroe Doctrine and to ensure United States profit and political influence in the New World. Many Radicals also argued that the southern rebellion and the French intervention were parts of a scheme to destroy liberal, republican government and to weaken the United States' power and economic position in the New World. Radical leaders Henry Winter Davis, Benjamin Wade, Nathaniel Banks, Zachariah Chandler, Thaddeus Stevens, Godlove Orth, and John Logan expressed varying degrees of support for a more dynamic policy aimed at removing the French from Mexico. Although many radicals believed President Johnson might introduce significant changes, they soon learned that no essential changes could be expected from the Johnson-Seward administration.

To the Radicals and the interests they represented, Seward's patient diplomacy was considered exasperating and undignified for a great nation. Consider General Grant's analysis submitted to the cabinet in late 1865:

To let the Empire of Maximilian be established on our frontier is to permit an enemy to establish himself who will require a large standing army to watch. Military stations will be at points remote from supplies, and therefore expensive to keep. The trade of an empire will be lost to our commerce, and Americans, instead of being the most favored people of the world throughout the length and breadth of this continent, will be scoffed and laughed at by their adjoining neighbors both north and south.[4]

Grant viewed huge military expenses, loss of trade and pride, and the curtailment of the United States position so aptly proposed in

4. Grant to Johnson, September 1, 1865, in *Official Records*, Vol. XLVIII, Pt. 2, p. 1221; and Perkins, *Monroe Doctrine*, 494–98.

the Monroe Doctrine as the probable results of permitting an empire to be built in Mexico. Naturally, those agreeing with a viewpoint similar to Grant's adopted a more insistent position regarding the termination of the French presence in Mexico.

For others, the Asian market was the goal and Latin America provided primarily the route. Thus, Professor Ernest Paolino has ably argued that Secretary of State Seward considered Middle America and the Caribbean the key areas necessary for firmly establishing and securing the Asian trade which was America's destiny. Since in the years 1865–1867 United States participation in the Asian market was neither large nor expanding rapidly, those sharing Seward's outlook saw no need for insistent action terminating French interference in the Caribbean region; rather they were content with the Lincoln-Seward-Johnson policy which called for avoiding an open break with the French. Seward intended to let French domestic, financial, and political problems, their European diplomatic problems, and the tenacious Mexican resistance combine with strong United States diplomatic pressure to force Napoleon to withdraw. The Monroe Doctrine per se would not be used as a lever to pry the French from Mexico. In addition, the Seward-Johnson supporters generally viewed the southern rebellion and the French intervention as unrelated problems. While it can be maintained that both factions wanted roughly the same result, they differed greatly in the proposed means to achieve the end and in their conception of the nature and urgency of the threat to United States interests.[5]

Given the wide differences in viewing the significance and urgency of removing the French, it is not unexpected that during the early Reconstruction years, the Mexican mission became a

5. Paolino, *Foundations of the American Empire*, 29, 39–40, 89, 105, 118–19, 145, 204–12; Charles Vevier, "The Collins Overland Line and American Continentalism," *Pacific Historical Review*, XXVIII (August, 1959), 237–53; Charles Vevier, "American Continentalism: An Idea of Expansionism, 1845–1910," *American Historical Review*, LXV (January, 1960), 323–35; and Thomas McCormick, *China Market: America's Quest for Informal Empire, 1893–1901* (Chicago, 1967), 8, 17–19, 178–79.

political football. In late 1865, as Radical pressure for decisive action to terminate the French intervention in Mexico mounted, Seward and Johnson recommended Radical favorite John A. Logan of Illinois, outspoken in his condemnation of French intervention in Mexico and the creation of Maximilian's empire, to fill the post. Realizing that his nomination represented a political maneuver rather than a change in administration policy, Logan was strongly inclined to refuse the mission. Meanwhile, the administration made political capital out of the pending nomination. Seward informed the French minister that Logan's nomination was only a political step, yet the mere mention of Logan's appointment caused consternation and concern in Maximilian's Mexico. Conversely, the Mexican Liberals used the nomination to sustain their claim to forthcoming United States support. After delaying three weeks, but convinced that he would not be instructed to pursue an aggressive Mexican policy, Logan declined in order to run for a Senate seat in 1866.[6]

Not surprisingly, given his large economic interests in Mexico, Edward L. Plumb also sought the Mexican post. After initial success in attaining the post of secretary of legation under United States Minister to Mexico Lewis D. Campbell, Plumb poured forth correspondence to political and business leaders interested in Mexican affairs and very pointed criticism of Campbell's weak, hesitant conduct in aid of Mexico. Having been instrumental in Campbell's removal, Plumb then actively sought the post of minister, now with considerable high-level support from his correspondents.[7]

6. Various correspondence and documents, folder labeled "Appointment as Minister to Mexico," in John A. Logan Papers, box 148, Library of Congress; William H. Corwin to Seward, December 3, 1865, in Seward Papers; Mariano Degollado to José Miguel Arroyo, November 22, 1865, Degollado to José Fernando Ramírez, December 15, 1865, in Luis García Pimental Collection, VII-1, carpeta 3-4; Viennot y Cia. to Editor of *Idea Liberal* November 23, 1865, Francisco Zarco to Editor of *Idea Liberal*, January 8, 1866, in Rafael García Papers, XXXVII, carpeta 1-3, Centro de Estudios de Historia de México; *Periódico Oficial del Gobierno Constitucional de la República Mexicana*, January 1, 4, 1866; and Blumberg, *Diplomacy of the Mexican Empire, 1863–1867*, p. 84.

7. James Mackie to Frederick Seward, August 10, 1866, in Seward Papers; J. Edgar Thomson to Plumb, July 8, 1867, George Wilkes to Plumb, July 18, 1867, Sumner to

The correspondence of prominent politicians mentioned many other names, often men with political reputations or men involved in Mexican communications and trade affairs, as potential candidates as minister to Mexico. Among those proposed were the United States consul-general in Mexico, Marcus Otterbourg; State Department employee Henry Roy de la Reintrie; Congressman Nathaniel Banks; John L. O'Sullivan, promoter and publicist; John Nugent, former senator from California; Caleb Cushing; General John McClernand; Charles L. Denman, former United States consul at Acapulco; and William L. King, New York *Herald* newspaper correspondent.[8]

The domestic political conflict related to Mexican affairs spread to many other areas besides the appointment of a minister to Mexico. Already in mid-1865, General Lew Wallace warned that "the opposition party soon to be formed will take up the question of our governmental relations with Maximilian, and assume the assertion of the Monroe Doctrine as their great political principle: carrying it eloquently before the people, who undoubtedly have it warmly at heart, will they not gain a hold upon public favor not easily shaken off?" Projecting that Mexican affairs would be a key political issue in the forthcoming months, Wallace did not wish to see President Johnson "lose ground upon that important issue." Similarly, whereas the Johnson-Grant split has often been analyzed in terms of the domestic political struggle between radical and moderate Republican factions and the Johnson administration, or as

Plumb, July 19, August 15, 18, 1867, all in Plumb Collection; Plumb to Cushing, June 20, 27, July 22, 1867, in Cushing Papers, box 98; Julius A. Skillon to Banks, July 13, 29, 1867, in Banks Papers, box 67; Plumb to William T. Sherman, September 3, 1867, in Plumb Papers.

8. De La Reintrie to William T. Sherman, June 23, 1865, in W. T. Sherman Papers; De La Reintrie to Seward, November 17, 1865, Samuel Ward to Frederick Seward, March 2, 1867, in Seward Papers; De La Reintrie to Banks, August 5, 1867 (private), in Banks Papers, box 67; and De La Reintrie to Romero, November 18, 1867, in Archivo Romero; R. S. Spofford to Cushing, July 9, 1867, Benjamin Butler to Cushing, July 11, 1867, S. L. M. Barlow to Cushing, July 16, 1867, Plumb to Cushing, July 22, 1867, all in Cushing Papers, box 98; Charles L. Denman to Juárez, June 22, 1867, in Archivo Juárez; William H. King to Andrew Johnson, June 18, 1867 (two telegrams), King to Johnson and Seward, June 19, 1867 (telegram), in Johnson Papers; and Sheridan to Plumb, June 18, 1867, in Plumb Collection.

part of a struggle between Johnson and Grant over control and reorganization of the army, Secretary of the Treasury Hugh McCulloch observed that Grant and Johnson had their first important differences upon the Mexican question.[9] In fact, a study of the Johnson-Grant split reveals that persistent foreign policy disagreement contributed significantly toward undermining their relationship, thereby seriously affecting reconstruction politics. Later, the early radical plans to impeach Johnson were shaped in part by differences over Mexican affairs.

The historians who have developed extensive and considered explanations of the Johnson-Grant split have relied almost exclusively upon domestic affairs to explain the break. Emphasizing Grant's vast popularity and Johnson's desire to use that popularity for his own purposes, they contended that Johnson pressured Grant into participating in the "swing-around-the-circle" in September, 1866. Then, later, when Johnson saw that Grant would not permit himself to be used, the president tried to get Grant out of the country on a trumped-up scheme requiring the general to accompany the United States minister, Lewis D. Campbell, on a mission to Mexico. They view the purpose of the mission to remove Grant from Washington so that Lieutenant-General William T. Sherman, whom Johnson believed to be in sympathy with his southern policy, could be made secretary of war. This thesis generally states that Grant's presidential aspirations became more pronounced after the "swing-around-the-circle." One historian, Harold Hyman, claimed that Secretary of War Edwin Stanton and Grant were working together to prevent Johnson from misusing the

9. McCulloch, *Men and Measures of Half a Century,* 387; Lewis Wallace to Seward, July 10, 1865, unsigned memorandum (confidential), August 16, 1865, in Seward Papers; Adam Badeau, *Grant in Peace: From Appomattox to Mount McGregor* (Philadelphia, 1866), 39–40; and Robert Dale Owen to Sumner, July 18, 1866, in Sumner Papers, box 78. For the intensity of Grant's commitment to a strong policy to remove the French from Mexico, see Matías Romero, *Speech of Señor Don Matías Romero . . . Read on the 65th Anniversary of the Birth of General Ulysses S. Grant, Celebrated at Washington, on the 25th of April, 1887* (New York, 1887), 7–8; Badeau, *Grant in Peace,* 52–53; William B. Hesseltine, *Ulysses S. Grant Politician* (New York, 1957), 82–89; and numerous summaries of Romero-Grant and Romero-Johnson conversations in Romero (comp.), *Correspondencia,* Vols. V–X.

"second army" (the one occupying the South) by involving it in politics, or, from threatening its existence by an early rearming of southern militia. Hyman contended that Johnson attempted to split Stanton and Grant by getting Grant to accept the Mexican mission, thereby opening up the possibility of removing Stanton. But when this did not work, Johnson towed Grant on the "swing-around-the-circle" in order to strengthen his position in the fall elections.[10] While offering variations of a thesis, these historians all view Mexican affairs as a trick or a tool used by Johnson to maneuver Grant out of Washington.

These traditional views are weakened by the fact that they ignore, slight, or misinterpret the role of Mexican policy in the split. For example, Hyman mistakenly dates Johnson's offer of the Mexican mission to Grant before the "swing-around-the-circle," when in fact the offer occurred four weeks afterwards. More important, Hyman's central thesis—the cooperation between Grant and Stanton to prevent Johnson's misuse of the army—was weakly supported by evidence. Stanton and Grant did not get along particularly well. Hyman admitted that Grant was not very frank and open in his relationship with Stanton, which would seem to weaken the case for their cooperation. Furthermore, in the summer of 1866, Grant and former Confederate lieutenant-general Richard Taylor together approached Johnson with a plan to reorganize the cabinet by the removal of Seward and Stanton.[11] Noteworthy is James Sef-

10. William Conant Church, *Ulysses S. Grant and the Period of National Preservation and Reconstruction* (New York, 1897), 341–51; Howard K. Beale, *The Critical Year: A Study of Andrew Johnson and Reconstruction* (New York, 1958), 304–11; Hesseltine, *Grant*, 70–80; and Harold M. Hyman, "Johnson, Stanton, and Grant: A Reconsideration of the Army's Role in the Events Leading to Impeachment," *American Historical Review*, LXVI (October, 1960), 85–100. See also Louis A. Coolidge, *Ulysses S. Grant* (Boston, 1922), 217–18, 238–39; and Martin E. Mantell, *Johnson, Grant, and the Politics of Reconstruction* (New York, 1973), 28–30.

11. Benjamin P. Thomas and Harold M. Hyman, *Stanton: the Life and Times of Lincoln's Secretary of War* (New York, 1962), 499–500; Beale (ed.), *Diary of Gideon Welles*, III, 72–73; Richard Taylor, *Destruction and Reconstruction* (New York, 1879), 251–55; and Grant to Sheridan, November 15, 1866, in Sheridan Papers, box 39. See also Cyrus B. Comstock manuscript diary, January 15, 1866, in Cyrus B. Comstock Papers, Library of Congress, box 8; and Blackburn, "Military Opposition," 177–78. Adam Badeau claimed Grant began to oppose Johnson as early as the spring of 1866, but offers no evidence. See *Grant in Peace*, 84.

ton's convincing argument that, while Congress was generating some problems for the army, Johnson did not particularly create problems for the military institution. Reflecting on Hyman's thesis that Johnson was misusing the army, Sefton concluded that the president was not abusing military power in 1866.[12] Moreover, in late 1865 and throughout 1866 Grant and Stanton disagreed on significant points regarding Mexican relations. While earlier interpretations of the Johnson-Grant break are very questionable, other, simpler, better substantiated explanations are available. Specifically the traditional interpretations are in error in viewing the Mexican maneuver only as a weapon in the conflict over domestic policy.

Regarding domestic policy, many historians agree that in mid-1865 Grant and Johnson held quite similar views on southern policy. Questioning this assumption, Hyman admitted that their views appeared to coincide, but he claimed that Grant's "secret views" actually differed from Johnson's. Yet, most historians argue that shortly after or during the "swing-around-the-circle" Grant either became alienated from Johnson or began to realize he had a chance to win the presidency. These historians claim that Johnson's conduct caused Grant to alter his opinion.[13]

In 1865 and much of 1866, Grant and Johnson apparently shared similar views on domestic policy, and perhaps on Mexican policy also, but they did not share the same urgency to implement a plan to terminate the French intervention in Mexico. Since the last days of the Civil War, Grant had publicly asserted that the French violation of the Monroe Doctrine deserved immediate and, if necessary, forceful counteraction. Many generals shared Grant's view that the French must withdraw or be driven out of Mexico.[14] Grant

12. For a convincing refutation of Hyman's thesis, see James E. Sefton, *The United States Army and Reconstruction, 1865–1877* (Baton Rouge, 1967), 73, 80–88, 115–16, 135–36, 155, 179–81.
13. Coolidge, *Grant*, 238–39; Beale, *The Critical Year*, 307–11; Hesseltine, *Grant*, 74–75; Thomas and Hyman, *Stanton*, 501–502; and Beale (ed.) *Diary of Gideon Welles*, II, 591–92.
14. Miller, "Matías Romero," 228, 235–36; Robert R. Miller, "Mexican Secret Agents in the United States, 1861–1867" (Ph.D. dissertation, University of California, Berkeley,

contended that the French intervention was part of the southern rebellion and, hence, until the French were compelled to leave, the rebellion was not completely ended. In June, 1865, Grant personally informed President Johnson "that he did not consider the Civil War completely terminated while the French remained in Mexico." Johnson claimed "he fully shared Grant's opinion." In fact, in mid-June, 1865, at Johnson's invitation, Grant presented his views on French intervention in Mexico to the cabinet. Grant argued before the cabinet that, since southern discontents would go to Mexico to prepare to renew the conflict with European aid, the French intervention in Mexico was a sign of open hostility to the United States.[15]

In mid-1865, Grant, Johnson, and Matías Romero had jointly and secretly worked up a plan to send an army of volunteers to fight under President Juárez against the French. At Romero's suggestion Grant had considered, for a short time, assuming command of the "volunteer" army of United States veterans, before deciding that as commanding general of the army he would be more valuable by encouraging men to go and by facilitating arms and supplies. Grant worked closely with Romero in seeking a competent officer to command the "volunteers," recommending Lieutenant-General William T. Shermen, Major-General Philip H. Sheridan, or Major-General John Schofield. Eventually, Schofield was selected to command this force. However, before the Grant-Romero-

---

1960); and Robert B. Brown, "Guns over the Border: American Aid to the Juárez Government During the French Intervention" (Ph.D. dissertation, University of Michigan, 1951); and Blackburn, "Military Opposition."

15. Romero to Ministro de Relaciones Exteriores, April 30, June 8, 18, and July 20, 1865, in Romero (comp.), *Correspondencia*, V, 280, 360–61, 390–93, 491–92; "General Grant on Mexican Affairs," *Chicago Tribune*, December 1, 1865; and "Our Continental Duty," *Harper's Weekly*, IX (August 26, 1865), 530. See also Beale (ed.), *Diary of Gideon Welles*, II, 317, 322, 333, 624; Dana and Wilson, *Life of Grant*, 377–78; McCulloch, *Men and Measures of Half a Century*, 387–89; Badeau, *Grant in Peace*, 52; Republican National and Congressional Committees, *Life and Services of General U. S. Grant, Conqueror of the Rebellion, and Eighteenth President of the United States* (Washington, 1868), 136; Theodore Stanton, *General Grant and the French* (n.p., [1890]), 20–21; and *Los Estados Unidos y Maximiliano* (n.p., 1865), 1–3, also found in *Periódico Oficial del Gobierno Constitucional de la República Mexicana*, May, 1865.

Johnson-Schofield plan could be implemented, on July 29, Johnson reversed his earlier agreement to keep knowledge of the plan from Seward, requesting Schofield to approach Seward with the details of the project. Although aware that the plan was in an advanced stage, Seward persuaded Schofield and Johnson to postpone military action. Seward argued that first Schofield should go to Paris to "get his legs under Napoleon's mahogany" and attempt a diplomatic solution. Schofield, flattered, accepted the offer. This turn of events greatly disgusted Grant and Romero.[16]

In September, 1865, Grant wrote again unavailingly to Johnson urging action in Mexican affairs. By the fall Grant, although assigning Seward chief responsibility for the delaying maneuver, had reason to suspect that Johnson was being persuaded by Seward's call for caution in Mexican affairs. By late October, 1865, Grant and Romero interpreted Seward's position as the dominating influence in the Johnson administration.[17] In an early November, 1865, interview that Johnson gave to Indiana intellectual Robert Dale Owen, the president asserted his desire to aid Mexico's Liberals. However, Romero observed that Seward could maintain his views "even against the desires and will of the President." Recognizing that while the United States remained neutral the president could not openly take sides in regard to aiding Mexico, Grant tried unsuccessfully to dissuade Johnson from adopting Seward's position on Mexican affairs.[18] Hence, Grant and Romero considered Sew-

16. Romero to Ministro de Relaciones Exteriores, May 8, 16, 30, June 5, 18, 27, 28, 29, July 12, 18, 20, 30, August 4, September 18, November 14, 1865, all in Romero (comp.), *Correspondencia*, V, 296–98, 315–16, 343–44, 360–61, 390–93, 424–28, 465, 475–76, 491–92, 513–19, 530–31, 632–33, and 785–86.

17. Romero to Ministro de Relaciones Exteriores, May 8, 18, and 30, 1865, in Romero (comp.), *Correspondencia*, V, 296–98, 315–16, 343–44; Daniel Woodhouse to Seward, July 21, 1866, in Seward Papers; Ignacio Mariscal to Pedro Santacilia, June 13, 1865, in Archivo Juárez; Grant to Johnson, July 15, and September 1, 1865, in *Official Records*, Vol. XLVIII, Pt. 2, pp. 1080–81, and 1221; Schofield, "The Withdrawal of the French from Mexico," 128–37; Romero to Ministro de Relaciones Exteriores, August 4, 1865, in Correspondencia General con los Estados Unidos; and Perkins, *Monroe Doctrine, 1826–1867*, 471, 498.

18. Romero to Ministro de Relaciones Exteriores, July 18, 19, and 30, and October 7, 23, and 28, 1865, in Romero (comp.), *Correspondencia*, V, 475–76, 479–80, 513–19, 675–76, 721–23, 741–42; and Robert Dale Owen's "Memorandum of a Conference held with Presi-

ard the chief villain and Johnson well-intentioned, but too weak to act. Thus began Grant's disillusionment with Johnson.

During the winter of 1865–1866 and throughout 1866, Grant attempted to give or sell arms and munitions to the Mexican republic. As early as July, 1865, Johnson informed Romero that he intended arms to be available for private purchase by Mexican Liberals. While Johnson voiced approval of arms transfers in meetings with Grant and Romero, invariably Seward and/or Stanton would persuade Johnson to sustain the secretary of state's objections against transferring war material to the Mexican republic's forces. Interestingly, Grant's official campaign biography in 1868 pointed out the general's frustrating efforts to send arms to the Mexican Liberals after the Civil War.[19] Again Grant and Romero held Seward responsible for these defeats, but they could not help but gradually realize that Johnson's support for a strong policy in Mexican matters was eroding.

Seward was not alone in opposing Grant's attempts to sell or give arms to the Mexican republican forces; Stanton also played a major role in constantly thwarting Grant's efforts throughout 1866.[20] Even when Grant tried to sneak past Stanton's roadblock by claiming he had previously obtained Johnson's verbal consent to send arms to Mexico, Stanton insisted upon resubmitting the re-

dent Johnson on Thursday morning, Nov. 9, 1865," enclosed with Romero to Ministro de Relaciones Exteriores, November 19, 1865, in Romero (comp.), *Correspondencia*, V, 811–12. See Van Deusen, *Seward*, 489–90 and footnotes for further information.

19. Republican National and Congressional Committees, *U. S. Grant*, 136–37; Romero to Ministro de Relaciones Exteriores, June 18, July 8, 18, and 19, and September 18, 1865, in Romero (comp.), *Correspondencia*, V, 390–93, 455–58, 475–76, 479–80, 632–33; Romero to Ministro de Relaciones Exteriores, April 11, 1866, in Romero (comp.), *Correspondencia*, VII, 406–407; Dana and Wilson, *Life of Grant*, 377–78.

20. Grant to Stanton, January 9, 1866, Andres Trevino to Grant, April 20, 1866, P. H. Sheridan to John A. Rawlins, July 17, 1866, Stanton draft note, July 17, 1866, in Edwin Stanton Papers, Library of Congress; Grant to Sheridan, May 2, 1866, Grant to Sheridan Letterbook, in Sheridan Papers, box 39; Sheridan to Rawlins, July 6, 1866, in Grant Papers, Series 5, Volume 54, p. 236, represent a sampling of a large body of letters, notes, endorsements, and so forth which reveal Grant's effort to send arms and munitions to Mexico. See also Grant to Sheridan, October 9, 1866, in Sheridan Papers, box 39. See also Blackburn, "Military Opposition," 117, 177–83; and Webster, "Texan Manifest Destiny and the Mexican Border Conflict, 1865–1880," 40–54.

quest for the president's formal approval. Apparently Grant had Johnson's tacit verbal approval to slip Juárez arms, but in order to avoid trouble with his secretary of state or his secretary of war and to preserve the appearance of neutrality, the president would not openly condone such weapon transfers. Grant could not escape the judgment that either he had been deceived by Johnson regarding his commitment to oust the French, or the president was slowly changing his mind.[21]

On April 8, 1866, after ten months of effort by Grant and Romero to persuade the government to permit the sale (or gift) of arms to the Mexican Liberal government, Romero obtained an interview with the president to complain about his frustrated attempts. So often approval had seemed granted, but no arms were forthcoming. Romero reported: "The President told me then, somewhat surprised, that he understood that arms had already been given us via Grant, to which I replied in the negative. Although the General... was prepared to accept the responsibility which might fall on him... the Secretary of War had encountered some difficulties which prevented the plan's realization. The President asserted then his positive desire that we receive arms... if it could be done in a manner honorable for the United States." In Romero's estimation, Johnson still had good intentions; however, his ability to implement them was in question.[22] Thus, Stanton joined Seward as opponents of the Grant-Romero venture to supply material aid to Mexico.

Indicative of Johnson's shifting, uncertain Mexican policy were several actions which the president took just prior to beginning his trip to the dedication of the Stephen Douglas statue in Chicago, which became known as the "swing-around-the-circle." On the eve of the "swing-around-the-circle," but six weeks after Maximilian had issued a decree closing Matamoros, Johnson proclaimed that decree null and void. While the response was as expected, the tim-

21. Grant to Stanton, March 28, 1866, and Stanton to Grant, March 29, 1866, in Stanton Papers; and Grant to Sheridan, May 2, 1866, in Sheridan Papers, box 39.
22. Romero to Ministro de Relaciones Exteriores, April 8, 1866, in Romero (comp.), *Correspondencia*, VII, 391–93; and Romero to Juárez, April 12, 1866, in Archivo Juárez.

ing of Johnson's proclamation, just a few days prior to his campaign trip to Chicago, coincided with that trip's concerted plan to use Mexican policy to attract support and votes to his administration.[23]

Then, Johnson took a difficult-to-explain, perhaps devious, step. In late August, 1866, after many unsuccessful attempts by Mexican imperial agents to be received by Seward or Johnson, the president permitted Mariano Degollado, consul general of the Mexican empire, to visit him secretly. According to Degollado, Johnson claimed Maximilian could not sustain himself without the French, adding however, that if by chance Maximilian succeeded in remaining in control after the French departed, his Mexican empire would be recognized by the United States.[24] The next week, Johnson and Seward, pointing to their support for Liberal Mexico, were extracting political capital from the presence of Grant and Romero on the "swing" west toward Chicago.

The "swing-around-the-circle" was, of course, a Seward-Johnson strategy to generate political support for the administration and for congressional candidates who supported the administration's policy. Their strategy, however, did not attempt to marshal support just by referring to domestic policy. Repeatedly during the "swing" the administration pointed to its success in compelling the French to withdraw from Mexico. To embellish this image, Romero was invited to travel west with Johnson's party. Romero's presence on the journey helps us to understand and clarify several matters. In a series of long, detailed dispatches he recorded how Seward and others constantly used him and Grant to produce cheers and applause for the administration's Mexican policy.[25]

---

23. Proclamation of August 17, 1866, enclosed with Seward to Bigelow, August 24, 1866, in U.S. Department of State, *Foreign Relations of the United States, 1866*, Pt. 1, pp. 338–39.

24. Mariano Degollado to Carlota Amalia, August 30, 1866, in Luis García Pimental Collection, VII-1, carpeta 4-4, #230, which reveals that the secretary of the interior, Orville Browning, also granted Degollado an interview.

25. On the campaign of 1866, see the following articles by Gregg Phifer: "Andrew Johnson Takes a Trip," *Tennessee Historical Quarterly*, XI (March, 1952), 3–23, "Andrew Johnson Argues a Case," *Tennessee Historical Quarterly*, XI (June, 1952), 148–70, "Andrew Johnson Delivers His Argument," *Tennessee Historical Quarterly*, XI (September, 1952), 212–

Since neither Grant nor Romero had faith in the Seward-Johnson Mexican policy, the attempt to attract support for it by using them must have upset and angered Grant as much as it did Romero.

Grant's relationship with Johnson altered notably during the active political campaign of 1866. Whereas Seward could be assigned major responsibility for defeating earlier Grant initiatives in aid of Juárez, Johnson could not escape his share of responsibility for the undesirable political turn which the "swing-around-the-circle" took. Secretary of the Navy Gideon Welles claimed that in several conversations with Grant during "the first week or ten days" of the "swing," the general agreed with the position Welles (and Johnson) held concerning a prompt reestablishment of the Union with "immediate representation by all the States." Hence, as the "swing" began, Grant still agreed with what he understood to be the basic goals of Johnson's reconstruction program, although not necessarily with the means or method of implementation. Yet, in the midst of the "swing," Grant wrote his wife: "I never have been so tired of anything before as I have been with the political stump speeches of Mr. Johnson from Washington to this place. I look upon them as a National disgrace. Of course you will not show this letter to anyone for so long as Mr. Johnson is President. I must respect him as such, and it is in the country's interest that I should also have his confidence."[26] But Grant's disillusionment did not stem entirely from his aversion to Johnson's method of presenting his program.

The general also rejected the administration's attempts to com-

34, "Andrew Johnson Loses His Battle," *Tennessee Historical Quarterly*, XI (December, 1952), 291–328; Everette Swinney, "Andrew Johnson's Swing Around the Circle" (Masters thesis, Pennsylvania State University, 1957); McKitrick, *Andrew Johnson and Reconstruction*, 421–47; Beale, *The Critical Year*, 304–311; and Thomas Schoonover, "The Mexican Minister Describes Andrew Johnson's 'Swing Around the Circle,'" *Civil War History*, XIX (June, 1973), 149–61, an introduction to and translation of Romero's dispatches describing the "swing."

26. Romero to Ministro de Relaciones Exteriores, September 7, 1866, in Correspondencia General con los Estados Unidos, also found in Romero (comp.), *Correspondencia*, VIII, 240–42, and translated in Schoonover, "The Mexican Minister Describes Johnson's 'Swing,'" 158–59; Beale (ed.), *Diary of Gideon Welles*, II, 591; Grant to Julia Grant, August 31, 1866, and September 9, 1866, in Grant Papers, Series 1A.

bine domestic and foreign policy. Thus, by mid-September, with the "swing" demonstrating that Johnson and Seward would use Grant for political purposes and that they intended to pursue their "successful," if to Grant objectionable, Mexican policy, it is not surprising that the Grant-Johnson relationship cooled noticeably. The often-noted drifting apart of the Grant-Johnson relationship during the election campaign of 1866 was the result of more than differing domestic politics.[27] Seward and Johnson had attempted to use their foreign policy to sustain their domestic program, but Grant only approved of the latter, not the former. When the two spheres of policy were combined into one, Johnson and Grant no longer agreed on the composite's desirability.

By the end of September, General John A. Rawlins, a close friend and staff officer of Grant's, admitted that the general's developing presidential aspirations widened the split with Johnson. Grant became increasingly convinced that Johnson and Seward could not form a successful political combination in 1868, and therefore his own possibilities appeared good. Later, Johnson analyzed this crucial split in the same terms.[28] While Grant refused to be a part of the Johnson administration's mild, diplomatic course in Mexican affairs, he had no intention of reducing his own efforts for a more forceful line of action. In early October, 1866, Grant revealed in a confidential letter to Sheridan, who commanded the United States forces along the Mexican border and shared Grant's views on French intervention in Mexico, that he did not intend to be stymied in his desires to assist the Liberal Mexican government. In spite of the continual moves of Seward, Johnson, and Stanton to block the general's attempts to extend aid, Grant insisted that although "no policy has been adopted by our Government which

27. Mantell, *Johnson, Grant, and the Politics of Reconstruction*, 28–30. See also Beale, *The Critical Year*, 307, 310–11; Coolidge, *Grant* 217–18, 238–39; Sefton, *The Army and Reconstruction*, 104; and Badeau, *Grant in Peace*, 89.

28. Johnson to Benjamin C. Truman, August 3, 1868, in Benjamin C. Truman, "Anecdotes of Andrew Johnson," *The Century Magazine*, LXXXV (1913), 438–40; Beale, *The Critical Year*, 310–11; and Blackburn, "Military Opposition," 182–83.

authorizes us to interfere directly on Mexican soil . . . there is nothing that I know of to prevent the passage of people and material going through our territory to the aid of the recognized government."[29] He would act regardless of administration wishes as long as no specific order prohibited his action. Naturally, with the presidential possibility looming before him, Grant would profoundly resent any move by the Johnson administration to use his reputation to sustain its political influence. Particularly Grant would resent any attempt to maneuver him into appearing to support a policy which he really opposed. Precisely this distortion had occurred in regard to Mexican policy during the "swing." It recurred, several weeks before the November elections, when the Johnson administration attempted to use Grant's popularity and international reputation by sending him on a special mission to Mexico.

In early October, 1866, still uncertain about the outcome of the fall elections, Johnson and Seward could not leave the domestic political situation as it stood after the "swing." If they intended to preserve their political control, they needed to continue the campaign for a more cooperative, pliable congress. About three weeks before the November, 1866, elections, Johnson held several conferences with Grant, requesting the general to accompany the recently designated United States minister on a journey to Mexico.[30] Ostensibly Grant was to be a special advisor to Campbell, but obviously his presence would indicate to the world the seriousness of the United States commitment to compel the French to leave, and by implication his own support of the Johnson administration's Mexican policy.

Johnson was persistent in his effort to commit Grant to the Mexican mission. The president offered Grant the assignment orally on October 17 and 20, which Grant politely refused in writing

29. Grant to Sheridan, October 9, 1866 (confidential), in Sheridan Papers, box 39; Romero to Ministro de Relaciones Exteriores, October 7, 1866, in Romero (comp.), *Correspondencia*, V, 675–76; and Webster, "Texan Manifest Destiny," 62.
30. Randall and Pease (eds.), *Diary of Orville H. Browning*, II, 101–104; William G. Moore Diaries, in Johnson Papers, Series 9A.

on October 21. Johnson then invited Grant to a cabinet meeting, where Seward read the instructions to Campbell which mentioned the general's role. Even though Jackson had received Grant's written refusal of the twenty-first, the president had primed some cabinet members before the meeting by informing them that Grant had previously consented to go. A heated scene took place at the meeting. Grant again declined the mission, whereupon Johnson requested the attorney-general to give an opinion on whether his order to Grant was legal. Before the attorney-general could reply, Grant dramatically answered the question: "I am an officer of the army, and bound to obey your military orders. But this is a civil office, a purely diplomatic duty that you offer me, and I cannot be compelled to undertake it. Any legal military order you give I will obey; but this is civil and not military, and I decline the duty." Then, Grant stormed out of the meeting. At a subsequent cabinet meeting, which Grant did not attend, Johnson obtained cabinet approval to "request" Grant to go to the Texas-Mexican border in order to place himself in position to advise Campbell. On October 27, Grant rejected the "request" citing his recent refusals of identical or similar missions.[31]

Grant would not support the Seward-Johnson Mexican policy, nor would he remove himself from the Washington political scene and perhaps create a situation allowing for Sherman's promotion over his head. So, on October 30, Johnson ordered Stanton to replace Grant with Sherman for the Mexican mission assignment. Disgusted with the Seward-Johnson group's late October machinations, Grant voiced strong resentment to his close friends Badeau

31. Randall and Pease (eds.), *Diary of Orville H. Browning*, II, 103–104; C. B. Comstock manuscript diary, in Comstock Papers, box 8; Beale (ed.), *Diary of Gideon Welles*, II, 621–22; and Comstock to Sheridan, October 31, 1866, in Sheridan Papers, box 5; St. George L. Sioussat, "Notes of Colonel W. G. Moore, Private Secretary to President Johnson, 1866–1868," *American Historical Review*, XIX (October , 1913), 98–132; Grant to Johnson, October 21, 1866, in Grant Papers, Series 5; Grant to Stanton, October 27, 1866, in Johnson Papers; George S. Boutwell, *Reminiscences of Sixty Years in Public Affairs* (New York, 1902), 109; and Johnson to Stanton, October 26, 1866, in RG 84, Post Archives of the Mexican Legation; and Badeau, *Grant in Peace*, 52–53. Badeau mistakenly places this confrontation in November.

and Comstock. Significantly, Grant's complaint that Campbell would receive orders from Seward and not from himself suggested that he might have considered the mission had he been given greater power to aid Mexico.[32]

What motivated Johnson to be so insistent regarding Grant's participation in the Campbell mission? Although the often-made claim that Johnson wanted to get Grant out of the country in order to promote General Sherman first to command of the army and then to the cabinet as secretary of war seems plausible, the timing of the proposed Grant-Campbell mission suggests other possibilities. The Mexican mission was to be made public about twelve days before the fall election in 1866. While the timing might have been purely coincidental, it is suspicious that Johnson's order to Secretary of War Stanton, selecting Grant to accompany Campbell, and Seward's long dispatch to Campbell, informing him of United States policy toward the French withdrawal and of Johnson's disposition to have Grant accompany him as advisor, were both printed. All the remaining State Department instructions to Campbell were handwritten.[33] Moreover, in the mid-nineteenth century, instructions to diplomats normally were nearly always handwritten by State Department clerks. The only exceptions to this policy would be circular orders and very rarely instructions which were intended for wide distribution. The printing of these instructions strongly suggests that the Johnson administration intended to give wide distribution to Grant's role in its Mexican policy. Moreover, Johnson's willingness to be satisfied if Grant would move into Texas, close to Mexico, indicated that Johnson

32. Johnson to Stanton, October 30, 1866, in RG 84, Post Archives of the Mexican Legation; Stanton to Sherman, October 30, 1866, in Stanton Papers; Comstock to Sheridan, October 31, 1866 (confidential), in Sheridan Papers, box 5; Badeau, *Grant in Peace,* 53–54; and Crook, *The North, the South,* 44–64.

33. All the Campbell-State Department correspondence in the microfilmed series of Diplomatic Dispatches and Diplomatic Instructions as well as the Post Archives of the Mexican Legation, RG 84, have been examined, and except for Circular Instructions which went to all or most legations, no other instructions to Campbell appear in printed form. See also William T. Sherman, *Memoirs of General W. T. Sherman* (2 vols.; New York, 1891), II, 416.

and Seward wanted to use Grant's reputation and popularity and his role in the Mexican mission to generate political support for their administration. Viewed in this way, the often-resurrected argument that Johnson wanted Grant out of the way so he could use the army to control the elections in 1866 seems less convincing.[34]

Most significantly, since the Johnson administration claimed confidence in Napoleon's February, 1866, assurances to initiate the evacuation of Mexico in November, 1866, Grant's mission promised to be a major success. Recognizing the relationship between a French withdrawal and domestic political success, Seward had sought since Napoleon's decision to extract his army to encourage the speediest possible compliance with this announced goal. When rumors circulated that the French might not withdraw in November, 1866, Seward refused to believe them; nevertheless, he informed the French that such a course would produce "a wide popular mistrust of even the Emperor's sincerity in making the engagement, and of his good faith in fulfilling it."[35]

True, in mid-1866, two United States agents, recently returned from France, former governor of Indiana Oliver Morton and General Schofield, expressed strong doubts that Napoleon really intended to withdraw.[36] Nevertheless, from the inner circle of the Johnson administration, Gideon Welles bears testimony to the fact that Johnson and Seward expected a diplomatic victory from the French withdrawal, only learning later, in mid-November, 1866, of

34. George S. Boutwell, "The Impeachment of Andrew Johnson from the Standpoint of One of the Managers of the Impeachment Trial," *McClure's Magazine*, XIV (1899–1900), 176–77; and Sefton, *The Army and Reconstruction*, 104–105.

35. Seward to Bigelow, November 23, 1866, in U.S. Department of State, *Foreign Relations of the United States, 1866*, Pt. 1, pp. 366–67.

36. Romero to Ministro de Relaciones Exteriores, March 20, June 5, 1866, in Romero (comp.), *Correspondencia*, VII, 330–32, 603; and George E. Church, *Mexico: Its Revolutions; Are They Evidence of Retrogression or of Progress?* (New York, 1866). This 84-page pamphlet, published in July, 1866, had first appeared as a series of articles in the New York *Herald* in May, 1866. Seward to de Montholon, April 25, 1866, and Seward to Bigelow, September 29, October 8, 1866, in U.S. Department of State, *Foreign Relations of the United States, 1866*, Pt. 1, pp. 358–59, 378–79. See also Romero to Ministro de Relaciones Exteriores, April 28, 1866, in Romero (comp.), *Correspondencia*, VII, 452–53; and Blackburn, "Military Opposition," 162–63.

the French decision to postpone withdrawal. So, at an October cabinet meeting Seward insisted that, upon arriving at Veracruz, the Campbell mission would find the French forces withdrawing and the road to the Mexican Liberal government in Mexico City open. Upon accepting the Mexican mission, Sherman indicated in correspondence with Grant that he considered the mission's success a foregone conclusion. He assumed his task was to find the best method to occupy or protect the major Mexican ports during the French withdrawal.[37] Would the Johnson administration send Grant on this glory-laden task, which would increase his fame, if it intended to subordinate him to Sherman afterwards? More realistically, the Johnson administration desired no less than to borrow Grant's world reputation in order to convince domestic doubters and the French government of its serious interest in Mexican affairs, and at the same time to profit from Grant's apparent support of the Johnson-Seward Mexican policy.

A nagging question remains: why did Grant refuse a mission that was supposed to end in a success he had been seeking for some time? Grant acted as if his role in the mission were meaningless, or as if the mission would succeed without his participation. As Seward's instructions to Campbell of October 25 indicated, Grant's role was delineated quite clearly. Several contingencies, important to the United States, were considered regarding French withdrawal. Seward recognized that "doubts have been entertained and expressed in some quarters upon the question whether the French government will faithfully execute this agreement." If the French

37. Romero to Ministro de Relaciones Exteriores, November 3, 1866, in Romero (comp.), *Correspondencia*, VIII, 530–32; Beale (ed.), *Diary of Gideon Welles*, II, 622–24; Randall and Pease (eds.), *Diary of Orville H. Browning*, II, 112; Sherman to Grant, November 2, 1866, in Grant Papers, Series 5; and Sherman to Grant, November 3, 1866, in W. T. Sherman Papers, box 104. See also Romero to Ministro de Relaciones Exteriores, May 11, 1866, in Romero (comp.), *Correspondencia*, VII, 516; and Church to Sherman, July 26, 1867, in William Conant Church Papers, Library of Congress. The French announcement of withdrawal produced a skelter of gratitude and jubilation among Latin American countries in favor of United States diplomacy. See Watson Webb to Seward, August 7, 1866, J. Kilpatrick to Seward, June 15, 1866, and Allan A. Burton to Seward, June 6, 1866, in U.S. Department of State, *Foreign Relations of the United States, 1866*, Pt. 2, pp. 320–21, 414–15 and Pt. 3, p. 536.

did not begin to withdraw, Seward's instructions indicated Grant's important role: "The General of the United States Army possesses already discretionary authority as to the location of the forces of the United States in the vicinity of Mexico," meaning the sizable military force in Texas. If, as Seward expected, the French initiated their evacuation, the northern border region and other areas within Mexico might undergo a period of anarchy or domestic civil war. In any case, Grant should advise Campbell "concerning such questions as may arise during the transition stage of Mexico from a state of military siege by a foreign enemy to a condition of practical self-government. At the same time it will be in his power, being near the scene of action, to issue any orders which may be expedient or necessary for maintaining the obligations resting upon the United States in regard to proceeding upon the borders of Mexico."[38] Although Grant could have considered his designated role meaningless and powerless, it is not necessary to accept his view. Potential domestic political advantages for Johnson, national security, and international power politics offer superior hypotheses for Grant's appointment to accompany Campbell.

Although Sherman later analyzed the October, 1866, Mexico maneuver as a move to put Grant "to one side," at that time he acted as if the mission was important. Recognizing that Johnson wanted to elevate him to secretary of war over Grant because he was considered more friendly to the administration, Sherman asserted Grant did not object, but that he refused to countenance that move. As the Campbell mission prepared to leave, Sherman requested Grant to expedite notice to Juárez that the mission was departing, and to inform General Henry Halleck, commanding in California, to prepare forces to undertake the temporary occupation of Acapulco as the French withdrew.[39] Why did Sherman make

38. Seward to Lewis D. Campbell, October 25, 1866, in RG 84, Post Archives of the Mexican Legation.

39. W. T. Sherman to John Sherman, October 21, 1866, in Rachel Sherman Thorndike (ed.), *The Sherman Letters: Correspondence Between General and Senator Sherman from 1837 to 1891* (New York, 1894), 279–82; Sherman to Grant, November 2, 1866, in Grant Papers, Volume 54; Sherman to Campbell, November 2, 1866, and Sherman to Grant, November 3, 1866, in Sherman Papers.

these preparations for a meaningless mission? If the Mexican mission had no intrinsic importance except as a means to remove Grant from Washington so that the pro-administration Sherman could rise to power, why did Johnson decide to send Sherman on a meaningless mission after Grant refused to go?

Indeed, as perplexing as the Grant appointment is the fact that when Grant refused the mission Sherman rather than some other general was chosen to accompany Campbell. Sherman even proposed to Johnson that either General Winfield S. Hancock, commanding in New Mexico, or General Philip H. Sheridan, commanding in Texas, be substituted for Grant, adding "in the event of neither of these alternates proving satisfactory to the Secretary of State, that I could be easier spared than General Grant."[40] Sheridan was also quite popular and as commander of the Mexican-Texas border area familiar with Mexican affairs, but like Hancock and many other major-generals, a determined, pronounced opponent of Johnson's "lenient" policy toward the South and a sharp critic of the Johnson-Seward Mexican policy. If Johnson wanted to send someone on a wild-goose chase, why select Sherman, second in command of the army, a popular figure, a supporter of Johnson's policy and one of the few generals not urging an aggressive Mexican policy?

Of course, if a chief function of the mission was to warn the French of the sincere United States interest in their withdrawal, Sherman, with a strong world military reputation derived from the great 1864–1865 campaign through the South, was almost as imposing a figure as Grant and vastly superior to Sheridan or Hancock, whose reputations were more national than international. According to Cyrus Comstock, Seward insisted upon "having some big military man" accompany the mission, suggesting a desire to apply additional diplomatic pressure upon the French rather than merely remove Grant from Washington.[41] Logically, after Grant

40. Sherman, *Memoirs*, II, 415; and Edward Lee Plumb diary of the Campbell-Sherman mission, November 14, 1866, in Plumb Papers.

41. C. B. Comstock to Sheridan, October 31, 1866 (confidential), in Sheridan Papers, box 5; and Blackburn, "Military Opposition," 162.

refused the mission, if Johnson merely wanted to get rid of a nuisance or fill a trumped-up post, Sheridan or some major-general opposed to the administration's policies would have gone; if he wanted to apply pressure on the French, Sherman was the best replacement. Hence, the choice of Sherman to replace Grant suggests the October mission was not merely trumped-up. Important matters were at stake, including the winning of congressional support for Johnson's followers. Grant refused to go because, in his view, his position as advisor possessed very limited power, his presence would not effectively aid Mexico, the election crisis demanded his attention, and by the fall of 1866 he had an increasing distrust and dislike of Johnson and Seward.

At the close of the fall, 1866, political campaign, Grant revealed his distrust or dislike of both Johnson and Seward. Grant explained to Sherman: "Whilst you were absent on your Mexican Mission I did not write to you because I did not know how to address you except through the Secretary of State and I have nothing to do with that functionary when it can be avoided." At the same time, as an outgrowth of the González Ortega incident, Grant revealed that he no longer trusted Johnson's determination on Mexican matters. When Mexican General Jesús González Ortega, residing in New York, claimed he was the legitimate president of the Mexican republic and attempted to return to Mexico to depose Juárez, Grant ordered Sheridan to arrest Ortega if he attempted to cross from Texas to Mexico, which Sheridan did. While approving Sheridan's action, Grant indicated his doubts about Johnson's firmness: "I believe it exactly agrees with the President's notion also, but whether that will be acknowledged or not I do not know."[42] Desiring a strong, aggressive policy to terminate French intrigues in Mexico, Grant had long ago lost confidence in Seward; now he was also judging Johnson to be unreliable.

42. Grant to Sherman, January 13, 1867, in Sherman Papers; Beale (ed.), *Diary of Gideon Welles*, II, 592; Comstock diary, in Comstock Papers, box 8; Badeau, *Grant in Peace*, 89; Hesseltine, *Grant*, 77; Grant to Sheridan, November 15, 1866, in Sheridan Papers, box 39; Romero to Ministro de Relaciones Exteriores, November 24, 1866, in Romero (comp.), *Correspondencia*, VIII, 625–26; and Plumb to Banks, June 20, 1866, in Banks Papers.

By late 1866, Grant's ability to influence the Johnson administration had waned. Although Romero had previously officially reported every interview with Grant, after the 1866 election campaign he explained to his government why he ceased to describe his
conversations with Grant: "Since Grant now has no influence with
the President, and since there is an almost open rupture between
him and Seward, his ideas and desires have for us no more than a
future interest, in case he might become President of the United
States."[43] The substance of the Grant-Johnson relationship was
gone by late 1866; only the shell remained, and that collapsed quite
easily in the Stanton removal crisis of August, 1867.

Although the Grant-Johnson crisis in the fall of 1866 had ended
the general's direct influence upon the president, it did not free
Johnson from the web of Mexican affairs. The mix of domestic
politics and Mexican affairs in the fall, 1866, election campaign set
in motion the events leading to the Radical Republicans' first effort
to impeach Johnson in the winter of 1866–1867. Already by early
1866 some Radicals were aware that the administration might use a
foreign dispute to divert attention from domestic problems. One
pondered whether "some of our potent politicians are on the *qui vive*
for a foreign war? And will not the President & his most flattering
advisers adopt such a step as an antidote to the odium of ignoring
the rights of the black men and as an opiate for the memory of his
late escapade? The Foreign Secretary, too, who is perhaps more
Johnsonian than the President himself—is he not feeling his way to
a European rupture?" Friction with either England or France was
considered the likely diversion.[44]

43. Romero to Ministro de Relaciones Exteriores, June 30, 1867, in Romero (comp.),
Correspondencia, IX, 644–45. Years later, Grant's services to Mexico in its struggle against
Maximilian were warmly recalled. See Mexico City Ayuntamiento, *Corona Funebre, Dedicado
a la Memoria del Gral. Ulises S. Grant* (Mexico, 1885), 16–18, 23, 37.

44. George Bemis to Sumner, February 26, 1866, in Sumner Papers, Volume 77. Sew-
ard had a long record of attempting to divert attention from domestic problems by calling
forth foreign ogres. See Crook, *The North, the South*, 44–64; Kinley J. Brauer, "Seward's
'Foreign War Panacea': An Interpretation," *New York History*, LV (April 1974), 133–157;
Paolino, *Foundations of the American Empire*; and Norman B. Ferris, *Desperate Diplomacy:
William H. Seward's Foreign Policy, 1861* (Knoxville, 1976).

Throughout the fall campaign in 1866, some people had suggested that the administration's best strategy was to turn attention from the domestic situation to foreign affairs. One of James Gordon Bennett's editorial writers passed on his chief's opinion to President Johnson: "He thinks you should strike out a fresh course on other questions; that a strong national policy in our foreign relations and affairs and an able financial policy would give éclât to your administration. This, he argues, would divert the public mind from the distracting and embittered partisan issues of the day and help to settle them." Another newspaperman suggested that a warlike stance, or even war, might divert attention from the domestic scene:

Your adversaries have thus far succeeded by speeches of war and vengeance. They have appealed to the passions of the people, and there is no doubt those passions have been greatly excited. Why not enlist their passions in another direction? Why not assume a hostile attitude toward England? . . . A foreign is better than an internecine war, if war should finally be resolved on. A declaration of war intentions, strongly expressed, immediately spread through the press, would immediately unite the whole people. They would care no more for these petty Congressmen and their stump speeches about Constitutional Amendments, negro slavery and southern butchery. They would cry "to arms," "our country is in danger" and this whole herd of miserable agitators would be brushed away in the popular ferment.

This Johnson well-wisher mentioned Mexico as an area for possible diversionary action.[45] Thus foreign affairs could be used to alter the course of domestic conflict.

Seasoned observers among the Radicals scored the administration's effort to save itself from the disaster facing its domestic policies by diverting attention to its Mexican policy. The editors of *Harper's Weekly* detected an administration effort to influence the November election through an active foreign policy. Referring to late October campaigning, an editorial noted: "There is some talk in

45. W. B. Phillips to Johnson, September 16, 1866 (confidential), Hiram Ketchum, Jr., to Johnson, October 13, 1866, and J. S. Baker to Johnson, July 5, 1866, in Johnson Papers.

the newspapers about a new heroic foreign policy to be adopted by the Administration. Payment in full is to be demanded of England for the *Alabama* piracies, and the French claims in Mexico are to be guaranteed, the Republican Government in the country recognized, and permission given to it to cede certain territory to the United States. If this is intended to affect the elections it is too late." Other journals agreed that the Johnson administration attempted to sway public opinion by drawing attention to its Mexican policy.[46]

In late November, 1866, James Speed, previously Johnson's attorney general, who had left the cabinet in mid-1866 and soon cooperated with the anti-Johnson forces, speculated in a letter to Charles Sumner,

From present appearances it looks like the President would try to retrieve his "lost cause" by some diversion of the public attention from our domestic affairs to our foreign policy—I know that you agree with me in thinking that this should not be permitted. We have enough to do this side of the Rio Grande. The President may well look upon that stream as Caesar did upon the Rubicon. I have great confidence in the calmness, dignity, and wisdom of this congress, and yet I sense that the folly called the "Monroe Doctrine" had a vague and undefinable charm for many of its best members.[47]

Several weeks later, the *Chicago Tribune* reacted similarly to the administration's Mexican policy. While noting the failure of the recent Mexican mission of Campbell and General Sherman, the *Tribune* editorial speculated that "the recent management of the Mexican question ... will neither add to Mr. Seward's reputation as a statesman, nor achieve what was doubtless a leading purpose, the rescue of Mr. Johnson's administration from merited contempt."[48] Contemporary observers clearly saw a relationship between Mexican affairs and domestic politics.

46. "Our Foreign Affairs," *Harper's Weekly*, X (November 10, 1866), 706; "The Mexican Affair," *The Nation*, III (November 29, 1866), 431–32; and the *Charleston Mercury*, December 13, 1866.
47. James Speed to Sumner, November 28, 1866, in Sumner Papers.
48. "The Mexican Muddle," *Chicago Tribune*, December 23, 1866.

Seward realized the profound negative effect which the November, 1866, unilateral French decision not to initiate withdrawal of its troops might have upon the domestic political setting. Several weeks after the election of 1866, when Seward received notice of the French decision not to withdraw some troops in November but to pull out the whole force in March, 1867, his dissatisfaction was complete. He found "the Emperor's decision to modify the existing arrangement without any understanding with the United States . . . in every way inconvenient and exceptionable. We cannot acquiesce." Then, Seward firmly instructed Bigelow to "state to the Emperor's government that the President sincerely hopes and expects that the evacuation of Mexico will be carried into effect with such conformity to the existing agreement as the inopportune complication which calls for this despatch shall allow." Finally, revealing the domestic impact of Napoleon's decision, Seward observed that the inauspicious French decision had been made "without full reflection upon the embarrassment it must produce here."[49]

For a long time the Radicals had distrusted Seward. He was considered "the marplot in Lincoln's cabinet" and continued giving his ill-advised and unacceptable views during Johnson's administration. Many Radicals knew Seward played a major role in Johnson's administration, advising, drafting speeches, and directing the efforts to create a new party in 1866 based upon conservative Republican and Democratic strength. Thus, long before the fall campaign of 1866, the Radical leaders received correspondence similar to the following: "There are I believe some intimations that you are about moving in relation to Mexican matters. One would think that it was high time, when we consider the truckling and contemptible course of Secretary Seward and his tool the President in these regards—as honest Americans, we must blush with shame at our own want of

49. Bigelow to Seward, October 12, November 8, 1866, and Seward to Bigelow, November 23, 1866, in U.S. Department of State, *Foreign Relations of the United States, 1866,* Pt. 1, pp. 359–60, 364–67.

spirit and manhood." Oliver Morton, like many opponents of the Johnson administration, considered Seward responsible for converting the president from a hard policy toward the South to a lenient one. In domestic affairs, the radicals held the secretary of state responsible for persuading Johnson to try to organize "a great middle party" which would eliminate radical and moderate Republican factions from power. In foreign affairs, Seward's evil influence worked to convert Johnson from a strong policy toward French intervention in Mexico to a slow, patient one. In both cases the Radical leadership became very disgusted with Seward's role and influence in Johnson's cabinet and desirous of removing him from power.[50]

Some Radicals noted with disgust that Seward assumed a major position in "the swing-around-the-circle." The *Chicago Tribune* editorial on September 5, 1866, described Johnson's "swing-around-the-circle" as "Seward's Railway Train," ascribing to Seward joint power with Johnson for running the train. At the end of the "swing" William Pitt Fessenden decided that "the truth is, Seward had destroyed the President, as well as himself.... I mourn over Andy. He began by meaning well, but I fear that Seward's evil counsels have carried him beyond the reach of salvation. Lost and disgraced himself, Seward seems to have no ambition but to destroy others. Him I cannot excuse or forgive." Later, during the fall election, Thomas L. McLain labeled "William H. Seward,

50. Maurice Wakeman to Banks, June 22, 1866, in Banks Papers, box 63; Foulke, *Life of Oliver P. Morton*, II, 464; clippings of the election of 1866, Edward McPherson Papers, Library of Congress, Volume 1, pp. 33–36, 64–65, 126–30, and Volume 2, p. 24; "Seward's Railway Train," "Seward on Loyalty," "Seward Among His Neighbors," and "The Impeachment Question," *Chicago Tribune*, September 5 and 12, October 2, and November 9, 1866; William P. Fessenden to Hugh McCulloch, September 11, 1866, McCulloch Papers; F. P. Blair (Sr.), to Frank (P. Blair, Jr.), June 25, 1866, and April 9, 1866, in Blair Family Papers, box 53 and box 8; James Russell Lowell, "The Seward-Johnson Reaction," *North American Review*, XXVIII (October, 1866), 523–28; Samuel C. Parks to Lyman Trumbull, January 30, 1866, George E. Eisenmeyer to Trumbull, September 17, 1866, in Lyman Trumbull Papers, Library of Congress; Wm. W. Thayer to Sumner, May 14, 1866 (confidential), in Sumner Papers, box 78, pt. 1; Zachariah Chandler to his wife, February 17 and 27, 1865, in Chandler Papers; Montgomery Blair to Johnson, August 9, 1866, in Johnson Papers; F. P. Blair to James R. Doolittle, July 20, 1866, in Seward Papers; and Van Deusen, *Seward*, 468.

the leader, the controller, the great power of this whole affair." Radicals often assigned Seward the role of "evil genius" or force for wrong who was leading the Johnson administration into erroneous policies and actions.[51] Unquestionably the Radicals had any number of reasons for wanting Seward's removal. Yet, although Johnson was aware of the strong opposition to Seward, it was also evident that the president had great respect for and trust in Seward's ability.[52] To some, it seemed that the easiest road to Seward's removal was the impeachment of Johnson.

The Radical dissatisfaction with the Johnson administration's foreign policy, particularly in regard to Mexico, played a significant role in producing support for the first impeachment effort.[53] Fur-

51. William P. Fessenden to McCulloch, September 11, 1866, in McCulloch Papers; Campaign of 1866 volumes of newspaper clippings, in McPherson Papers, Volume I, pp. 126-30; William Frank Zornow, *Lincoln and the Party Divided* (Norman, Oklahoma, 1954), 48, 101; T. Harry Williams, *Lincoln and the Radicals*, 19, 205, 280; William R. Brock, *An American Crisis: Congress and Reconstruction, 1865-1867* (London, 1963), 119; R. M. T. Hunter to Seward, September 27, 1865, in Hunter Papers; F. P. Blair (Sr.) to Frank Blair (Jr.), December 9, 1866, in Blair Family Papers, box 53; Maurice Wakeman to Nathaniel Banks, June 22, 1866, in Banks Papers; Edward L. Pierce (ed.), *Memoirs and Letters of Charles Sumner* (4 vols.; Boston, 1894), IV, 300; Foulke, *Life of Oliver P. Morton*, II, 464; Sheridan, *Personal Memoirs* II, 215-19; and Milton Lomask, *Andrew Johnson: President on Trial* (New York, 1960), 221.

52. Moore diaries, in Johnson Papers, Ser. 9A, pp. 4, 26-27; Lucius Q. Washington to R. M. T. Hunter, November 17, 1866, and John L. Dawson to R. M. T. Hunter, January 15, 1867, in Hunter Papers; Matías Romero to Ministro de Relaciones Exteriores, September 7, 1866, in Correspondencia General con los Estados Unidos; and John H. and Lawanda Cox, "Andrew Johnson and his Ghost Writers," *The Mississippi Valley Historical Review*, XLVIII (December, 1961), 460-79. See also R. W. Johnson to Andrew Johnson, July 23, 1866, in Johnson Papers; Alfred Iverson to Seward, November 26, 1866, in Seward Papers; Robert Winston, *Andrew Johnson, Plebian and Patriot* (New York, 1924), 364-66, 369; Zornow, *Lincoln and the Party Divided*, 48, 96, 101; Brock, *An American Crisis*, 119-21; Lawanda and John H. Cox, *Politics, Principles, and Prejudice 1865-1866: Dilemma of Reconstruction America* (London, 1963), viii, 44-46; Williams, *Lincoln and the Radicals*, 19-20, 205-12; Van Deusen, *Seward*, 449-51, 463-64, 468.

53. Historians who have treated Johnson's impeachment in depth invariably focused upon the second impeachment move. See Michael Les Benedict, *The Impeachment and Trial of Andrew Johnson* (New York, 1973); Raoul Berger, *Impeachment: The Constitutional Problems* (Cambridge, Mass., 1973); Irving Brant, *Impeachment: Trials and Errors* (New York, 1972); Trefousse, *The Radical Republicans*, 366-69, 380-404; McKitrick, *Andrew Johnson and Reconstruction*, 486-709; Lomask, *Johnson on Trial*; George F. Milton, *The Age of Hate: Andrew Johnson and the Radicals* (Hamden, Conn., 1956), 382-425; Claude G. Bowers, *The Tragic Era* (Cambridge, Mass., 1929), 156-96; David Miller Dewitt, *The Impeachment and Trial of Andrew Johnson* (Madison, 1967); and Charles Ernest Chadsey, *The Struggle Between President Johnson and Congress over Reconstruction* (New York, 1896).

thermore, there are very strong indications that the early Radical move for impeachment was not aimed at President Johnson alone, but also, and perhaps principally, at Secretary of State William H. Seward.

Although historians have usually noted the Radical dislike and distrust of Seward which led to repeated attempts to remove the secretary from office, not even those historians who assign Seward a role as a major influence in the Johnson administration have suggested the possibility that impeachment was aimed at removing Seward's influence. Nevertheless, in mid-November, 1866, Charles G. Halpine, editor of the *New York Citizen*, informed Johnson that "I find the radical leaders, so far as I can judge, enlisted not against you but against Mr. Seward." Then, in early December, 1866, John Gilligan warned Seward that the impeachment effort was aimed at both Johnson and Seward.[54]

Romero revealed the early impeachment effort as a step to remove Seward's influence from the Johnson administration. On December 2, 1866, fifteen days before Ohio Congressman James M. Ashley's first impeachment move in the House, Romero visited various Radical leaders who were his close friends and confidants.[55] In a dispatch to his government he described the conversations in this manner:

I visited various of the principal senators and representatives and from the conversations I had with them I believe that the radical faction of the Republican party is disposed to impeach the President. Their plan is to force the resignation of the president pro tempore of the Senate, Mr. [Lafayette] Foster [of Connecticut], a moderate Republican, who has just failed reelection in his state, and to put in his place Senator [Benjamin] Wade of Ohio, a Radical Republican. If they can count on two thirds of the Senate, which is necessary in order to impeach the President, it appears to me that they are disposed to do it, and in that case the presidency will fall on Mr. Wade. . . .

54. Van Deusen, *Seward*, 468, 474; Cox and Cox, *Politics, Principle, and Prejudice*, viii, 44–46; Brock, *An American Crisis*, 119–21; Zornow, *Lincoln and the Party Divided*, 18–22, 48, 96, 101–103; Charles G. Halpine to Johnson, November 15, 1866, in Johnson Papers; John Gilligan to John Henry Martindale, December 3, 1866, in Seward Papers.
55. Goldwert, "Matías Romero and Congressional Opposition."

I note on the part of the representatives and senators a great disgust with the President, and very especially with Mr. Seward, for whom they have a concentrated detestation. They have given credit, in general, to the rumors that this Government has offered to assume payment of the French debt, retaining in exchange some of our states, and they [the congressmen and senators] manifest a decided opposition to this arrangement, which they categorize as undignified and nocuous. Others believe that the President and Mr. Seward wish to provoke, at any price, a foreign war in order to exit from the bad situation in which they find themselves, and these others are disposed to impede the development of the plans [of Johnson and Seward].[56]

Romero detected a sense of caution in the Radical leaders. They did not intend to make the move unless they were assured of success—"if they can count on two thirds of the Senate." In addition to the Radical disgust with Seward's role in the administration and the speculation that Seward was the target of this first impeachment plan, Romero's observations raise related questions regarding the seriousness and goals of the first impeachment effort and Wade's role in the project.

Romero's belief that a serious Radical plan to impeach existed at this time was independently sustained by Secretary of the Interior Browning, Secretary of the Navy Welles, and others. Browning expressed his fears of a Radical impeachment effort to several cabinet members—Seward, Secretary of the Treasury McCulloch, and Postmaster-General Alexander W. Randall—during a meeting at the White House on November 15, 1866, only to find that none of those present shared his apprehensions. However, two weeks later, Welles confided to his diary that he suspected a "conspiracy" among the impeachment forces. Later, after the actions of Ashley and other Radicals in December, 1866, and early January, 1867,

56. Romero to Ministro de Relaciones Exteriores, December 3, 1866, in Romero (comp.), *Correspondencia*, VIII, 693–94. A search of the Archivo Histórico de Matías Romero, Banco de México, the Archivo Benito Juárez, Biblioteca Nacional, and the Archivo de la Secretaría de Relaciones Exteriores failed to reveal who the "principal senators and representatives" were.

Welles again insisted that "a committee is sitting in secret, a foul conspiracy."[57]

Whereas Welles's use of the word "conspiracy" to describe what he considered a carefully planned impeachment effort in the winter of 1866–1867 overdramatizes the Radical position, numerous others observed that a serious, planned effort was under way. On January 19, 1867, Henry Cooke described to his brother Jay Cooke a Radical plot which was similar to the one Romero revealed. Henry wrote:

I am reluctantly coming to the conclusion that the Radicals intend to force through the impeachment against Johnson as a political measure. This is nothing more nor less than revolution. We may as well look the facts in the face. The intention is to get rid of Johnson, and to put Wade or Fessenden, probably Wade, in as President of the Senate and he in turn will become acting President under a law of Congress depriving the President of the exercise of the functions of his office while on trial.[58]

In early January, 1867, Radical Congressman James Garfield wrote a close friend:

If we could succeed in an impeachment of the President it would be a blessing, probably, but it is perfectly evident that with the Senate constituted as it is, we cannot effect an impeachment. Still Ashley and such like impeachment men, are determined to push the insane scheme of making the attempt and settling the country in a ferment.

Garfield believed many were involved in the first effort to impeach Johnson to do "some absurdly extravagant thing to prove their radicalism." While he felt the constant agitation about impeachment was "ruinous both to the party and to the general peace of the country," Garfield asserted "that there is a very formidable attempt being made to impeach Johnson." Writing long after the events, Radical leader George W. Julian agreed that when Congress met in December, 1866, impeachment came in for considerable discussion

57. Beale (ed.), *Diary of Gideon Welles*, II, 627, III, 19–20; Randall and Pease (eds.), *Diary of Orville Hickman Browning*, II, 109–110.

58. Henry Cooke to J. Cooke, January 19, 1867, quoted in Ellis Paxon Oberholtzer, *Jay Cooke: Financier of the Civil War* (2 vols.; Philadelphia, 1907), II, 25–26.

and "both houses seemed ready for all necessary measures."[59] Thus, this first effort was considered a serious, planned one.

In mid-January, 1867, in the midst of the first impeachment inquiry, Senator Jacob M. Howard, one of the senators who had sought the honor of proposing the impeachment resolution, made a speech condemning the administration's Mexican policy, observing that "the state of war has interrupted our trade with Mexico; it has greatly involved our relations with the legitimate Government of that republic; and our own interests, the interest of our commerce, the interest of our own citizens, the interest of mankind generally, require that it should be brought to a speedy close." Howard even charged that the Johnson administration contemplated arranging an understanding with the interventionists regarding recognition of Maximilian.[60] The indictment of Johnson would not rest solely on domestic issues, although domestic political manipulations might increase the size of the anti-administration factions, moving the president closer to political doom.

Benjamin Wade's role in the early impeachment effort is instructive and enlightening. Wade had long been a confidant of Romero and an outspoken and active figure in the drive to force the United States government into a more vigorous insistence upon French withdrawal from Mexico. When it appeared Wade might be elevated to president of the United States, Romero described Wade to his superiors as "one of the best friends that we have in this country." This judgment was based upon knowledge Romero had accumulated over a period of four years of continual contact with Wade.[61]

59. James Garfield to Burke Aaron Hinsdale, January 1, 1867, in Theodore Clarke Smith, *The Life and Letters of James Abram Garfield* (2 vols.; New Haven, Conn., 1925), I, 396–97; Garfield to Hinsdale, January 20, 1867, in Mary L. Hinsdale (ed.), *Garfield-Hinsdale Letters: Correspondence Between James Abram Garfield and Burke Aaron Hinsdale* (Ann Arbor, Mich., 1949), 88, 94; and George W. Julian, *Political Recollections, 1840–1872* (Chicago, 1884), 303–304. See also [?] to Seward, November 26, 1866, in Seward Papers, enclosing newspaper clipping suggesting that Foster was perhaps too "weak kneed" for impeachment.

60. *Congressional Globe*, 39th Cong., 2nd Sess., 458–60, 487.

61. Romero to Ministro de Relaciones Exteriores, March 9, and April 17, 1867, in Romero (comp.), *Correspondencia*, IX, 181, 296. For Romero's contact with Wade between

Wade's promotion to president pro tempore of the Senate was pushed even before the November elections, supporting the contention that an impeachment plan existed which would elevate Wade to the presidency. John W. Forney, influential Pennsylvanian newspaperman and Radical, urged Senator Zachariah Chandler to give his "attention to the necessity of electing Judge *Wade* President of the Senate, in the first week of the session. It seems to me he is the man for the impending exigency. Politeness to the incumbent should have nothing to do with the discharge of this great duty. Our friends everywhere should move, and move instantly towards the election of a patriot firm enough to meet every crisis and upon whom the whole country would rely. His election would give peace and security to all business circles and would consolidate our ranks more than anything else." At the beginning of the session, Wade's niece had written to his wife: "What about impeachment of the President? Will it be done or [are] there too many wavering ones; we are all wishing to see uncle Frank in Mr. Foster's place so in case the President is deposed we shall have an incorruptible one in his place."[62] The urgency to get Wade into the effective vice-president slot in lieu of lame-duck Senator Foster only makes sense if impeachment were seriously contemplated.

The plan which Romero described and others affirmed helps us clear up another shadow-filled incident, Benjamin Wade's midnight effort to sneak the bill for the admission of Colorado through the Senate. Senator James Doolittle attempted to block the late-night consideration of Colorado's admission by hinting that Wade was involved in some nefarious plot: "The people of the United States know what is transpiring in this body; and there are peculiar reasons which connect themselves with the Senator from Ohio, which will draw some attention to him, and to the course he is pursuing on

January, 1864 and January 1865, see Emma Cosío Villegas (ed.), *Diario de Romero*, 584–85, 595, 600–602, 604, 607, 609–12, 647, 650, 652. See also Edward Pierrepont to Bigelow, June 16, 1866, quoted in Blackburn, "Military Opposition," 175.

62. John W. Forney to Chandler, November 3, 1866 (private), in Chandler Papers; and Maggie G. Wade to "My Dear Aunt," December 9, 1866, in Wade Papers.

this occasion. We all know, time and again, that Senator, in pressing this matter of Colorado, has said over and over that his purpose was to reenforce a majority in this body, already more than two thirds. And for what, sir?" Benjamin Wade's recent biographer, after judiciously assessing the evidence, decided that Senator Doolittle's veiled assertion that Wade maneuvered in such a manner out of personal motives is incorrect. Wade wanted Colorado and Nebraska admitted because their votes would be useful to the Radicals in the contest over reconstruction policy.[63] But the Radicals already had more than the two-thirds majority necessary to implement a congressional reconstruction.

While the Radicals may have expected to command the two-thirds majority needed to override the president's veto when the Fortieth Congress met, it was generally conceded that their majority in the Senate would be considerably reduced in an impeachment effort. In November, 1866, an observer had noted that "most likely there will be a Radical Party in Congress to impeach President Johnson. Still it is thought a necessary two-thirds vote cannot be obtained in the Senate, that such men as Fessenden, Trumbull and others of the party, will oppose it." Garfield recognized that the Radical strength in the Senate was most likely insufficient for a successful impeachment.[64] While the evidence is not as strong as might be desired, it is plausible that Wade pushed for the admission of four strong Radical Senators from Colorado and Nebraska in order to assure his ascension to the presidency via impeachment.

Many years ago, historian David Miller Dewitt first recognized the possibility of a long-range Radical plan to impeach Johnson, beginning in February, 1866. However, due to lack of available evidence, Dewitt could do little more than sketch the possibility. He suggested, however, that Wade's efforts to make Nebraska and Colorado states were part of his plan. Recently, historian James E.

63. *Congressional Globe*, 39th Cong., 2nd Sess., 1922; and Hans L. Trefousse, *Benjamin Franklin Wade: Radical Republican from Ohio* (New York, 1963), 277–78.
64. Garfield to Hinsdale, January 1, 1867, in Hinsdale (ed.), *Garfield-Hinsdale Letters*, 88; Joseph Swift to Emily Balch, November 18, 1866, in Balch Family Papers, box 2.

Sefton has concurred that Wade's action regarding Colorado's admission is more understandable if an impeachment plan existed.[65]

By late January, 1867, Romero was reporting that his "best sources" were informing him "that there is no object of pushing [impeachment] through for the present, and certainly not before the 40th Congress meets."[66] Although Romero gives no indication why his sources gave him a different story on impeachment in January, 1867, than they had two months earlier, in the interval the French had publicly stated their decision to withdraw their whole force from Mexico within the next few months. In fact, the French army had begun concentrating its army in Mexico City and moving units and supplies to Veracruz. On the domestic scene, Johnson had taken no important action indicating a change in heart, mind, or plans on his part which would justify the softer approach toward him. The anti-administration forces, waiting for the Fortieth Congress and a stronger anti-Johnson majority, might have decided to wait until it could act effectively. By early 1867, the Mexican issue dividing the political factions appeared headed toward a solution. The domestic issues were intensifying, however, and it became increasingly clear that Johnson shared responsibility for the unacceptable actions of his administration. The ultimate more serious clash between Johnson and his opponents would center on their domestic differences.

The divisive impact of Mexican policy upon the Johnson-Grant split and the politics of the first impeachment attempt suggest the significance of Mexican affairs in domestic United States politics. Specifically, quarrels arose between administration and anti-administration factions over the transfer of arms and war materials to Mexico, the raising of United States volunteer forces for service with Juárez, the use of Grant's name and reputation in the "swing-around-the-circle," and the attempted use of his reputation for the

65. Dewitt, *Impeachment of Johnson*, 54, 66–86, 91, 149, 174–77; and James E. Sefton, "The Impeachment of Andrew Johnson: A Century of Writing," *Civil War History*, XIV (June, 1968), 122–23, 136–37.

66. Romero to James W. Beekman, January 25, 1867, in James W. Beekman Papers.

Campbell mission to place a sign of approval upon the administration's Mexican policy. These differences prompted the most active anti-administration forces to use a failing Mexican policy as a lever to pry Johnson and Seward out of political power during the first impeachment. Faced with an angry congressional and popular outburst in the United States over French violation of the agreement, the Johnson administration became more insistent; and the French, informed of the reaction against their policy, decided to withdraw all their forces in March, 1867. But the termination of the French intervention in Mexico resolved only one foreign relations problem facing the United States.

One can speculate that special problems threatening to limit future United States expansion, such as the desire for Canadian annexation, fisheries and reciprocal tariff problems with Canada, the *Alabama* claims negotiations, access to naval stations in Santo Domingo and Haiti, rising interest in a Central American canal, or the general interest of bankers, exporters, farmers, and manufacturers in expanding United States trade and investment opportunities abroad, all had their effect upon "domestic events." Further study of the Reconstruction years, not only in terms of the domestic positions of the chief political forces, but also of their positions on foreign relations, might well reveal more clearly how strongly party and factional bonds or cleavages rested in part on shared or disputed foreign policies.

During the early post–Civil War years, many Republicans became convinced that improper influences were obstructing domestic order, and in addition, pursuing a foreign policy which could seriously threaten the security as well as future commercial growth of the United States. If a militarily powerful and ideologically unacceptable government controlled Mexico, all United States' trade lines with the Caribbean, Central America, South America, the Pacific coast states, and Asia would be threatened. During the Civil War and Reconstruction years, United States interest in expansion into Mexico revealed a new impulse. Land was no longer the prime objective; it was replaced by investment, exploitation, and commercial goals. Economic expansion, nearly universally accepted within the United States, raised questions regarding which interest groups would participate in the expansion and to what extent. From 1864 through 1867, numerous United States politicians, merchants, investors, and speculators examined the possibilities of economic activity in Mexico.

IX Dollars over Dominion:
The Developing
United States Economic Interests
in Mexico, 1861–1867

D URING the last twenty years several historians have carefully examined United States investment in railroad and mining activity in Mexico following the American Civil War, but only a few scholars have discussed earlier capital investment interests, and no one has studied the period from 1861 until 1867 in Mexican–United States economic relations.[1] In spite of the American Civil War and Mexico's fifty-year history of disorder, revolution, and civil war, capped in 1861 by the intervention of France, England,

1. David M. Pletcher has described specific aspects of United States economic penetration of Mexico following the American Civil War in "Mexico Opens the Door to American Capital, 1877–1880," *The Americas*, XVI (July, 1959), 1–14, and "The Development of Railroads in Sonora," *Inter-American Economic Review*, I (March, 1948), 3–45. Broader studies of the years after 1867 are Pletcher, *Rails, Mines, and Progress;* David M. Pletcher, "México, campo de inversiones norteamericanas, 1867–1880," *Historia Mexicana*, II (January–March, 1953), 564–74; Frank A. Knapp, Jr., "Precursors of American Investment in Mexican Railroads," *Pacific Historical Review*, XXI (February, 1952), 43–64; and Francisco R. Calderón, *Historia Moderna de México: La República Restaurada—La Vida Económica* (Mexico, 1955), esp. 711–42. For pre-1861 United States investment interest in Mexico, see David M. Pletcher, "A Prospecting Expedition Across Central Mexico, 1856–1857," *Pacific Historical Review*, XXI (February, 1952), 21–41; and J. Fred Rippy, "Diplomacy of the United States and Mexico Regarding the Isthmus of Tehuantepec, 1848–1860," *Mississippi Valley Historical Review*, VI (March, 1920), 503–531. The best broad studies of American expansionism in the mid- and late nineteenth century are LaFeber, *The New Empire;* Williams, *The Roots of the Modern American Empire;* Plesur, "America's Outward Thrust"; and Wehler, *Aufstieg des amerikanischen Imperialismus.*

and Spain, American speculators, opportunists, capitalists, and promoters launched an intense campaign to gain concessions and investment opportunities during the years from 1861 to 1867. Although their successes were few, the promoters gained considerable business experience and information about Mexico's economy.

Why these unlikely years witnessed the unleashing of a pack of American capitalists and speculators is not entirely clear. Certainly a key event was the arrival to power of the Republican party, with its emphasis in foreign relations upon profit and gaining political influence for the United States through commerce and investment in contrast to the earlier territorial expansion promoted by the Democratic party. Another factor was that President Juárez' Liberal government came to power in 1861 and, while opposed to American territorial expansion, encouraged, even sought, United States investment to further Mexico's economic modernization. In addition, United States moral and material aid in support of the Mexican republic against the French produced a positive, even friendly atmosphere for American investors.[2] However, these years were marked by a hesitant, inconsistent development that defines them as a transitional era between the heyday of private and public efforts to annex all or part of Mexico and a period when most North Americans sought trade and investment rather than territorial annexation.

During the course of the Civil War, State Department officials and United States businessmen demonstrated considerable interest in Mexico. The visible activity of the businessmen was often significantly influenced by the less obvious conduct and views of State Department personnel in Mexico. Thomas Corwin believed that either of the two loan agreements which he had negotiated with Mexico would prevent European intervention in Mexico, while providing an opening for United States capital. On August 20, 1861, he took another step to aid American businessmen by asking

2. For the Mexican liberals' commitment to economic modernization, see Sinkin, "Modernization and Reform in Mexico, 1855–1876."

all United States consuls in Mexico to provide detailed information about importation and banking activities in Mexico.[3] Support for United States businesses also came from Marcus Otterbourg, consul in Mexico City from 1861 to 1866, who suggested ways that American capital could undermine the German, English, French, and Spanish commercial positions while at the same time increasing United States investments.[4]

Corwin's and Otterbourg's desire to expand American commercial activity in Mexico reflected a changing view of consular duties. During the pre-Civil War years when the Democrats were in power, consular officers in Mexico and Central America usually limited their activity to such traditional diplomatic matters as annexation schemes and protection of American life. So far as commercial activity was concerned, they were ordinarily interested only in their personal business holdings. After 1861, however, the emphasis shifted as newly appointed Republican consuls began arguing that the United States should increase its commercial activity in areas south of the border.

The Republican consuls in Mexico suggested many steps to improve Mexican–United States economic relations. Among other things, they proposed the establishment of communications and transportation networks aimed at making northern Mexico more accessible to North American mining interests, especially those in San Francisco. The consuls, supported by Governor Frederick F. Low of California and other important federal and state officials in California, also urged the creation of more consular positions with salaries high enough to attract men capable of promoting economic opportunity for North Americans.[5]

3. Circular of August 20, 1861, in Corwin to Seward, August 28, 1861, in Diplomatic Dispatches, Mexico, RG 59, NA.

4. Marcus Otterbourg to Seward, November 29, 1861, and September 28, 1862, in Consular Dispatches, Mexico, RG 59, NA.

5. This summary is excerpted from the United States consular dispatches from Mexico during the period 1861–1867. See specificially Reuben W. Creel to Seward, December 10, 1863, September 18, 1864, March 17 and June 29, 1865, and August 18, 1866, in Consular Dispatches, Chihuahua, RG 59, NA; F. B. Elmer to Seward, April 6, 1863, October 20,

Still, the man most responsible for establishing the ideological basis for the encouragement to United States economic involvement in Mexico during the 1860s and after was Secretary of State Seward. Strongly opposed to overt annexation, he believed that laissez-faire capitalism would spread United States influence in Mexico and eventually lead to the absorption of that country into the Union. Thus, Seward's belief that his fellow citizens no longer desired territorial acquisition derived from his conviction that they had learned to "value dollars more, and dominion less."[6]

Investors with views similar to Seward's found themselves appointed to important diplomatic positions. Edward Lee Plumb, later to serve as secretary of the legation and chargé d'affaires in Mexico from 1866 to 1868, had been active in mining and railroad development in Mexico since the mid-1850s. In early 1862, however, the continuing American Civil War and the initiation of European intervention in Mexico forced Plumb to reveal his concern for the future of the United States in Mexico. He did so in a memorandum—prepared at the request of Senator Charles Sumner, chairman of the Senate Foreign Relations Committee—on Corwin's first draft agreement of November, 1861, for a direct United States government loan to Mexico. The Corwin proposal, argued Plumb, would not only counter European influence, but also ensure that "commerce... would be revived and stimulated, and... flow into our hands in place of the present European channels." The loan, he believed, would also increase the possibility of Mexico's eventually joining the United States.[7] Plumb, like Seward

1864, March 31, October 10 and 20, 1865, in Consular Dispatches, La Paz, RG 59, NA; William L. Blake to Seward, March 28, 1865, and September 30, 1866, in Consular Dispatches, Manzanillo, RG 59, NA; Richard L. Robertson to Seward, May 24, 1863, and F. W. Freelon to Seward, August 28, 1863, in Consular Dispatches, Mazatlán, RG 59, NA.

6. Whelan, "Seward: Expansionist," 9–23, 143–44; Rippy, *The United States and Mexico*, 252, 277; LaFeber, *The New Empire*, 28; and Van Deusen, *Seward*, 366, 511–14, 526. For a less convincing analysis of Seward's views, see A. Curtis Wilgus, "Official Expression of Manifest Destiny Sentiments Concerning Hispanic America, 1848–1871," *Louisiana Historical Quarterly*, XV (July, 1932), 486–506.

7. Memo to Charles Sumner on the Corwin loan treaty (written sometime early in 1862), enclosed in E. L. Plumb to Nathaniel Banks, May 9, 1866, in Plumb Papers. For

and many others, believed Mexico would ultimately be absorbed peacefully, and the process could be hastened by encouraging commercial and investment ties.[8]

Ranking members of Mexico's Liberal party shared the desire for greatly increased commercial and financial relations with the United States, though they rejected the idea of ultimate amalgamation. The Liberal party's interest in developing economic ties with the United States was revealed in January, 1861, when, under specific instructions from the Juárez government, Matías Romero traveled to Springfield to congratulate Lincoln upon his election. Not only did Mexico look to the United States as its model for political and economic modernization, he told Lincoln, but it also "proposed to dispense complete protection to United States' citizens and concede them every form of facilities which tend to develop the commercial and other interests of both republics."[9] Thus, though the future would reveal that Romero and Seward disagreed completely on how active a role the United States should play in removing foreign intervention from Mexico, their views on United States–Mexican commercial relations remained quite similar.

Romero's concept of Mexican-American relations, particularly in regard to potential economic ties, was amplified for Postmaster-General Montgomery Blair in early 1862:

Mexico expected that the present administration has a policy more elevated than that followed until recently of acquiring our territory ... with

additional information on Plumb's economic and political involvement in Mexico, see the Archivo Romero and Romero (comp.), *Correspondencia*. See also Pletcher, *Rails, Mines, and Progress*, Chapter 3, for a sketch of Plumb's later activity in Mexico.

8. Plumb to Seward, August 15, 1866, Plumb to Charles Sumner, July 26 and August 26, 1867, Plumb to William T. Sherman, September 3, 1867, all in Plumb Papers; and *Congressional Globe*, 39th Cong., 2nd Sess., 458–60, 487. For the argument that the United States did not adequately recognize Latin America's economic potential, see Carlos Butterfield to William Steuben De Zang, June 24, 1867, in Seward Papers.

9. Romero to Ministro de Relaciones Exteriores, January 23, 1861, in Romero (comp.), *Correspondencia*, I, 686–87; Matías Romero, *Estudio sobre la anexión de México*, 18. On Mexican economic thought and policy for this period, see Sinkin's "Modernization and Reform in Mexico, 1855–1876." See also Harry Bernstein, *Matías Romero, 1837–1898* (Mexico, 1973), a weak biography. Robert Ryal Miller is presently writing a biography of Romero.

the sole object of introducing slavery into it, or they would not entertain for a moment such projects [of economic cooperation].... The United States would receive more benefit from Mexico as an independent nation than... inside the Union... since then the lack of homogeneity of population, which has been the cause of the present civil war, would... present more difficulties in preserving the Union.... We can celebrate... commercial arrangements, in virtue of which the manufacturing states of the North acquire in Mexico the market they have lost in the South, and from which they have been prohibited until now because of the natural jealousy and distrust with which Mexico has viewed the United States. Since our political tendencies and interests are identical, we can make other arrangements... which will result in the United States obtaining all of the advantages... [of] annexing Mexico to the American Union, but without suffering any of the inconveniences.[10]

Romero's statement signaled the Mexican Liberals' policy, stressing the benefits of mutual economic relations and the dangers of annexation or amalgamation. This position contrasted with the earlier policy of the Mexican conservative party which, though it had also feared annexation, opposed closer economic ties. Key Mexican officials reiterated the Mexican Liberal party's position during the course of the 1860s. On March 29, 1864, speaking in New York at a dinner given in his honor, Romero suggested that the geographic nearness of the two nations and their common frontier presented the United States with the opportunity "to develop the great natural resources of Mexico." President Juárez read this speech six weeks after Romero delivered it and raised no objections to any part of it.[11] Juárez' interest in attracting United States capital was publicized in October, 1865, when Juan Navarro, Mexico's consul in New York, published a letter in the New York *Herald* announcing

10. Romero to Ministro de Relaciones Exteriores, February 1, 1862, in Romero (comp.), *Correspondencia*, II, 32–34.

11. Matías Romero (comp.), *Proceedings of a Meeting of Citizens of New York, to Express Sympathy and Respect for the Mexican Republican Exiles. Held at Cooper Institute, July 19, 1865. With an Appendix Containing the Speeches of the Hon. Matías Romero* (New York, 1865), 52–53; Juárez to Romero, April 20 and May 15, 1864, in Jorge L. Tamayo (ed.), *Epistolario* (Mexico, 1957), 262–67. See also Plumb to Romero, March 18, 1864, and Romero to Plumb, March 24, 1864, in Plumb Papers; and I. D. Andrews to Romero, October 10, 1867, in Archivo Romero.

that Juárez sought North American capital to develop Mexico's economy. Later, on June 22, 1866, Secretary of Foreign Relations Sebastián Lerdo de Tejada affirmed his government's desire that United States capital develop Mexico.[12] In February, 1867, as the French intervention drew to a close, the powerful general and politician Porfirio Díaz, later dictator in Mexico, was advised to seek the active cooperation of the United States in developing his country's economy.[13]

The wish of Díaz, Romero, Juárez, Lerdo de Tejada, and many other leading Mexican Liberals for closer economic ties between Mexico and the United States found limited support in the United States Congress. In early 1866, Romero and Corlies and Company, Mexico's financial agent in the United States, made plans to secure from Congress a guaranty of a Mexican bond issue, thus facilitating Mexico's entry into the private United States money market to raise funds for purchasing war materials to fight the French. Romero, assured that Thaddeus Stevens of Pennsylvania and other congressmen would support a resolution calling for a loan guaranty, persuaded Robert C. Schenck, Republican congressman from Ohio, to introduce it. Later, in March, 1866, learning of Seward's opposition to the guaranty, Romero informed Juárez that until Seward resigned or was removed from the cabinet, the guaranty would not pass.[14]

Seward and many congressmen felt the French might react adversely to the United States guaranteeing a Mexican loan, even to the point of refusing to implement their agreement to withdraw from Mexico by 1867. Nevertheless, despite some opposition in the House Foreign Affairs Committee, two proposals to assist Mexico's search for a loan reached the House floor near the end of the ses-

12. Juan Navarro to the editor of the New York *Herald*, October 20, 1865, Luis García Pimental Collection, VII-1, folder 3-4, no. 155.
13. [?] to Porfirio Díaz, February 27 and May 20, 1867, in Archivo Juárez.
14. Romero to Ministro de Relaciones Exteriores, February 14, 1866, in Romero (comp.), *Correspondencia*, VII, 156–58; Romero to Juárez, March 3, 1866, in Archivo Juárez; Romero to Plumb, May 5, 6, and 9, 1866, in Plumb Collection; and J. M. Iglesias to Juan Zambrano, May 14, 1866, in Archivo Romero.

sion. Thaddeus Stevens' resolution, introduced on June 16, 1866, inquired into the propriety of the United States government directly lending Mexico $20 million. Two days later, the resolution of Republican Congressman William D. Kelley from Pennsylvania called for the United States to guarantee up to $50 million in Mexican government bonds. Neither resolution was acted upon before the session ended.[15]

When Congress reconvened in December, 1866, the Louisiana Tehuantepec Company, a group of capitalists interested in building a railroad in Mexico and represented by Joseph N. Maddox, supported a loan guaranty by the United States government in order to stabilize Mexico. Aware that he could obtain a railroad concession only by impressing Romero with his group's solid economic and political position, and thus their potential utility in aid of a loan guaranty for Mexico, Maddox claimed the Louisiana Tehuantepec Company had the support of Nathaniel P. Banks, Republican from Massachusetts and chairman of the House Foreign Affairs Committee; Thaddeus Stevens; Samuel S. Cox, Democrat and minority leader from Ohio; Godlove S. Orth, Republican from Indiana; William D. "Pig Iron" Kelley; and other congressmen.[16] Those financially involved in this railroad scheme, according to Maddox, were Generals James B. Steadman, William Woods Averell, and W. G. M. Davis; John T. Pickett, former Confederate agent in Mexico; E. W. Bruce of New York; a Mr. Bail, president of the Bank of the Commonwealth, New York; Alexander Holland, American Express Company, New York; Judge William Marvin, United States senator-elect from Florida; and Waterhouse, Pearl

15. Romero to Ministro de Relaciones Exteriores, June 8 and 18, 1866, in Romero (comp.), *Correspondencia*, VII, 611, 693–96; *Congressional Globe*, 39th Cong., 1st Sess., 3217–18, 3251.

16. Maddox to Romero, December 12 and 13, 1866, in Archivo Romero. The other congressmen on Maddox' list of alleged supporters were Amos Myers, Republican from Pennsylvania; Robert C. Schenck; Columbus Delano, Republican from Ohio; James Falconer Wilson, Republican from Iowa; Martin Russell Thayer, Republican from Pennsylvania; and Governor Sewell. Maddox' first name appears as both James H. and Joseph H. in Romero's papers. He signed his letters simply J. H. Maddox, Maddox to Romero, December 3, 1866, in Archivo Romero.

and Company, a New York bank.[17] Romero asked Juan Navarro to investigate the character and financial position of the politicians and investors on Maddox's lists in order to gauge the seriousness of the proposal. Navarro reported that, while his informants considered Samuel Cox "a low politician," they believed the others on the lists were "good people." However, Navarro's informants rated the railroad venture as speculative and "without the possibility of bringing any advantage" to Mexico. Nonetheless, because of the important politicians involved, Romero gave Maddox a letter of introduction to Juárez, but refused, in spite of several bribe offers, to write a letter expressing confidence in the scheme.[18]

Although Romero withheld full confidence in the railroad project, Maddox nevertheless informed Romero of his plan to get the "dominant party," the Radical Republicans, indirectly to endorse his project by obtaining their support. While Romero's correspondence does not reveal the details of Maddox's plan, Romero expressed satisfaction with it. Two weeks later, after conversing with several congressmen about Mexican affairs, Romero informed his government that financial aid was now more likely because of Maddox's influence. Yet, in spite of the combined efforts of Romero, Maddox, and their congressional allies, in mid-February, 1867, the House Foreign Affairs Committee tabled the resolution guaranteeing the Mexican bonds. This action, Nathaniel Banks explained to Romero, reflected an increasingly widespread belief that the money would end up in the hands of American speculators.[19]

17. Unsigned note and list, in Archivo Romero, folio 01437. Another copy of the list is found in Juan Navarro to Romero, November 8, 1866, in Archivo Juárez. See also Resolution of Board of Trustees, Tehuantepec Transit Co., July 13, 1867, Causten-Pickett Papers, Volume 101, Library of Congress.

18. Romero to Juárez, October 31 and November 13, 1866, Romero to Navarro, November 2, 1866, and Navarro to Romero, November 5 and 8, 1866, in Archivo Romero; Romero to Juárez, November 17, 1866, in Archivo Juárez.

19. Maddox to Romero, December 3, 1866, Romero to Juárez, February 16, 1867, and Romero to Plumb, February 17, 1867, in Archivo Romero; Romero to Ministro de Relaciones Exteriores, December 15, 1866, in Romero (comp.), *Correspondencia*, VIII, 745–46; Romero to Ministro de Relaciones Exteriores, February 15 and 23, 1867, in Romero (comp.), *Correspondencia*, IX, 136, 152–53. See also U. C. Chaffee to Banks, May 22, 1866, E. L. Norton to Banks, February 5, 1867, in Banks Papers, box 63.

The Senate was much less occupied with a Mexican loan guaranty, though Romero did succeed in persuading Senator Benjamin Wade to introduce the Kelley resolution. However, the Seward-Sumner combination in the Senate, which agreed upon pursuing a Mexican policy that would not agitate the French, was too powerful. After holding the resolution in committee for seven months, Sumner killed the measure by requesting that the Foreign Relations Committee be discharged from further consideration of it.[20]

Partly due to Romero's direct lobbying with House and Senate leaders, numerous friends of Mexico were selected for the Senate Foreign Relations Committee and the House Foreign Affairs Committee during the second session of the Fortieth Congress. Romero was now more confident Mexico might obtain the loan guaranty.[21] Nevertheless, before the second session of the Fortieth Congress convened, the French intervention terminated and Romero returned to Mexico; so the Liberal government no longer actively pursued a United States loan guaranty. Although important leaders in Congress were interested in Mexico's fate, lack of knowledge about Mexican conditions plus the unsettled state of United States domestic affairs during the early months of Reconstruction produced a cautious approach which defeated the loan guaranty resolutions.

In any event, the attitudes and actions of State Department officials and congressmen were not as significant as the plans and actions of businessmen and concession seekers. There were many entrepreneurs and economic adventurers who sought to take advantage of Mexico's receptiveness to United States capital. Along with such well-known figures as Edward Lee Plumb, Caleb Cushing (former minister to China and former attorney general), Robert L.

20. *Congressional Globe*, 39th Cong., 2nd Sess., 1954, 3650; Van Deusen, *Seward*, 367, 495; and Donald, *Charles Sumner*, 142–43, 356–57.
21. Romero to Plumb, February 28 and March 13, 1867, Romero to Juárez, March 11, 1867, in Archivo Romero; Romero to Ministro de Relaciones Exteriores, March 12, 1867, in Romero (comp.), *Correspondencia*, IX, 194–95.

McLane (former minister to Mexico), Nathaniel Banks, Thaddeus Stevens, Thomas A. Scott (former assistant secretary of war and Pennsylvania railroad magnate), Generals John C. Frémont, John Schofield, Ulysses S. Grant, Orville E. Babcock, and Lew Wallace, Romero's dispatches to the minister of foreign relations mention scores of other financiers, engineers, speculators, soldiers, and politicians, all claiming they had aided or could aid Mexico.

Among those who sought concessions for their alleged services, no one negotiated a more impressive or grandiose contract for economic development in Mexico than John C. Frémont. In return for unspecified future services in marketing a Mexican loan and in obtaining a United States government guaranty of this loan, Mexican agent Gaspar Sánchez Ochoa offered Frémont Mexican government aid in constructing and maintaining a railroad in northern Mexico, vast mining and land grants, $6 million in bonds, plus other concessions. Frémont planned to link his proposed Mexican railroad with the Memphis and El Paso Railroad and thereby create an imposing transcontinental railroad empire dominating the southwestern United States and northern Mexico. Such generous concessions, in return for so little (Frémont was not bound to any specific action or conduct), led the Juárez government to instruct Romero to supervise and control all Mexican agents in the United States, including the authority to approve and countersign all contracts negotiated by Juárez' agents in the United States. Naturally, Romero, after reviewing the Ochoa-Frémont contract, in which Ochoa exceeded his authority, refused approval, but the general was too prominent a person with too many influential friends to be lightly brushed aside. Romero, willing to pay well, if less, for Frémont's services as a congressional lobbyist, offered him a smaller contract, substituting for a guaranteed railroad concession a promise to recommend the general's railroad project to Juárez. Furthermore, in the new contract, results (specific services rendered and goals achieved), not promises, were to be compensated. Frémont verbally agreed to Romero's terms and then changed his mind, refusing to sign the new contract and reasserting his belief in the validity of the Ochoa contract even without Romero's signature. But Frémont did not get his railroad concession, and Mexico never received his assistance. Frémont's role in this affair has been aptly summarized by historian Robert W. Frazer: "There was nothing altruistic in his attitude toward republican Mexico. He had an end in view, the railway grant, and he did not care particularly how he attained it."[22]

Others besides Frémont sought railroad grants from Mexico during the 1860s. Benjamin H. Cheever, New England lawyer and businessman, described to Romero a newly formed company, which planned "to connect the [Union] Pacific Road Eastern Division, the Kansas branch, with El Paso and thence through Chihuahua and Sonora to Guaymas." This group included such financially and politically influential people as J. D. Perry, president of the Union Pacific Railroad; Colonel Thomas A. Scott; Judge Justin Rice Whiting; C. A. Ropello; George E. Church of the New York *Herald*; and Frank Macmanus, a businessman in Chihuahua, Mexico. They sought the revalidation of a recently acquired old railroad concession which had been terminated in August, 1866, claiming the completion of 270 miles of survey work before Indian raids forced a halt. By October, 1867, more settled conditions had returned to Mexico, and Cheever's group wanted to complete the undertaking.[23] The grant was, however, not revalidated, perhaps because of Frank Macmanus' earlier efforts to negotiate a similar railroad grant with Maximilian's government. In October, 1865, Mexico's consul in New York, at Romero's instigation, had publicly warned concession seekers and holders that

22. Miller, "Gaspar Sanchez Ochoa," 321–22; and Frazer, "The Ochoa Bond Negotiations," 399–414 (the quotation is from p. 414).
23. Benjamin H. Cheever to Plumb, October 23, 1867, in Plumb Collection. The long, reasoned decree voiding the concession is found in *Colección de Leyes, Decretos y Circulares Expedidas por el Supremo Gobierno de la República*, III, 77–82, or in the *Periódico Oficial del Gobierno Constitucional de la República Mexicana*, August 13, 1866. See also George E. Church to Romero, October 22, 1867, and Cheever to Romero, October 23, 1867, in Archivo Romero.

negotiations with the empire would be detrimental to their concessions.[24]

Groups seeking railroad concessions expressed renewed interest during this period in the Tehuantepec Isthmus. Since the 1830s a route across Mexico had been considered among the quicker means of getting from the East Coast of the United States to California and Oregon. In the late 1840s, American capitalists had purchased from British interests their concession to build a road or railroad across the narrow Tehuantepec Isthmus. The grant was subsequently declared void in September, 1857, by Mexican President Ignacio Comonfort on the grounds that the concessionaires had not met the stipulated terms. A second charter was then granted to other United States interests. Since the group holding the original transit charter did not recognize the validity of Comonfort's 1857 decree, the existence of two charters led to an extended conflict for control of the transit route. Interesting facts in the case are that Judah Benjamin, later Confederate secretary of state, was a lawyer for and partner in the new charter group, located in New Orleans under the name Louisiana Tehuantepec Company, while Thomas Corwin, later United States minister to Mexico, served as one of the lawyers for the New York-based Tehuantepec Transit Company, whose charter had been declared void.[25] With the outbreak of the Civil War, tension heightened because now competing nations rather than competing firms maneuvered to validate these charters.

On March 8, 1861, Romero warned his government of the delicate situation that might develop over control of the Tehuantepec

24. John S. Cripps to Reuben W. Creel, October 1 and 5, 1866, in Records of the Mexico City Consulate, Letterbook, Volume 9, RG 84, NA. Otterbourg's certification, dated June 30, 1866, of a September 11, 1865, bill of sale is found in Records of the Mexico City Consulate, Miscellaneous Record Book, Volume 10, RG 84, NA. See also Juan Navarro to the editor of the New York *Herald*, October 1865, in García Pimental Collection, VII-1, folder 3-4, No. 155.

25. Meade, *Judah P. Benjamin*, 84, 121–23; Romero to Ministro de Relaciones Exteriores, March 13, and December 14, 1861, in Romero (comp.), *Correspondencia*, I, 315–16, 645–46.

transit rights. Romero had just received a copy of a memorial from the lawyers of the Tehuantepec Transit Company to Secretary of State Seward in which the company asserted the validity of its grant and the invalidity of Mexican President Comonfort's cancellation decree. Seward pointedly informed Romero of his desire to prevent these potentially valuable economic and military transit rights from passing to Confederate interests. Seeking to purchase Mexican acquiescence, Seward suggested a mutually agreeable sum be paid for the transit rights, perhaps during the loan negotiations between Corwin and the Mexican government. Romero, however, maintained that the Tehuantepec Transit Company's grant could only be renegotiated, not revived.[26] There the matter rested until after the Civil War when, both railroad grants having been declared void, the two groups maneuvered to have their charters reaffirmed.

By late 1866, when the French were withdrawing and Juárez and the Liberals were nearing victory, a resolution of the conflict between the two companies seeking to build a Tehuantepec railroad seemed feasible. On October 15, 1866, Juárez declared the Louisiana Tehuantepec Company's grant forfeited because the firm had not met construction deadlines. Juárez' action may have been in part a direct response to this latter company's flirtation with French and imperial interests, which had led to Maximilian's decree of October 12, 1866, reaffirming the Louisiana Tehuantepec Company's grant.[27] The Louisiana Tehuantepec Company's involvement with the empire, and the difficulty experienced by the Tehuantepec Transit Company in raising the $100,000 owed the Mexican gov-

26. James Wiles to Romero, March 8, 1861, and memorial of Benjamin H. Cheever and James Wiles to Seward, March 8, 1861, both enclosed in Romero to Ministro de Relaciones Exteriores, March 8, 1861, and December 14, 1861, in Romero (comp.), *Correspondencia*, I, 309–10, 645–46.

27. Matías Romero, *The Tehuantepec Isthmus Railway* (Washington, D.C., 1894), 10. See also Romero to Ministro de Relaciones Exteriores, December 27 and 29, 1866, in Romero (comp.), *Correspondencia*, VIII, 786–88, 800–901; and John S. Cripps' certification of Maximilian's October 12, 1866, decree, Records of the Mexico City Consulate, RG 84, Vol. 10. From the beginning of 1861, the Louisiana Tehuantepec Company attempted to sell its rights to the French. See the Marquis de Radepont Papers, files 7, 8, 9, and 22, Houghton Library, Harvard University. See also *El Mexicano*, October 18, 1866, p. 150.

ernment to fulfill the company's initial obligation under its newly drafted charter, convinced Romero that a merger of the two companies offered the best chance to combine the capital, energy, and organization required for success. From late 1866 on, Romero tried unsuccessfully to persuade Marshall O. Roberts, chief spokesman for the Louisiana Tehuantepec Company (which had now moved north to New York to find a new home, partners, and political support), and Charles Knapp, president of the New York-based Tehuantepec Transit Company, to merge their forces.[28]

United States domestic political maneuvers reinforced Romero's conviction that the two companies should work together. Grant had written a letter in support of Benjamin Cheever of the Tehuantepec Transit Company. Grant's wishes could not be overlooked, but then neither could Romero and Mexico take lightly the wishes of Nathaniel Banks, chairman of the House Foreign Affairs Committee, and Thaddeus Stevens, House majority leader. Banks had written a warm letter of support for Marshall O. Roberts of the Louisiana Tehuantepec Company, and Simon Stevens, Thaddeus Stevens' nephew, was an attorney for that company. Additional endorsements and correspondence involving other politically powerful people further confused and strained the Mexican diplomat's ability to arrive at a solution to the conflicting claims of the two companies.[29] Since a merger could not be worked out and the $100,000 was not forthcoming, the Tehuantepec Transit Company

28. Romero to Plumb, January 18, 1867, Romero to José María Iglesias, February 16 and April 6, 1867, in Archivo Romero; Romero to Ministro de Relaciones Exteriores, November 28, 1866, in Romero (comp.), *Correspondencia,* VIII, 661–62; Romero to Ministro de Relaciones Exteriores, January 13 and 29, February 16, March 17, April 5, and June 17, 1867, in Romero (comp.), *Correspondencia,* IX, 28–30, 96–98, 139–40, 205–206, 254.

29. Grant to Romero, May 15, 1866, enclosed in Romero to Ministro de Relaciones Exteriores, May 15, 1866, in Romero (comp.), *Correspondencia,* VII, 526–28; Henry Wikoff to Johnson, October 25, 1866, in Johnson Papers; Cheever to Cushing, November 10, 1866, S. L. M. Barlow to Cushing, December 13, 1866, George W. Searle to Cushing, February 12, 1867, E. L. Stone to Cushing, March 17, 1867, and Cheever to Cushing, August 14, 1867, all in Cushing Papers; Schofield to Juárez, October 11, 1867, Schofield to Romero, October 11, 1867, and Orville E. Babcock to Schofield, November 22, 1867, all in Schofield Papers, box 77. The Wade Papers, box 18, also contain material on the Tehuantepec Transit Company, although Wade's relationship to the company is not clear.

lost its charter on August 26, 1867. A new concession was granted on October 6, 1867, to a third group represented by Émile la Sère of New Orleans. La Sère kept his grant, altered in form, for twelve years, but he also failed to construct the required all-weather road or a railroad.[30]

In 1862, still another group had expressed interest in a Mexican railroad project. This scheme was inspired by A. C. Allen, United States consul at Minatitlán, who was deeply involved in Mexican economic and political affairs, in part through his close ties with Manuel Doblado, the Mexican foreign minister. In 1862, Juárez and Doblado offered Allen a railroad concession in the Tehuantepec Isthmus, if the United States would approve the April, 1862, Corwin-Doblado loan treaty. Viewing the loan as an essential step toward strengthening the forces south of the Rio Grande which favored United States development of Mexico's economic potential, Allen suggested that his railroad project would produce the defeat of Napoleon's plan to dominate Mexico, and hence should be supported by the United States government. Allen presumed that government-subsidized steamship lines, running to and from both ends of his Tehuantepec railroad concession, would produce sufficient cargo to make the railroad profitable. However, with the Senate's rejection of the Corwin-Doblado treaty in late 1862, Allen's hope for a railroad concession was lost.[31]

While some promoters sought an international transcontinental railroad to facilitate United States commerce with Mexico's Pacific

30. Romero to Ministro de Relaciones Exteriores, March 17, April 5, and June 17, 1867, in Romero (comp.), *Correspondencia*, IX, 205–206, 254, 604–606; Romero, *The Tehuantepec Isthmus Railway*, 10–11. For later United States participation in Mexican railroad development, see Pletcher, *Rails, Mines, and Progress*, and John H. McNeely, *The Railways of Mexico: A Study in Nationalization* (El Paso, 1964).

31. Allen to Seward, June 20 and October 8, 1862, Plumb to Seward, May 4, 1862, in Seward Papers; Corwin to Sumner, April 14, 1862, in Sumner Papers; Corwin to Seward, April 16, 1862, enclosed with Corwin to Seward, April 16 and 28, 1862, in Diplomatic Dispatches, Mexico, RG 59, NA; Bruno von Natzmer to Seward, April 8 and 26, 1862, in Consular Dispatches, Minatitlán, RG 59, NA; Allen to Doblado, March 24 and April 22, 1862, Manuel Doblado Correspondence; Romero to Ministro de Relaciones Exteriores, June 23, 1862, in Correspondencia General con los Estados Unidos.

Coast and to exploit the resources and commerce of northern Mexico, others wished to establish permanent mail-steamship service between Veracruz and New York, and Acapulco and California. Regular communications, contended Marcus Otterbourg, would generate an increase in Mexican–United States commerce and replace British economic influence with American. Another important figure encouraging ocean communication with Mexico was California Senator James McDougall, Romero's first ally in Congress, who promoted a Pacific Coast steamship line concession to benefit his home state. In December, 1866, Robert M. McLane, former minister to Mexico, presented one Mexican-California steamship project to Romero, in the form of a solicitation by his brother, Louis McLane, an investor in steamship lines, to create a Pacific coast line. While it is not possible to determine which interest groups were successful, two steamship companies had been operating regular service to several west coast Mexican ports prior to 1860 and several new lines began service in the 1860s. Businessmen like Plumb, Roberts, and others argued that closer steamship communication ties were necessary to facilitate economic entrance into Mexico.[32]

Mines and minerals were another attraction to concession seekers. The interest in Mexican mines was probably related to the gold and silver bonanza existing in the United States between 1848 and 1880. In addition to gold and silver, copper, coal, and petro-

32. Corwin to Seward, August 28, 1861, February 5, 1862, in Diplomatic Dipatches, Mexico, RG 59, NA; Otterbourg to Seward, September 28, 1862, in Consular Dispatches, Mexico, RG 59, NA; Romero to Ministro de Relaciones Exteriores, July 6, 1865, and Iglesias to Lerdo de Tejada, September 8, 1865, in Ramo de Fomento, Desagües, Volume 19 and expediente 56, Archivo General de la Nación; and Romero to Robert McLane, June 7, 1867; Benjamin Cheever to Romero, September 22, 1866, and McLane to Romero, October 10, 1867, in Archivo Romero. See also Samuel L. M. Barlow to Montgomery Blair, November 3, 1866, in Blair Family Papers, box 8; S. L. M. Barlow to Caleb Cushing, December 13, 1866, in Cushing Papers; [?] to Díaz, February 27, 1867, in Archivo Juárez; and Plumb to Sumner, September 4, 1867, in Plumb Papers; William E. Curtis, *Trade and Transportation Between the United States and Latin America*, in *Senate Executive Documents*, 51st Cong., 1st Sess., No. 54, pp. 123–45; and John Haskell Kemble, "Mail Steamers Link the Americas, 1840–1890," in Adele Ogden and Engel Sluiter (eds.), *Greater America: Essays in Honor of Herbert Eugene Bolton* (Berkeley, 1945), 490–95.

leum tempted numerous engineers and investors. The number of requests for mining rights and the importance of the men making these requests indicate that the interest shown during and after the Civil War in Mexico's mining areas was markedly greater than during earlier years.[33]

Although the French intervention was producing instability and insecurity in eastern Mexico, in 1864 the United States consul at Guaymas, Farrelly Alden, described a boom in mining and related activities in Sonora. He estimated the value of the silver and copper mines owned by American citizens to be more than a million dollars. The Nacosari mine, according to Alden, contained over fourteen million tons of copper and silver ore. In June, 1865, Alden's successor estimated that more than two million dollars had been invested in Sonoran mining by United States citizens during the preceding three-year period. Northern and western Mexico witnessed such increased North American interest in mining that by 1865 thirty United States mining firms had invested in northern Mexico.[34]

Petroleum, a mineral recently discovered to be very useful as a lubricant and source of power, also attracted investors. In early 1865, Wedworth Clarke, an oilman from New York, asked Romero's help in obtaining a concession to drill for oil in Mexico. Clarke's agents called upon Romero with three nearly identical petitions for petroleum grants. The first asked for the grant for all of Mexico; the second for the states of Veracruz, Tabasco, and Cam-

33. For a general view of the quickening intensity of United States interest in Mexican mines, see the consular dispatches from Mazatlán, La Paz, Guaymas, and Chihuahua. See also John C. Ten Eyck to Romero, May 17, 1867, mentioning the Volcanic Mining Company interest in Mexican mines, and Romero to Charles Miles, April 11, 1867, noting the interest of the Guadalupe and Sacramento Gold and Silver Mining Company, both in Archivo Romero. See also Plumb to Fessenden, July 20, 1866, in Banks Papers, box 63. For the origins of United States interest in Mexican mining areas, see P. L. Bell and H. Bentley Mackenzie, *Mexican West Coast and Lower California: A Commercial and Industrial Survey* (Washington, D.C., 1923), xv; Marvin D. Bernstein, *The Mexican Mining Industry, 1890–1950: A Study of the Interaction of Politics, Economics, and Technology* (Albany, N.Y., 1964), 17–19; and Pletcher, "A Prospecting Expedition across Central Mexico," 21–41.

34. Alden to Seward, September 30 and December 18, 1864, Edwin Conner to Seward, June 12, 1865, all in Consular Dispatches, Guaymas, RG 59, NA; and Bernstein, *Mexican Mining Industry*, 19.

peche; and the third for Veracruz and the Isthmus of Tehuantepec. The Clarke group sought petroleum rights which it claimed would "greatly augment the commercial importance of Mexico and contribute to the aggrandizement of that country, which was not only in the aspirations of the Mexican people, but also in the cordial desires of all citizens of our Republic." Romero informed Clarke that he might obtain a concession based on a modification of his third, or least extensive, petition. Since Clarke undoubtedly wanted as broad a concession as possible, Romero's reply discouraged him.[35]

Although the Clarke group did not obtain a grant, other parties continued to seek oil concessions, and oil was eventually produced in the Tehuantepec Isthmus. The first United States interest in oil occurred in early April, 1865, when M. Protos of Portland (Maine?), claiming he had drilled four wells in Tabasco, requested an exclusive petroleum privilege for all of Mexico. Unfortunately, the loss of many official Mexican republic records for the years 1864 to 1866 do not allow this grant request, nor many others, to be followed to its final disposition. But other American oil prospectors left paths which can be traced. In November, 1866, Rollin C. M. Hoyt, United States consul at Minatitlán, petitioned the minister of public works for an oil concession. Hoyt sought rights to drill on the Isthmus of Tehuantepec, claiming that without an official concession no capital could be attracted to initiate the project. Although no evidence exists as to whether Protos, Clarke, or Hoyt were responsible for the drilling, in mid-1866 the imperial newspaper *El Mexicano* claimed a significant strike had been made in the region which all three Americans had sought to explore, the Tehuantepec Isthmus.[36] United States oilmen, intrigued by the

35. Romero to Ministro de Relaciones Exteriores, April 13, 1865, enclosing John Adams and Wedworth Clarke to Romero, April 8, 1865, and Romero to Ministro de Relaciones Exteriores, April 25, 1865, in Correspondencia General con los Estados Unidos.

36. Romero to Ministro de Relaciones Exteriores, April 5, 1865, in Correspondencia General con los Estados Unidos; Rollin C. M. Hoyt to Romero, November 10 and December 13, 1866, in Archivo Romero; Hoyt to Seward, December 13, 1864, John L. Cilley to Seward, May 19 and July 12, 1865, and John Y. Bryant to Seward, November 14, 1865, all in Consular Dispatches, Minatitlán, RG 59, NA; and "Petróleo," from *Párajo Verde*, quoted in *El Mexicano*, May 31, 1866, p. 335.

prospects for Mexican oil discoveries, were hesitant to act without very favorable concessions and a more stable political situation to aid in raising capital.

Cotton culture was one economic activity which thrived on the political crisis in both the United States and Mexico, because the instability drove raw cotton prices up, thereby attracting the capital necessary to develop cotton production on Mexico's west coast. This area furnished significant supplies of raw cotton for the New England textile mills. Moreover, United States consuls on Mexico's west coast were reporting significant involvement of American citizens in supplying capital and technology to the cotton agriculture. The machinery was imported from the United States; Americans were purchasing the cotton land, growing the cotton, and preparing it for export; and finally, Americans were purchasing most of the export crop. The United States consul at Acapulco reported a cotton export to the United States for the third quarter of 1862 of 7,095 bales, or 1,036,444 pounds, a sizable export crop from an area that had just entered the world's raw cotton trade. By 1864, Mexico had altered its pre–Civil War cotton trade pattern with the United States. Whereas in the 1850s Mexico imported about 7.5 million pounds of southern cotton each year, by the mid-1860s it was exporting yearly about 15 million pounds of cotton, grown on its west coast, to New England. This trade not only benefited New England's cotton-starved textile industry, it also supplied some of the specie needed by the Juárez government to resist the French intervention.[37]

Mexico's unsettled lands also attracted adventurers. In March, 1863, Jacob Leese's Lower California Company sought a concession for an agricultural and mining settlement on vacant land in Baja California. When the concession was granted on March 13, 1864, Mexico added extra mining and fishing rights in return for $100,000

37. Lewis S. Ely to Seward, September 25, 1862, in Consular Dispatches, Acapulco, RG 59, NA; Thomas Schoonover, "Mexican Cotton and the American Civil War," *The Americas*, XXX (April, 1974), 429–47.

in advance cash payments.[38] In 1867, when the French intervention had produced a dire financial condition for the Mexican republic, the Lower California Company, taking advantage of this weakness, offered cash payments in exchange for complete control over all mines on the lands of the original grant and, in addition, for a similar concession in that part of Sonora bordering on the United States. When the request to increase the concession was presented to Romero in mid-1866, he recommended it be denied. There is no record of any enlargement of the Leese concession before it was canceled in 1871.[39]

Most of the military leaders connected with the several schemes to send Union and Confederate veterans into Mexico to aid in ousting Maximilian requested concessions as compensation for their services. Generals Schofield and Grant, both involved in the military plans to drive out the French, are representative of these military leaders. Grant and Romero decided on General Schofield to command a joint United States volunteer army to aid Juárez. Romero promised Schofield a concession in return for his services. Later, in June, 1867, Schofield sent his chief-of-staff, General William Mackey Wherry, with a private, confidential letter to Romero mentioning his interest in Mexican mines and land and requesting favorable consideration. While suggesting that first Schofield bring together capital and engineers, and then approach the Mexican government about a mining concession, Romero warned that a land grant would not include mineral or mining rights. When Schofield's mining venture did not develop, a mone-

---

38. Zorrilla, *Relaciones*, I, 448; George Wilkes to Romero, May 4, 1867, in Archivo Romero; Romero to Ministro de Relaciones Exteriores, November 10, 1865, in Romero (comp.), *Correspondencia*, V, 775–76; Romero to Ministro de Relaciones Exteriores, March 22, 1867, in Romero (comp.), *Correspondencia*, IX, 211–14. Ruth Elizabeth Kearney, "The Magdalena Bubble," *Pacific Historical Review*, IV (March, 1935), 25–38, chronicles Leese's Lower California Company.

39. Romero to Ministro de Relaciones Exteriores, March 8 and 21, and May 4, 1866, in Romero (comp.), *Correspondencia*, VII, 258–60, 272–73, 314–16, 475–81; Iglesias to Romero, January 18, 1866, Romero to Duncan, Sherman and Co., May 8, 1867, and Romero to Iglesias, June 28, 1867, in Archivo Romero.

tary payment for his services was agreed upon, though Schofield later claimed that only one installment on this settlement was ever paid.[40]

General Grant's friendship with Romero went far beyond the crisis period of the 1860s and ended only with Grant's death in 1885. Grant never requested personal consideration, but, mainly in the 1870s and 1880s, he solicited favors for members of his staff. In his May 15, 1866, letter, supporting Benjamin Cheever's efforts to obtain a railroad concession, Grant made early use of his influence.[41]

One group of concession seekers, including Generals Rufus Ingalls and Orville E. Babcock, close friends and advisers to Grant, sought to draw upon Grant's reputation with the Juárez government, when they offered immediate cash, annual payments, and the equivalent of coast guard services for Mexico's Pacific coast area in return for fishing rights. However, since Ingalls and Babcock were sensitive to their public positions and refused to permit public use of their names, the inquiry about a fishing concession was made in the name of L. Brooke of Portland, Oregon. Romero had to deny the group's petition, since the monopoly fishing rights it sought were unconstitutional in the Mexican republic.[42]

40. Romero to John M. Schofield, June 13, 1867 (two letters), and April 14, 1872, Schofield to Romero, February 26, 1872, in Archivo Romero; Romero to Ministro de Relaciones Exteriores, September 8, 1867, in Correspondencia General con los Estados Unidos. Another Civil War general, Lew Wallace, also active in planning and organizing a military force to free the Mexican Republic, sought concessions for mining and to lay a telegraph line. Wallace did not realize any of his projects. See the Wallace Papers.

41. Grant to James Longstreet, April 15, 1867, enclosed in Romero to Ministro de Relaciones Exteriores, May 24, 1867, in Correspondencia General con los Estados Unidos, explains why Grant refused to permit his name to be used in conjunction with any enterprise at that time. See also Grant to Romero, May 15, 1866, enclosed in Romero to Ministro de Relaciones Exteriores, May 15, 1866, in Romero (comp.), Correspondencia, VII, 526–28.

42. L. Brooke to Romero, September 3, 1867, and Romero [to Brooke?], September 4, 1867, enclosed in Romero to Ministro de Relaciones Exteriores, September 4, 1867, in Correspondencia General con los Estados Unidos. Babcock obtained an impressive list of recommendations in an attempt to obtain a transit railroad concession. However, upon arriving in Mexico, he discovered that several weeks earlier, a concession had been granted to Emile La Sère's group. See W. T. Sherman to Plumb, October 7, 1867, in Plumb Collection; Schofield to Juárez, and Schofield to Romero, October 11, 1867, Babcock to Schofield, November 22, 1867, in Schofield Papers; Babcock to Romero, October 16, 1867 (telegram), Díaz to Romero, December 27, 1867, in Archivo Romero.

The drive for investment or commercial activity on the part of United States promoters was not limited to Juárez' Mexico. The archives of Maximilian's imperial government contain many petitions from American citizens for concessions for railroads, canals, steamship lines, and other activities.[43]

While United States speculators represented an aggressive, modernizing economic system, expanding outward due to rapidly increasing agricultural and industrial surpluses, even the Confederacy's traditional agrarian-based society revealed interest in closer trade and communication ties with neighboring Mexico. While northern promoters were active in Mexican economic life, only a few Confederates demonstrated an awareness of the political and economic potential of closer ties with Mexico. John Forsyth, Confederate agent to the United States government and former United States minister to Mexico, in a long dispatch to Jefferson Davis on March 20, 1861, urged the establishment of political and commercial relations between Mexico and the Confederacy. To facilitate commercial ties, Forsyth understood that Colonel Carlos Butterfield, who already possessed a contract for a subsidized mail-steamship line from the Mexican government, would soon submit a proposal for regular steamship service between Mexico and the Confederacy. The Confederate government, desiring access to the Pacific, rapidly developed its own project for a transcontinental

43. For a sampling of such activity, see Archivo General de la Nación, Ramo de Fomento, Desagües, Volume 9, expediente 139, Volume 18, expedientes 37, 38, and 49; Ferrocarriles, Volume 19, expedientes 259, 289, and 293, Volume 20, expediente 279, Volume 22, expedientes 296, 297, and 302, Volume 23, expediente 315, Volume 26, expediente 387, Volume 27, expedientes 2–7, and legajo 9. A United States group, including Senator William Sprague, Rhode Island, and Congressmen Oakes Ames and John Bartley, both of Massachusetts, offered Maximilian a most intriguing railroad project. See Archivo General de la Nación, Ramo de Fomento, Ferrocarriles, Volume 22, expedientes 297 and 302 cited above. For the interest of several United States citizens in coal mining under Maximilian's empire, see the agreement among Samuel Dunbar, John White, and George F. Henderson, signed January 24, 1865, in Records of the Mexico City Consulate, Miscellaneous Record Book, Volume 10, RG 84, NA. On Maximilian's effort to propagandize his internal improvements in the United States, see Plumb to Lerdo de Tejada, February 21, 1865, in Plumb Papers, and Robert W. Frazer, "Maximilian's Propaganda Activities in the United States," *Hispanic American Historical Review*, XXIV (1944), 4–29. A private United States reaction to Franco-Mexican economic policy is found in Joshuah D. Abbot to Wade, April 6, 1867, in Wade Papers, Volume 13.

railroad connecting Texas with Mazatlán. In the summer of 1861, the talented Confederate diplomat assigned to northern Mexico, José A. Quintero, discussed a transcontinental railroad project with Governor Santiago Vidaurri of Nuevo León. A railroad through this area would bind northern Mexico to the Confederacy and be the shortest route to the Pacific. Moreover, the railroad would service an important mining area which was also significant for its agricultural productivity. The cool relations which existed between the Mexican Liberal government and the Confederacy delayed action at that time. When Maximilian, rumored to be sympathetic to the South, accepted the Mexican crown, the Confederate government acted. In January, 1864, Secretary of State Judah Benjamin instructed William Preston, Confederate commissioner to Mexico, "to secure for our people some more convenient access to the Pacific Ocean than that provided by the Gadsden Purchase." Benjamin suggested a route traversing the mining country and ending in Guaymas, but undoubtedly any route to the Pacific would have been acceptable.[44] The failure of the Preston mission to reach Mexico, because Maximilian refused to receive a Confederate envoy, and the end of the Civil War shortly thereafter doomed Confederate dreams for a transcontinental railroad.

At the Civil War's end, disgruntled and defeated Confederates sought refuge in Maximilian's unsettled mining and agricultural lands. Confederate leaders sponsored several colonization projects. William M. Gwin, former senator from California, planned an immense mining and agricultural colony in northern Mexico. His proposal seemed to have the favor of Napoleon in 1863–1865, but was ultimately "defeated by... [the] fear of American opposition and the overwhelming power of Mexican nationalism." Several

---

44. John Forsyth to Jefferson Davis, March 20, 1861, in Pickett Papers; Quintero to R. M. T. Hunter, August 20, 1861, "Memorandum [addressed to Quintero] on the true route of the Pacific Rail Road" [n.d.], signed by General Hugh McLeod, and Benjamin to Preston, January 7, 1864, all in Records of the Confederate States of America, the first two items in Vol. VIII, and the last item in container 17.

other agricultural colonies of Confederate refugees had temporary success before ultimately failing.[45]

United States economic expansion into Mexico between 1861 and 1867 was largely the work of a highly active private business sector that was quietly encouraged by Congress and the State Department and welcomed by Mexico. Matías Romero, Sebastián Lerdo de Tejada, Benito Juárez, and other Mexican leaders believed that American capital would greatly benefit Mexico's economic development. William H. Seward, Thomas Corwin, Marcus Otterbourg, Edward Lee Plumb, and many United States consuls in Mexico were convinced that a policy which produced economic profit and increased American political influence in Mexico was more advantageous to future United States–Mexican relations than a policy of territorial expansion. Moreover, towards the end of the 1860s, with southern expansionism shattered, the northern merchant-manufacturing alliance could safely obtain its economic and national security objectives in Mexico without annexation. Thus, developing American economic and political interests in Mexico over the next decades would reduce the likelihood that threats to United States security and to the Monroe Doctrine, such as the French intervention, would recur.

The businessmen's accomplishments may appear few. Nevertheless, there were significant successes for North American investment in mining (in Sonora and northwestern Mexico) and agriculture (particularly cotton), and isolated minor accomplishments in mail-steamship communications and the petroleum industry. More important, however, while the United States experienced the Civil War and Reconstruction, and while the Mexican republic

45. Regarding Mexican imperial projects for economic development, see Hanna and Hanna, *Napoleon III and Mexico*, Chaps. 1, 16, and 20; Carl C. Rister, "Carlota: A Confederate Colony in Mexico," *Journal of Southern History*, XI (May, 1945), 167–89; George D. Harmon, "Confederate Migration to Mexico," *Hispanic American Historical Review*, XVII (November, 1937), 458–87; and Hallie M. McPherson, "The Plan of William McKendree Gwin for a Colony in North Mexico, 1863–1865," *Pacific Historical Review*, II (December, 1933), 357–86.

fought the French and brought down Maximilian's empire, these businessmen succeeded in acquainting themselves with virtually every phase of Mexican economic life.[46] This is a considerably more active record in Mexico during the 1860s than is traditionally assigned to the United States.

46. For manifestations of rising United States economic penetration of Mexico in the post-Civil War years, see Webster, "The Mexican Border, 1865-1880"; Pletcher, *Rails, Mines, and Progress;* and Jorge Espinosa de los Reyes, *Relaciones Económicas entre México y los Estados Unidos, 1870-1910* (Mexico, 1951).

Epilogue

IN EARLY 1867 the United States government attempted diplomatically to soften what it feared might be excessive Mexican repression aimed at Maximilian and his supporters. The State Department sought clemency for Maximilian also to prevent a revenge-seeking renewal of conflict between Mexico and the European powers. Both France and Austria might attempt to obtain satisfaction for their offended honor if Maximilian were executed. Although the requests for leniency were made with circumspection, Romero, Lerdo de Tejada, and Juárez resented the United States government initiating this request. Thus, when Seward asked Romero to communicate the wish that Maximilian be treated well if taken prisoner, Romero responded that the United States had not notified the French to treat Juárez well if caught in 1864 and 1865.[1]

The long, determined resistance of Juárez and his followers from 1862–1867, the rise of Prussia, the end of the United States Civil War, all operated together to end the French experiment in New World empire. In the spring of 1867 the French army with-

1. Romero to Ministro de Relaciones Exteriores, April 6, 1867, in Romero (comp.), *Correspondencia*, IX, 257; and Romero to Juárez, June 1, 1867, and July 6, 1867, in Archivo Romero.

drew while Maximilian first wavered between remaining and departing and then decided to stay it alone. Alone he was. His imperial forces crumbled within weeks; his capture and execution followed.[2]

Later, when the Senate debated a resolution ostensibly sustaining the Juárez government's decision to execute Maximilian, the discussion focused upon the nature of the conflict in Mexico and its relationship to the United States. In a long speech, Michigan Senator Zachariah Chandler condemned the intervention in Mexico as "part and parcel of our rebellion." Chandler observed that those expressing friendship to Mexico now had been loyal during the rebellion, while those condemning Juárez' actions were former rebels, traitors, or northerners who sympathized with the Confederacy. Moreover, if the United States adopted the proper supportive policy toward liberal Mexico, Chandler projected a profitable future, since the "other nations that have heretofore monopolized the trade and the political influence in Mexico propose to cast her off" and "all the commerce of that republic would naturally fall as a matter of course into the hands of the people of the United States, who stand by her in her hour of trial." Senator Fowler blamed Seward for the sorry state of United States relations with Mexico and for the ailing United States support of the Liberal government. Praising the Mexicans for their long struggle to obtain liberal republicanism and warning that Juárez' enemies were the enemies of republican institutions, Fowler regretted the United States refusal to aid her sister republic.[3]

Taking exception to the remarks of Chandler and Fowler,

2. J. M. Thompson, *Louis Napoleon and the Second Empire* (Oxford, England, 1954), 218–21; Van Deusen, *Seward*, 492–96; Malloy, "The United States and French Intervention," 278; Isidro Fabela, *Las Doctrinas Monroe y Drago* (Mexico, 1957), 201; Fernando Iglesias Calderón, *El egoismo norte-americano durante la intervención francesa* (Mexico, 1905), 12–15, 289–307, 343–51; and Claude A. Duniway, "Reasons for the Withdrawal of France from Mexico," in American Historical Association, *Annual Report* I (1902), 315–28. See also Richard B. McCormack, "James Watson Webb and French Withdrawal from Mexico," *Hispanic American Historical Review*, XXXI (May, 1951), 274–86.

3. *Congressional Globe*, 40th Cong., 1st Sess., 600–601.

Senator Reverdy Johnson of Maryland noted that Maximilian's government was recognized everywhere in the civilized world except the United States. After all, Maximilian had accepted the Mexican crown in order to revive and stabilize Mexico, not to interfere with United States affairs. Responding to Senator Johnson, Senator James Warren Nye of Nevada asserted that the effort to overthrow republicanism in the New World was the result "of consultation among the crowned heads of Europe." With all Europe, except Russia, participating in this nocuous decision, Nye sympathized with the struggling Mexican republicans. Disappointed at the lack of American aid for the Liberals, Nye defined the threat which French intervention in Mexico posed by answering the rhetorical question "What did France want with Mexico? She wanted to break the commercial power of this mighty nation that faces the Pacific for four thousand miles." Seconding Nye's presentation, Senator Howard voiced his opinion that in Mexico's struggle against imperialism, Maximilian's fate had been just.[4]

Chandler's July speech drew warm praise from *New York Times* editor Henry Raymond: "I desire to express my admiration of the bold and straight forward manner in which you saw fit to present the sentiments of the *American Nation* upon Mexican affairs in general and Maximilian's fate in particular, in the U.S. Senate... I believe this to be a peculiarly opportune season for this nation to speak out the national sentiment and determination in regard to establishing Monarchical govts. on this continent." Raymond expected a strong stand to be taken against foreign interference which would be forcefully sustained in the future.[5]

In the summer of 1867, the *Chicago Tribune* analyzed Maximilian's end in this fashion:

When the Austrian gave his sword to Escobedo at Querétaro, the last rebel army surrendered. The invasion of Mexico by the French, and the strug-

---

4. *Ibid.*, 598–605.
5. Henry Raymond to Chandler, July 18, 1867, in Chandler Papers. For another expression of sympathy and approval of Mexico's course, see E. George Squier to Romero, July 12, 1867, in Archivo Romero.

gle of Maximilian to build up an Empire on this continent, were in fact, a branch of the Southern rebellion; they were entered upon and undertaken on a false estimate of the result of the great revolt against the power of the United States. . . . All through the war Mr. Seward and Napoleon understood each other perfectly. If the rebellion should be successful, of course this Government would have neither the strength nor motive to attempt the expulsion of the invaders of Mexico. If the rebellion failed, Napoleon would be compelled to abandon his undertaking, for he well knew that with the Union restored, the United States would never consent to see a monarchy set up by foreign bayonets, on this continent. That enterprise was, therefore, a part and parcel of the southern rebellion, with which its beginning and end are identities. . . . In the American mind the failure of the Southern rebellion and of Napoleon and Maximilian in Mexico will be linked together as events depending upon each other, and inseparably connected; and whoever shall write the history of the Great Rebellion will not complete it until he has traced to its final termination the effort of the Austrian Archduke to establish himself on the throne of a Mexican Empire.

Written after the United States Civil War and the French intervention were past, this editorial portrayed a widely held view of the forces moving North American history in the 1860s.[6]

Demonstrative of the friendly United States wishes for the firm establishment of a liberal regime in Mexico were Seward's instructions to United States Minister Otterbourg in mid-1867 that it was not compatible with American interests to press claims against the Mexican government. Since "it is the desire of the United States not to hinder but to favor the consolidation of republican institutions in Mexico," Otterbourg was not to take any action regarding claims unless specifically directed to do so. Granting a period for Mexico's stabilization and recovery was considered in the interest of the United States.[7]

The long struggle against the Franco-Maximilian forces, officially recognized by most European governments, left Mexico isolated from Europe and, in a sense, dependent upon the United

6. "Maximilian and the Rebellion," *Chicago Tribune*, June 13, 1867, p. 2.
7. Seward to Otterbourg, August 8, 1867, in U.S. Department of State, *Foreign Relations of the United States, 1867*, Pt. 2, p. 445.

States for trade and investment capital. During the intervention, Juárez had expressed gratitude for acts of solidarity and support by New World republics. Then, when victorious, he took special care to reiterate his thanks to the "American republics," including the United States, for their steady support of Mexico. Juárez also evaluated Mexico's struggle as part of a conflict of European monarchy against the American republics. But while in some respects the dominant position the United States inherited by default was disadvantageous for Mexico, it did carry certain compensating factors as well. An *El Siglo Diez y Nueve* editorial singled out the rupture of relations with Europe as one advantage incurring to Mexico from the intervention. The old treaties had placed Mexico in a state of wardship, particularly the "most favored nation" clause which, while exempting foreigners from some of the internal taxes and levies, favored foreign merchants over nationals. With revived nationalism, the editorial proclaimed: "The foreigners who come to our country, ought to submit to our laws, without demanding advantages over the nationals, because it is not just that the foreigner has preeminence nor enjoys advantages over the son of the house." In the best liberal tradition, security and opportunity should be provided for all in Mexico, even foreigners, but special privilege to none. The possibility of redefining Mexico's relationship with the European countries eventually became too high a price to pay for the rapidly increasing influence of United States trade and investment dollars in Mexico's economic life. By the 1880s Mexico sought to reestablish diplomatic ties with Europe.[8]

In late 1869, soon after ending his service as secretary of state, Seward was invited by Juárez to tour Mexico and visit the govern-

---

8. Juárez' speeches to the Mexican Congress of April 15 and May 31, 1862, and December 8, 1867, in *Un Siglo de Relaciones Internacionales de México*, 98–100, 106; Lacrete, "Great Britain and Mexico," 231; Guillermo Tardiff, *Historia General del Comercio Exterior de México* (2 vols.; Mexico, 1970), II, 723; "Los Estrangeros," *El Siglo Diez y Nueve*, July 24, 1867; and Jorge Espinosa de Los Reyes, *Relaciones económicas entre México y los Estados Unidos, 1870–1910* (Mexico, 1951), 53–54. For a gesture of friendship toward the United States by the Mexican Republic, see Albert S. Evans, *Our Sister Republic: A Gala Trip through Tropical Mexico in 1869–70* (Hartford, Conn., 1870), 255–56.

ment in Mexico City. In the course of this trip, Seward made a series of speeches which revealed his analysis of the role of the United States in the New World and of the significance of the French intervention in Mexico. Clearly, Seward considered the French intervention an element in the worldwide conflict between liberalism and conservatism. He observed that since the eighteenth century the American states were moving toward independence and away from European colonialism, and that these independent American states were participating in social and political movement away from "imperial or monarchical governments" toward "republican governments," but that during his lifetime, these changes were being "contested in Europe and on the battlefield throughout America." The United States had taken the lead in encouraging this change in system. But the efforts of the South American countries to follow the United States model had "encountered the resistance of a long-cherished and powerful conservatism, animated and sustained by European influence and intervention." And it is to be expected that if the republican system is successful in the New World "the same great system may be accepted by other nations throughout the world." The French intervention, and Spanish invasion of Santo Domingo and seizure of the Peruvian Chincha Islands forced the United States and all republican states of the New World to form bonds of friendship and alliance. Seward then predicted that "every part of the continent must sooner or later be made entirely independent of all foreign control, and of every form of imperial or despotic power—the sooner the better." Based upon the mutual cooperation in producing a liberated, liberal republican New World, Seward recognized "that loyalty and patriotism on the part of a citizen of one American Republic is, in my judgment, not only consistent but congenial with the best wishes for the welfare, prosperity and happiness of all other American Republics." [9]

9. Speeches by Seward, delivered in Colima, Guadalajara, and Mexico City and quoted in full in Evans, *Our Sister Republic*, 61–63, 152–54, 276–77, 283–87. See also E. George Squier to Romero, July 12, 1867, in Archivo Romero.

Seward's speeches in Mexico—a post-crisis analysis—clearly and emphatically interpreted the Civil War–French intervention era as the turning point in the clash between the New World republican "system" and the Old World, "conservative," monarchical and aristocratic "system." The result of this battle was now clear. New World republicanism had won, and, under United States guidance and leadership, naturally, the road to material prosperity and happiness lay before the American republics. Seward took pains to assure the Mexican audience that the United States had no more territorial desires against those American nations it had recognized, holding open, however, the possible acquisition of some of the remaining Old World colonies. Thus, in the future, dollars not dominion would define United States relations with its American sister republics in the new liberal age adawning.

The execution of Maximilian and his generals Miguel Miramón and Tomás Mejía on a hill outside Querétaro ended the seven-year-long conservative threat to the republican political institutions and liberal ideology of both Mexico and the United States. After a brief pause to settle their disturbed domestic situations, the two nations could try to build a new relationship limited by the legacy of the past, but sharing a liberal's dream for social, political, and material progress in the future.

Bibliography

I. PRIMARY MATERIALS

A. Archival Materials

1. Austria

Haus-, Hof- und Staatsarchiv. Emperor Maximilian von Mexiko.
  Staatsarchiv. Politisches Archiv.
    Vereinigte Staaten.
    Mexiko
2. Mexico

Archivo de la Cámara de Diputados
  Actas de las Sesiones Secretas
Archivo General de la Nación
  Folletería
  Ramo de Fomento
  Ramo de Gobernación
Archivo Histórico de la Secretaría de Relaciones Exteriores
  Correspondencia General con los Estados Unidos, 1861–1867
  Expedientes, miscellaneous
  Expediente Personal de Thomas Corwin
  Expediente Personal de Manuel Doblado
  Expediente de Consules Extranjeros
  Sucesos entre México y los Estados Unidos de América: Relaciones con Texas
    y otros Estados Limítrofes
Banco de México.
  Archivo Histório de Matías Romero
Biblioteca Nacional
  Archivo Benito Pablo Juárez
  Archivo Lafragua

Centro de Estudios de Historia de México. Condumex
    Ignacio Aguilar y Marocho Papers
    Rafael García Papers
    Luis García Pimental Papers
    Luis Gutiérrez Canedo Papers
    Reforma, Intervención y Imperio Collection
    Segundo Imperio Collection
Museo Nacional de Antropología. Archivo Histórico
    Documentos Varios

3. United States

Brown University
    Samuel S. Cox Papers
Dallas Historical Society
    Franklin Chase Papers
Duke University, William R. Perkins Library, Durham, N.C.
    Thomas Corwin Papers
    Jefferson Davis Papers
    Jubal A. Early Papers
    John Berkely Grimball Papers
    Darius Starr Papers
Harvard University, Houghton Library, Cambridge, Mass.
    Marquis de Radepont Papers
    Charles Sumner Papers
Indiana Historical Society Library, Indianapolis, Ind.
    Lew Wallace Collection
Library of Congress, Washington, D.C.
    Nathaniel Banks Papers
    Edward Bates Papers
    Blair Family Papers
    Benjamin Butler Papers
    Simeon Cameron Papers
    Campbell-Preston Papers
    Causten-Pickett Papers
    William Chandler Papers
    Zachariah Chandler Papers
    Salmon P. Chase Papers
    William Conant Church Papers
    Schuyler Colfax Papers
    Cyrus B. Comstock Papers
    Caleb Cushing Papers
    James R. Doolittle Papers
    William P. Fessenden Papers
    Hamilton Fish Papers
    Giddings-Julian Papers

Ulysses S. Grant Papers
Adam Gurowski Papers
Andrew Johnson Papers
Joshua Leavitt Papers
Abraham Lincoln Papers
John Logan Papers
Hugh McCulloch Papers
Edward McPherson Papers
James Murray Mason Papers
Matthew F. Maury Papers
Miscellaneous MS Collections
Alfred Mordecai Papers
Justin Lot Morrill Papers
John C. Nicolay Papers
John T. Pickett Papers
James Shepherd Pike Papers
Edward Lee Plumb Papers
Records of the Confederate States of America
John M. Schofield Papers
Carl Schurz Papers
Philip H. Sheridan Papers
John Sherman Papers
William T. Sherman Papers
Edwin Stanton Papers
Alexander H. Stephens Papers
Thaddeus Stevens Papers
Ambrose W. Thompson Papers
Lyman Trumbull Papers
Benjamin Wade Papers
Elihu B. Washburne Papers
Gideon Welles Papers
Manhattanville College of the Sacred Heart, New York City
Alexander H. Stephens Papers
National Archives, Washington, D.C.
Records of the State Department. Record Group 59
Consular Dispatches, 1861–1867
Acapulco (National Archives Microcopy No. M143)
Campeche (M286)
Chihuahua (M289)
Ciudad del Carmen (Laguna de Terminos, Isla del Carmen) (M308)
Ciudad Juárez (M184)
Guaymas (T210)
La Paz (M282)
Manzanillo (M295)
Matamoros (M281)

Mazatlán (M159)
Mérida (M287)
Mexico City (M296)
Minatitlán (M298)
Monterrey (M165)
San Blas (M301)
Tabasco (M303)
Tampico (M304)
Tehuantepec (M305)
Veracruz (M183)
Zacatecas (M307)
Diplomatic Dispatches, 1861–1867
    Mexico (M97)
Diplomatic Instructions, 1861–1867
    Mexico (M77)
Special Agents
Foreign Post Records. Record Group 84
Legation in Mexico
Consulate in Acapulco
Consulate in Guaymas
Consulate in La Paz
Consulate in Matamoros
Consulate in Mexico City
Consulate in San Luis Potosí
Consulate in Tampico
Consulate in Veracruz
New York Historical Society
James W. Beekman Papers
Ohio Historical Society Archives
Lewis D. Campbell Papers
Stanford University Library
Edward Lee Plumb Collection
Plácido Vega Papers
University of Rochester. Rush Rhees Library, Rochester, N.Y.
William H. Seward Papers
University of Texas. Latin American Collection
Ignacio Comonfort Papers
Santos Degollado Correspondence
Manuel Doblado Correspondence
Juan Antonio de la Fuente Correspondence
Jesús González Ortega Correspondence
Teodosio Lares Collection
Francisco Mejía Papers
Mariano Riva Palacio Papers
Vincente Riva Palacio Papers

Matías Romero Letters (National Archives Microfilm)
Jesús Terán Correspondence
University of Virginia, Alderman Library, Charlottesville, Va.
    Balch Family Papers
    Robert M. T. Hunter Papers
    Alexander H. H. Stuart Papers
Virginia Historical Society, Richmond, Va.
    Alexander Caldwell Jones Papers
    Robert E. Lee Papers
    W. B. Phillips Papers
Yale University Archives
    James Watson Webb Papers. William Seward to Webb Correspondence

B. Newspapers and Journals

Atlantic Monthly (Boston), 1861–1867
La Bandera Nacional (Matamoros), 1864
El Boletín Republicano (Mexico), 1867
Charleston Mercury, 1861–1867
Chicago Tribune, 1861–1867
Diario del Gobierno de la República Mejicana (Mexico), 1863
Eco del Comercio (Veracruz), 1864
El Globo (Mexico), 1867
Harper's New Monthly Magazine (New York), 1861–1867
Manchester Guardian, 1861–1867
El Mexicano (Mexico), 1866
El Monitor Republicano (Mexico), 1861–1862, 1867
The Nation (New York), 1866–1867
New York Evening Post, 1861
North American Review (New York and Boston), 1861–1867
El Pájaro Verde (Mexico), 1861
Periódico Oficial del Gobierno Constitucional de la República Mexicana (Chihuahua and
    Paso del Norte), 1864–1866
La Reforma (Mexico), 1861
La Reforma Social (Veracruz), 1859–1860
La Revista (Veracruz), 1864
El Siglo Diez y Nueve (Mexico), 1861–1863, 1867
La Sociedad (Mexico), 1863
Le Trait d'Union (Veracruz), 1860, (Mexico), 1862

C. Printed Document Collections

Cleven, N. Andrew N. "The Corwin-Doblado Treaty, April 6, 1862." *Hispanic
    American Historical Review*, XVII (November, 1937), 499–506.
Colección de leyes, decretos y circulares expedidas por el Supremo Gobierno de la República. 3
    vols. Mexico: Imprenta del Gobierno, 1867.
Congressional Globe. 37th Cong.–40th Cong.

Confederate States of America. "Proceedings of the Confederate Congress." *Southern Historical Society Papers.* New Series, Vols. VI–XI. Richmond: Southern Historical Society, 1923–1943. New Series, Vols. XII–XIV. Richmond: Virginia Historical Society, 1953–1959.

Democratic Party. *Official Proceedings of the Democratic National Convention, held in 1864 at Chicago.* Chicago: The Time Steam Book and Job Printing House, 1864.

John H. Haswell, comp. *Treaties, Conventions, International Acts, Protocols and Agreements Between the United States of America and Other Powers.* Washington: Government Printing Office, 1889.

House Executive Documents. 38th Cong.–39th Cong.

Journal of the Congress of the Confederate States of America. 7 vols. Washington: Government Printing Office, 1904–1905.

Lefefre, E. *Documentos Oficiales recogidos en la Secretaría privada de Maximiliano: Historia de la intervención francesa en México.* 2 vols. Brussels and London: n. p., 1869.

Mexico City Ayuntamiento. *Corona Funebre, Dedicado a la Memoria del Gral. Ulises S. Grant.* Mexico: Imprenta Litografía de Dublan y Cía., 1885.

Porter, Kirk Harold, and Donald Bruce Johnson. *National Party Platforms, 1840–1956.* Urbana: University of Illinois Press, 1956.

Proceedings of a Meeting of Senators, Representatives, and Citizens held in the Reception Room of the United States Senate Chamber, in Memory of Hon. Thomas Corwin, Washington, D.C., December 19, 1866. Washington: Philip and Solomons, 1866.

Republican National and Congressional Committees. *Life and Services of General U. S. Grant, Conqueror of the Rebellion, and Eighteenth President of the United States.* Washington: Philip & Solomons, 1868.

Republican party. *Proceedings of the National Union Convention held in Baltimore, Md., June 7th and 8th, 1864.* New York: Baker and Godwin, 1864.

Richardson, James D., comp. *A Compilation of the Messages and Papers of the Presidents, 1789–1897.* Vol. VI. Washington: Government Printing Office, 1898.

———, ed. *The Messages and Papers of Jefferson Davis and the Confederacy, Including Diplomatic Correspondence, 1861–1865.* 2 vols. New York: Chelsea House-Robert Hector Publishers, 1966.

Romero, Matías, comp. *Correspondencia de la legación mexicana en Washington durante la intervención extranjera.* 10 vols. Mexico: Imprenta del Gobierno, 1870–1892.

———. *Estudio sobre la anexión de México a los Estados Unidos.* Mexico: Imprenta del Gobierno Federal, 1890.

———, comp. *Proceedings of a Meeting of Citizens of New York, to Express Sympathy and Respect for the Mexican Republican Exiles. Held at Cooper Institute, July 19, 1865. With an Appendix Containing the Speeches of the Hon. Matías Romero.* New York: J. A. Gray and Green, 1865.

———. *The Situation of Mexico: Speech Delivered by Señor Romero . . . at a Dinner in the City of New York, on the 16th of December, 1863.* New York: Wm. C. Bryant & Co., 1864.

———. *Speech of Señor Don Matías Romero . . . Read on the 65th Anniversary of the Birth of General Ulysses S. Grant, Celebrated at . . . Washington, on the 25th of April, 1887.* New York: 1887.

Senate Executive Documents. 51st Cong., 1st Sess.

Sanger, George P., ed. *Treaties concluded by the United States of America, with Foreign Nations and Indian Tribes.* Boston 1862. In *United States Statutes at Large,* 36th–37th Congress (1859–1863).

United States Department of Commerce. Bureau of the Census. *Historical Statistics of the United States: Colonial Times to 1957.* Washington: Government Printing Office, 1960.

United States Department of State. *Papers Relating to the Foreign Relations of the United States.* Washington: Government Printing Office, 1862–1868.

United States Navy Department. *War of the Rebellion: Official Records of the Union and Confederate Navies.* 30 vols. Washington: Government Printing Office, 1894–1922.

United States Treasury Department. *Statistical Abstract of the United States, 1880.* Washington: Government Printing Office, 1881.

United States Treasury Department. *Statistical Abstract of the United States, 1895.* Washington: Government Printing Office, 1896.

United States War Department. *War of the Rebellion: Official Records of the Union and Confederate Armies.* 128 vols. Washington: Government Printing Office, 1880–1901.

Un siglo de Relaciones Exteriores: A Través de los Mensajes Presidenciales. No. 39, Archivo Histórico Diplomático Mexicano. Mexico: Secretaría de Relaciones Exteriores, 1935.

D. Autobiographies, Correspondence, Diaries

Altamirano, Ignacio. *La Nota de Campbell.* Toluca, Mexico: Tipógrafo del Instituto Literario, 1867.

Ambler, Charles Henry. *Correspondence of Robert M. T. Hunter, 1826–1876. American Historical Association Annual Report, 1916.* Vol. II. Washington: Government Printing Office, 1918.

Basler, Roy P., ed. *The Collected Works of Abraham Lincoln.* 8 vols. and index. New Brunswick, N. J.: Rutgers University Press, 1953.

Beale, Howard K., ed. *The Diary of Edward Bates, 1858–1866. American Historical Association Annual Report, 1930.* Vol. IV. Washington: Government Printing Office, 1933.

———, ed. *Diary of Gideon Welles.* 3 vols. New York: W. W. Norton and Company, 1960.

Blaine, James G. *Twenty Years of Congress: From Lincoln to Garfield.* 2 vols. Norwich, Conn.: The Henry Bill Publishing Company, 1884–1886.

Boutwell, George S. "The Impeachment of Andrew Johnson from the Standpoint of One of the Managers of the Impeachment Trial." *McClure's Magazine,* XIX (1899–1900), 176–77.

———. *Reminiscences of Sixty Years in Public Affairs.* New York: McClure, Phillips and Company, 1902.

Chambrun, Adolphe, Marquis de. *Impressions of Lincoln and the Civil War: A Foreigner's Account.* Translated by Adelbert de Chambrun. New York: Random House, 1952.

Chase, Salmon Portland. *Diary and Correspondence of Salmon P. Chase. American Historical Association Annual Report, 1900.* Vol. II. Washington: Government Printing Office, 1902.

Cosío Villegas, Emma, ed. *Diario personal de Matías Romero, 1855-1865.* Mexico: El Colegio de México, 1960.

Cox, Samuel Sullivan. *Eight Years in Congress, from 1857 to 1865: Memoir and Speeches.* New York: D. Appleton and Company, 1865.

————. *Three Decades of Federal Legislation—Union—Disunion—Reunion, 1855 to 1885.* Providence, R.I.: J. A. and R. A. Reid, 1894.

Davis, Henry Winter. *Speeches and Addresses Delivered in the Congress of the United States and on Several Public Occasions.* New York: Harper and Brothers, 1867.

Davis, Jefferson. *The Rise and Fall of the Confederate Government.* 2 vols. New York: Thomas Yoseleff, 1958.

Dennett, Tyler, ed. *Lincoln and the Civil War in the Diaries and Letters of John Hay.* New York: Dodd, Mead and Company, 1939.

Donald, David, ed. *Inside Lincoln's Cabinet: The Civil War Diaries of Salmon P. Chase.* New York: Longmans, Green and Company, 1954.

Evans, Albert S. *Our Sister Republic: A Gala Trip through Tropical Mexico in 1869-70.* Hartford, Conn.: Columbian, 1870.

Grant, Ulysses S. *Personal Memoirs.* 2 vols. New York: L. Webster & Co., 1892.

Gurowski, Adam. *Diary.* Vol. I. Boston: Lee & Shepard, 1862. Vol. II. New York: G. W. Carleton & Co., 1864.

Hinsdale, Mary L., ed. *Garfield-Hinsdale Letters: Correspondence Between James Abram Garfield and Burke Aaron Hinsdale.* Ann Arbor: University of Michigan Press, 1949.

Hoar, George F., ed. *Charles Sumner: His Complete Works.* 20 vols. Boston: Lee and Shepard, 1900.

Iglesias, José María. *Refutación del Discurso pronunciado por Mr. Billault Ministro sin Cartera en el Cuerpo Legislativo Francés sobre la política del Emperador en México.* Mexico: Imprenta de Vincente García Torres, 1862.

————. *Revistas históricas sobre la intervención francesa en México.* Mexico: Editorial Porrua, 1966.

Juárez, Benito Pablo. *Discursos y manifestos.* Mexico: A. Pola, 1905.

————. *Exposiciones.* Mexico: F. Vasquez, 1902.

————. *Miscelanea.* Edited by Angel Pola. Mexico: A. Pola, 1906.

Julian, George W. *Political Recollections, 1840-1872.* Chicago: Jansen, McClurg and Company, 1884.

McCulloch, Hugh. *Men and Measures of Half a Century: Sketches and Comments.* New York: Charles Scribner's Sons, 1900.

Mowry, Duane. "Doolittle Correspondence." *Publications of the Southern History Association,* IX (July, 1905), 242-43.

Nevins, Allan, and Milton H. Thomas, eds. *The Diary of George Templeton Strong.* 4 vols. New York: Macmillan, 1952.

Pecquet du Bellet, Paul. *The Diplomacy of the Confederate Cabinet of Richmond and its Agents Abroad: Being Memorandum Notes Taken in Paris during the Rebellion of the*

Southern States from 1861 to 1865, No. 23, Confederate Centennial Studies Series. Tuscaloosa, Ala.: Confederate Publishing Company, 1963.

Phillips, Ulrich Bonnell, ed. *The Correspondence of Robert Toombs, Alexander H. Stephens, and Howell Cobb. American Historical Association Annual Report, 1911.* Vol. II. Washington: Government Printing Office, 1913.

Pierce, Edward L., ed. *Memoirs and Letters of Charles Sumner.* 4 vols. Boston: Roberts Brothers, 1877–1893.

Randall, James G., and Theodore C. Pease, eds. *The Diary of Orville Hickman Browning.* 2 vols. Springfield: Illinois State Historical Library, 1933.

Regan, John H. *Memoirs with Special References to Secession and the Civil War.* Edited by Walter F. McCaleb. New York and Washington: The Neale Publishing Co., 1906.

Reed, William B. *A Review of Mr. Seward's Diplomacy. By a Northern Man.* Philadelphia: n. p., 1862.

Russell, William H. *My Diary: North and South.* Edited by Fletcher Pratt. New York: Harper and Brothers, 1954.

Santacilia, Pedro. *Juárez y César Cantú: Refutación de los cargos que hace en su última obra el historiador italiano contra el benemérito de América.* Mexico: Imprenta del Gobierno, 1885.

Schofield, John. *Forty-Six Years in the Army.* New York: The Century Company, 1897.

———. "The Withdrawal of the French from Mexico." *Century Illustrated Magazine,* New Series XXXII (May-October, 1897), 128–37.

Schurz, Carl. *The Reminiscences of Carl Schurz.* 3 vols. Garden City, N.Y.: Doubleday, Page, 1913.

Seward, Frederick W. *Seward at Washington, 1861–72 as Senator and Secretary of State.* New York: Derby and Miller, 1891.

Sheridan, Philip H. *Personal Memoirs of P. H. Sheridan: General United States Army.* 2 vols. New York: Charles L. Webster & Co., 1888.

Sherman, William T. *Memoirs of General W. T. Sherman.* 2 vols. New York: Charles L. Webster & Co., 1891.

Sioussat, St. George L. "Notes of Colonel W. G. Moore, Private Secretary to President Johnson, 1866–1868." *American Historical Review,* XIX (October, 1913), 98–132.

Smith, Theodore Clarke. *The Life and Letters of James Abram Garfield.* 2 vols. New Haven, Conn.: Yale University Press, 1925.

Tamayo, Jorge L., ed. *Benito Juárez: Documentos, Discursos y Correspondencia.* 14 vols. completed. Mexico: Secretaría del Patrimonio Nacional, 1964–1970.

———, ed. *Epistolario.* Mexico: Fondo de Cultura Económica, 1957.

Taylor, Richard. *Destruction and Reconstruction.* New York: D. Appleton, 1897.

Thorndike, Rachel Sherman, ed. *The Sherman Letters: Correspondence Between General and Senator Sherman from 1837 to 1891.* New York: Charles Scribner's Sons, 1894.

Truman, Benjamin C. "Anecdotes of Andrew Johnson." *Century Magazine,* LXXXV (1913), 438–40.

Washington, Lucius Q. "The Confederate State Department." *Independent*, LIII (September, 1901), 2218–24. Also in *Southern Historical Society Papers*, XXIX (1901), 341–49.

Weed, Harriet A., ed. *Autobiography of Thurlow Weed*. Boston, New York: Houghton, Mifflin and Company, 1883–1884.

Williams, Mary Wilhelmine, ed. "Letter from Colonel John T. Pickett, of the Southern Confederacy, to Señor Don Manuel de Zamacona, Minister of Foreign Affairs, Mexico." *Hispanic American Historical Society*, II (November, 1919), 611–17.

Zambrano, Juan A. *Apunto sobre Caminos de Fierro y Facilidad de Hacerlos*. Mexico: Imprenta de Vicente García Torres, 1867.

Zarco, Francisco. *Textos políticos*. Edited by Xavier Tevera Alfaro. Mexico: Universidad Nacional Autónoma de México, 1957.

Zavala, F. J. *Informe a la vista leído por el C. Lic. F. J. Zavala el 16 del presente ante el Juez I° de lo criminal de esta ciudad, en el juicio de Imprenta que contra el periódico titulado: "La Verdad," sigue el C. Lic. Ignacio L. Vallerta*. Guadalajara, Mexico: Tipógrafo de Brambila, 1867.

II. SECONDARY MATERIALS

A. Unpublished Material

Arrowood, Flora R. "United States-Mexican Foreign Relations from 1867–1872." M.A. thesis, University of Texas, 1934.

Auer, John Jeffery. "Tom Corwin: King of the Stump." 2 vols. Ph.D. dissertation, University of Wisconsin, 1947.

Blackburn, Charles Byron. "Military Opposition to Official State Department Policy Concerning the Mexican Intervention, 1862–1867." Ph.D. dissertation, Ball State University, 1969.

Bock, Carl Heinz. "The Negotiation and Breakdown of the Tripartite Convention of London of 31 October 1861." 2 vols. Ph.D. dissertation, Philipps-Universität, Marburg, Germany, 1961.

Boyd, Willis. "Negro Colonization of the National Crisis, 1860–1870." Ph.D. dissertation, University of California, Los Angeles, 1953.

Brown, Robert B. "Guns over the Border: American Aid to the Juárez Government During the French Intervention." Ph.D. dissertation, University of Michigan, 1951.

Caldwell, Edward Maurice. "The War of 'La Reforma' in Mexico, 1858–1861." Ph.D. dissertation, University of Texas, 1935.

Casebier, Gertrude. "Trade Relations Between the Confederacy and Mexico." M.A. thesis, Vanderbilt University, 1931.

Durham, Marvin L. "American Expansionism into Mexico, 1848–1862." Ph.D. dissertation, Fletcher School of Law and Diplomacy, 1962.

Fenner, Judith Anne. "Confederate Finances Abroad." Ph.D. dissertation, Rice University, 1969.

Frazer, Robert W. "Matías Romero and the French Intervention in Mexico 1861–1867. Ph.D. dissertation, University of California, Los Angeles, 1941.

Gerrity, Francis X. "American Editorial Opinion of French Intervention in Mexico, 1861–1867." Ph.D. dissertation, Georgetown University, 1952.

Henry, Milton Lyman, Jr. "Henry Winter Davis and the Radical Republican Use of Foreign Policy." Paper presented at the Organization of American Historians Convention, Chicago, April 1973.

Lacrete, Robert Kenneth. "Great Britain and Mexico in the Age of Juárez, 1854–1876." Ph.D. dissertation, Case Western Reserve University, 1971.

Maisel, Jay M. "The Origin and Development of Mexican Antipathy toward the South, 1821–1867." Ph.D. dissertation, University of Texas, 1955.

Malloy, George Wallace. "The United States and French Intervention in Mexico, 1861–1867." Ph.D. dissertation, University of California, 1937.

Miller, Robert R. "Mexican Secret Agents in the United States, 1861–1867." Ph.D. dissertation, University of California, 1960.

Ogden, John Patton. "The Labors of Matías Romero, 1861–1867." M.A. thesis, Duke University, 1941.

O'Rourke, Sister M. M. "The Diplomacy of William H. Seward During the Civil War: His Policies as Related to International Law." Ph.D. dissertation, University of California, 1963.

Pendergraft, Darly. "The Public Career of Thomas Corwin." Ph.D. dissertation, University of Iowa, 1943.

Peterson, Hal. "The Concept of Freedom: A Study in the Liberal Values of Buckle, Acton and Lecky." Ph.D. dissertation, Northern Illinois University, 1972.

Sheaver, Ernest Charles. "Border Diplomatic Relations Between the United States and Mexico, 1848–1860." Ph.D. dissertation, University of Texas, 1940.

Sinkin, Richard N. "The Mexican Constitutional Congress, 1856–1857: A Statistical Analysis." Paper read at the 86th Annual Meeting of the American Historical Association, New York, December 1971.

———. "Modernization and Reform in Mexico, 1855–1876." Ph.D. dissertation, University of Michigan, 1972.

Southerland, James Edward. "Mexican–United States Relations, 1857–1860: The Failure of Manifest Destiny." Ph.D. dissertation, University of Georgia, 1970.

Stout, Joseph A., Jr. "The Last Years of Manifest Destiny: Filibustering in Northwestern Mexico, 1848–1862." Ph.D. dissertation, Oklahoma State University, 1971.

Swinney, Everette. "Andrew Johnson's Swing Around the Circle." M.A. thesis, Pennsylvania State University, 1957.

Webster, Michael Gordon. "Texan Manifest Destiny and the Mexican Border Conflict, 1865–1880." Ph.D. dissertation, Indiana University, 1972.

Wheat, Raymond C. "Francisco Zarco: The Liberal Spokesman of La Reforma." Ph.D. dissertation, University of Texas, 1957.

Whelan, J. G. "William Henry Seward, Expansionist." Ph.D. dissertation, University of Rochester, 1959.

B. Published Material

Abbot, Gorham D. *Mexico and the United States: Their Mutual Relations and Common Interests.* New York: G. P. Putnam & Son, 1869.

Adams, Henry M. *Prussian-American Relations, 1775–1871.* Western Reserve, Ohio: Press of Western Reserve University, 1960.

Altamirano, Ignacio M. *Historia y política de México, 1821–1882.* Mexico: Empresas Editoriales, 1947.

Alvarez, Ignacio. *Estudios sobre la historia general de México.* 6 vols. Zacatecas, Mexico: Imprenta de M. Ruiz de Esparza, 1869–1877.

Armstrong, William M. *E. L. Godkin and American Foreign Policy, 1865–1900.* New York: Bookman Associates, 1957.

Auer, John Jeffery. "Lincoln's Minister to Mexico." *Ohio Archeological and Historical Quarterly,* LIX (April 1950), 115–28.

Badeau, Adam. *Grant in Peace: From Appomattox to Mount McGregor.* Philadelphia: Hubbard Brothers, 1866.

Bailey, Richard Eugene. "The French in Mexico in the Nineteenth Century: The Franco-Mexican Political and Commercial Contacts; French Influence on Society." *Mexican Review,* IV (Winter, 1943-Summer, 1944), 15–23.

Bancroft, Frederic. "The French in Mexico and the Monroe Doctrine." *Political Science Quarterly,* XI (March, 1896), 30–43.

Bancroft, Hubert H. *History of Mexico.* 6 vols. San Francisco: A. L. Bancroft & Co., 1883–1888.

Barker, Nancy Nichols. "France, Austria, and the Mexican Venture, 1861–1864." *French Historical Studies,* III (Fall, 1963), 224–45.

Barney, William L. *The Road to Secession: A New Perspective of the Old South.* New York: Praeger Publishers, 1972.

Bazant, Jan. *Historia de la deuda exterior de México, 1823–1946.* Nueva Serie 3, Centro de Estudios Históricos. Mexico: El Colegio de México, 1968.

Beale, Howard K. *The Critical Year: A Study of Andrew Johnson and Reconstruction.* New York: F. Ungar Publishing Company, 1958.

Beisner, Robert L. *From the Old Diplomacy to the New, 1865–1900.* New York: Thomas Y. Crowell, 1975.

Belenki, A. B. *La Intervención Extranjera en México, 1861–1867.* Translated from Russian by María Teresa Francés. Mexico: Fondo de Cultura Popular, 1966.

Bell, P. L., and H. Bentley Mackenzie. *Mexican West Coast and Lower California: A Commercial and Industrial Survey.* Washington: Government Printing Office, 1923.

Bemis, Samuel Flagg. *The Latin American Policy of the United States.* New York: Harcourt, Brace and Co., 1943.

Benedict, Michael Les. *A Compromise of Principle: Congressional Republicans and Reconstruction, 1863–1869.* New York: W. W. Norton, 1974.

————. *The Impeachment and Trial of Andrew Johnson.* New York: W. W. Norton, 1973.

Benjamin, Ruth L. "Marcus Otterbourg, United States Minister to Mexico in 1867." *American Jewish Historical Society Publications,* XXXII (1932), 65–98.

Benson, Lee. *The Concept of Jacksonian Democracy.* New York: Atheneum, 1969.

Berger, Raoul. *Impeachment: The Constitutional Problems.* Cambridge, Mass.: Harvard University Press, 1973.

Bernath, Stuart L. *Squall Across the Atlantic: American Civil War Prize Cases and Diplomacy.* Berkeley: University of California Press, 1970.

Bernstein, Harry. *Matías Romero, 1837–1898.* Mexico: Fondo de Cultura Económica, 1973.

Bernstein, Marvin D. *The Mexican Mining Industry, 1890–1950: A Study of the Interaction of Politics, Economics, and Technology.* Albany: State University of New York Press, 1964.

Blanchot, Charles. *L'intervention française au Mexique.* 3 vols. Paris: Libraire Emile Nourry, 1911.

Blumberg, Arnold. *The Diplomacy of the Mexican Empire, 1863–1867.* New Series, Vol. LXI, Pt. 8 (1971) of *Transactions of the American Philosophical Society.* Philadelphia: American Philosophical Society, 1971.

————, ed. "A Swedish Diplomat in Mexico, 1864." *Hispanic American Historical Review,* XLV (May, 1965), 275–86.

————. "United States and the Role of Belgium in Mexico, 1863–1867." *Historian,* XXVI (February, 1964), 206–227.

————. "William Seward and Egyptian Intervention in Mexico," *Smithsonian Journal of History,* I (Winter, 1966–1967), 31–48.

Blumenthal, Henry. "Confederate Diplomacy: Popular Notions and International Realities." *Journal of Southern History,* XXXII (May, 1966), 151–71.

————. *France and the United States. Their Diplomatic Relations, 1789–1914.* Chapel Hill: University of North Carolina Press, 1970.

————. *A Reappraisal of Franco-American Relations, 1830–1871.* Chapel Hill: University of North Carolina Press, 1959.

Bosch García, Carlos. *Historia de las Relaciones entre México y los Estados Unidos, 1819–1848.* Mexico: Universidad Nacional Autónoma de México, 1961.

Bowers, Claude G. *The Tragic Era.* Cambridge, Mass.: Houghton, Mifflin, 1929.

Brant, Irving. *Impeachment: Trials and Errors.* New York: Alfred A. Knopf, 1972.

Brauer, Kinley J. "Gabriel García y Tassara and the American Civil War: A Spanish Perspective." *Civil War History,* XXI (March, 1975), 5–27.

————. "Seward's 'Foreign War Panacea': An Interpretation." *New York History,* LV (April, 1974), 135–57.

Bravo Ugarte, José. *Historia de México.* Mexico: Editorial Jus, 1959.

————. *México Independiente.* Barcelona, Spain: Salvat Editores, 1959.

Brock, William R. *An American Crisis: Congress and Reconstruction, 1865–1867.* London: St. Martins Press, 1963.

————. *Conflict and Transformation: The United States, 1844–1877.* Baltimore: Penguin Books, 1973.

Brom, Juan O. "Las ideas políticas de Ignacio Ramírez." *Anuario de Historia,* VI–VII (1966–1967), 41–64.

Buchanan, Russell. "James A. McDougall: A Forgotten Senator." *California History Society Quarterly,* XV (September, 1936), 199–212.

Burke, Ulick R. *A Life of Benito Juarez, Constitutional President of Mexico.* London: Remington and Company, 1894.

Butler, Pierce. *Judah P. Benjamin.* Philadelphia: G. W. Jacobs, 1907.

Calderón, Francisco R. *Historia Moderna de México: La República Restaurada: La Vida Económica.* Edited by Daniel Cosío Villegas. Vol. II. Mexico, Buenos Aires: Editorial Hermes, 1955.

Callahan, James Morton. *American Foreign Policy in Mexican Relations.* New York: Macmillan, 1932.

————. *The Diplomatic History of the Southern Confederacy.* Baltimore: Johns Hopkins Press, 1901.

————. *Evolution of Seward's Mexican Policy.* Morgantown: West Virginia University, 1909.

Callcott, Wilfred Hardy. *Liberalism in Mexico, 1857–1929.* Stanford: Stanford University Press, 1931.

Campbell, A. E. "An Excess of Isolation: Isolation and the American Civil War." *Journal of Southern History,* XXIX (May, 1963), 161–74.

Carman, Harry J., and Reinhard H. Luthin. *Lincoln and the Patronage.* New York: Columbia University Press, 1943.

Carreño, Alberto María. *La Diplomacía Extraordinaria entre México y los Estados Unidos, 1789–1947.* 2 vols. Mexico: Editorial Jus, 1951.

Carroll, Daniel B. *Henri Mercier and the American Civil War.* Princeton, N.J.: Princeton University Press, 1971.

Case, Lynn, and Warren Spencer. *The United States and France: Civil War Diplomacy.* Philadelphia: University of Pennsylvania Press, 1970.

Castañeda Batres, Oscar. *Francisco Zarco.* Mexico: Club de Periodistas de México, 1961.

Castillo Negrete, Emilio del. *México en el siglo XIX.* 26 vols. Mexico: Imprenta en las Escalerillas, 1875–1888.

Chadsey, Charles Ernest. *The Struggle Between President Johnson and Congress over Reconstruction.* New York: Columbia University Press, 1896.

Church, George E. *Mexico: Its Revolutions; Are They Evidence of Retrogression or of Progress?* New York: Baker and Godwin, 1866.

Church, William Conant. *Ulysses S. Grant and the Period of National Preservation and Reconstruction.* New York: G. P. Putnam's Sons, 1897.

Cohen, Barry M. "The Texas-Mexican Border, 1858–1867: Among the Lower Rio Grande Valley During the Decade of the American Civil War and the French Intervention in Mexico." *Texana,* VI (July, 1968), 153–65.

Coleman, Evan J. "Gwin and Seward—a Secret Chapter in Ante-Bellum History." *Overland Monthly,* XVIII (November, 1891), 465–71.

Connell-Smith, Gordon. *The Inter-American System.* London: Oxford University Press, 1966.

Coolidge, Louis A. *Ulysses S. Grant*. Boston: Houghton, Mifflin, 1922.

Cordova, Luis. "Proteccionismo y librecambio en el México Independiente (1821–1847)." *Cuadernos Americanos,* CLXXII (September-October, 1970), 135–53.

Cortés Conde, Roberto. *The First Stages of Modernization in Spanish America*. New York: Harper and Row, 1974.

Corti, Egon Caesar. *Maximilian and Carlotta in Mexico*. Translated by Catherine Alison Phillips. 2 vols. New York: Alfred A. Knopf, 1928.

Cosío Villegas, Daniel. *Historia Moderna de México: La República Restaurada: La Vida Política*. Vol. I. Mexico, Buenos Aires: Editorial Hermes, 1955.

Cotner, Thomas E., and Carlos E. Castañeda, eds. *The Charles Wilson Hackett Memorial Volume: Essays in Mexican History*. Austin: Institute of Latin American Studies, University of Texas, 1958.

Cox, John H., and Lawanda Cox. "Andrew Johnson and his Ghost Writers." *The Mississippi Valley Historical Review,* XLVIII (December, 1961), 460–79.

————. *Politics, Principles, and Prejudice 1865–1866: Dilemma of Reconstruction America*. New York: Atheneum, 1963.

Crook, Carland E. "Benjamin Theron and French Designs in Texas during the Civil War." *Southwestern Historical Quarterly,* LXVIII (April, 1965), 432–54.

Crook, Donald P. *The North, the South, and the Powers, 1861–1865*. New York: John Wiley and Sons, 1974.

Cue Canovas, Agustín. *El Tratado McLane-Ocampo, Juárez, los Estados Unidos y Europa*. 3rd ed. Mexico: Editorial Libros Económicos, 1968.

Dabbs, Jack A. *The French Army in Mexico, 1861–1867: A Study in Military Government*. The Hague: Mouton, 1963.

Dana, Charles A., and James H. Wilson. *The Life of Ulysses S. Grant, General of the Armies of the United States*. Springfield, Mass.: Gurdon Bill & Co., 1868.

Delaney, Robert W. "Matamoros, Port for Texas During the Civil War." *Southwestern Historical Quarterly,* LVIII (April, 1955), 473–87.

Dewitt, David Miller. *The Impeachment and Trial of Andrew Johnson*. Madison: The State Historical Society of Wisconsin, 1967.

Diamond, William. "Imports of the Confederate Government from Europe and Mexico." *Journal of Southern History,* VI (November, 1940), 470–503.

"Diplomacy of Seward, 1861." *Continental Monthly,* I (February, 1862), 199–209.

Donald, David. *Charles Sumner and the Rights of Man*. New York: Alfred A. Knopf, 1970.

Donaldson, Jordon, and Edwin J. Pratt. *Europe and the American Civil War*. Boston and New York: Houghton Mifflin and Comp., 1931.

Dorman, Frederick J. "General William Preston." *Filson Club History Quarterly,* XLIII (October, 1969), 301–310.

Dozer, Donald Marquand. "Anti-Expansionism during the Johnson Administration." *Pacific Historical Review,* XII (September, 1943), 253–75.

DuBose, John W. "Confederate Diplomacy." *Southern Historical Society Papers,* XXXII (1904), 102–116.

Dunbar, Edward E. *The Mexican Papers*. Nos. 1–4, New York: J. A. H. Hasbrouck & Co., 1860–1861; No. 5, New York: Rudd & Carleton, 1861.

Duniway, Claude A. "Reasons for the Withdrawal of France from Mexico." *American Historical Association Annual Reports, 1901*. Vol. I. Washington: Government Printing Office, 1902.

Dunn, Frederick S. *The Diplomatic Protection of Americans in Mexico*. New York: Columbia University Press, 1933.

Espinosa de Los Reyes, Jorge. *Relaciones económicas entre México y los Estados Unidos, 1870–1910*. Mexico: Nacional Financiera, S.A., 1951.

Everett, Edward. *The Monroe Doctrine, Reprinted from the New York Ledger*. New York: Loyal Publication Society, 1863.

Fabela, Isidro. *Las Doctrinas Monroe y Drago*. Mexico: Universidad Nacional Autónoma de México, 1957.

———. "La Doctrina Monroe y la segunda intervención francesa en México." *Cuadernos Americanos*, año 16, XCV:5 (September-October, 1957), 201–214.

Fehrenbacher, Don E. *The Era of Expansion: 1800–1848*. New York: John Wiley and Sons, 1969.

Ferris, Nathan L. "The Relations of the United States with South America during the American Civil War." *Hispanic American Historical Review*, XXI (February, 1941), 51–78.

Ferris, Norman B. *Desperate Diplomacy: William H. Seward's Foreign Policy, 1861*. Knoxville: University of Tennessee Press, 1976.

Fischer, LeRoy H., and B. J. Chandler. "United States-Spanish Relations during the American Civil War." *Lincoln Herald*, LXXV (Winter, 1973), 134–47.

Foner, Eric. *Free Soil, Free Labor, Free Men: The Ideology of the Republican Party Before the Civil War*. New York: Oxford University Press, 1970.

Foulke, William Dudley. *Life of Oliver P. Morton*. 2 vols. Indianapolis: Bowen-Merrill Company, 1899.

Frazer, Robert W. "Latin-American Projects to Aid Mexico during the French Intervention." *Hispanic American Historical Review*, XXVIII (August, 1948), 377–88.

———. "Maximilian's Propaganda Activities in the United States." *Hispanic American Historical Review*, XXIV (February, 1944), 4–29.

———. "The Ochoa Bond Negotiations of 1865–1867." *Pacific Historical Review*, XI (December, 1942), 397–414.

———. "The Role of the Lima Congress, 1864–1865, in the Development of Pan-Americanism." *Hispanic American Historical Review*, XXIX (August, 1949), 319–48.

———. "Trade Between California and the Belligerent Powers during the French Intervention in Mexico." *Pacific Historical Review*, XV (December, 1946), 390–99.

———. "The United States, European and West Virginia Land and Mining Company." *Pacific Historical Review*, XIII (March, 1944), 28–40.

Frías y Soto, Hilarión. *Juárez glorificado y la intervención y el imperio ante la verdad histórica; refutando con documentos la obra de Francisco Bulnes intitulada: El verdadero Juárez*. Mexico: Imprenta Central, 1905.

Fuentes Mares, José. *Juárez y los Estados Unidos.* Mexico: Libro Mex, 1961.
————. *Juárez y el Imperio.* Mexico: Editorial Jus, 1963.
————. *Juárez y la Intervención.* Mexico: Editorial Jus, 1962.
————. *Poinsett, Historia de una Gran Intriga.* Mexico: Editorial Jus, 1958.
————. "Washington, Paris y el Imperio Mexicano." *Historia Mexicana,* XIII (October-December, 1963), 244–71.
García Cantú, Gastón. "Las dos políticas exteriores de México." *Cuadernos Americanos,* año 18, CVI:5 (September-October, 1959), 41–55.
Genovese, Eugene D. *The Political Economy of Slavery.* New York: Vintage Books, 1967.
Goebel, Julius, Jr. *The Recognition Policy of the United States.* Columbia University Studies in History, Economics and Public Law, No. 158. New York: Columbia University Press, 1915.
Goetzmann, William H. *When the Eagle Screamed: The Romantic Horizon in American Diplomacy, 1800–1860.* New York: John Wiley and Sons, 1966.
Goldman, Henry H. "Southern Sympathy in Southern California: 1860–1865." *Journal of the West,* IV (October, 1965), 577–86.
Goldwert, Marvin. "Matías Romero and Congressional Opposition to Seward's Policy Toward the French Intervention in Mexico." *The Americas,* XXII (July, 1965), 22–40.
Gonzales, John E. "Henry Stuart Foote: Confederate Congressman and Exile." *Civil War History,* XI (December, 1965), 384–96.
Gordon, Leonard. "Lincoln and Juárez—A Brief Reassessment of Their Relationship." *Hispanic American Historical Review,* XLVIII (February, 1968), 75–80.
Graebner, Norman A. *Empire on the Pacific: A Study in American Continental Expansion.* New York: The Ronald Press, 1955.
————. "Northern Diplomacy and European Neutrality." *Why the North Won the Civil War,* edited by David Donald. Baton Rouge: Louisiana State University Press, 1960.
Green, George D. *Finance and Economic Development in the Old South: Louisiana Banking, 1804–1861.* Stanford: Stanford University Press, 1972.
Hale, Charles A. *Mexican Liberalism in the Age of Mora, 1821–1853.* New Haven: Yale University Press, 1968.
Hale, Edward E., Jr. *William H. Seward.* Philadelphia: G. W. Jacobs & Co., 1910.
Halperin-Donghi, Tulio. *The Aftermath of Revolution in Latin America.* Translated by Josephine de Bunsen. New York: Harper and Row, 1973.
Hammond, Bray. *Banks and Politics in America from the Revolution to the Civil War.* Princeton, N.J.: Princeton University Press, 1957.
Hanna, Alfred J. "A Confederate Newspaper in Mexico." *Journal of Southern History,* XII (February, 1946), 67–83.
Hanna, Alfred J., and Kathryn A. Hanna. *Napoleon III and Mexico: American Triumph over Monarchy.* Chapel Hill: University of North Carolina Press, 1971.
Hanna, Kathryn A. "The Roles of the South in the French Intervention in Mexico." *Journal of Southern History,* XX (February, 1954), 3–21.

Harmon, George D. "Confederate Migration to Mexico." *Hispanic American Historical Review*, XVII (November, 1937), 458–87.

Hendrick, Burton J. *Statesmen of the Lost Cause: Jefferson Davis and his Cabinet.* New York: The Literary Guild of America, 1939.

Hertz, Emanuel. "Lincoln's Diplomacy, an Unwritten Chapter." *Magazine of History with Notes and Queries*, XLVI (March, 1932), 3–16.

Hesseltine, William B. *Ulysses S. Grant Politician.* New York: F. Ungar, 1957.

Hockett, Homer C. "Thomas Corwin." *Dictionary of American Biography.* Vol. IV. New York: Charles Scribner's Sons, 1946.

Holt, William S. *Treaties Defeated by the Senate.* Baltimore: Johns Hopkins Press, 1933.

Hyman, Harold M. "Johnson, Stanton, and Grant: A Reconsideration of the Army's Role in the Events Leading to Impeachment." *American Historical Review*, LXVI (October, 1960), 85–100.

Iglesias Calderón, Fernando. *El egoismo norteamericano durante la intervención francesa.* Mexico: Imprenta Económica, 1905.

Iturribarria, Jorge Fernando. "El 'Diario' de Don Matías Romero." *Historia Mexicana*, XI (January-March, 1962), 382–415.

Jenkins, Brian. *Fenians and Anglo-American Relations during Reconstruction.* Ithaca, N.Y.: Cornell University Press, 1969.

Johnson, Ludwell H. "Fort Sumter and Confederate Diplomacy." *Journal of Southern History*, XXVI (November, 1960), 441–77.

Jones, Oakah L., Jr. *Santa Anna.* New York: Twayne Publishers, 1968.

Jordan, Donaldson, and Edwin J. Pratt. *Europe and the American Civil War.* Boston and New York: Houghton, Mifflin Company, 1931.

Kasson, John. *Evolution of the Constitution of the United States of America and History of the Monroe Doctrine.* Boston: Houghton, Mifflin Company, 1904.

Kearney, Ruth Elizabeth. "The Magdalena Bubble." *Pacific Historical Review*, IV (March, 1935), 25–38.

Kemble, John Haskell. "Mail Steamers Link the Americas, 1840-1890." *Greater America: Essays in Honor of Herbert Eugene Bolton*, edited by Adele Ogden and Engel Sluiter. Berkeley: University of California Press, 1945.

Kennedy, Philip W. "Union and Confederate Relations with Mexico." *Duquesne Review*, XI (Spring, 1966), 47–63.

Kirkland, Edward Chase. *Industry Comes of Age: Business, Labor and Public Policy, 1860–1897.* Chicago: Quadrangle Books, 1967.

Knapp, Frank A., Jr. *The Life of Sebastián Lerdo de Tejada, 1823–1883.* Austin: University of Texas Press, 1951.

———. "Precursors of American Investment in Mexican Railroads." *Pacific Historical Review*, XXI (February, 1952), 43–64.

LaFeber, Walter. *The New Empire: An Interpretation of American Expansion, 1860–1898.* Ithaca, N.Y.: Cornell University Press, 1963.

Leavitt, Joshua. *The Monroe Doctrine.* New York: Sinclair Tousey, 1863.

Lee, Fitzhugh. "The Failure of the Hampton Conference." *Century Magazine*, LII (July, 1896), 476–78.

Leopold, Richard W. *Robert Dale Owen: A Biography*. Cambridge, Mass.: University of Harvard Press, 1940.

Lomask, Milton. *Andrew Johnson: President on Trial*. New York: Farrar, Straus, 1960.

Lowell, James Russell. "The Seward-Johnson Reaction." *North American Review*, CCXIII (October, 1866), 523–28.

Luraghi, Raimundo. "The Civil War and the Modernization of American Society: Social Structure and Industrial Revolution in the Old South before and during the War." *Civil War History*, XVIII (September, 1972), 230–50.

Luz, Nícia Vilela. *A Amazônia para os Negros Americanos*. Rio de Janeiro: Editôra Saga, 1968.

Lynch, Sister M. Claire. *The Diplomatic Mission of John Lothrop Motley to Austria, 1861–1867*. Washington: University of America Press, 1944.

McBride, G. McCutchen. *The Land System of Mexico*. New York: American Geographic Society, 1923.

McCaleb, Walter F. *The Public Finances of Mexico*. New York, London: Harper and Brothers, 1921.

MacCorkle, Stuart Alexander. *American Policy of Recognition Towards Mexico*. The Johns Hopkins University Studies in Historical and Political Science, Series LI, No. 3. Baltimore: The Johns Hopkins Press, 1933.

McCormack, Richard B. "Los Estados Confederados y México." *Historia Mexicana*, IV (January-March, 1955), 337–57.

———. "James Watson Webb and French Withdrawal from Mexico." *Hispanic American Historical Review*, XXXI (May, 1951), 274–86.

McCormick, Thomas. *China Market: America's Quest for Informal Empire, 1893–1901*. Chicago: Quadrangle, 1967.

McKee, Irving. *"Ben Hur" Wallace: The Life of General Lew Wallace*. Berkeley: University of California Press, 1947.

McKitrick, Eric L. *Andrew Johnson and Reconstruction*. Chicago: University of Chicago Press, 1960.

McNeely, John H. *The Railways of Mexico: A Study in Nationalization*. Vol. II, Southwestern Studies. El Paso: Texas Western College, 1964.

McPherson, Hallie M. "The Plan of William McKendree Gwin for a Colony in North Mexico, 1863–1865." *Pacific Historical Review*, II (December, 1933), 357–86.

Manning, William R. *Early Diplomatic Relations Between the United States and Mexico*. Baltimore: Johns Hopkins Press, 1916.

Mantell, Martin E. *Johnson, Grant, and the Politics of Reconstruction*. New York: Columbia University Press, 1973.

Martin, Percy F. *Maximilian in Mexico*. London: Constable & Co., 1914.

Meade, Robert Douthat. *Judah P. Benjamin, Confederate Statesman*. New York: Oxford University Press, 1943.

Mecham, J. Lloyd. "The Origins of Federalism in Mexico." *Hispanic American Historical Review*, XVIII (May, 1938), 154–82.

————. *A Survey of United States-Latin American Relations.* Boston: Houghton, Mifflin Company, 1965.

Miller, Robert R. "The American Legion of Honor in Mexico." *Pacific Historical Review,* XXX (August, 1961), 229–41.

————. "Gaspar Sanchez Ochoa: A Mexican Secret Agent in the United States." *Historian,* XXIII (May, 1961), 316–29.

————. "Herman Sturm: Hoosier Secret Agent for Mexico." *Indiana Magazine of History,* LVIII (March, 1962), 1–15.

————. "Lew Wallace and the French Intervention in Mexico." *Indiana Magazine of History,* LIX (March, 1963), 31–50.

————. "Matías Romero: Mexican Minister to the United States during the Juárez-Maximilian Era." *Hispanic American Historical Review,* XLV (May, 1965), 228–45.

————. "Plácido Vega: A Mexican Secret Agent in the United States." *The Americas,* XIX (October, 1962), 137–48.

Milton, George F. *The Age of Hate: Andrew Johnson and the Radicals.* Hamden, Conn.: Archon, 1956.

Monaghan, Jay. *Diplomat in Carpet Slippers.* Indianapolis: Bobbs-Merrill Company, 1945.

Moreno, Daniel. "Mr. E. L. Plumb en México y la acción en las cumbres de Acultzingo 1862." *Boletín del Archivo General de la Nación,* 2^d Serie, III (1962), 175–98.

Morrow, Josiah. *Life and Speeches of Thomas Corwin.* N.p., 1896.

Moseley, Edward H. "Indians from the Eastern United States and the Defense of Northwestern Mexico, 1855–1864." *Southwestern Social Science Quarterly,* XLVI (December, 1965), 273–80.

————. "The Religious Impact of the American Occupation of Mexico City, 1847–1848." *Militarists, Merchants and Missionaries: United States Expansion in Middle America,* edited by Eugene R. Huck and Edward H. Moseley. University: University of Alabama Press, 1970.

————. "A Witness for the Prosecution: the Pickett Incident." *Register of the Kentucky Historical Society,* LXVIII (April, 1970), 171–75.

Mosse, W. E. *Liberal Europe: The Age of Bourgeois Realism, 1848–1875.* London: Harcourt Brace Jovanovich, 1974.

Mowry, Duane, ed. "Doolittle Correspondence." *Publications of the Southern History Association,* IX (July, 1905), 241–48.

Neiman, Simon I. *Judah P. Benjamin.* Indianapolis: Bobbs-Merrill Company, 1963.

Newton, Thomas W. *Lord Lyons, A Record of British Diplomacy.* 2 vols. London: Edward Arnold, 1913.

Nichols, Jeanette P. "The United States Congress and Imperialism, 1861–1897." *Journal of Economic History,* XXI (December, 1961), 526–38.

Nichols, Roy. *The Stakes of Power, 1845–1877.* New York: Hill and Wang, 1961.

Nicolay, John G., and John Hay. "Abraham Lincoln: A History; Blair's Mexican Project; the Hampton Road's Conference; the XIIIth Amendment." *Century Magazine,* New Series XVI (October, 1889), 838–56.

Niles, Blair. *Passengers to Mexico.* New York: Farrar and Rinehart, 1943.

North, Douglass C. *Growth and Welfare in the American Past: A New Economic History.* Englewood Cliffs, N.J.: Prentice-Hall, 1966.

Nuermberger, G. A. "The Continental Treaties of 1856: An American Union Exclusive of the United States." *Hispanic American Historical Review,* XX (February, 1940), 32–55.

Oberholtzer, Ellis Paxon. *Jay Cooke: Financier of the Civil War.* 2 vols. Philadelphia: G. W. Jacobs, 1907.

Ocaranza, Fernando. *Juárez y sus amigos, colección de ensayos.* Mexico: Stylo, 1942.

Orozco, Luis. ed. *Maximiliano y la restitución de la esclavitud en México.* Vol. XIII. Mexico: Secretaría de Relaciones Exteriores, 1961.

Osterweis, Rollin G. *Judah P. Benjamin: Statesman of the Lost Cause.* New York, London: G. P. Putnam's Sons, 1933.

"Our Diplomacy During the Rebellion." *North American Review,* XII (April, 1866), 446–72.

Owsley, Frank L. *King Cotton Diplomacy.* Rev. ed. Chicago: University of Chicago Press, 1959.

Paolino, Ernest. *Foundations of the American Empire: William Henry Seward and U.S. Foreign Policy.* Ithaca, N.Y.: Cornell University Press, 1973.

Parkes, Henry Bamford. *A History of Mexico.* 3rd ed., Boston: Houghton, Mifflin Company, 1960.

Patrick, Rembert W. *Jefferson Davis and His Cabinet.* Baton Rouge: Louisiana State University Press, 1944.

———. *Reconstruction of the Nation.* New York: Oxford University Press, 1967.

Perez-Maldonaldo, Carlos. "La pugna Juárez-Vidaurri en Monterrey, 1864." *Memoria de la academía de la historia* (January-March, 1965), 57–91.

Perkins, Dexter. *The Monroe Doctrine, 1826–1867.* Baltimore: Johns Hopkins Press, 1933.

Petin, Hector. *Les Etats-Unis et la Doctrine de Monroe.* Paris: Arthus Rousseau Editeur, 1900.

Pflaum, Rosalynd. *The Emperor's Talisman: The Life of the Duc of Morny.* New York: Meridith Press, 1968.

Phelan, John Leddy. "Pan-Latinism, French Intervention in Mexico (1861–1867) and the Genesis of the Idea of Latin America." *Conciencia y Autenticidad Históricas.* Mexico: Universidad Nacional Autónoma de México, 1968.

Phifer, Gregg. "Andrew Johnson Argues a Case." *Tennessee Historical Quarterly,* XI (June, 1952), 148–70.

———. "Andrew Johnson Delivers His Argument." *Tennessee Historical Quarterly,* XI (September, 1952), 212–34.

———. "Andrew Johnson Loses His Battle." *Tennessee Historical Quarterly,* XI (December, 1952), 291–328.

———. "Andrew Johnson Takes a Trip." *Tennessee Historical Quarterly,* XI (March, 1952), 3–23.

Phillips, Ulrich B. *The Life of Robert Toombs.* New York: Macmillan, 1913.

Plesur, Milton. *America's Outward Thrust: Approaches to Foreign Affairs, 1865–1890.* De Kalb: University of Northern Illinois Press, 1971.

Pletcher, David M. "The Development of Railroads in Sonora." *Inter-American Economic Review*, I (March, 1948), 3-45.
──────. *The Diplomacy of Annexation; Texas, Oregon, and the Mexican War.* Columbia: University of Missouri Press, 1973.
──────. "México, campo de inversiones norteamericanas, 1867-1880." *Historia Mexicana* II (January-March, 1953), 564-74.
──────. "Mexico Opens the Door to American Capital, 1877-1880." *The Americas*, XVI (July, 1959), 1-14.
──────. "A Prospecting Expedition Across Central Mexico, 1856-1857." *Pacific Historical Review*, XXI (February, 1952), 21-41.
──────. *Rails, Mines, and Progress: Seven American Promoters in Mexico, 1867-1911.* Ithaca, N.Y.: Cornell University Press, 1958.
Potter, David M. "Civil War." *The Comparative Approach to American History*, edited by C. Vann Woodward. New York: Basic Books, 1968.
Powell, Fred W. *The Railroads of Mexico.* Boston: Stratford Company, 1921.
Powell, T. G. *El liberalismo y el campesinado en el centro de México, 1850-1876.* Mexico: Sep Setentas, 1974.
Quirarte, Martín. *Historiografía sobre el Imperio Maximiliano.* Mexico: Universidad Nacional Autónoma de México, 1970.
Randall, James G., and David Donald. *The Civil War and Reconstruction.* Lexington, Mass.: D. C. Heath, 1969.
Reed, Merle E. *New Orleans and the Railroads: The Struggle for Commercial Empire, 1830-1860.* Baton Rouge: Louisiana State University Press, 1966.
Reinders, Robert C. *End of Era: New Orleans, 1850-1860.* New Orleans: Pelican Publishing Company, 1964.
Republican National and Congressional Committees. *Life and Services of General U. S. Grant, Conqueror of the Rebellion, and Eighteenth President of the United States.* Washington: Philip and Solomons, 1868.
Reuter, Paul H., Jr. "United States-French Relations Regarding French Intervention in Mexico: From the Tripartite Treaty to Queretaro." *Southern Quarterly*, VI (July, 1968), 469-89.
Reynolds, G. "Mexico." *Atlantic Monthly*, XIV (July, 1864), 51-63.
Rippy, James Fred. "Diplomacy of the United States Regarding the Isthmus of Tehuantepec, 1848-1860." *Mississippi Valley Historical Review*, VI (March, 1920), 503-531.
──────. "Mexican Projects of the Confederates." *Southwestern Historical Quarterly*, XXII (April, 1919), 291-317.
──────. *The United States and Mexico.* New York: Alfred A. Knopf, 1926.
Rister, Carl C. "Carlota: A Confederate Colony in Mexico." *Journal of Southern History*, XI (May, 1945), 167-89.
Roeder, Ralph. *Juárez and His Mexico.* 2 vols. New York: Viking Press, 1947.
Rolle, Andrew F. *The Lost Cause: The Confederate Exodus to Mexico.* Norman: University of Oklahoma Press, 1965.
Romero, Matías. *Mexico and the United States. A study of subjects affecting their political, commercial and social relations made with a view to their promotion.* Vol. I. New York: G. P. Putnam's Sons, 1898.

———. "The Philosophy of the Mexican Revolutions." *North American Review*, CLXII (January, 1896), 33–47.

———. *The Tehuantepec Isthmus Railway*. Washington: n.p., 1894.

Russell, Addison P. *Thomas Corwin: A Brief Sketch*. Cincinnati: R. Clarke and Company, 1881.

Santovenia, Emeterio S. *Lincoln: El Precursor de la Buena Vecindad*. La Habana: Editorial Uniclad, 1951.

Schmitt, Karl M. *Mexico and the United States, 1821–1973: Conflict and Coexistence*. New York: John Wiley & Sons, 1974.

Schofield, John M. "The Withdrawal of the French from Mexico." *Century Illustrated Magazine*, New Series XXXII (May-October, 1897), 128–37.

Scholes, Walter V. *Mexican Politics during the Juárez Regime, 1855–1872*. University of Missouri Studies, Vol. 30. Columbia: University of Missouri Press, 1957.

Schonberger, Howard B. *Transportation to the Seaboard: The "Communications Revolution" and American Foreign Policy, 1860–1900*. Westport, Conn.: Greenwood Publishing Corporation, 1971.

Schoonover, Thomas. "Documents Concerning Lemuel Dale Evans' Plan to Keep Texas in the Union in 1861." *East Texas Historical Journal*, XII (Spring, 1974), 35–38.

———. "Mexican Cotton and the American Civil War." *The Americas*, XXX (April, 1974), 429–47.

———."The Mexican Minister Describes Andrew Johnson's 'Swing Around the Circle.'" *Civil War History*, XIX (June, 1973), 149–61.

Sefton, James E. "The Impeachment of Andrew Johnson: A Century of Writing." *Civil War History*, XIV (June, 1968), 120–47.

———. *The United States Army and Reconstruction, 1865–1877*. Baton Rouge: Louisiana State University Press, 1967.

Sepulveda, Cesar. "Sobre Reclamaciones de Norteamericanos a México." *Historia Mexicana*, XI (October-December, 1961), 180–206.

Sheridan, Philip J. "The Committee of Mexican Bondholders and European Intervention in 1861." *Mid-America*, XLII (January, 1960), 18–29.

Sierra, Justo, ed. *México, Su Evolución Social*. 3 vols. Mexico: J. Ballesch & Co., 1900–1902.

Silbey, Joel H. *The Transformation of American Politics, 1840–1860*. Englewood Cliffs, N.J.: Prentice-Hall, 1967.

Smart, Charles A. *Viva Juárez!* New York, Philadelphia: J. B. Lippincott Company, 1963.

Smith, Elbert B. *The Death of Slavery: The United States, 1837–1865*. Chicago: University of Chicago Press, 1967.

Sowle, Patrick. "A Reappraisal of William H. Seward's Memorandum of April 1, 1861, to Lincoln." *Journal of Southern History*, XXXIII (May, 1967), 234–39.

Stanton, Theodore. *General Grant and the French*. N.p., [1890].

Steiner, Bernard C. *Henry W. Davis*. Baltimore: John Murphy Company, 1916.

Stern, Phillip van Doren. *When the Guns Roared: World Aspects of the American Civil War*. Garden City, N.Y.: Doubleday and Co., 1965.

Sydnor, Charles S. *The Development of Southern Sectionalism, 1819–1848.* Vol. V of *A History of the South.* Edited by Wendell Holmes Stephenson and E. Merton Coulter. Baton Rouge: Louisiana State University Press, 1948.

Tardiff, Guillermo. *Historia General del Comercio Exterior Mexicano.* 2 vols. Mexico: Imprimir de Gráfica Panamericana, 1968–1970.

Teja Zabre, Alfonso. *Guía de la Historia de México.* Mexico: Secretaría de Educación Pública, 1944.

———. *Historia de México.* Mexico: Secretaría de Relaciones Exteriores, 1935.

Thomas, Benjamin P., and Harold W. Hyman. *Stanton: The Life and Times of Lincoln's Secretary of War.* New York: Alfred A. Knopf, 1962.

Thompson, James Matthew. *Louis Napoleon and the Second Empire.* Oxford: Blackwell's, 1954.

Thompson, Samuel B. *Confederate Purchasing Operation Abroad.* Chapel Hill: University of North Carolina Press, 1935.

Thompson, William Y. *Robert Toombs of Georgia.* Baton Rouge: Louisiana State University Press, 1966.

Torrea, Juan Manuel. "Sebastián Lerdo de Tejada." *Memoria de la Academia Nacional de Historia y Geografía,* No. 2 (1946), 28–50.

Trefousse, Hans L. *Benjamin Franklin Wade: Radical Republican from Ohio.* New York: Twayne Publishers, 1963.

———. *The Radical Republicans: Lincoln's Vanguard for Racial Justice.* New York: Alfred A. Knopf, 1969.

Tyrner-Tyrnauer, A. R. *Lincoln and the Emperors.* London: Rupert Hart-Davis, 1962.

Turlington, Edgar. *Mexico and Her Foreign Creditors.* New York: Columbia University Press, 1930.

Turner, Frederick C. *The Dynamic of Mexican Nationalism.* Chapel Hill: University of North Carolina Press, 1968.

Tyler, Alice Felt. *Freedom's Ferment.* New York: Harper and Brothers, 1962.

Tyler, Ronnie C. *Santiago Vidaurri and the Southern Confederacy.* [Austin]: Texas State Historical Association, 1973.

van Alstyne, Richard W. *The Rising American Empire.* Chicago: Quadrangle, 1965.

Van Deusen, Glyndon G. *William Henry Seward.* New York: Oxford University Press, 1967.

Vargas, Fulgencio. *Estudio biográfico sobre D. Manuel Doblado.* Guanajuato, Mexico: Universidad de Guanajuato, 1965.

Vasconcelos, José. *Breve Historia de México.* Mexico: Edición Botas, 1944.

Vevier, Charles. "American Continentalism: An Idea of Expansionism, 1845–1910." *American Historical Review,* LXV(January, 1960), 323–35.

———. "The Collins Overland Line and American Continentalism." *Pacific Historical Review,* XXVIII (August, 1959), 237–53.

Voegeli, V. Jaques. *Free but not Equal: The Midwest and the Negro during the Civil War.* Chicago: University of Chicago Press, 1968.

Washington, Lucius Q. "The Confederate State Department." *Independent,* LIII (September, 1901), 341–49.

Weinert, Richard. "Confederate Border Troubles with Mexico." *Civil War Times Illustrated*, III (October, 1964), 36–43.

Wehler, Hans Ulrich. *Der Aufstieg des amerikanischen Imperialismus: Studien zur Entwicklung des Imperium Americanum, 1865–1900*. Göttingen, Germany: Vanderhocht & Ruprecht, 1974.

Weisberger, Bernard A. *The New Industrial Society*. New York: John Wiley and Sons, 1969.

Wheat, Raymond C. *Francisco Zarco: El Portavoz Liberal de la Reforma*. Mexico: Editorial Porrua, 1957.

Wilgus, A. Curtis. "Official Expression of Manifest Destiny Sentiment Concerning Hispanic America, 1848–1871." *Louisiana Historical Quarterly*, XV (July, 1932), 486–506.

Williams, James. *The Rise and Fall of "The Model Republic."* London: Richard Bently, 1863.

Williams, T. Harry. *Lincoln and the Radicals*. Madison: University of Wisconsin Press, 1960.

Williams, William A. *The Contours of American History*. Chicago: Quadrangle, 1966.

———. *The Roots of the Modern American Empire*. New York: Vintage Books, 1969.

Wilson, Major L. "Ideological Fruits of Manifest Destiny: The Geopolitics of Slavery Expansion in the Crisis of 1850." *Journal of the Illinois Historical Society*, LXIII (Summer, 1970), 132–57.

Winston, Robert. *Andrew Johnson, Plebian and Patriot*. New York: Henry Holt, 1924.

Yearns, Wilfred Buck. *The Confederate Congress*. Athens: University of Georgia Press, 1960.

Younger, Edward. *John A. Kasson: Politics and Diplomacy from Lincoln to McKinley*. Iowa City: State Historical Society of Iowa, 1955.

Zamacois, Niceto de. *Historia de México desde sus tiempos más remotos hasta nuestros días*. 22 vols. Barcelona: J. F. Parres, 1876–1902.

Zornow, William Frank. *Lincoln and the Party Divided*. Norman: University of Oklahoma Press, 1954.

Zorrilla, Luis G. *Historia de las Relaciones entre México y los Estados Unidos*. 2 vols. Mexico: Editorial Porrua, 1965–1966.

Index